Printed in Great Britain
by Amazon

38920764R00131

About the Author

Markus Thielen is the Head of Research and Strategy for Matrixport, a leading digital-asset investment firm. Before joining Matrixport, Markus was the Chief Investment Officer at the digital-asset investment firm IDEG Asset Management, and before that the founder and Chief Investment Officer at Jomon Investment Management. Previously Markus was a Portfolio Manager at Millennium Capital Partners and JP Morgan Investment Group. He started his career at Morgan Stanley, where he set up and ran the Quant & Derivatives Strategies Group in Asia. Markus has a degree from the ESCP Business School in Paris and a Certificate in Sustainable Finance from the University of Cambridge.

Markus Thielen

Crypto Titans:

How trillions were made and billions lost

in the cryptocurrency markets

Books are available at a discount when purchased in quantity for sales promotions or corporate use. Special editions, which include personalized covers, excerpts, and corporate imprints, can be created when purchased in large quantities. For more information, please email info@markusthielen.com.

LIBRARY OF CONGRESS CATALOGING-IN-PUBLICATION DATA

LIBRARY OF CONGRESS CATALOG

Library of Congress Control Number: 2023906614

ISBN digital version 979-8-9877797-0-5

ISBN paperback version 979-8-9877797-1-2

ISBN hardback version 979-8-9877797-2-9

© 2023 Markus Thielen

First Edition: May 2023

Cover design by Aaron Meng

Visit the author's website at www.markusthielen.com

"I don't have time to try to convince you, sorry"

(Satoshi Nakamoto, Bitcoin developer)

Contents

Foreword

I am pleased to write the foreword for this book. As an industry veteran I can attest to the value of understanding the past to navigate better the present and future of this rapidly evolving field. My journey in crypto began in 2011, and two years later I cofounded Bitmain, the largest Bitcoin mining rig manufacturer in the world. In 2019 I cofounded Matrixport, which became Asia's most prominent crypto-asset management firm after its competitors collapsed like dominoes during the 2022 crypto financial crisis mentioned in this book. In 2021 I cofounded Bitdeer.

I have experienced the ups and downs of the market cycles described in this book, and I can confidently say that much is to be learned from these experiences. Markus has led the research team at Matrixport, and the company's clients have greatly appreciated his reports. So when he approached me two months before the publication of this book, I was intrigued.

Reading through the manuscript has been like reliving every moment of my life in this industry. Markus brings a unique perspective, with a deep understanding of both traditional asset classes and the emerging crypto market. His knowledge of the Wild West days of crypto and the current highly regulated TradFi (traditional finance) environment is second to none.

This book is essential reading for anyone interested in understanding the history of crypto—not just the headline-grabbing news stories but the underlying mechanisms and practices that have shaped this field. As the industry continues to grow and expand into every corner of the world with a libertarian spirit, the dynamics of community will continue to evolve. Understanding the history and future of crypto is crucial for institutional researchers, regulators, and crypto practitioners alike.

From its early days as a pirate ship to its current status as a trillion-dollar industry, crypto has come a long way. When I first joined an early crypto forum, there were only around twenty thousand members. Today there are hundreds of millions of investors and users worldwide. With essential information from the early days of the peer-to-peer payment system right through to the current boom in NFTs (non-fungible tokens) and DeFi (decentralized finance), this book is an invaluable resource for anyone, whether a newcomer or a seasoned veteran, who wants to comprehensively understand the history of Bitcoin and the cryptocurrency landscape as a whole.

Markus has done an excellent job covering all the important names and stories that have shaped the crypto industry, consistently hitting the nail on the head with accurate analysis to help readers understand the motivations and personal characteristics. I highly recommend this book to anyone who wants to learn more about this fascinating and constantly evolving field.

This book will help a person just starting out in crypto to command the same level of knowledge as a crypto "OG" (original). Despite the challenges, the cyclical nature of bull and bear markets in crypto is part of what makes this industry so fascinating. Whether you are a miner, trader, builder, or investor, navigating the market cycles and capitalizing on the opportunities presented by each cycle is essential to success in the crypto industry. This book provides valuable insights into the cyclical nature of the crypto market. It offers practical advice on managing risk and making informed business decisions by understanding the factors that drive the market cycles and how to take advantage of them.

At the end of the book the bursting of the bubble of the 2021 bull cycle is described, along with the FTX fiasco. If you have read the entire book, like me, you will feel the charm of the cyclical nature of bull and bear markets in crypto and be full of expectations for the next bull market cycle in crypto.

Markus's book leads the reader to understand an essential aspect of the crypto industry: the formation and bursting of crypto bubbles. In contrast other crypto proponents may only emphasize the technology and its potential impact. Furthermore Markus has a strong understanding of the technology side of the blockchain space and the financial sector, which is essential in comprehending the history of crypto.

When I advocated for Bitcoin in 2011, I found that only a few people could understand computer science and finance. As crypto is the intersection of both fields, Markus is able to guide readers to grasp the history of crypto much better than someone who only understands one side of the coin.

In conclusion I am honored to have the opportunity to write this foreword. Out of politeness, and knowing that I was a part of some controversial history regarding the Bitcoin protocol debates documented in this book, Markus asked me whether I wanted to delete anything in the book, but I did not make any changes. I hope readers will find this book a valuable and informative resource as they navigate the exciting and ever-changing world of crypto.

Jihan Wu

Introduction

This book explains how the crypto industry started and evolved, and how everything in crypto is ultimately connected. It introduces the major players behind the three-trillion-dollar industry (at its peak) and tells how billions of dollars were lost. Cryptocurrencies have become a new asset class, and many want to understand how crypto markets evolved.

Each of the four crypto bull markets of 2011, 2013, 2017, and 2021 unfolded differently, but they were all shadowed by violent price corrections during bear markets. The last three years have been the most significant, with the adoption level for crypto reaching not only individuals but also asset managers and corporate executives—only to be dominated by cataclysmic bankruptcies of multi-billion-dollar crypto lending firms and the misappropriation of eight billion dollars in customer funds by the executives of the FTX crypto exchange.

Figure 1: The four crypto bull markets of 2011, 2013, 2017, and 2021

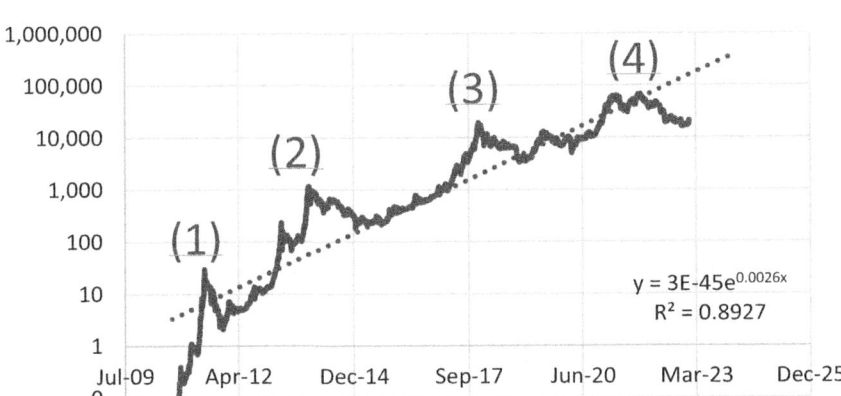

$y = 3E\text{-}45e^{0.0026x}$

$R^2 = 0.8927$

Bitcoin evolved from its early start as a peer-to-peer payment system to become the subject of many speculative manias. While crypto cycles tend to be tremendously volatile, the chronological investigation in this book lists the drivers of these cycles and explains why exuberant bull markets were occasionally interrupted by violent bear markets. These points may help the reader to identify the next crypto bull market.

This book fills the gap in understanding how the crypto industry evolved and which events led to its spectacular rise to become a multitrillion-dollar industry. Each bull market has brought in more people as the underlying blockchain technology progresses. Some 420 million people are now believed to own cryptocurrencies. Despite hurdles crypto continues to evolve and push forward. But if people lack an understanding of the industry's beginnings and evolution, it could easily be dismissed as a temporary phenomenon.

No other industry has become more mesmerizing than the crypto industry, which lies at the intersection of technological innovation, human imagination, and financial regulation. The building blocks of trust, money, and technology have motivated players worldwide to rebuild the global financial system after the 2008 financial crisis.

The intensity of Bitcoin price movements has become more critical as the industry has gained recognition from the financial sector and the most innovative people in leading universities worldwide. This value creation has attracted an ever larger number of students, early adopters, startup founders, and venture capitalists, fueling the drive to provide crypto services for the masses.

Explosive growth and scandals

While the crypto industry has created trillions of dollars within four major bull markets, billions have also been lost in bankruptcies, misappropriation of customer funds, cyberattacks, and hacks. For some the wealth created is incomprehensible; for others it is simply an illusion. The combination of get-rich-quick schemes, technological curiosity, and the incentive to make enormous amounts of money has attracted charlatans and turned decent people into bad actors.

Many crypto exchanges and crypto firms have come and gone over the years. Some cash-grabbing individuals have disappeared as quickly as they entered the crypto world. Meanwhile a core group of die-hard early adopters and enthusiasts have shaped the industry over the last decade. Many believe a year in crypto is synonymous with five years in traditional finance (TradFi), as everything in crypto tends to move faster without strict regulatory oversight. When oversight has been deemed necessary, regulators have acted forcefully, but this has never stopped the industry from adjusting as crypto has become a global phenomenon.

Numerous exchanges have seen explosive growth without appropriate compliance rules being enforced. Many crypto exchanges only require an email address for identity verification, as cryptocurrency traders tend to value their anonymity. This has attracted not only users who cherish secrecy for libertarian reasons but also bad actors with criminal motives.

In TradFi, brokers must keep client funds separate from other company assets. In crypto, on the other hand, many rules are yet to be established and those that have been established have often been loosely implemented.

Crypto markets are dominated by asymmetric, non-public information that can be exploited—a perfect feeding ground for "pump-and-dump" schemes. But while regulation in crypto is only in its infancy compared to TradFi, it does not mean that every aspect of the crypto ecosystem is legal.

The value in crypto exchanges comes from being fully vertically integrated. But this makes the user's funds vulnerable, because a crypto exchange is not simply a trading venue that matches buyers with sellers. Crypto exchanges also provide leverage, listing services, prime broker services, custody services, and balance-sheet extension services. The latter are of particular interest, as often customer funds sitting idle on an exchange have been lent out to trading firms without the explicit consent of the exchange's clients, even if this was justified by the fine print in the terms and services agreement buried somewhere on the exchange's website.

Bringing fiat dollars into the cryptocurrency arena is called an onramp. This process tends to be controlled by a handful of institutions with banking licenses and funding relationships. Stable banking relationships have been the most significant and pressing problem for crypto firms, as many financial institutions avoid setting up and maintaining service relationships with the crypto industry.

The stablecoin Tether is presumed to be backed one-to-one by fiat assets. It has often become the crypto instrument of choice for exchanges and crypto without suitable banking relationships. It may have been the most remarkable invention to circumvent the banking system and compliance rules, such as know-your-customer (KYC) procedures and anti-money-laundering (AML) orders.

According to the Boston Consulting Group crypto adoption numbers are expected to reach one billion by 2030. While many have already embraced crypto as a new asset class, numerous individuals, corporate executives, regulators, and politicians have been watching from the sidelines, curious about what crypto is all about and how blockchain might impact them. Insiders call crypto adoption inevitable, as it is simply an extension of the technological improvement of our daily lives.

Crypto has no borders and, often, no limitations. It has raced over regulatory hurdles and circumvented the compliance barriers of the traditional banking system. Despite the intimidating complexity of the crypto software stack and the risk of losing funds to state-sponsored North Korean hackers, interest in crypto has remained robust. Crypto is mystical and addictive. It operates at the intersection of money and trust, and has thus attracted many visionaries as well as exploiters over the years, many of whom feature in this book.

Technologists and die-hard libertarians were the early crypto adopters. But as crypto trading became highly valuable, it attracted different individuals as well. Crypto has now reached a sizable market capitalization and is continuously gathering interest, with the main adoption hurdle often said to be education. This book helps to educate the reader, regardless of his/her level of experience, sophistication, or motivation.

Figure 2: The value of the fifty leading crypto tokens (billion dollars)

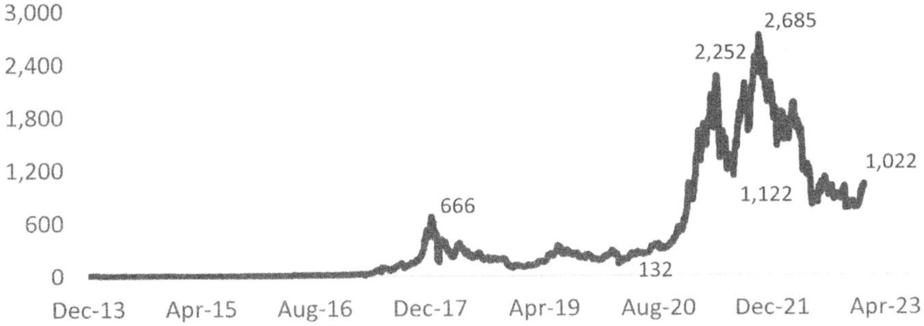

Overview of the book

The first part of the book describes how Bitcoin started as a peer-to-peer payment system, and how the first crypto bubble was facilitated by onramp payment companies in 2011, which mainly funneled money into the notorious Mt. Gox exchange in Japan, eventually leading to investors' funds being stolen. The first leveraged Bitcoin exchange was set up by a student whose crypto exchange's source code was subsequently leaked. A copycat site then became one of the most important crypto exchanges, and later the backbone of the Tether stablecoin.

The second part of the book analyzes how China embraced Bitcoin and hailed it as a new form of money, setting off a massive speculative bubble in 2013. Chinese entrepreneurs set up industrial-scale Bitcoin mining operations that allowed them to control the network. Although China eventually restricted its banks from transacting with crypto exchanges, the Hong Kong central bank classified Bitcoin as a commodity that did not require regulation. This made the city the hub of choice for crypto firms and speculation. BitMEX became the largest crypto exchange, setting a precedent for other businesses to offer leveraged crypto trading.

The third part of the book describes how Ethereum started, and how it set off the period of initial coin offerings (ICOs) that led to the third bull market in 2017. Despite Ethereum's success the project would have failed without the support of a Chinese corporate investor. The U.S. Securities and Exchange Commission (SEC) used the Howey Test, a legal outcome from 1946, to classify some ICOs as illegal money-raising exercises. As crypto achieved a one-trillion-dollar market capitalization, North Korean hackers became regular cyber exploiters with the help of Russia-based money laundering firms. Meanwhile Tether became the essential stablecoin, despite the nearly one-billion-dollar disappearance of its affiliate firm.

The fourth part of the book shows how decentralized finance (DeFi) started, and how the speculative mania set off by COVID stimulus checks reached a peak. Binance became the largest crypto exchange despite its controversies, effectively dethroning BitMEX. Corporations started to use Bitcoin as part of their treasury reserves. Meanwhile the NFT (non-fungible token) bubble extended the bull market as large buyers with vested interests drove up the prices for digital art. Some crypto hedge funds and trading firms—influenced by the crypto "supercycle" theory, which was driven by a belief in the institutional adoption of crypto and the overall democratization of finance—were confident enough to deploy billions of dollars of borrowed capital near the top of the cycle.

The fifth part of the book takes a deep dive into the 2022 bear market, exploring how crypto spectacularly crashed from a multitrillion-dollar valuation and why the implosion of the Terra stablecoin caused sixty billion dollars to vanish within a few days. The crypto hedge fund Three Arrows Capital had once controlled ten billion dollars in assets but was later on the hook for three billion dollars as it could not repay the firms that had lent to it, uncollateralized. Crypto lending firms often used customer funds that promised to pay depositors high rates. But most of the funds disappeared, and many of the crypto lending firms went under in short succession. Several of them were rightfully accused of misusing customer funds.

The sixth part of the book contemplates the events that led to the implosion of the crypto exchange FTX after a meteoric four-year rise. Once valued at thirty-two billion dollars, the exchange went under amid an ongoing spat with its main competitor, Binance. FTX misappropriated at least eight billion dollars in user funds and offered its affiliated trading firm, Alameda Research, a sixty-five-billion-dollar credit facility. When the exchange's customers realized that their funds had been misused, large withdrawal requests caused a liquidity crunch. Billions of dollars of tightly controlled tokens were used as collateral that quickly evaporated as the exchange went bust within days. Sam Bankman-Fried (SBF), the CEO of FTX and cofounder of Alameda, will stand trial on October 2 2023.

PART ONE: THE FIRST CRYPTO BULL MARKET (2011)

1

"Running Bitcoin"
(Hal Finney, first Bitcoin recipient)

It was on Halloween, Friday October 31, 2008 that Satoshi Nakamoto sent his white paper "Bitcoin: A Peer-to-Peer Electronic Cash System" to a mailing list started by a group of "cypherpunks", who were initially interested in cryptography and privacy-enhancing technologies, not electronic cash systems specifically. While Nakamoto stated that the writing of the code for Bitcoin had begun in 2007, on August 22 2008 he had started emailing Wei Dai, the author of "b-money", and sometime before that he had contacted Adam Back, whose proof-of-work system is used in the Bitcoin code.

The Bitcoin peer-to-peer payment system (2008–13)

When Nakamoto released his white paper, the initial reaction was muted. There had been too many people before him who had claimed to have found a double-spending solution. Nevertheless, by November 16 2008 Nakamoto had shared a pre-release version of the Bitcoin code with several members of the cryptography mailing list, including James A. Donald, Ray Dillinger, and Hal Finney.

Finney had created the first reusable proof-of-work system in 2004 and was the recipient of the first Bitcoin transaction. He also lived for ten years in the same town (Temple City, California) as the Japanese American physicist Dorian Satoshi Nakamoto, adding to speculation that he may have been Bitcoin's creator—something that he always denied. Diagnosed with amyotrophic lateral sclerosis (ALS) in 2009, Finney died in 2014.

Nakamoto's last public message was posted on April 26 2011: "I wish you would stop talking about me as a mysterious shadowy figure. The press just turns that into a pirate currency angle. Maybe instead make it about the open-source project and give more credit to contributors. It helps motivate them."[1]

The release of the Bitcoin software (2009)

The Bitcoin software was implemented as open-source code and released in January 2009. The first block of the Bitcoin chain is called the genesis block and was mined by Nakamoto himself on January 3. Embedded in the coinbase of this first block was the text "The Times 03/Jan/2009 Chancellor on brink of second bailout for banks." This reference to the British newspaper *The Times* has been interpreted as a time stamp for the start of the crypto era, while at the same time being seen as a criticism of the fractional-reserve banking system and an expression of disapproval of the bailing out of elite bankers. By contrast, Bitcoin favors liberalism and self-governance.

The 2008 Global Financial Crisis and the years that followed have been associated with government-led bailouts and the protecting of overleveraged bankers. The system appeared to be rigged, a theme that resurfaced in the Occupy Wall Street Movement in the United States in 2011 and the forced "bail-in" of retail bank depositors in Cyprus in 2013, at the peak of the European Debt Crisis. Against this backdrop Bitcoin offered a new approach to a different type of money outside the traditional banking system.

Bitcoin was presented as a peer-to-peer electronic cash system that solved the double-spend problem, a key concern associated with electronic payment systems. Instead of lengthy settlement systems to verify who spent what and who owned which amount, it was seen as offering an instant settlement solution—a public ledger.

Hal Finney, who had created the first reusable proof-of-work system in 2004, was the first receiver of Bitcoins—ten in total—from Nakamoto on January 12 2009. The first known commercial transaction using Bitcoins occurred the following year, when programmer Laszlo Hanyecz bought two pizzas for ten thousand Bitcoins from Jeremy Sturdivant on March 23 2010. It is estimated that Nakamoto himself mined about one million Bitcoins before disappearing in 2011. These coins might be lost forever.

The Bitcoin exchange Mt. Gox was launched in 2010 in Japan and was handling over seventy percent of all Bitcoin transactions worldwide until February 2014, when the exchange noticed that it had been hacked over an unspecified period, losing 750 thousand Bitcoins. A Japanese trustee of Mt. Gox holding close to 142 thousand Bitcoins—a fraction of the overall number of coins stolen—is expected to start paying them out to creditors from mid-2023 onwards, almost nine years after the exchange filed for bankruptcy protection. Customer funds lost by crypto firms have a history of lengthy settlement procedures.

Initially the black-market site Silk Road was the major user of Bitcoins, accepting them exclusively as a method of payment. The site took in nearly ten million Bitcoins (worth about 214 million dollars at the time). It hosted four thousand vendors and had more than 146 thousand customers buying goods and services. Nearly 1.3 million transactions were completed on the site, generating a total revenue of 183 million dollars from sales and a total commission of 614 thousand Bitcoins.

Ross Ulbricht, the creator and operator of Silk Road, was arrested on October 1 2013 by the FBI, which seized thirty thousand Bitcoins from the site. The seized Bitcoins would later be auctioned off by the U.S. government to the Silicon Valley venture capitalist Tim Draper, who bought them for 18.7 million dollars in June 2014.

In September 2012 twenty-two-year-old James Zhong had used Silk Road to buy cocaine. He exploited a vulnerability in Silk Road's payment processing system to transfer fifty thousand Bitcoins from the platform's address into his own without ever providing any goods or services in return.[2] "I accidentally double-clicked the withdraw button and was shocked to discover that it resulted in allowing me to withdraw double the amount of Bitcoin I had deposited."[3] Zhong had funded nine different accounts with two hundred to two thousand Bitcoins and then triggered 140 withdrawal transactions in rapid automatic succession, exposing a lag in the Silk Road transaction system that did not update the ledger escrow account immediately. At the time the transferred Bitcoins were worth 620 thousand dollars, each about twelve dollars. Zhong sat on them for nearly five years, before exchanging some to launch a real-estate development business. Even after the Bitcoin Cash and SV forks Zhang was able to convert the coins into another 3,500 Bitcoins. In 2017 Zhang, using the alias "Loaded," had tried to contact the Bitcoin investor Roger Ver on the Bitcoin Forum to trade "at least 60k" in Bitcoin Unlimited.[4] Also in 2017 he started spending sixteen million dollars on real estate and Lamborghinis.

In 2019 Zhong reported a burglary at his house, saying a briefcase with 400 thousand dollars in cash was stolen. On November 9 2021 law enforcement officers executed search warrants at Zhong's residences in Georgia, U.S. They seized over fifty thousand Bitcoins with a market value of 3.35 billion dollars, and laptops containing detailed ledgers of Zhong's cryptocurrency transactions, including the Silk Road proceeds. In 2022 Zhong voluntarily surrendered another 860 Bitcoins that he had unlawfully obtained from Silk Road. On November 4 2022 he pleaded guilty to one count of substantive wire fraud. On April 14 2023 Zhong agreed to forfeit 42.7 million dollars in additional Bitcoin and property and was sentenced to one-year prison sentence.[5] The authorities indicated that all 9.9 million Bitcoins that had passed through Silk Road were confiscatable.

The use of Bitcoin as a hedge against deposit bail-ins (2013)

On March 18 2013, at the height of the European Debt Crisis, the Republic of Cyprus, a small island in the eastern Mediterranean that had joined the European Union in 2004, closed all its banks. The banks were fighting insolvency, and individuals had been withdrawing large amounts from their deposits, causing even more stress for the beleaguered banks. A bank run had been inevitable, as two of the biggest Cypriot banks had lost a combined 3.5 billion euros on Greek bonds the previous year—more than ten percent of the annual GDP of Cyprus.

A week later, on March 25, Cyprus was bailed out, and the country's second-largest bank was closed indefinitely. To finance the bailout, Cyprus agreed to sell 400 million euros of its gold reserves. The Cypriot government also announced that all savers' deposits would be subject to a haircut. The deposit tax took 6.75 percent from insured deposits of 100 thousand euros or less, and 9.9 percent from uninsured amounts above 100 thousand euros.

Figure 3: Bitcoin prices surged following the "bail-in" of bank depositors in Cyprus

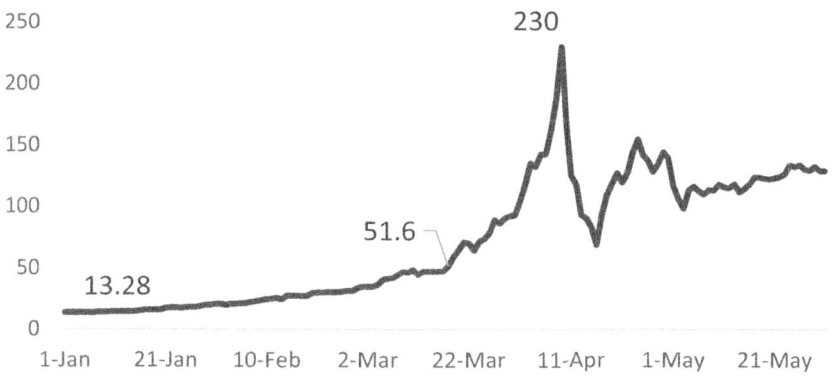

Bitcoin prices started to explode as depositors from over-indebted countries across Southern Europe searched for alternative ways to store their money. In anticipation of the events in Cyprus Bitcoin prices had already rallied from thirteen dollars on January 1 to fifty-one dollars at the time of the bailout. Worried that their deposits would be taxed like those of their Cypriot counterparts, individuals from countries from Greece to Spain became enthusiastic buyers of Bitcoin, with volumes on the crypto exchange Mt. Gox increasing from ten thousand to twenty thousand transactions within days.[6]

Cypriot banks remained shut down for nearly two weeks to prevent a run on deposits, only reopening on March 28 under tight restrictions and with a cash withdrawal limit of three hundred euros per day.[7] Bitcoin prices continued to rally, peaking at 230 dollars on April 9, when European lawmakers intervened to provide some insurance for depositors.

In Bitcoin's brief history, prices have tended to rise parabolically during periods of potential bank runs and defaults, such as the European Debt Crisis and the COVID pandemic, when the U.S. government debased its currency by printing an enormous amount of dollars. These were exactly the events that Satoshi Nakamoto had foreseen in establishing Bitcoin as the basis for an alternative financial system.

2

"Bitcoin is a stateless currency"
(Julian Assange, WikiLeaks)

Often crypto bull markets are driven by the combination of a technical innovation and an improved process to buy crypto currencies on exchanges. This is why the history of crypto is interlinked with technologists on the one side and crypto exchange operators on the other.

BitPay, founded in May 2011 by Tony Gallippi and Stephen Pair, is a company that provides Bitcoin and Bitcoin Cash payment processing services for merchants. While the company only started to get venture capital funding and gain traction a few years later, it was part of a wave of companies which were providing services between Bitcoin holders and merchants who could and would accept crypto for payments.

Meanwhile some non-profit groups also started accepting Bitcoin as donations. These groups included the Electronic Frontier Foundation and WikiLeaks, which started taking Bitcoins in January and June 2011 respectively. The involvement of WikiLeaks and the association with payment services on the Silk Road darknet website have helped to paint a picture of Bitcoin being used for illicit activities. During a secret meeting on June 23 2011, before he took refuge in the Ecuadorian embassy in the UK, the founder of WikiLeaks, Julian Assange, described Bitcoin to Eric Schmidt, then executive chairman of Google, as "a stateless currency."[8]

Figure 4: The first crypto bull market peaked in June 2011

TradeHill: an early Bitcoin exchange (2011–13)

Without appropriate regulation it was difficult to facilitate a seamless onramp from fiat money into crypto as banks were unwilling to transact with crypto companies. A problem that would exist for at least the next decade was that most crypto firms failed to set up reliable and recognized banking relationships. A few companies have tried to step in over the years to fill this void, but most encountered problems with strict anti-money laundering (AML) and know-your-customer (KYC) compliance rules.

Although the first wave of Bitcoin adopters and innovators were US-based entrepreneurs, the crypto industry would eventually be scaled in Asia. Back in 2011 one of the few methods to buy Bitcoin was on Mt. Gox in Japan, which processed about seventy percent of all Bitcoin transactions globally at the time. Buyers had to send an international wire transfer into the personal bank account of CEO Mark Karpelès, a process in which foreign exchange risk and delays in trade confirmations were common.

On June 8 2011 Jered Kenna launched a Bitcoin exchange called TradeHill, which was very similar to Mt. Gox but based in San Francisco in the U.S. Kenna had first bought Bitcoins in a batch of five thousand at 0.20 dollars each and immediately became hooked.[9]

Within two months TradeHill was already reporting anomalies with its onramp payment company Dwolla, which had stopped accepting deposits. On August 10 the exchange resumed its service, providing methods for SEPA (Single Euro Payments Area) transfers for both deposits and withdrawals. SEPA is a quicker payment system than the standard SWIFT transfers.

Even though TradeHill was based in the U.S., buyers still had to wire money to Kenna's personal ING bank account, and everything was manually verified. The process was very cumbersome, and handling money required various licenses that were costly and time-consuming to obtain. Then the Financial Crimes Enforcement Network (FinCEN), a bureau of the U.S. Department of the Treasury, released regulation on virtual currencies that would force TradeHill, and other US-based Bitcoin exchanges, to register as a money transmitter with the federal government. This meant that if TradeHill wanted to operate in the U.S., it was required to receive licenses from each state individually—and most states had different rules, so the process was complicated and costly.

TradeHill shut down on February 13 2012 due to increased regulatory scrutiny and because Dwolla removed over 100 thousand dollars in "chargebacks" from its account without notice. TradeHill sued Dwolla, but the charges were dismissed to allow for alternative dispute resolution as stipulated in Dwolla's terms of use. TradeHill had become the second-largest exchange and Bitcoin prices fell from 5.50 to 4.40 dollars, a decline of twenty percent when TradeHill shut down.[10]

On June 29 2012 FinCEN issued efforts to establish a regulatory framework for new payment methods[11] and on March 18 2013 FinCEN issued its first comprehensive discussion of virtual currency and how it fits into the Bank Secrecy Act (BSA) regulatory structure.[12] The report confirmed that anyone selling units of a decentralized virtual currency to another person for real currency, or its equivalent, is categorized as a money transmitter and therefore needs to be licensed.

TradeHill reopened after launching a new service called Prime, a business-to-business digital exchange intended to facilitate the exchange of digital currencies between businesses and large investors. However the firm was still ill-equipped to handle the regulatory burden, and in August 2013 it suspended trading due to "operational and regulatory issues" faced by its bank, the Internet Archive Federal Credit Union (IAFCU).

As mentioned above, procuring a money transmitter license is a costly and time-consuming endeavor as different states in the U.S. work under different rules and regulations. Estimates vary, but the time needed to acquire all the licenses is approximately two years and the cost is around 1.0–1.5 million dollars.[13] A New York money transmitter license alone would cost anywhere from ninety to 100 thousand dollars per annum to maintain.

The effect of the FinCEN license requirement was to push Bitcoin trading offshore, with some U.S.-based companies focusing on the onramp from fiat (U.S. dollars) to crypto instead of offering exchange services. BitInstant, meanwhile, built a business model around faster integration with the largest exchange, Mt. Gox.

BitInstant: a "fast Mt. Gox" (2011–14)

In early 2011 Charlie Shrem, who was born and raised in Brooklyn, New York, discovered the TradeHill website and wired some money to try it out. But the account got shut down, and he feared that the site was a scam. He called TradeHill and talked to Jered Kenna for three hours.

Shrem had an idea for a crypto start-up, and he ran it by Kenna. The idea was for a "fast Mt. Gox". Instead of wiring U.S. dollars to Japan and using Mt. Gox, Shrem's company BitInstant would help with the onramp so that customers could put money faster into Bitcoin exchanges.

Shortly after the conversation with Kenna, Shrem launched BitInstant, "a processing company that would engage with the four largest Bitcoin exchanges."[14] BitInstant charged a fee for users to purchase and make purchases with Bitcoin. It also provided temporary credit to speed up transactions. Users could buy Bitcoin on the BitInstant exchange with fiat currencies without sending them across the world to Japan.

BitInstant was launched with a ten thousand dollars loan from Shrem's mother. Shortly afterward it received 125 thousand dollars from angel investor Roger Ver in exchange for a ten-percent share of the company, followed by another 1.5 million dollars from a group of investors led by Winklevoss Capital Management. Ver, who had spent ten months in federal prison in 2002–03 for selling fireworks without a license, asked that Shrem hire his friend Erik Voorhees, who became BitInstant's head of marketing.

Voorhees would later set up other crypto ventures, such as SatoshiDice, a Bitcoin gambling game site; Coinapult, a site that allows users to transfer Bitcoin via SMS and email; and ShapeShift, a Bitcoin and altcoin exchange. In July 2013 he sold SatoshiDice to an anonymous investor for 126,315 Bitcoins (valued at 11.5 million dollars back then).

BitInstant partnered up with the peer-to-peer and cross-border money transfer companies MoneyGram and Softpay, enabling it to reach many retail outlets in the U.S. The company also allowed its customers to purchase Bitcoin through more than 700 thousand stores, including Walmart, CVS, and Walgreens.

BitInstant was an instant hit, and by early 2013 it was processing approximately thirty percent of all Bitcoin transactions. In June 2013 the company announced its integration with Jumio, an online payment and credentials company, a move which enabled it to verify customers' identities.

In July 2013, however, BitInstant abruptly suspended its services to "improve the code based on trends they noticed."[15] Shortly afterward it received around 17,300 customer service complaints, followed by class action lawsuits charging the company with false representation and failure to perform services. As a result the company was forced to shut down trading operations.

On January 26 2014 Shrem was arrested at New York's JFK airport. Prosecutors alleged that he and Robert Faiella had conspired to launder one million dollars' worth of Bitcoins to help users of the Silk Road marketplace make illegal purchases anonymously. Faiella operated a Bitcoin exchange on the black-market site and received a discount from BitInstant for high-volume trades of Bitcoin that he purchased for Silk Road buyers.

In September 2018 the Winklevoss twins filed a lawsuit against Shrem for thirty-two million dollars, claiming that he had stolen thousands of Bitcoins from them back in 2012. Early in 2013 the twins had bought 108 thousand Bitcoins—one percent of the 10.8 million Bitcoins that had been mined up until then.

Despite the early attempts of TradeHill and BitInstant the three largest Bitcoin exchanges in 2013 were BTC-e, Bitstamp and Mt. Gox. BTC-e— which was launched in July 2011 by two Russians, Alexander Vinnik and Aleksandr Bilyuchenko—had around eight percent of global volume, while Bitstamp—founded in August 2011 by Slovenian entrepreneurs Nejc Kodric and Damian Merlak—had around twenty percent. But the bulk of Bitcoin trading remained in Asia, with Mt. Gox still accounting for around seventy percent of the overall trading volume.

Mt. Gox: the Bitcoin exchange in Japan (2010–14)

In July 2010 programmer Jed McCaleb read about Bitcoin on the social news website *Slashdot* and decided to reuse a website he had previously built for trading cards in the virtual world, *Magic: The Gathering Online*. A few years earlier he had purchased the web domain *Mt. Gox*—short for

Magic: The Gathering Online eXchange—and on July 18 Mt. Gox launched its exchange and price quoting service.

Initially Mt. Gox used PayPal as the main funding option, but because of a chargeback fraud the exchange switched to Liberty Reserve on October 10 2010. Liberty Reserve was a Costa Rica-based centralized digital-currency payment processor company that was shut down in May 2013 by U.S. federal prosecutors due to its lax security and for operating without a money transmitting business license.

Liberty Reserve was started back in 2002 in the U.S. by Arthur Budovsky and Vladimir Kats. In 2007 the duo received a five-year prison sentence for operating an illegal financial business, but the sentence was reduced to five years' probation. Budovsky and Kats subsequently moved to Costa Rica, where they operated Liberty Reserve until they were arrested in 2013. Budovsky went on to receive a twenty-year prison sentence, after U.S. prosecutors had accused the company of handling six billion dollars of criminal proceeds.[16]

Meanwhile, in February 2011 McCaleb had transferred the Mt. Gox site, in return for twelve percent of the shares in the new company, to French software developer and network administrator Mark Karpelès, who had been living in Japan since 2009. In 2011 Bitcoin was trading at 1.0 dollar and volumes had started to pick up, leading to Mt. Gox recording around twenty thousand transactions per day.

On June 13 2011, however, the Mt. Gox exchange was robbed of twenty-five thousand Bitcoin (400 thousand dollars) from 478 accounts. Then, on June 17, Mt. Gox's user database was leaked for sale to Pastebin, a text storage site which was used by hackers to post data.

On June 19 many fraudulent trades caused the nominal price of Bitcoin to drop from seventeen dollars to 0.01 dollars. The hackers then started buying Bitcoin at this artificially low price, using the private hot-wallet keys of Mt. Gox customers and obtaining about two thousand Bitcoins in the process. The Mt. Gox private key had been unencrypted, and potentially stolen, earlier in 2011. Mt. Gox's poor accounting procedures disguised the extent of the hack, and it is still unclear whether this information was obtained through a hack or with the help of an insider. Over the next three years the hackers succeeded in skimming at least 650 thousand Bitcoins from customer accounts without the exchange noticing.

Analysis by WizSec, a Bitcoin security specialist firm that matched up most of Mt. Gox's deposit and withdrawal logs, showed that the discrepancy between the exchange's expected and actual Bitcoins had started to widen as early as 2011.[17] Bitcoins appeared to have left Mt. Gox without going through a valid withdrawal process, and from there they would be either resent to the exchange, moved into a different account or moved to other crypto exchanges, such as BTC-e or Bitcoinica.

By February 2013 Mt. Gox was handling most of its Bitcoin transactions globally, and the site had nearly 1.1 million active accounts from 239 countries, with about thirty percent of customers coming from North America. On some days the exchange handled upwards of ninety percent of all Bitcoin trading worldwide, ultimately generating forty million dollars in fees in 2013.

In 2012 Mt. Gox had formed a partnership with CoinLab, a Bitcoin project incubator and tech firm, to handle all of its North American services. CoinLab was a Seattle-based start-up working on projects involving Bitcoin and had been launched by Peter Vessenes, Mike Koss, and Tihan Seale, with Silicon Valley venture capitalist Tim Draper being the prominent 500 thousand dollar angel investor who had helped to get the firm off the ground. In May 2013 CoinLab, which also provided Bitcoin software and technology products, sued Mt. Gox for seventy-five million dollars, claiming breaches of contract relating to the parties' exclusivity agreements and revenue sharing provisions, among others.[18]

By then Mt. Gox was also under investigation by the U.S. Department of Homeland Security due to claims that one of the exchange's subsidiaries was operating without a license in the U.S. In order to accept funds in dollars, Mt. Gox had opened a Wells Fargo business account under its subsidiary Mutum Sigillum, but the company had failed to report that it was engaged in money services. The Department of Homeland Security issued a seizure warrant to Dwolla for the money in Mt. Gox's Dwolla account, and CEO Mark Karpelès was facing up to five years in prison for failing to register Mutum Sigillum properly as a money service business.

During the summer of 2013 Mizuho Bank in Tokyo, which handled Mt. Gox's transactions, pressured the exchange to close its banking account. As a result the Mt. Gox fiat onramp and banking relationships were slowly cut off. Then, on February 7 2014, Mt. Gox halted withdrawals after detecting unusual activity on its Bitcoin wallets. Bitcoin prices plunged, and 24,750 former customers ultimately sought compensation.

A Cyprus-registered company, Sunlot Holdings, tried to resurrect Mt. Gox without success, after buying McCaleb's twelve-percent stake for one Bitcoin. Brock Pierce, the main person behind the Sunlot Holdings company, was a former child actor who, while initially focused on the gaming industry, went on to become a leading figure in crypto. Pierce would later be a cofounder of Tether, Blockchain Capital, and Block.one, as well as a vocal proponent of establishing Puerto Rico as a crypto enclave.

The Mt. Gox hack is still not fully resolved, although a U.S. grand jury has indicted BTC-e cofounder Alexander Vinnik, accusing him of receiving funds from the Mt. Gox hack and laundering them. There is, however, no reliable accounting available on how much Bitcoin was stolen while the Mt. Gox exchange was still operational, and it took until 2023 before some of the stolen Bitcoins were expected to be returned to investors.

BTC-e: the notorious Russian Crypto Exchange (2011–17)

Between September 2011 and May 2014 Alexander Vinnik and his co-conspirators at BTC-e allegedly stole 530 thousand Bitcoins. Vinnik, who used the nickname WME in forums, was responsible for financial operations at the company, while his cofounder Alexandr Bilyuchenko was responsible for the technical part of the exchange.

BTC-e is estimated to have handled nine billion dollars in Bitcoin transactions between 2011 and its closure in July 2017, when Vinnik was arrested in Greece. Vinnik was subsequently extradited to France in 2020, where he was sentenced to five years in prison for operating an international money laundering scheme responsible for the laundering of four billion dollars, or 300 thousand Bitcoins.

The BTC-e exchange quickly became popular, largely due to the absence of any user verification system (user registration only required an email address—a strategy which has repeatedly been used by new crypto exchanges over the years to grow user numbers quickly). BTC-e also had no anti-money-laundering (AML) controls in place.

In March 2014 BTC-e began to offer trading in Chinese yuan. The move came after the Chinese crypto exchange BTER announced that it would be halting deposits from banks due to expected stricter controls and a potential ban. BTER had been launched in 2012 by Lin Han, a former postgraduate student in Canada with a PhD in optics focusing on high-performance computing, and the company was officially operated by Jinan Manwei Information Technology.

BTER had 230 thousand registered accounts, half of which came from China, and it processed transactions worth 890 thousand Bitcoins. However, in February 2015 it was on the verge of closing after two hacks, one of which caused a loss of 7,170 Bitcoins. The hack involved the company's cold wallet, a cryptocurrency wallet that stores private keys on a hardware device offline. BTER traced the stolen Bitcoins to the mixer platform Bitcoin Fog, which allows users to mix their Bitcoins in a wallet with those of other users to prevent the source of the Bitcoins from being traced back to the Users.

Roman Sterlingov, a dual Russian-Swedish national, is believed to have operated Bitcoin Fog from 2011 to April 2021, when he was arrested at Los Angeles International Airport by the U.S. Department of Justice.

During this time he is thought to have moved over 1.2 million Bitcoins, valued at 335 million dollars. According to his arrest warrant the bulk of these Bitcoins came from darknet marketplaces, including Silk Road and AlphaBay, and were tied to illegal narcotics, computer fraud, abusive activities, and identity theft.

Within six months of the first two hacks BTER suffered another hack and was unable to repay its customers. But while the exchange managed to keep operating by negotiating a bounty with the hacker, it finally closed after China introduced a ban on ICOs in 2017—only to be reopened after dropping fiat trading and rebranding itself as Gate.io, an exchange which focuses on crypto-to-crypto and Chinese yuan over-the-counter (OTC) trading.

Capital controls were always a major reason behind the fast adoption of Bitcoin by Chinese users, since Bitcoin offered a faster option and a seemingly less traceable way to move money out of the country. Investment opportunities in China were seen as being limited to real estate and the stock market. So after it started offering trading in Chinese yuan, BTC-e quickly became one of the world's most successful exchanges. In 2015 it was handling around three percent of the global Bitcoin exchange volume.

Despite BTC-e's success, its links to the Mt. Gox hack eventually brought law enforcement closer to shutting it down. From the Mt. Gox hack three BTC-e accounts received thirty thousand Bitcoins, while the rest went into digital wallets through the TradeHill exchange in San Francisco and back into Mt. Gox wallets controlled by Vinnik's account.[19]

Authorities believe that the Russian cybercrime group Fancy Bear was among BTC-e's clients, and the exchange is suspected of having ties to Russia's military intelligence unit, the GRU, as well. After Vinnik was arrested in 2017, the BTC-e exchange stopped working. At the time it held sixty-five thousand Bitcoins and other currencies worth more than one billion dollars.

In April 2018 BTC-e moved over thirty thousand Bitcoins out of its service wallet, with around fifty million dollars' worth transferred to the cryptocurrency OTC broker SUEX OTC, S.R.O. (SUEX). Registered in the Czech Republic[20] without any known physical presence, SUEX claims that it can convert crypto holdings into cash. Based on data from Chainalysis,[21] since becoming active in February 2018 SUEX has received 481 million dollars in Bitcoin, including funds associated with ransomware, scam operators, and darknet markets. It has also been sanctioned by the U.S. Treasury's Office of Foreign Assets Control (OFAC) after being found to have moved hundreds of millions of dollars' worth of crypto into cash at physical branches located in Moscow and St. Petersburg in Russia.

In 2020 the authorities in New Zealand froze ninety million dollars from Canton Business Corporation, a company belonging to Vinnik, and a wallet linked to the BTC-e exchange was found to have moved ten thousand Bitcoin (165 million dollars) to unknown wallets in 2022.[22]

WEX: the BTC-e clone (2017–18)

To repay BTC-e's customers after its servers had been seized by the FBI in mid-2017, a clone exchange was started under the name WEX. The idea to revive the exchange was suggested to Alexandr Bilyuchenko by Dmitry Vasiliev, a major client of BTC-e who had primarily traded on behalf of Chinese investors. Vasiliev became the owner of the official legal entity behind the new exchange, World Exchange Services (WEX).

The WEX crypto exchange bought out and migrated the BTC-e user base along with their digital profiles, and created the WEX tokens, which were used to represent customers' seized funds. However, despite its new internet address, the WEX website resembled the old BTC-e one by design, functionality and even trading pair options.

By the end of 2017, WEX had eighty million dollars in daily turnover and was one of the top twenty most popular crypto exchanges.[23] BTC/USD prices were quoted thirty-five percent higher, at a premium, than on other international exchanges. After a year of operation, WEX froze all withdrawals and shut down overnight after claiming to have "completed schedule maintenance".

CEO Dmitri Vasilev announced that he had sold the exchange to Dmitri Khavchenko. The exchanges wallets were drained of millions of dollars' worth of crypto before and after shutting down. In 2019, Alexei Bilyuchenko confessed to being the WEX administrator and claimed that he was forced to transfer all the money, 450 million dollars at the time, to Russia's Federal Security Service (FSB).

Both Russian exchanges, BTC-e and WEX had near non existent KYC and AML compliance procedures and become a natural hub for illicit Bitcoin trading. While some money was recovered from the Mt. Gox hack, users of BTC-e and its clone lost most of their funds.

Mt. Gox files for bankruptcy (2014)

On February 28 2014 in Tokyo Mt. Gox filed a form of bankruptcy protection from creditors, reporting that it had liabilities of sixty-five million dollars. The company admitted to losing almost 750 thousand of its customers' Bitcoins and around 100 thousand of its own Bitcoins, a total of around seven percent of all Bitcoins mined back then.

Mt. Gox CEO Mark Karpelès was arrested on August 1 2015 by Japanese police on suspicion of having accessed the exchange's computer system to falsify data on its outstanding balance. On March 14 2019 the Tokyo Court found Karpelès guilty and sentenced him to 30 months in prison.

When Mt. Gox imploded, the bulk of its Bitcoin trading volume went to three Chinese exchanges—Huobi (based in Beijing), OKcoin (also based in Beijing), and BTC China (based in Shanghai)—while most of the U.S. dollar-based trading gravitated to Bitfinex (based in Hong Kong) and Bitstamp (the Slovenian company, which since April 2013 had been registered in the UK).

Roger Ver—the angel investor in BitInstant, who is known as "Bitcoin Jesus" for his longtime evangelism for Bitcoin—was also an early investor in CoinLab and a customer of Mt. Gox. In addition he was a user of Bitcoinica, a New Zealand–registered Bitcoin derivatives exchange based in Singapore, where he stored nearly twenty-five thousand Bitcoins. Bitcoinica's bankruptcy claim against Mt. Gox was filed with sixty-five thousand Bitcoins.

Meanwhile Tihan Seale, one of the cofounders of CoinLab, was focused on bringing deal flow to the CoinLab incubator. He also scouted investments for other firms, and in late 2011 he came across Bitcoinica as well.

3

"Free your money, one Bitcoin at a time"
(Bitcoinica)

Bitcoinica was launched on September 8 2011 by Zhou Tong, a seventeen-year-old high-school student in Singapore. Originally from China, Zhou had received a scholarship from the Ministry of Education in Singapore to go and study in the city-state, where coding became his only passion.

Bitcoinica: the first leveraged Bitcoin exchange (2011–12)

Zhou started Bitcoinica on Heroku, a cloud infrastructure that initially only supported the Ruby programming language, which is not an ideal language for financial trading. Zhou outsourced system administration, security, banking, and everything he could not handle to third parties, but still spent less than 100 dollars a month processing millions of monthly page requests.

Bitcoinica was started as an experiment to help users trade Bitcoins with the advanced features of traditional leveraged foreign-exchange markets. The exchange offered Bitcoin margin trading and was the first to allow people to short, or bet against, the price of Bitcoin.

Bitcoinica made a lot of money from position liquidations—except for huge and forced liquidations, where accounts went negative and the exchange would be on the hook as they could not go after users with negative balances. Forced liquidations often take place at relatively unfavorable prices within the trading range, and if the exchange does not liquidate positions fast enough, users' accounts can become negative. This is the risk that the exchange takes by offering excessive leverage to its users. While some have said over the years that volatility is a feature and not a problem for crypto, it is remarkable how often exchanges eventually lose out when overleveraged client accounts lose money.

During its early months of trading Bitcoinica pocketed fifty-three thousand dollars per month from trading operations, with revenue increasing steadily. It was a lucrative business for a high-school student who did not have any professional training and was not aware of the regulatory environment of running a crypto exchange. At its peak the exchange's volumes may even have been comparable to those of Mt. Gox, with net profit increasing to six digits per month.

As with foreign-exchange trading Bitcoinica took no commission, offering only bid-and-offer spreads, which tended to be 1.7 percent wide. As a comparison Mt. Gox charged 0.6 percent fees and BTC-e 0.2 percent fees, while Bitcoinica itself paid 0.25 percent fees to trade on Mt. Gox.

Bitcoinica soon became the leading exchange for leveraged trading in Bitcoin. Within months it was matching 600 thousand Bitcoins per month, pocketing ten thousand Bitcoins per month in the process. With an exchange rate of 5.3 dollar per Bitcoin, its fifty three-thousand dollars in monthly revenue could also have been substantially more if prices had climbed higher.

The Bitcoinica site reached forty million dollars in transaction volume within just six months, with users depositing a total of one million dollars in assets on the platform. Users could leverage their bets up to a ratio of ten-to-one. However some quickly lost money through trading with excessive leverage. In fact *'zhoutonged'* became Bitcoin slang for losing your position on a margin call or being financially ruined. Some Bitcoinica accounts were wiped out with negative value because the exchange could not close positions fast enough during highly volatile periods. And while Zhou insisted that users should honor negative balances, these clients never returned, leaving their accounts negative.

Just two months after Bitcoinica launched, Tihan Seale, the investment scout who had cofounded CoinLab, came across Zhou. While identifying

Bitcoinica as a promising start-up in the Bitcoin space, Seale pointed out that the exchange was experiencing growing pains as its success had outgrown the capacity of a lone student. Due to the regulatory concerns that Seale outlined, Zhou agreed to a sell out to the Wendon Group, an investment fund that Seale represented, with the official handover time being January 2012.

Seale facilitated the Bitcoinica takeover for an undisclosed amount, setting up Core Credit Limited as its general partner on February 9 2012. Zhou was paid eight thousand dollars a month to operate Bitcoinica part-time while Seale looked for a management team willing to run the exchange and manage Wendon's investment.

Then, on March 1 2012, Linode, a New Jersey–based web and cloud hosting company that managed Bitcoinica's data, had an internal security breach that gave the attacker access to a wallet in which Bitcoinica stored some of its funds. A vulnerability in Linode's customer system was used to obtain administrator access to many popular Bitcoin servers. In total eight accounts dealing with Bitcoin businesses were targeted, with Bitcoinica being the largest one impacted.

More than forty-three thousand Bitcoins, worth 228 thousand dollars at the time, were stolen by the hacker.[24] Bitcoinica said that they would cover the losses for their customers as the company had now been acquired by Core Credit. Seale, who represented Core Credit, was under the impression that the exchange's "cracking out six-figure profit" per month would continue after its acquisition of Bitcoinica.[25] However monthly profits quickly went from one-hundred thousand dollars to zero by March 2012 as the exchange experienced numerous issues, including constant problems with the algorithm that executed buy-and-sell orders for Bitcoinica on Mt. Gox.

Zhou wrote down several security and technological improvements that Bitcoinica urgently needed to make. But as he was still a student, he did not have the time, the professional capacity, or the skills to upgrade the exchange. As for Seale, he thought that the issues could all be resolved once the new management was on board, as "in the meantime, any company expense would be coming directly from user deposits" (by then the net financial position of the company had changed to monthly losses of forty-thousand dollars and then eighty-eight thousand dollars).[26]

Eventually Donald Norman, Patrick Strateman, and Amir Taaki agreed to help improve Bitcoinica's technological infrastructure. The trio, who had set up the Bitcoin spot exchange Intersango, would not take any salary until the exchange's losses had turned into profits again.

Intersango was a popular exchange, trading forty-five thousand Bitcoins in Europe across different BTC-currency pairings, with Euro and Sterling the most active pairs. When TradeHill shut down in February 2012, Intersango became the second-largest exchange after Mt. Gox. But in July 2012 Intersango's UK bank, Metro Bank, halted its ability to send and receive payments, causing weeks of delays for users to get their funds. The exchange also suffered after the Bitcoin Savings & Trust (BST) company closed down on August 17 2012.

The Intersango trio, especially core developer Patrick Strateman, had become known in the industry for pointing out vulnerabilities and inconsistencies at other Bitcoin exchanges. At Bitcoinica Strateman found a vulnerability that would have allowed him to withdraw the exchange's hot wallet, which was accessible over the internet. This was brought to the attention of Seale, who struck a deal with the trio, allowing them to manage the Bitcoinica exchange.

In exchange for giving Norman, Strateman, and Amir a combined interest of twenty-five percent in Bitcoinica LP, the Wendon Group acquired 250 shares in Intersango. Seale also set up a new entity called Bitcoinica Consultancy, which gave twenty-five percent of the business to the trio and the remaining seventy-five percent to Wendon. The trio's early involvement with Bitcoin, their experience operating a Bitcoin exchange, and their reputations for expertise in online security provided great reassurance to Seale.

Norman, Strateman, and Amir accepted responsibility for Bitcoinica on April 24 2012. As the three executives of Bitcoinica Consultancy, they had exclusive legal authority to act on behalf of the company. They also had exclusive responsibility for Bitcoinica's daily operations in all respects, including security and hot-wallet management. In addition the trio became owners and operators of Bitcoinica LP, through a separate consultancy agreement to be set up on April 24 as well.

Christopher Heaslip, an accounting professional in New Zealand, assisted with the formation of the new company. Bitcoinica LP set up a new corporate structure and completed registration as a financial service provider in the legal jurisdiction of New Zealand. This license was ideal for receiving third-party funds for deposit, opening accounts for clients, and engaging in leveraged currency trading activities.

From the time of the verbally agreed consultancy agreement until all the documents were signed and approved by the New Zealand regulator, Norman, Strateman, and Amir discussed with Zhou and Seale how to improve the Bitcoinica site. The plan was that Strateman, as the core developer, would rewrite the whole site, while Norman would help with the logic for the hedging bot—the algorithm behind the exchange. The management team also wanted to set up partnerships to increase traffic and work closer with Bitcoin.com, a website which Roger Ver eventually gained control of in April 2014.

In early May 2012 Zhou pointed out to the Bitcoinica management that users had built huge short positions and that open interest was about 180 thousand Bitcoins. The exchange's profit potential was high because the market could move in either direction and users could be forced to stop out. Bitcoin exchanges have made vast profits by stopping out and liquidating customers—a reason why so many exchanges have been set up and why exchanges tend to be profitable beyond the bid-offer price quotations. However, by some estimates forty-five percent of Bitcoin exchanges have failed within the first three years of launching.

As a new business initiative Zhou proposed to set up a "secure loans" system where customers could settle Bitcoin loans between themselves, with the loans being two-hundred-percent overcollaterized. This system would increase the velocity of U.S. dollars and Bitcoin on the platform as users could trade with more leverage. The plan was to rely less on Mt. Gox and let customers trade more against each other.

But on May 11 2012 Bitcoinica was robbed again. An intruder broke into the site and proceeded to lift 18,547 Bitcoins from the company's hot wallet. Zhou discovered an entry into Bitcoinica's Rackspace server through a compromised email address. The hacker took the entire site content down, while also deleting the backups in cloud files.[27] Without proper backup and accounting records, processing claims was nearly impossible.

Bitcoinica had an internet mailing list called *info@bitcoinica.com* which was the login email for the website and all the company's sensitive accounts. Several people had access to this mailing list, including Zhou, Seale, Strateman, Norman, and Amir. It was Strateman's personal email that was actually compromised. However, at the time of the intrusion the Intersango trio were not technically general partners, as the paperwork to establish the Bitcoinica Consultancy had not been completed—something that Seale suspected was a deliberate delay. This made the timing of the attack suspicious. And while accusations mounted that Zhou was behind the theft,[28] some people blamed the "anarchist" Amir, who in 2015 would join the People's Defense Units (YPG) "to offer his skills to the revolution" in Syria.[29]

Whoever was behind the Rackspace intrusion, Strateman, Norman, and Amir claimed that they had no liability for it, nor any authority to initiate the claims process. The site was eventually taken offline, and users were notified that they would receive fifty percent of their deposits.

Shortly afterward Bitcoinica was hit with another disaster, when its source code was leaked online in July 2012. Again some suspected that Amir was behind the leak, which led to the loss of forty thousand more Bitcoins. The loss was caused by the fact that the source code contained the Bitcoinica–Mt. Gox API (application programming interface) key, which was subsequently used to steal funds from the exchange. By this time Zhou had already moved on, leaving Norman, Strateman, and Amir as the remaining Bitcoinica operators.

After the Rackspace hack all compromised passwords were changed—except for the LastPass password for Bitcoinica's accounts, as it had not been compromised. The attack had only been possible because the LastPass account storing all the passwords needed to access the Mt. Gox account had been set to the same password as the one the Mt. Gox API key used by the Bitcoinica server to access funds. This password belonged to Zhou, who communicated it only to Seale (while they were meeting at the Chimelong Hotel in Guangzhou, China in February 2012, when Zhou sold the site to the Wendon Group), raising suspicions that Seale could have given the password to someone else who then exploited the site.

However several Bitcoinica users provided evidence that Zhou was behind the hack himself. Within hours of these accusations being posted online, Zhou claimed that his former business associate Chen Jianhai was behind the hack and that he (Zhou) was able to recover most of the coins. On July 26 2012 Zhou pointed out that "Chen was familiar with credit card fraud and … was quite active in the financial black markets".[30] For most Bitcoinica users this was all too suspicious.

Bitcoinica eventually collapsed, sparking civil litigation. On August 1 2012 Seale and the Wendon Group, as the general creditor to Bitcoinica LP, announced that it would appoint a receiver under New Zealand law. In response some users filed a complaint on August 6 in San Francisco stating that "Bitcoinica is an entity of unknown form and origin".[31] This was only the second Bitcoin-related lawsuit filed in the U.S., after TradeHill had sued Dwolla for two million dollars in March 2012.

On August 19 2013 Bitcoinica underwent liquidation proceedings in New Zealand. The company had 500 thousand dollars' worth of U.S. dollars and Bitcoin on hand and owed 1.2 million dollars to customers. While these amounts were relatively small, it should be remembered that leveraged Bitcoin trading was still in its infancy in 2012. Also it has been estimated that by the time it shut down, forty-four percent of Bitcoinica's user deposits had already been stolen.

When Zhou was later asked what he had learned from his experience of launching Bitcoinica, he said that a tech start-up founder must be a developer, as he believed the best way to make money is to generate value for others and take a cut. He also advised, "Never outsource core competency, and always outsource incompetency."[32]

In hindsight, it's incredible how a seventeen-year-old student built a Bitcoin futures exchange within a week with limited resources by himself. There was clearly a market for futures trading back then but suitable security as well as checks and balances were not the site's priority. However, the biggest impact of the Bitcoinica exchange came from its leaked source code, as in addition to enabling the hacker to steal forty thousand Bitcoins, it offered another person, Raphael Nicolle, the chance to rebuild the exchange under a different name.

ICBIT: the first Bitcoin futures exchange that matched users' orders (2011–16)

In August 2012 Vitalik Buterin, who would later be seen as the inventor of Ethereum, wrote that "ever since Bitcoinica shut down, the Bitcoin economy has lacked a way of betting for or against Bitcoin price at leverage."[33] This was because, while Bitcoinica was powering ahead, nobody paid much attention to ICBIT, a competitor futures exchange which launched just two months after the Bitcoinica exchange sprang up in Singapore.

While Bitcoinica had users trade with the exchange, employing an algorithm to buy and sell on Mt. Gox to cover its users' positions, ICBIT allowed orders to be matched between users, thereby shielding the exchange from the risk of individual trader bankruptcies.[34]

When Bitcoinica went under, user activity started to pick up at ICBIT, and the exchange was soon processing two thousand spot Bitcoin transactions per day, while the "futures" section traded 1,500 Bitcoin transactions per day. ICBIT was therefore the first Bitcoin "futures" exchange to use the "difference contract" method, whereby users could trade Bitcoin and futures on Bitcoin on the same exchange. This opened the door to arbitrage strategies between futures and spot.

ICBIT invented the inverse Bitcoin-USD futures contract, which years later would become popular on the BitMEX crypto exchange. During the first few years the futures cash-and-carry trade yielded two-hundred percent premium per annum as futures prices traded far above spot prices. ICBIT took a flat fee of 0.005 Bitcoin per Bitcoin (0.5 percent) in each contract as revenue. Over the next five years twelve thousand customers would execute 11.6 million trades on the platform.

In 2014 BitMEX and several other crypto exchanges—such as 796 (based in Guangzhou), Huobi and OKcoin (based in Beijing), and BTC China (based in Shanghai)—all launched similar versions of the ICBIT inverse futures structure. Since high leverage could cause severe losses for the exchange if trades were not liquidated fast enough, these exchanges set up a system where in extreme cases losses were socialized among the traders.

Users could trade on ICBIT anonymously, without any know-your-customer (KYC) or anti-money laundering (AML) compliance requirements. This eventually led to the exchange's closure, as without any KYC or AML identification users could not withdraw U.S. dollars. The Bitfinex team later solved this problem with the creation of Tether, as exchanges needed a way to fund their margin accounts without touching the banking system. The lack of reliable banking relationships due to crypto exchanges' rudimentary, or even nonexistent, compliance infrastructure has caused many crypto platforms to rely on stablecoins to account for inflows.

As a result of the lack of identification requirements, volumes at ICBIT remained quite low. And with low liquidity, prices could easily be manipulated. While ICBIT set daily price limits of plus or minus ten percent, several users complained that the "administrator" of the site manually overwrote this feature on several occasions to perform "manual clearing" of the order book. In *Bitcoin Magazine*, Vitalik Buterin wrote that, according to several sources, "ICBIT may be engaging in hidden market manipulation against their customers' interest."[35]

Nevertheless ICBIT was one of only a few crypto exchanges that was never hacked or lost users' funds through missteps by the exchange's operators. ICBIT's offsetting futures exchange model did not require a lot of Bitcoins in a hot wallet, which kept security risk at a minimum. However the lack of KYC and AML requirements kept volumes low, as the exchange was also not registered anywhere as a financial service provider.

In 2016 the Sweden-based crypto broker Safello acquired BT Technology, including the ICBIT futures exchange platform, having raised 685 thousand dollars the previous May in a crowdfunding campaign backed by Barry Silbert's Digital Currency Group (DCG).[36] ICBIT's founder and CEO, Aleksey Bragin, joined Safello as Chief Technology Officer.

Bitfinex: the exchange with peer-to-peer borrowing and lending (2012–)

Bitfinex started off as a spin-off on the back of the leaked source code of Bitcoinica, redeveloped by French IT technician Raphael Nicolle. After three years as a systems administrator, Nicolle got involved in the Bitcoin ecosystem by building the Bitfinex trading platform, allowing people to trade Bitcoin on margin and lend in U.S. dollars and Bitcoin.

Nicolle became known in the Bitcoin Forum with the username "unclescrooge",[37] openly discussing with other members Bitcoinica's bugs and how Bitfinex should be improved from the leaked source code.[38] Bitfinex's key innovation was popularizing a peer-to-peer borrowing and lending market for fiat and crypto. This enabled traders to effectively engage in margin trading—something that Zhou had also proposed for Bitcoinica but had not been able to implement before it was shut down. Bitfinex also allowed users any form of collateral to fund their margin trades.

When a Forum user wanted to know how Bitfinex handled private keys and databases, Nicolle responded that the Bitfinex wallet and private keys were encrypted.[39] "I have a copy on my work computer (Fedora Linux) to process withdrawal,"[40] he replied. "I have a paper backup, 2 digital backups on two of our computers, 1 on a physical drive. The wallet is encrypted by a random passphrase, which is written down on paper (my partner loves papers) and in a GPG encrypted text file (which is a file encrypted by a master password we cannot forget while not being easily bruteforcable [*sic*]). The only copy of this wallet, which contains all the addresses generated by the Bitfinex server, is backed up every hour (although there [is] not much point to it)."

Only Nicolle and his wife had the keys and credentials to allow the sending of Bitcoins from Bitfinex's wallet to banks and the Mt. Gox exchange, where Bitfinex actively traded. Initially there was no "dead man's switch", so if both Nicolle and his wife had been unable to return to a computer, all the Bitfinex coins and funds would have been lost.

On November 22 2012, only months after Bitcoinica's collapse, Vitalik Buterin wrote an article about Bitfinex in *Bitcoin Magazine*, putting the exchange on the radar for the Bitcoin trading community.[41] In the article Buterin described how, unlike Bitcoinica, Bitfinex would not have a hot wallet; instead it would process withdrawals manually at the end of each day to limit the risk of being hacked. The API (application programming interface) keys, meanwhile, would only be used for trading, and not to withdraw coins—as a way of preventing a replay of Bitcoinica's hack in July 2012. In addition Bitfinex would offer two-factor authentication from the start.

Buterin also explained that instead of trading purely on the exchange, Bitfinex orders could also be "routed" in an attempt to match them with opposing orders on the site—a move which enabled Bitfinex to lower the execution fee to only 0.1 percent. The exchange also set up an interest rate system where users could earn up to 16.5 percent annual yields in exchange for providing liquidity.

As with Bitcoinica, however, the cap on leverage was set at ten-to-one, which meant that users could post a small amount of Bitcoin as margin in order to take out huge leverage. If they correctly guessed the direction of the Bitcoin price movement, they would win. But the platform might sit on the losses if the prices moved in the opposite direction and the exchange could not liquidate the account in time. It all depended on the exchange's algorithm.

In his article Buterin also compared Bitfinex's policy of not having a hot wallet to that of a bucket shop, because it created "perverse incentives." A hundred years ago the legendary Wall Street trader Jesse Livermore described the bucket shop approach, which allowed customers to build huge leveraged positions only to then stop those customers out.[42] As trades were only settled at the end of the day, the bucket shop could run up as much risk as customers could stomach, before engineering a cascading reversal in prices by simply making an order on the market large enough to significantly bump the price up or push it down, and then liquidating all of its users with opposite positions at high leverage and keeping all of their profits.

Buterin also warned about Bitfinex's founder, who in the summer of 2012 had been "strongly supporting" Trendon Shavers (aka "Pirateat40"), the U.S. entrepreneur who had operated Bitcoin Savings and Trust (BTCST) before eventually being sentenced to eighteen months in prison for running a Ponzi scheme. The Shavers Ponzi scheme was the first U.S. criminal securities fraud case related to Bitcoin.[43] Prosecutors alleged that from 2011 to 2012 Shavers had raised at least 764 thousand Bitcoins for BTCST, which at the time were worth more than 4.5 million dollars.

BTCST was operated from Shavers' home and offered online-related Bitcoin investments. Shavers promised seven-percent interest rates per week to investors who loaned Bitcoin to BTCST while he pursued a "market arbitrage strategy." However he largely used new investors' Bitcoins to pay back prior investors— a classic Ponzi scheme. At BTCST's peak Shavers controlled about seven percent of all the Bitcoins in public circulation. Prosecutors alleged that he also "misappropriated Bitcoins to purchase a BMW car, buy a steakhouse dinner in Las Vegas and used some money for spas and casinos".[44]

Bitfinex appeared to have started in a similar way. Nicolle was twenty-six years of age and living in Lyon, France when he started the site. According to one of his blog posts, "[W]hen I need more coins than I have to fill an order, I will ask everyone that previously 'registered' with me to lend me some BTC. After 7 days, I will return all of it, principal + 2% interests [per week]. … Now the questions you might have: What could you do to make so much profit? Let just say that I do "arbitrage": I buy low and sell high."[45]

Over the years it would always be "riskless arbitrage" that captured investors' imagination of risk-free profits, only for them to realize that the arbitrage strategy had a lot of hidden or even explicit risk embedded. While arbitrage often exists in less mature markets, it tends to occur only temporarily and attracts other traders motivated by the profit potential, which removes the arbitrage from the market over time.

Nicolle openly defended Shavers' business practices. "Pirate turns growth in demand for bitcoins (ie USD flows to bitcoins) into bitcoins profit. That's why he needs massive (at bitcoin scale) capital," he wrote on a Bitcoin forum, adding elsewhere that, "I have no problem with ponzi talks and whinnings [sic], but don't drag the parasites that be into this, thanks."[46] At the time, in 2012, Nicolle might have been under the impression that Bitcoin was outside the law, or perhaps that Ponzi schemes were simply legitimate.

While the Bitfinex project was initially started in October 2012, the site gained publicity in 2013 once a more experienced manager had taken over. Giancarlo Devasini became a partner in Bitfinex in late 2012 and moved the company to Hong Kong, where jurisdiction and taxation were more favorable. Officially he served as Bitfinex's chief financial officer.

Devasini started to get interested in cryptocurrencies in 2012, when he was looking to sell DVDs and CDs for 0.01 Bitcoins, or roughly eleven cents, promising free shipping for bulk orders. Born in Turin, Italy in 1964 and trained as a doctor at the University of Milan, Devasini quit his job as a plastic surgeon just two years out of college in 1992. According to his Bitfinex profile, he built a group of companies in Italy which grew over one-hundred million Euros in revenue and which he claimed to have sold shortly before the 2008 crisis. However Italian company documents show that revenues were just twelve million Euros and that the firm closed after a devastating fire in Devasini's warehouse and offices in February 2008. The parent company, Solo, went into liquidation in June 2008, while the subsidiaries were written down to a nominal value of one Euro only.

This was not the only interesting detail in Devasini's résumé. In December 1996, following a yearlong investigation, he paid sixty-five thousand dollars in a settlement with Microsoft after admitting that he had sold a thousand copies of counterfeit software.[47] The investigation, which had followed a complaint for breach of copyright and trademark rights in respect of more than forty people, led to a series of raids across Italy and the seizure of more than twenty-five thousand counterfeit disks (OEM floppy-disk versions of Microsoft products).

In December 2007 Toshiba also sued one of Devasini's companies, Acme, for alleged infringement of its patents for DVD format specifications, while in 2006 another of Devasini's companies, Alcosto, had bought 1,575 memory chips from a U.K. business regarded by a 2016 U.K. tax tribunal as "linked to fraudulent tax losses."[48] Then, in March 2010 one of Devasini's Monaco-based entities, Perpetual Action Group, was banned from the online used-electronics marketplace Tradeloop after a buyer had claimed to have received a box from the company filled with wood instead of memory chips.

Before joining Bitfinex, where he ran the exchange's trading and risk management operations, Devasini had also briefly launched a food delivery service called Delitzia. Although he had shown exceptional business sense throughout his career, it was Bitfinex that catapulted him into a different league, especially as Hong Kong was about to benefit from Bitcoin's explosive growth in Mainland China.

In 2013 Bitcoin interest in China went through the roof, and Bitfinex was a major beneficiary due to Hong Kong's proximity to the Mainland. Devasini actively engaged with Bitfinex's clients, developing a lively dialogue with Philip Potter, one of the exchange's initial and most active clients. Potter, who had Wall Street experience, had many suggestions for how Bitfinex could be improved, and he eventually joined the exchange as its Chief Strategy Officer.

In late 2013 Bitfinex became the fourth-largest Bitcoin exchange, with eight-percent market share, after BTC-e (twenty-five percent), Bitstamp (thirty-one percent), and Mt. Gox (thirty-four percent). Early the following year crypto news website *CoinDesk* included Bitfinex in its Bitcoin Price Index (BPI) benchmark calculation, increasing the exchange's credibility within the crypto trading community. And when Mt. Gox went under in 2014, all the volume was transferred to Bitfinex.[49] As a result, by March 2014 Bitfinex was the third-largest Bitcoin exchange, with twenty-seven-percent market share, after BTC-e twenty-nine percent and Bitstamp forty-three percent.

In 2014 Bitfinex launched the stablecoin Tether, and while there is common ownership and similar management of the two companies, their relationship is not widely known or disclosed. This is because the companies are run from different locations around the world, operating in a decentralized way with different senior people working out of different jurisdictions. However the Paradise Papers data leak in 2017 revealed that

Tether was actually set up on September 5 2014 by Devasini and Potter in the British Virgin Islands.[50]

Devasini appears to have listed addresses in Switzerland, Italy, and the French Riviera as his residence. Referring to Devasini, Sam Bankman-Fried (SBF) the former CEO of FTX and cofounder of Alameda Research, has said that "he's responsive 24/7, and he's not just responsive to crises or unbelievable opportunities, he's responsive to day-to-day operations"[51]—notably coordinating the purchase and redemptions of Tether tokens for customers like Alameda Research with Deltec Bank, the Bahamas financial institution which is also the bank of both Bitfinex and Tether.

Tether gained popularity in 2017, when Bitcoin exchanges were banned in China and when Bitfinex was struggling with its own banking relationships. And when, in September 2019, Binance—the world's largest crypto exchange since 2018—also set all its crypto pairs against Tether's USDT (the so-called "digital dollar") instead of fiat, USDT demand and issuance started to explode.

When Bitstamp was hacked in 2015 for a modest amount of five million dollars (nineteen thousand Bitcoins), Bitfinex became the single largest exchange for non–Chinese yuan trading. The exchange benefited tremendously from the mass adoption that was happening across the border from Hong Kong in Mainland China, where in 2013 the government had appeared to fully embrace Bitcoin through several TV documentaries putting cryptocurrencies in a positive light, and where the commercial sector had begun accepting Bitcoin as a payment method.

PART TWO: THE SECOND CRYPTO BULL MARKET (2013)

4

"Bitcoin has already reached into our daily lives"
(Baidu, Chinese web service company)

C hina dominated Bitcoin trading in 2013. Its share of global Bitcoin trading volumes rose from 1.5 percent during the summer of 2012 to 10.8 percent in 2013 and 70.8 percent in 2014.[52] There were many reasons for this rise, from capital controls and availability of capital to the build-out of large-scale Bitcoin mining sites, as well as the speculative Chinese mindset and support from government-sponsored media channels.

Chinese state TV and companies embrace Bitcoin (2013)

A whole nation supported Bitcoin, because by buying Bitcoin with Chinese yuan and selling it into other currencies, Chinese nationals could effectively evade capital controls and move money around the world.

In 2002, seventeen years before Facebook (now Meta) announced its intention to create a currency called Libra (which it eventually withdrew following a regulatory outburst), the popular Chinese instant-messaging service Tencent QQ launched a virtual currency called QQ Coin. QQ Coins became popular in 2007 and were widely accepted by online vendors in exchange for "real" merchandise such as small gifts. But the People's Bank of China (PBC), China's central bank, tried to crack down on QQ Coins, prompting Tencent to claim that they were a "mere regular commodity, and … therefore, not a currency."[53] The attempted crackdown, however, only caused the value of QQ Coins to rise as third-party vendors increasingly started to accept them.

There is a crucial difference between a commodity, which tends to be loosely regulated, and a currency, which is usually only issued by the sovereign state itself. Crypto, especially Bitcoin, has tried to separate the state from money creation, stripping away the sovereign's monopolistic powers. This has obviously raised scrutiny and led to pushbacks from governments. It has also prevented institutional adoption without a regulatory framework, which governments are unwilling to provide.

Figure 5: The second crypto bull market peaked in December 2013

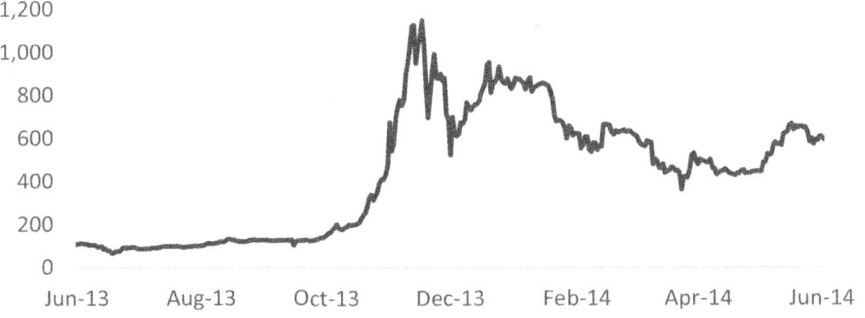

The Chinese government eventually decided to regulate QQ Coins in 2009, making it illegal to redeem them for above the purchase price, and only allowing their use for the purchase of digital items. Since then buying real-world goods with any virtual currency has been illegal in China. Nevertheless the early experience with QQ Coins certainly helped with the lightning-fast adoption of Bitcoin a few years later.

But the real catalyst for the Bitcoin bull market in China was when a Chinese charity, One Foundation, started accepting Bitcoins to help raise funds for earthquake victims in Lushan, Sichuan province on April 20

2013. Within a few days the charity had received 233 Bitcoins, and it subsequently received Bitcoins worth a total of 30 thousand dollars.

By May 2013 print and TV media channels had started to pick up on Bitcoin and the people's "generosity," something that China's state media were eager to report on. *The People's Daily Online* ran a story on May 7, when one Bitcoin was worth 759 Chinese yuan (122 dollars), outlining that Bitcoin "had great powers and that it could be exchanged for real banknotes and also could be directly used for shopping."[54] The story listed online merchants accepting Bitcoins for payments, such as Garage Café in Beijing[55] as well as some Taobao stores (part of a popular online shopping platform owned by Alibaba).

Also in May 2013 China's state-owned TV channel CCTV 2 broadcast a thirty-minute documentary on digital currencies, which sparked local interest and started the country's Bitcoin boom. According to data from SourceForge China's download volume of Bitcoin-Qt (the original Bitcoin client software) rose from 103 thousand downloads in January 2013 (making it fifth globally, behind the U.S. with 635 thousand) to 712 thousand downloads in January 2014 (making it second globally, behind the U.S. with 1.4 million).[56] This was a sevenfold increase during a period when the download volume in the U.S. only doubled.

During the Bitcoin boom many people in China also became interested in Bitcoin mining. The Chinese tech community began constructing mining rigs on a grand scale, recouping their setup costs within a few weeks as Bitcoin prices had their strongest rally in 2013. By September the number of Chinese Bitcoin validation nodes (any computer running a Bitcoin implementation program and storing the entire blockchain) had catapulted China into the number two position of Bitcoin validators globally.

BTC China: the country's first Bitcoin exchange capitalizes on the bull market (2013)

Originally set up in 2011, BTC China was the country's first major Bitcoin exchange. The platform offered no-fee trading for starters, with the only fees that users paid being a 0.5 percent Tenpay (China's version of PayPal) cash in/out fee and a one percent bank transfer fee.

In April 2013 Bobby Lee, a Chinese native residing in the U.S., took over BTC China after approaching the company's then two-person team and agreeing to invest his own money in the equity of the exchange. After graduating from the elite prep school The Lawrenceville School in New Jersey, Lee had attended Stanford University, where he graduated with a bachelor's and master's degree in computer science in 1998. Having previously worked for IBM, Microsoft, Yahoo, and Walmart, Lee brought international experience as well as technological expertise to the newly launched Bitcoin industry in China.

Interestingly Lee's brother Charlie, who is also a computer scientist, is the creator of Litecoin—one of the earliest "altcoins" built on top of the Bitcoin network. Charlie graduated from the Massachusetts Institute of Technology (MIT) with a bachelor's and master's degree in computer science in 2000. Prior to creating Litecoin, he worked for Google and Coinbase.

When Bobby Lee took over BTC China, he quickly secured a five million dollar investment from Lightspeed China Partners, an offshoot of the Silicon Valley venture capital firm Lightspeed Venture Partners. The exchange grew quickly until "two aggressive, well-supported competitors emerged" later that year: OKcoin and Huobi. [57] Nevertheless, by November 2013 BTC China's global market share in Bitcoin trading had reached 32.5 percent.

Bitcoin adoption goes full steam (2013)

The Chinese are known for being passionate gamblers. Officially gambling has remained illegal in most parts of the country, apart from the state-owned national lotteries and a few betting sites. Internet sites were also blocked for Chinese users, so Bitcoin offered a new way for the

Chinese to speculate back in 2013. From early 2010 to late 2013 the Chinese stock market declined by thirty-five percent, while in 2013 alone Bitcoin prices increased 5,738 percent from thirteen to 746 dollars, making crypto an attractive value proposition. So instead of buying stocks, Chinese investors started buying Bitcoin.

When Baidu—China's version of Google, and the country's largest internet site by traffic—announced in October 2013 that it would accept Bitcoin for payment services,[58] China's share of global Bitcoin trading volume exploded from 10.8 to 70.8 percent. According to Baidu Bitcoin had "already reached into our daily lives." It was "a new kind of electronic currency, a digital transfer medium, which has already received a high degree of international recognition, and ... is considered quite 'trendy.'"[59] At the time the price of Bitcoin was just under 160 dollars.

By early November BTC China was trading 110 thousand Bitcoins per week, compared to the UK-based Bitstamp exchange, which was trading ninety-three thousand plus seventy-six thousand on Mt. Gox. Wenzhou, the east coast city known for its entrepreneurial and speculative culture, saw an especially large interest in Bitcoin trading.

In China most Bitcoin trading happened on spot and not on futures markets. Institutional activity was minimal as the scene was dominated by retail traders. Bobby Lee, CEO of BTC China, explained the appeal of Bitcoin in China as follows: "China has been known as a nation of savers, who are always saving for a rainy day. Bitcoin is a digital asset, like real estate, gold, or stock. It is just one more option now. With Bitcoin hard-coded to be limited, it's like a collectible."[60]

Capital controls in China prevented the two-way convertibility of the Chinese yuan proceeds of BTC-USD trading. Bitcoin prices tended to trade at a thirty-percent premium in countries with capital control restrictions, so speculators could buy Bitcoin at Mt. Gox in U.S. dollars, send them to BTC China, and sell them there for yuan. However converting them back from yuan to U.S. dollars was difficult—although this was not a serious problem, as most traders were primarily concerned with sending money out of China. As a result the Bitcoin premium remained for some time.

To get money out of China, trade invoices were often falsified, the movement of speculative cash being disguised as payments for goods and services. In the first quarter of 2013 alone China estimated that fake trade invoices accounted for a total of seventy-five billion dollars.[61] According to world trade data China exported 320 billion dollars' worth of goods to Hong Kong in 2013, while Hong Kong imported 266 billion dollars—a discrepancy of fifty-four billion dollars.[62] Some of these capital outflows could easily have been used to take advantage of large-scale speculative Bitcoin arbitraging from corporations, until Chinese financial institutions were eventually banned from using Bitcoin.

In the meantime many crypto exchanges and platform providers started to appear, with several turning out to be scams as the lack of regulation attracted many bad actors. GBL, for example, was a Chinese Bitcoin trading platform that claimed to be based in Hong Kong although investigators had shown that the company's server was actually based in Beijing. The platform appeared to have launched in May 2013 but shut down just a few months later, in November. GBL registered as a company with the Hong Kong authorities in June but never received a financial services license there. Yet, despite these red flags, a thousand Mainland Chinese investors sent GBL 4.1 million dollars, which subsequently disappeared.

Meanwhile Inputs.io, a digital wallet company, was hacked for 1.2 million dollars in two separate attacks on October 23 and 26. After this the Chinese authorities became much more wary about scams, hacks, and speculative behavior that was beyond their control. Bitcoin's rampant price increase had become a real concern, as the government was worried about the abuse of its capital controls and the threat to social harmony posed by the ongoing scams. So on December 5, less than seven months after state media had first promoted Bitcoin as a financial innovation, the Chinese central bank prohibited all Chinese financial institutions from using

Bitcoin. The move was followed by Baidu's halting acceptance of Bitcoins for certain services.

Following the central bank's lead, major Chinese banking institutions such as the Industrial and Commercial Bank of China (ICBC), the Agricultural Bank of China (AgBank), the China Construction Bank (CCB), and the China Merchants Bank (CMB) all announced that they would close all accounts related to Bitcoin businesses. While the People's Bank of China (PBC) did not ban Bitcoin outright, prices fell from 1,150 dollars to just 500 dollars within two weeks as Chinese crypto exchanges lost their banking relationships.

Chinese crypto entrepreneurs start to control Bitcoin mining (2013)

There was some confusion about the implications of PBC's ban for crypto traders and exchanges. Most banks stopped working with crypto companies, but trading in Bitcoin was still allowed and crypto adoption continued as more individual traders and private businesses started to engage with Bitcoin.

Bitcoin adoption had initially started in the U.S. through the pursuits of hobbyists, but China took it to another level as industrial-scale Bitcoin mining machines (CPUs and later GPUs) were set up in huge Bitcoin mining farms. Bitcoin mining became a competitive business requiring large capital expenditure—like the secretive high-frequency-trading "arms race" that quant trading firms had engaged in.

The code for mining Bitcoin with GPUs was released to the public in October 2010, but it was only when field programmable gate arrays (FPGAs) were introduced that Bitcoin mining started to scale, as FPGAs are more power-efficient than GPUs. Then, in June 2012 the U.S. company Butterfly Labs announced a breakthrough in mining hardware that used ASIC (application-specific integrated circuit) technology, where chips are customized for a specific use, rather than being general-purpose.

According to Butterfly Labs ASIC mining machines "could mine Bitcoins one thousand times faster."[63] As a result twenty thousand customers placed orders and Butterfly Labs collected between twenty and fifty million dollars in pre-orders. In the second half of 2012 the Bitcoin hash rate increased from ten to twenty-five terahashes per second.[64]

Inspired by Butterfly Labs, on August 7 2012 Jiang Xinyu (also known as "roasted cat") and Fan Dawei raised 167 thousand dollars through a crowdfunding approach for their ASICMiner shares, with an issue price of 0.1 Bitcoin per share.[65] Jihan Wu and Xiao Qiang both invested one thousand Bitcoins, receiving twelve thousand five hundred shares. Wu was born in 1986 and graduated from Peking University in 2009. Two years later he discovered Bitcoin and purchased nine hundred coins. Together with Chang Jia he founded Babite, the first Bitcoin community site in China. He was also the first person to officially translate Satoshi Nakamoto's Bitcoin white paper into Chinese.

Also inspired by Butterfly Labs, Guo Yifu, together with Zhang Nanxuan (also known as "Pumpkin Zhang") created the first dedicated Bitcoin mining machine chip in China.[66] Named Avalon, the miners first appeared in January 2013—one month ahead of the ASICMiners.[67] They were officially produced by Canaan Technology (Beijing Jianan Zhizhi Information Technology Co., Ltd.) and were capable of mining ten Bitcoins per day, with backers recouping their investments within two days. But with only 1,500 units assembled, the overall production capacity was low.

Yang Yaorui, one of the original creators of Renren (the Chinese version of Facebook), set up another Bitcoin mining hardware company, ASICME, on June 2 2013. The company, which had forty employees in Beijing, set the price for its machines at the one-month return-of-investment period. During the first month alone ASICME sold 833 thousand dollars' worth of mining equipment.[68]

The new Bitcoin miners made mining with desktop computers obsolete. Demand was so high that initially most equipment firms kept the machines for themselves, as they could make more money mining Bitcoin than selling the miners. As a result waiting periods for machines tended to be eight months for delivery to customers.[69]

Li Xiaolai, a former English teacher who was believed to be the largest holder of Bitcoins in China, also invested in ASICMiner. The manufacturer was able to build one machine for 328 dollars and sell it for 6,560 dollars, and by July 2013 the ASICMiner shares was trading at five Bitcoins per share—about five hundred times the original value. This led the company to distribute 140 thousand Bitcoins to its shareholders.

By October 2013 Jihan Wu had quit his day job as an investment analyst, establishing Bit China and cofounding Bitmain Technology with Micree Zhan. In November Bitmain introduced its first Bitcoin mining rig, the Antminer S1, which had a hash rate of 180 gigahashes per second. A few months later the Antminer S2 was released, with a significantly higher hash rate of one terahash per second. In 2014 alone Bitmain would introduce four new versions of the Antminer, and by 2020 the Antminer S19 Pro had appeared, with a hash rate of 110 terahashes per second. In 2017 Bitmain made one billion dollars in profits, and another billion dollars during the first six months of 2018. By this time Bitmain controlled eighty percent of the Bitcoin hardware market, with the company raising 500 million dollars at an eighteen-billion-dollar valuation.[70]

Meanwhile, in 2013 "roasted cat" had set up a "roasted cat mine" in Shenzhen, where the machines were so efficient that they accounted for forty-two percent of the total Bitcoin network—and sometimes even more than fifty percent. But as competition increased, the mine started to have problems, falling behind with dividend payments by January 2015. Investors came to the building every day to ask for answers, and the last time "roasted cat" logged onto the Bitcointalk forum was on January 26. After that he went missing. On March 3 nineteen thousand Bitcoins, with a value of five million dollars, were transferred out of three addresses linked to "roasted cat." Two years later two other accounts associated with "roasted cat" moved nearly eighteen thousand Bitcoins with a value of 160 million dollars.[71] The disappearance of "roasted cat" remains a mystery.

By the end of 2013 China's global Bitcoin mining market share had grown to seventy-five percent, giving Chinese Bitcoin mining firms a large amount of Bitcoin to speculate with on exchanges and to hedge their exposure. This enabled them to effectively control the global Bitcoin network. But while the Chinese Bitcoin mining machines became hugely successful, Butterfly Labs was shut down by the U.S. Federal Trade Commission (FTC) as the company failed to deliver a workable product amid accusations of fraud and misrepresentation.[72]

Meanwhile ever-increasing Bitcoin mining difficulty and increased competition caused mining profitability to decline, necessitating huge capital expenditure. In 2013 it took just thirteen hours to mine one Bitcoin using a normal personal computer. By 2014 the time had extended to twenty-three days, and in 2021 it was as much as ten years.[73]

As Bitcoin prices rallied in 2013, however, the payback time for Bitcoin mining equipment was as low as three days, although it largely fluctuated between ten and a hundred days in 2013 and 2014. This made it extremely attractive for entrepreneurs to raise capital for large-scale Bitcoin mining sites.[74]

One of China's earliest large-scale Bitcoin mining facilities, the so-called Ordos mine in Inner Mongolia, was set up in 2014. By 2017, when Bitcoin prices had reached four thousand dollars, the facility was mining Bitcoins with a market value of 280 thousand dollars per day and consuming thirty-nine thousand dollars in daily electricity, accounting for four percent of the processing power of the Bitcoin network.[75] At Ordos fifty employees slept on-site, watching over twenty-five thousand Bitcoin mining machines which were hosted in eight different buildings. In 2015 the mine had been bought by Bitmain.

But restrictions by the Chinese central bank, followed by limitations on commercial banks' engagement with Bitcoin exchanges, caused Bitcoin prices to fall into a steep bear market. Bitcoin's second major bull market, driven by China, was over. Bitcoin prices peaked out at 948 dollars in

December 2013 and dropped to 222 dollars in June 2015. The next bull market would not start until October 2015.

5

"If you want to get forked up check this out"
(Arthur Hayes, BitMEX)

On January 11 2014 China Central Television (CCTV) broadcast an overwhelmingly negative documentary centered on Bitcoin. The documentary, called *Outrageous Bitcoin*, compared Bitcoin to a Ponzi scheme and the Dutch Tulip Mania of 1634–37. It featured Mingxing "Star" Xu, CEO of the crypto exchange OKcoin, telling a story of someone who had lost half his investment during the Bitcoin crash, and Chandler Guo and his wife Jin Yangyang, the hosts of a popular Bitcoin videocast, speaking about people crying on the phone for help while they could do little to comfort them. [76] The documentary received harsh criticism as the interviews had been heavily edited to represent only the TV station's viewpoint.

China restricts banks from transacting with crypto exchanges (2014)

In March 2014 rumors started circulating that the Chinese government would penalize any bank transacting with Bitcoin exchanges after April 15. At the time Mainland Chinese people were collectively buying ten thousand Bitcoins an hour—far more than any other nation—according to FiatLeak, a site which tracks Bitcoin sales. Then, in May, the CEOs of the five major Bitcoin exchanges in China, including Star Xu and BTC China's Bobby Lee, all withdrew from the Global Bitcoin Summit that was scheduled in Beijing that month.

As a result of the ban on banks transacting with Bitcoin exchanges, in April 2014 one of China's largest Bitcoin exchanges, BTC38, announced to its users that the company would be suspending the use of third-party payment processors. Without third-party onramp possibilities Bitcoin exchanges had very few options to take Chinese yuan as payment for Bitcoin—hence the growth of stablecoins a few years later.

Hong Kong emerges as a global crypto hub (2014)

Another result of the ban on banks transacting with Bitcoin exchanges was the relocation of some Mainland Chinese crypto firms across the internal border to Hong Kong, where payments using Bitcoins were legally accepted, and where the Hong Kong Monetary Authority (HKMA)—the de facto central bank—took a more hands-off approach. According to law firm DLA Piper there was no governmental body in charge of regulating crypto currencies in Hong Kong and no indication that there would be any legislation or policies specifically targeting the crypto industry anytime soon. Indeed the HKMA even took Bitcoin out of its regulatory agenda, a move that was interpreted by some as the regulator turning a blind eye on crypto firms. This prompted DLA Piper to state that, "With an independent legal system and a high level of autonomy with the local currency, Hong Kong offers a goldmine of opportunities for tech start-ups and companies in the digital world to venture into bitcoin-related businesses."[77]

On February 28 2014 the crypto exchange Asia Nexgen (ANXBTC) opened the doors to the first physical Bitcoin shop in the world. Located in Hong Kong, the shop allowed customers to buy Bitcoin after providing government identification and proof of address. As part of the promotion launch for the shop ANXBTC gave away seventy thousand dollars in Bitcoin through a lucky draw. In an interview with the *South China Morning Post* cofounder Lo Ken-bon said, "The biggest issue people have right now is buying bitcoins ... people have to put money in and trade it through an online exchange."[78]

The HKMA viewed Bitcoin as a virtual commodity rather than a virtual currency. Therefore ANXBTC was seen as operating a vending machine and was not regarded as a currency transmitter, which would have required operating licenses and business approvals.

A few weeks after the opening of the ANXBTC Bitcoin shop Bitcoin ATMs (BTMs) also started to appear in Hong Kong, with three different companies competing to win customers. BTMs are ATMs that allow users to buy Bitcoins and transfer Bitcoins to someone else, with some even letting users sell Bitcoins and withdraw cash. The first BTM in the world was launched by Robocoin in a coffee shop in Vancouver in October 2013.

By the end of 2015 there were 443 BTMs worldwide. In 2018 there were four thousand—sixty percent of which were in the U.S., where BTMs are big business as regulatory scrutiny limits crypto exchanges' growth options. To operate BTMs in the U.S., a federal money transmission license is required from the Department of the Treasury, but it only takes fifteen minutes to receive the license through an online registration process on the department's website.

In 2018 Cottonwood Vending operated ninety-one BTMs in the U.S., generating annual revenues of thirty-five million dollars with just thirteen employees. The company paid five hundred dollars a month per machine to place the BTMs in stores, and charged users a nineteen-percent premium above the normal Bitcoin price as transaction fees and store owners' fees were added to the operating costs. This was still cheaper, however, than the estimated thirty-percent fees that money launderers might charge for illicit cash transactions.

Bitcoin of America, meanwhile, ran a BTM in northwest Detroit, one of the most dangerous neighbourhoods in the U.S. During six months of 2016 the BTM brought in 808 thousand dollars—which, thanks to a fifteen-percent transaction fee, resulted in cash revenue of more than 120 thousand dollars for the operators.

The number of BTMs in the U.S. peaked at just over thirty-four thousand in August 2022 according to Coin ATM Radar, while the amount of money funneled through BTMs globally fell to 230 million dollars in the following October, down from a high of 349 million in January 2021. This was despite the fact that, according to Chainalysis, the number of BTMs installed tripled during that time, indicating a seventy-five-percent drop in value generated per machine. This, in turn, signaled that a structural peak in BTM usage was occurring by 2022.

Back in Hong Kong BitFX launched its first retail store in November 2014 under Chairman Kevin Fong. Hong Kong consumers could now buy Bitcoin with cash instantly, making the city a viable hub for virtual currencies. Many Mainland Chinese frequently traveled to Hong Kong, bringing bags of cash with them. Officially travelers are allowed to take up to five thousand dollars of foreign currency or twenty thousand Chinese yuan in or out of the Mainland every trip. This became especially attractive after the People's Bank of China (PBC) prohibited Chinese banks and financial institutions from dealing with Bitcoin companies in December 2013.

Back then the average life span of a virtual-currency business was only nine months, as companies quickly ran into trouble or founders misappropriated funds. Hong Kong saw numerous crypto businesses being launched during this period. Daniel Wang, for instance, founded Coinport, offering Bitcoin payment processing services and a multi-currency exchange, while Aurélien Menant launched Gatecoin, another Bitcoin exchange.

Bitcoin exchanges were being launched all over Asia too. In South Korea Ki Hyun Joo launched Coinplug in August 2013, an exchange that is still in business today. Also in South Korea Bithumb launched in 2014, becoming the country's largest exchange with eight million registered users and a cumulative transaction volume of one trillion dollars. Meanwhile, in Indonesia Oscar Darmawan founded the Bitcoin Indonesia exchange in May 2013, which quickly gained over a million users and is also still in business today.

The impact of the Chinese currency devaluation (2015)

For ten years from 2005 the Chinese yuan had steadily appreciated by thirty-three percent, making the country's exports less and less competitive. The currency devaluation by the PBC in August 2015 was a desperate attempt to boost exports as domestic economic growth was slowing. But the Chinese people worried that a weaker yuan would erode their purchasing power, and since the country had—and still has—capital controls in place, many moved their money into cryptocurrencies. According to data from Statista the annual share of Bitcoin trading volume in China rose from sixty-six percent in August 2015 to ninety-three percent by August 2016.

After a ban on local exchanges in 2017 many Chinese traders turned to foreign crypto exchanges, via VPNs (virtual private networks) that circumvented China's great internet firewall. But on September 24 2021 the Chinese authorities announced new measures to curb crypto adoption. As a result Ethereum's second-largest mining pool, SparkPool, suspended operations three days later. Binance, by then the world's largest crypto exchange, also announced that it would be halting fiat deposits and spot crypto trading for Singapore accounts, while Huobi said that it would be retiring existing Mainland China–based user accounts by the year-end.

After the September 2021 ban Chainalysis noticed a disproportional inflow into DeFi (decentralized finance) protocols from Asia-based users, with the key beneficiaries being the decentralized exchanges Uniswap and dYdX, where users can swap stablecoins into other crypto assets. Mainland Chinese would also travel across the internal border to Hong Kong and deposit cash in one of the physical Bitcoin machines, or they would bring the money directly to an OTC (over-the-counter) crypto trading house that accepted cash, converting it into either Bitcoin or Tether's stablecoin USDT.

BitMEX: the 100x-leverage Bitcoin exchange (2014–)

BitMEX was founded in 2014 by Arthur Hayes, Ben Delo, and Samuel Reed in Hong Kong, and was operated by HDR Global Trading out of the Seychelles. In 2016 the exchange introduced perpetual futures, which would become the standard derivatives contract for all other Bitcoin exchanges.

After graduating from Wharton Business School with a bachelor's in economics and finance in 2008, Arthur Hayes joined Deutsche Bank on the day the investment bank Lehman Brothers went under. He moved to Hong Kong to work first at Deutsche Bank and then at Citibank, where he was a delta one trader. In this capacity he traded exchange-traded funds (ETFs), sold futures when they were trading at a premium, hedging his book by buying stocks and simultaneously trading one instrument against another. It was often a profitable arbitrage trading strategy, but it was quite boring and, relatively speaking, amounted to pennies every day. And in mid-2013 he was laid off.

Complaining that he had missed the golden days of finance, Hayes dedicated himself to trading Bitcoin with his own money. Back in 2013 the Bitcoin price in China was twenty to forty percent higher than in the rest of the world because of restrictions on the convertibility of the Chinese yuan. Hayes could sell Bitcoin in Mainland China for yuan, bring up to twenty thousand yuan (or, alternatively, five thousand dollars) back to Hong Kong and deposit it into his bank account, which accepted yuan and was able to convert it back into Hong Kong dollars.

Hayes also discovered the ICBIT futures exchange platform, where futures traded at a substantial premium to the actual Bitcoin price. Taking his delta-one trading strategy, he sold the Bitcoin futures that traded at a premium and hedged himself by buying spot Bitcoin. Then he waited until the futures expired to see if the strategy had been profitable. However he had much bigger plans than making money through arbitrage trading; he wanted to build a futures exchange himself.

Within six months of founding their company Hayes, Delo, and Reed had a beta version off the ground and had settled on the name BitMEX. This was short for Bitcoin Mercantile Exchange and was named after the famous Chicago Mercantile Exchange, where most traditional financial futures are traded. Initially the team raised 180 thousand dollars to start the company, through a combination of contributions from friends, family, and the venture capital (VC) arm of Chinaccelerator, an intensive start-up accelerator based in Shanghai.

BitMEX began its Asia push in mid-2015 through the Chinaccelerator program—which, Hayes explained, taught him and his cofounders how to crack the Chinese market as foreigners. The three cofounders also worked on getting Korean and Japanese traders onto the platform, working the social-media channels to win over potential users. Approachability was their currency.

Nevertheless, during the first twelve months of BitMEX's operation the number of registered users was relatively small—only 3,400. But these users traded upwards of 250 million dollars in exchanging volume by mid-2016,[79] as Hayes focused on winning over active traders to the platform. To drive traffic and create a sense of competitiveness, the company launched paper-trading competitions and established a leaderboard to show off the best traders' profits.

By early 2016 BitMEX was trading five million dollars a day and offering derivatives contracts with 100x leverage. Hayes wanted to make BitMEX a fully featured trading platform, and in April 2016 he told reporters that "BitMEX is the Goldman Sachs of Bitcoin."[80] Within three years the company would be trading close to one trillion dollars, having moved into Hong Kong's most expensive offices in Cheung Kong Center—the same building as Goldman Sachs.

BitMEX invented the perpetual swap (or "perp"), a futures contract that did not need to be rolled every month or quarter. The contracts started trading in May 2016. The following year Bitcoin went from one thousand to twenty thousand dollars, and BitMEX's exchange volume increased by

8,500 percent. Despite the market crash in 2018 volumes went up another six hundred percent that year, as BitMEX's users were able to bet on rising and falling markets—a great business model during volatile market periods and bear markets. All the exchange needed was volume, and while many spot exchanges closed during the two-year bear market as their volumes declined drastically, BitMEX continued to thrive.

Contrary to other exchanges BitMEX only allowed withdrawals once a day and with human oversight. This made it less attractive for hackers. But BitMEX was subject to numerous lawsuits from former customers alleging engagement in market manipulation, money laundering, trading against its customers, and breaking international compliance laws.[81]

Over the years BitMEX would eventually lose market share, with a turning point coming on March 13 2020, when Bitcoin prices fell by fifty percent within twenty-four hours and the exchange liquidated 1.1 billion dollars of customer positions—the highest number in eighteen months. [82] The exchange's order book at the time showed 1.4 billion dollars in sell orders versus just 131 million in buy orders. If these sell orders had been switched to market orders, Bitcoin prices could have crashed to zero as there was nobody willing to buy and money could not have been moved quickly enough onto the exchange to purchase low-priced Bitcoin. This is because ownership is updated every time a new block is mined on the Bitcoin network, and this tends to take ten minutes per block—too slow to move Bitcoin around during a market crash. In 2020 stablecoins were still not common, but their usage would explode after the March market crash.

BitMEX's stabilization fund, the last defense against a crypto exchange becoming bankrupt and socializing losses, only lost 4.6 percent in March 2020. The insurance fund for Deribit, the Panama-based options exchange, by contrast, was nearly wiped out, its value dropping ninety-two percent to just 227 thousand dollars. Deribit "went down" as a result, — along with Gemini, Huobi, and Bithumb, which all had similar issues.

During the market crash a DDoS (distributed denial-of-service) attack caused thirty minutes of downtime on the BitMEX exchange, during which traders could not manage their positions.[83] A DDoS attack is a malicious cyberattack that attempts to disrupt normal traffic to a web property. "Between 02:16 and 02:40 UTC March 13 2020," BitMEX subsequently informed its customers, "we became aware of a hardware issue with our cloud service provider causing BitMEX requests to be delayed. Normal service resumed at 03:00 UTC."[84] During the downtime prices started rallying sharply.

Some industry players accused BitMEX of liquidating holders and causing Bitcoin prices to hit multi-month lows. BitMEX dismissed these allegations as "conspiracy," blaming two DDoS attacks for the steep Bitcoin price decline on its platform. The company eventually refunded 156 accounts, paying out only 200 thousand dollars.

On the same day as the DDoS attack Sam Bankman-Fried tweeted, "Insane theory of the day: there was no BitMEX hardware issue."[85] Since there was an insufficient order book size for the number of automatic liquidations on the BitMEX exchange, prices were pushed down as the liquidation engine searched for liquidity. As traders became uncertain, prices gapped uncontrollably lower, and at a certain point BitMEX stopped lowering the prices where they wanted to sell. "They just sat there … hoping that someone would lift it. But no one did," SBF would write.[86]

Controversy also arose over the relationship between BitMEX the trading platform and the affiliated entity that engaged in market making, an entity known as Arrakis Capital.[87] As rumors spread, customers started complaining that their positions had been liquidated at unfavorable levels, because when BitMEX's auto-liquidation algorithm was switched off, Bitcoin prices rebounded.

As with SBF's own crypto exchange, FTX, a few years later, BitMEX needed a trading unit to start providing liquidity on its exchange. So the company funded an entity that would provide market prices on new products. That entity was expected to scale back when liquidity improved, and other market makers were attracted to provide pricing. If the market-making business was making too much money, BitMEX claimed that the team would tighten spreads and increase the amount of liquidity, thus acting in the best interest of its clients.

The BitMEX market-making desk was run by Nick Andrianov, a Ukrainian national who had previously worked at Deutsche Bank's equity flow and exotic options trading desk. There were accusations that Andrianov was represented on BitMEX's trader leaderboard under the pseudonym "quick-grove-mind", and that he had the ability to manipulate the BitMEX market.

Arthur Hayes stated that BitMEX's market-making business should be at best a break-even operation, and that its "earnings are comprised of a service fee paid by the business [the BitMEX exchange]." This encouraged it to participate in unprofitable trading and wash trading, and to inflate exchange volume. The market-making business was also the only entity allowed to sell options initially, giving it a unique status as sky-high implied option volatility caused option prices to be overvalued, giving BitMEX's users low probabilities of making money. Bitcoin option selling has been a profitable trading strategy for many years, as buyers tend to overpay for the chance of making outsized returns. According to some studies BitMEX option prices were five to ten times above the fair market price,[88] with contracts on crypto options exchange specialist Deribit being significantly cheaper.[89]

There were also accusations that BitMEX's trading affiliation had more bandwidth API (application programming interface) request allowances than that of other users. API requests determine how many orders per second the user is allowed to send to the exchange. Anecdotal evidence suggests that other institutional trading firms have repeatedly asked BitMEX for more bandwidth, but their requests have been denied. Four years later FTX ran into similar problems and accusations. However BitMEX appears never to have moved customer funds or to have given its market-making arm access to client positions.

Controversy also arose around BitMEX's insurance fund, which only temporarily decreased in size. The fund had 200 million dollars to protect the exchange and prevent the socializing of losses from overleveraged traders. Over the years BitMEX struggled with controversy due to the enormously high 100x leverage that its traders could play around with. Many of these traders failed to understand that when liquidity vanishes on an instrument, the bid-offer prices quickly widen and a stop-on-trading price can quickly get filled when the stop-loss price is set too tight. With the mark price on futures often swinging between premium and discounts, futures prices could deviate from spot prices frequently. This was the arbitrage play that many of the exchange's liquidity providers were playing with, and when traders were stopped out, the positions would normally be taken over by the liquidation engine.

On October 1 2020 the U.S. Commodity Futures Trading Commission (CFTC) and federal prosecutors charged BitMEX with illegally operating a virtual-currency exchange and breaking anti-money laundering (AML) laws while conducting business out of the U.S. and allowing U.S. customers to trade on the BitMEX platform. The U.S. Attorney for the Southern District of New York announced that Hayes, Delo, and Reed, along with BitMEX's first employee Gregory Dwyer, were being charged with violating the U.S. Bank Secrecy Act (BSA). The CFTC alleged that BitMEX had received some eleven billion dollars in Bitcoin deposits and made more than one billion dollars in fees while conducting a significant part of its business from the U.S.

On May 21 2022 Hayes was sentenced to two years' probation after pleading guilty to one account of violating the BSA in February 2022. Having pleaded guilty to charges stating that he had willfully failed to implement an AML program at the exchange, Hayes faced a maximum sentence of ten years in prison, but because he was a first-time offender with a long track record of charitable work the Probation Department recommended a period of probation with no incarceration.[90] BitMEX cofounders Delo and Reed also pleaded guilty to the charges.

BitMEX agreed to pay a 100 million dollar fine to settle separate charges for breaching the BSA. As the company struggled with accusations of market manipulation and rumors that the U.S. government would start prosecuting its executives, BitMEX slowly lost its spot as a leading derivatives exchange.

PART THREE: THE THIRD CRYPTO BULL MARKET (2017)

6

"It's a full house"
(Fenbushi Capital, Chinese venture capital firm)

The third crypto bull market, which occurred in 2017, was fueled to a large degree by one single innovation: the ICO (initial coin offering). ICOs are a blockchain-based approach to fundraising which helps to fund the development of the initial protocol. During ICOs investors buy digital "coins" used on crypto platforms which might give them voting rights or an entitlement to some sort of revenue stream from the protocol. However, contrary to IPOs (initial public offerings), where companies raise money by selling stocks, ICOs do not necessarily lead to an ownership share in the entity itself.

One selling point of ICOs was that they could offer instant—or at least faster—liquidity, as companies were keen to get their tokens listed. In addition large tech companies usually stayed away from blockchain investments as it would invite regulatory scrutiny. This allowed smaller players to build crypto businesses without the large tech players monopolizing specific segments of the crypto market.

Mastercoin: the second Bitcoin (2013)

The person who started the ICO period was J. R. Willet, a software engineer from Seattle who had grown up in Oregon and started coding when he was ten years old. Willet orchestrated the first ICO in 2013, when he created the Mastercoin (now Omni) protocol on top of the Bitcoin blockchain. He was also credited as the inventor of algorithmically stabilized stablecoins, while his friend Craig Sellars was the inventor of the first asset-backed stablecoin. Sellars, a computer scientist based initially in Santa Monica, was the founder and CTO of Tether (as well as the CTO for Bitfinex from January 2015 until May 2016), although he would later transition to an advisory role in the company.

Willet's "The Second Bitcoin Whitepaper" was published on January 6 2012.[91] In the paper Willet described how the existing Bitcoin network could be used as a protocol layer on top of which new currency layers with new rules could be built without changing the foundation, making it possible for anyone to create "interoperateable" tokens backed by the protocol. "Smart contracts would regulate those new tokens issued on top of Bitcoin," Willet wrote. Vitalik Buterin, then still a journalist writing for *Bitcoin Magazine*, wrote an article about Willet's white paper. A few years later he would create Ethereum based on Willett's ideas.

Figure 6: The third crypto bull market peaked in December 2017

Mastercoin's ICO was announced on July 31 2013. Mastercoin was seen as an extension of Bitcoin, and received 500 thousand dollars in Bitcoin as "funding," which was intended to be used for development and paying bounties for projects around the Mastercoin ecosystem. The ICO was a big success, and within four months Mastercoin had increased tenfold in Bitcoin value and twentyfold from its original USD value.

Mastercoin subsequently evolved into the Mastercoin Foundation and then, in March 2015, the Omni Foundation. Omni is a platform and software layer built for creating and trading custom digital assets and currencies. Omni transactions are Bitcoin transactions that enable next-generation features on the Bitcoin blockchain. For example Tether's USDT is a cryptocurrency asset that can be issued on the Bitcoin blockchain via the Omni Layer protocol. The Omni Layer acts as a bridge between "altcoins" (such as Mastercoin, which is regarded as the first altcoin), smart contracts and smart properties, and the Bitcoin blockchain.

In March 2014 Bitcoin added the OP_RETURN field, which enabled the addition of metadata to a Bitcoin transaction. Using this extra space, Omni could attach the details of smart contracts and smart properties without altering the foundation layer.

Instead of creating an entirely new blockchain, Mastercoin was seeking to create a completely new network on top of Bitcoin currencies, commodities, and securities. The company would use the Bitcoin blockchain to store every transaction. The key insight was that Mastercoin would be able to leverage Bitcoin's high degree of security and make it much easier to create protocols that would interact between Bitcoin and Mastercoin in the future, thereby enhancing the value and success of the foundational Bitcoin protocol. In this way Mastercoin envisioned supporting user-defined currencies, decentralized exchanges, on-blockchain price feeds, on-blockchain bets, savings addresses, and so on.

The Mastercoin protocol became the initial technological foundation of the Tether stablecoin. Later Tether stablecoins would be upgraded and issued on the Ethereum, EOS, TRON, Algorand, and OMG blockchains. The precursor of Tether, Realcoin, was announced in July 2014 by Craig Sellars, Brock Pierce, and Reeve Collins, and the project was renamed Tether on November 20. Pierce was one of the founding members of the Mastercoin Foundation, while Sellars subsequently became its CTO.

Pierce, an active angel investor, was an early adopter and advocate of Bitcoin, who had started mining as early as 2009. He was also an early investor in the Chinese crypto exchange BTC China, and in 2013 had joined Bart and Brad Stephens in founding the venture capital firm Blockchain Capital. In March 2014 Pierce and a group of investors had filed an offer to purchase the assets of Mt. Gox, using a Cypriot entity called Sunlot Holdings. The bid was unsuccessful. Pierce would end his involvement with Tether in 2015 and would later become a cofounder of Block.one in 2017, resigning a few months later in March 2018.

In 2017 Pierce had moved to Puerto Rico, which offered no federal personal income taxes, no capital gains tax, and favorable business taxes without having to renounce U.S. citizenship. In 2016 Puerto Rico had declared bankruptcy, with a large portion of the debt owed to U.S. hedge funds. Then, in September 2017, Hurricane Maria had caused enormous damage to the territory, prompting crypto investors to come to the island to build a "crypto utopia." Many of these investors were libertarians who saw crypto as a tool to circumvent taxes and other forms of government oversight, and many made the most of the opportunities, as oversight in Puerto Rico was relatively relaxed.

In June 2021 Pierce led an international delegation to El Salvador, to advise the Salvadoran government on its formal adoption of Bitcoin as the national currency. The country, which has pegged its currency to the U.S. dollar since 2001, adopted Bitcoin as a legal currency in October 2021.

While Pierce has undoubtedly become a leading personality in crypto, his early involvement in Mastercoin, which set off the ICO period and the era of smart contracts, was likely the most instrumental part of his career.

Ethereum: another expansion of Bitcoin's underlying technology (2014)

In 2010 Peter Thiel started the Thiel Foundation to provide young entrepreneurs with 100 thousand-dollar grants over two years if they skipped college for twenty-four months. Along with nineteen others, twenty-year-old Toronto-based Vitalik Buterin was awarded the fellowship on June 5 2014. His Ethereum project sought to expand the applications of Bitcoin's underlying technology into the field of smart contracts and decentralized finance applications.

Buterin was born on January 31 1994 in Kolomna, Russia, where he lived until the age of six, when he immigrated to Canada with his parents. In 2011 he started writing about Bitcoin for a blog, earning around five Bitcoins per article. He went on to write articles for *Bitcoin Magazine*, which was cofounded later that year by Mihai Alisie, a Romania-based Bitcoin enthusiast.

In 2013 Buterin shared a white paper on Ethereum, which he initially described as a digital currency. About thirty people reached out to him to discuss the concept. Six of these are regarded as part of Ethereum's founding team, along with Buterin. These include the four initial cofounders: Mihai Alisie, who helped to establish Ethereum's base in Switzerland; Anthony Di Iorio, who would later become the chief digital officer of the Toronto Stock Exchange and the CEO of Decentral; Amir Chetrit, who had worked briefly with Buterin at an Israeli startup called Colored Coins, which aimed to tokenize real-world assets; and Charles Hoskinson, Ethereum's CEO, who played a leading role in setting up the Ethereum Foundation, and who would later launch the Cardano token, an Ethereum competitor.

While these were the four initial Ethereum cofounders, two others would join the team shortly afterward: Gavin Wood, a British computer programmer who was introduced to Buterin's white paper through Amir Taaki, the British-Iranian anarchist who had been involved with Bitcoinica; and Joseph Lubin, who would later launch ConsenSys, an incubator for other blockchain startups. Lubin made contact with Ethereum through Anthony Di Iorio and the Bitcoin Alliance of Canada, while Wood got in touch with Buterin directly, offering to implement Ethereum in the C++ programming language. Wood met the founding team just before the North American Bitcoin conference in January 2014, where Ethereum was unveiled to the public. He would later propose Ethereum's native programming language Solidity. Like Jeffrey Wilcke, who was working on Mastercoin in the Netherlands, Wood wrote Ethereum's implementation in Google's Go programming language.

There were endless tensions among the various Ethereum cofounders, notably between those that wanted to build a commercial, for-profit business and those that wanted to make the company a mission-driven, non-profit organization. Lubin wanted to build a commercial business, and Hoskinson was eventually expelled from the group over the issue. Wood also left after repeated disputes. The first Ethereum transaction on the blockchain had been between Wood and Hoskinson, but both would later run Ethereum rivals—in Wood's case two: Polkadot and Kusama.

Hoskinson called himself Ethereum's CEO. He idolized Steve Jobs and started calling Buterin "kind of a Communist. He's not a capitalist."[92] On May 28 2014 he was fired by Buterin, along with Amir Chetrit, who had still been focusing on his Colored Coins project. Years later Di Iorio would also be fired. Hoskinson would later say that Ethereum became "a *Lord of the Flies*-style situation, where … whoever was most persuasive to Vitalik was the one who won."[93]

On July 2014 Ethereum raised thirty-one thousand Bitcoins (18.3 million dollars) through an ICO token sale. By this time the vision for Ethereum had changed slightly, as the founding team had realized that it was relatively easy to create decentralized file storage and concepts like name registry with a few lines of code on a blockchain. But as Bitcoin prices dropped through the summer of 2014 and the Ethereum Foundation failed to convert the Bitcoin into U.S. dollars, the company "suffered roughly nine million dollars in lost potential capital," Buterin wrote in his blog.

While Ethereum initially struggled, it was Buterin's links to China that eventually helped the project to take off. Because just when he appeared to be running out of money, Buterin met Feng Xiao, a tremendously influential investor from China.

Fenbushi Capital: the company that saved Ethereum

On September 30 2015 the Chinese conglomerate Wanxiang Group, the nation's largest auto parts manufacturer, announced its intention to invest fifty million dollars in Blockchain technology to improve its product lines.[94] The managing director of Wanxiang-owned subsidiary Datayes had purchased 416 thousand Ethers for a total investment of 500 thousand dollars. The investment included establishing two entities dedicated to promoting blockchain technologies. The first was a non-profit entity called Blockchain Labs, which was cofounded by Buterin along with BitShares cofounder Bo Shen and Feng Xiao from Wanxiang's investment arm. The second was a fifty million dollar venture capital fund named Fenbushi Capital—*fenbushi* meaning "distributed" in Chinese—with Wanxiang the sole limited partner (LP).

As a result of these developments Feng introduced Buterin to his investor network. Buterin spent months in China going to karaoke bars with venture capitalists and developers, his Chinese becoming so good that he started correcting his Chinese translators. He also made friends with many influential crypto people in China.

The Chinese loved Ethereum's open, decentralized nature. While most of the company's core development was happening in North America, most of the funding came from China. As a result Buterin became very active in the Chinese crypto community, always making himself available to speak to them. So when the ICO craze came in 2017, Ethereum was able to reach industry-leading status as Ether prices kept climbing higher.

In May 2017 the ICO for a new web browser called Brave generated about thirty-five million dollars in token interest in under thirty seconds. Then messaging-app developer Kik raised 100 million dollars in September. By November there were fifty ICOs a month, with the highest grossing coming in September 2017, when the decentralized storage network Filecoin raised 257 million dollars—200 million of which came within the first hour of the token sale.

Ethereum was the leading blockchain for ICO token sales like these, with a market share of eighty percent. This was because the tokens for new projects were generally based on the Ethereum ERC-20 standard, enabling the company to establish itself as the industry's base layer during the ICO craze.

The scale of this craze can clearly be seen by comparing the data for 2016–18. In 2016 forty-three ICOs raised over ninety-five million dollars, with the Waves Tech ICO alone raising sixteen million. In 2017 453 ICOs raised 6.6 billion dollars, the most notable being for Hdac, which raised 258 million dollars; Filecoin, which raised 257 million dollars; Tezos, which raised 232 million dollars; Sirin Labs, which raised 157 million dollars; Bancor, which raised 153 million dollars; and Polkadot, which raised 144 million dollars. Then, in 2018 a massive 1,082 ICOs raised twenty-one billion dollars, with Telegram raising 1.7 billion and Petro 735 million. But the clear standout was Block.one, raising 4.2 billion dollars over the period of a year.

Block.one: the four billion dollar ICO (2017)

Block.one was founded by Brendan Blumer and Dan Larimer and is best known for developing the EOS.IO protocol in 2017 (and subsequently releasing it as open-source software in 2018). In December 2017 Blumer, Block.one's CEO, promised to invest one billion dollars from its ICO through an investment arm called EOS VC, to grow the blockchain technology underpinning EOS and foster the startups that intended to build applications for the EOS protocol. But, instead, the company devoted its funds to unrelated ventures—including Bitcoin investments, which became hugely valuable over time—leading some to argue that Block-one had misled its ICO investors.

Block.one's aim was to facilitate efficient and scalable decentralized applications (dApps). This was a reasonable goal, as its blockchain works in a similar way to that of the Ethereum platform, But, despite an aggressive marketing campaign, it failed to attract other projects to make it a really valuable underlying layer.

The marketing campaign for EOS was stage-managed by another cofounder, Brock Pierce—the crypto investor who had previously been involved with Mastercoin and Tether. According to a former executive, from the very start Block.one's chairman, Kokuei Yuan, had made it clear that the company was a "marketing organization selling a token," Yuan is reported as saying that Block.one needed "to put up the minimum software necessary and then get out."[95]

At Block.one Blumer surrounded himself with people he knew from before and who he knew would not challenge him. Andrew Lewis, the company's chief strategy officer, was a childhood friend of Blumer, while Blumer's sister oversaw communications. As for Yuan, he had worked with Blumer at OKAY.com, a Hong Kong real-estate agency platform that Blumer had founded in 2005.

In 2019 EOS suffered congestion issues resulting in slow transaction times and high fees, which disappointed both users and developers. At the same time the U.S. Securities and Exchange Commission (SEC) announced a twenty-four million dollar settlement with Block.one over allegations that the ICO had been an unregistered securities sale that included US-based investors. Many of these investors wondered what the company was doing with the money that had been raised at the ICO. Some blamed the impending SEC lawsuit for the absence of developments, while others blamed the 2018 crypto bear market for making Blumer cautious in putting the funds to work.

In May 2019 Block.one revealed that it was holding 140 thousand Bitcoins, and that most of its holdings were in liquid fiat assets, while only 174 million dollars had gone into venture investments. In the same month the company announced a buyback, which valued it at 2.3 billion dollars—up from forty million during the 2017 seed round.[96] A private buyback is unusual and is often a sign that the company sees limited growth opportunities, or that it is trying to calm early investors disappointed by its growth trajectory.

Research by John Griffin of the University of Texas has pointed out that Block.one's one-year ICO sale was accompanied by suspicious trading. Griffin alleged that the sale saw many transactions that could be classified as "wash trades." A wash trade occurs when one entity executes both sides of the trade, buying and selling at the same time. The result is an inflated market value and a misrepresentation of investor interest. In the Block.one ICO recycled funds amounted to 815 million dollars based on Griffin's analysis.[97]

In December 2020 Block.one's cofounder Dan Larimer, who was also the company's CTO, resigned. In the following May the company announced the launch of its subsidiary Bullish, a cryptocurrency exchange. The launch caused the EOS token temporarily to surge fifty percent in value. The initial funds for the exchange were raised from Block.one's capital injection of 164 thousand Bitcoins, twenty million EOS, and 100 million dollars, as well as an additional 300 million dollars raised from a private funding round that included Peter Thiel, hedge fund managers Alan Howard and Louis Bacon, and Hong Kong tycoon Richard Li. Most of the investors in this funding round had also participated in Block.one's ICO in 2017.

In November 2022 Blumer purchased a 9.3 percent stake in Silvergate Bank, a crypto specialist.[98] Block.one also bought a 7.5 percent stake, making Blumer the bank's largest shareholder. By this time the EOS price had plummeted to 0.88 dollars, from fifteen dollars in May 2018.

While Block.one settled with the SEC in 2019, the ICO bubble burst shortly after the company finished its ICO, as the SEC had established that federal securities laws could be applied to token sales. The Block.one ICO had started just before the SEC released its Report of Investigation into The Decentralized Autonomous Organization created by Slock.it,[99] and in line with the findings of this report it judged that Block.one was required to register its ICO as a security offering as it had raised money from U.S. investors. According to Steven Peikin, a codirector of the SEC's Division of Enforcement, the company had also failed to provide its ICO investors with the information they were entitled to as participants in a securities offering.[100]

The Howey Test: a law from 1946 legislating crypto today

According to the SEC an "investment contract exists when there is the investment of money in a common enterprise with a reasonable expectation of profits to be derived from the efforts of others."[101] This is the so-called Howey Test, which refers to the U.S. Supreme Court case from 1946 determining whether a transaction qualifies as an investment contract. The Howey Test applies to "any contract, scheme, or transaction, regardless of whether it has any of the characteristics of typical securities". If a transaction is found to be an investment contract, it is considered a security and requires strict rules and guidelines for capital raising and marketing to protect investors.

The Howey Test is so vague, it is easy to put any form of crypto or financial asset under it. And by 2017 it had become clear that regulators, such as the SEC, were starting to crack down on protocols and companies' approaches to raising capital through ICOs without proper disclosures. This resulted in the third major bear market for crypto. Fortunately for the crypto industry, however, the regulators were short-staffed and crypto was not yet seen as potentially causing a systemic risk to either the financial system or the economy. As a result fines or settlements only resulted in minor punishments.

7

"Ending 2017 with incredible momentum"
(Brad Garlinghouse, Ripple Labs)

In July 2017 the U.S. Securities and Exchange Commission (SEC) indicated that it could apply federal securities law to initial coin offerings (ICOs). The SEC had investigated whether The DAO, a decentralized autonomous organization created by Slock.it, had violated U.S. law. It eventually decided not to pursue an enforcement action against Slock.it's cofounders, a decision which helped the crypto bull market to extend its life until December.

Slock.it was launched in 2015 by Stephan Tual, who had left his position as chief communications officer (CCO) at the non-profit Ethereum Foundation because he wanted to set up a for-profit business. Tual's vision was to create a "universal sharing network" with the Ethereum blockchain at its core. He aimed to do this by connecting all kinds of smart locks to the blockchain to enable users to receive payments directly and rent, sell, or share just about anything.

In November 2015, at an Ethereum Developer Conference in London (DevConL) Slock.it's cofounder Christoph Jentzsch described his proposal for The DAO, a venture which resembled a crowdfunding project but did not meet the requirements of a crowdfunding project under the U.S. JOBS Act of 2012. The idea was for participants to send Ethereum to The DAO to purchase DAO tokens which would permit them to vote and entitle them to rewards. Jentzsch likened this to "buying shares in a company and getting dividends." [102] All funds would be held at an

Ethereum blockchain address associated with The DAO, which planned to invest them in projects and distribute the anticipated earnings.

The DAO aimed to run through a set of independent curators who would put investment proposals forward. Many well-known experts from the Ethereum community volunteered to participate, giving the project additional traction. Within the four-week offering period The DAO raised twelve million Ethers—roughly 150 million dollars at the time, or ten percent of the overall supply. But before the venture was able to commence any funding projects, an attacker used a flaw in its code to steal a third of its assets.[103]

The Ethereum hack that split the community

On June 5 2016 Christian Reitwiessner discovered an anti-pattern in Ethereum's programming language Solidity which could have led to attacks on smart contracts. While Gavin Wood was credited with proposing Solidity, it was the team around Reitwiessner that later developed it. Solidity is a statistically typed programming language designed for developing smart contracts that run on the Ethereum Virtual Machine (EVM), and Reitwiessner had become a smart-contract advisor at Slock.it in December 2015.

On June 9 Peter Vessenes, cofounder of CoinLab and the Bitcoin Foundation, wrote a blog about Reitwiessner's discovery, which brought broader attention to the flaw. A few days later MakerDAO hacked itself and moved the code's funds into a safe "multisig" (a crypto wallet requiring two or more signatures before a transaction can be executed). Meanwhile, on June 12 Eththrowa had found the same anti-pattern in the rewards section of The DAO.

Slock.it submitted a DAO Security Proposal on May 26,[104] but the process required a two-week voting time, and on June 17 a hacker began moving 3.6 million Ethers into a ChildDAO address under his/her control. But the hacker was prevented by The DAO's code from moving the Ethereum from that address for twenty-seven days, and the Slock.it cofounders proposed a hard fork to the Ethereum blockchain to restore The DAO token funds. A hard fork is a branching of a cryptocurrency's blockchain that splits a single cryptocurrency into two chains.

On July 15 a short-notice on-chain vote was held on the DAO hard fork, with eighty-seven percent (representing 5.5 percent of the overall supply, or 3.9 million Ethers) voting for and thirteen percent against the fork.[105] Twenty-five percent of the votes in favour of the fork came from a single address.

On July 20, after the majority of the Ethereum network had adopted the necessary updates, the newly forked Ethereum blockchain became active. Surprisingly the old chain received continued support, so crypto exchanges started to list the tokens from the old chain under the name Ethereum Classic.

The SEC applies the Howey Test to ICOs (2017)

In December 2017 the SEC issued an order stating that the utility tokens marketed by California-based company Munchee for a planned fifteen million dollar token sale were classified as a security.[106] Munchee had wanted to improve an existing iPhone app centered on restaurant reviews by creating an ecosystem in which participants would be able to buy and sell goods and services using MUN tokens, which could be either purchased by users or earned by writing restaurant reviews on the app. Munchee was also in talks with restaurants to accept the tokens for meals and to sell advertising in exchange for tokens.

The SEC judged that investors could reasonably expect a return on their investment in MUN tokens, which would classify them as a security under the Howey Test. But since Munchee stopped the offering immediately after the SEC had contacted it, and before any tokens had been delivered to investors, no penalties were imposed. Nevertheless the intervention was significant as it showed that the SEC would respond to ICOs if it thought that they closely resembled IPOs for conventional securities.

In 2017 the SEC also created a Cyber Unit, which filed its first ICO charges against PlexCorps, a company which had allegedly defrauded investors with the ICO for its "next decentralized worldwide cryptocurrency" PlexCoin.[107] PlexCorps had already raised fifteen million dollars from investors before the SEC stopped the sale with an emergency asset freeze in December. PlexCorps' founder Dominic Lacroix was sent to prison for two months for making false statements, including the promise of returns of over 1,345 percent.

In April 2018 the SEC then charged two cofounders of the crypto firm Centra Tech with running a fraudulent ICO that had raised more than thirty-two million dollars in 2017. The company had received endorsements from boxer Floyd Mayweather and rapper DJ Khaled.

By this time the perception among many investors was that private markets were offering higher returns than were available in the stock market. The perception was reinforced by the valuation of the ride-sharing company Uber, which had remained private, at sixty-nine billion dollars in March 2017, and was further supported by the fact that access to private deals was restricted to high-net-worth individuals, institutions, and asset managers.

In addition to these benefits ICOs promised investors part of a company's revenue stream, like equity ownership in startups. Another major selling point was the promise of almost instant liquidity, as tokens were usually listed and could be traded immediately after the ICO period.

But without clarity on regulation and enforcement of the securities law, ICOs became a huge vehicle for scams and fraud. According to a survey conducted by Bitcoin.com, nearly half of the ICOs in 2017 went bust within four months of the ICO offering, with a majority of them failing by February 2018.[108]

China bans ICOs (2017)

At the same time as U.S. regulators were enforcing securities law on ICOs, Chinese regulators started to crack down on ICOs as well. This caused the bull market to reverse and set off another "crypto winter" (a prolonged decline in crypto prices).

One of the main players in the ICO boom in China was Chandler Guo, one of the country's earliest Bitcoin adopters, who traveled around China in a bus signing up projects to take part in ICOs. Guo, whose Chinese name is Guo Hongcai, is a well-known figure in China who appeared alongside his wife, Jin Yangyang, in the *Outrageous Bitcoin* documentary broadcast by China Central Television (CCTV) in 2014. In 2018 he and his family moved to Silicon Valley, which he believed was the real crypto valley, buying a one-hundred thousand-square-foot mansion with 500 Bitcoins and spending another 160 Bitcoins on two Rolls Royces.

Guo graduated from high school, but his grades were not good enough for Tsinghua University. So instead of attending the university, he moved close to the campus and made money by copying audio and video material from the Shuimu Tsinghua BBS forum, burning it onto CD-ROMs and selling them. He married early and had two kids, and when his family moved to Beijing, his wife came across the Garage Café, which functioned as a tech incubator space for aspiring entrepreneurs. There she attended a Bitcoin sharing meeting held by Li Xiaolai in March 2013. Li was a famous English teacher with New Oriental Education & Technology Group who had been allowed to buy a small number of pre-IPO shares before the company was listed in 2006 on the New York Stock Exchange. He subsequently sold these shares, investing first in shares in Apple and then in Bitcoin. Li was mostly living off royalties from previously published test-prep books that were paying him 7,200 dollars per year after taxes.[109] He is quoted as saying that "English teaching is essentially selling a dream".[110]

Li started buying Bitcoin in 2011, purchasing 2,100 Bitcoins when the value was just one dollar, before buying an additional 100 thousand six months later on the Mt. Gox exchange in Japan. He had many sleepless nights and subsequently branched out into Bitcoin mining, achieving a net worth of 100 million dollars before the 2014 Bitcoin crash. "This is the first time in history that human beings have found a way to ensure the inviolability of personal property," Li would say.[111]

In 2013 Li founded BitFund, a venture capital firm for which he was raising 3.3 million dollars. He also founded the crypto exchange Yunbi, before going on to focus on lending as a guarantor between two counterparties. In July 2017 Li raised eighty-two million dollars during the PressOne ICO. He was also an investor in both Block.one and EOS.

In a leaked recording in 2018 Li called Binance a "scam exchange,"[112] claiming the main reason behind its success was that when all the exchanges were forced to shut down during the 2017 crypto ban, "Binance managed to stick around."[113] In the recording he also revealed his own approach to cutting "leeks" (inexperienced buyers): using his celebrity status to hype up projects and "harvest retail and newbie investors."[114] Li would later be described as "China's richest Bitcoin billionaire," with an estimated net worth of 1.5 billion dollars in 2018 and 3.5 billion dollars in 2023.

After hearing Li speak at the Garage Café, Jin Yangyang bought five hundred Bitcoins at a price of two hundred Chinese yuan. When Bitcoin rose in value to 1,000 yuan, Guo realized that there was money to be made in Bitcoin and asked his wife to introduce him to Li. In 2013 Guo and Jin then cofounded China's earliest Bitcoin self-media company. Guo put all his money into Bitcoin, also borrowing money from friends and mortgaging his father's house so that he could go to Inner Mongolia and build BitBank, one of the largest Bitcoin mines in China. The "mine," which consumed 500 thousand yuan (eighty-two thousand dollars) in electricity every day, suffered during the 2014 bear market, forcing Guo to sell it and start preaching Bitcoin instead. Nevertheless, by December 2015 three of the four largest Bitcoin mining pools in the world were based in China, thanks to easy access to cheap electricity and highly efficient ASIC mining equipment. The three mines possessed a combined global hash-rate power of sixty percent, which had increased to seventy percent by the end of 2017.

Guo soon became an internet celebrity in the crypto field. In 2016 he was invited to the Davos Forum in Switzerland, where he told the elite audience that "in the future people will no longer trust gold, cash, or dollars; people will believe in blockchain technology."[115] By this time Guo believed that crypto was no longer just about Bitcoin, and that alternative blockchains would drive prices higher. His conviction was based on his experience at the Money20/20 conference in Las Vegas in October 2015, where he had assumed that everybody would be focusing on Bitcoin, only to find that they were actually talking about blockchain, the technological backbone of Bitcoin.

In the meantime Guo had gotten rich by doing product endorsements for a one-percent endorsement fee. He endorsed some 100 projects overall, notably Stellar, Fcoin, and Bytom (BTM). Most of these projects plummeted after they were launched, but Guo may still have earned as much as twenty-five million dollars through his ICO endorsements alone.

The ICO boom ultimately lifted Bitcoin out of the bear market. China was initially a major market for ICOs. During the first seven months of 2017 China-based crypto startups collected nearly 400 million dollars through sixty-five token sales. But then, on September 2, the Office of the Leading Group for the Special Rectification of Internet Financial Risks issued a "Notice on the Clean-Up and Rectification of Token Issuance and Financing,"[116] stating that ICOs were essentially unapproved illegal public financings and therefore suspected of being vehicles for illegal fundraising, illegal issuance of securities, illegal sale of tokens, and involvement in financial fraud and pyramid schemes.[117]

Two days later seven Chinese financial regulators officially banned all ICOs within China, with a list of sixty major ICO platforms provided for local financial regulatory bodies to inspect and report on. Ethereum, considered the biggest beneficiary of the ICO boom, fell twelve percent that day.[118] Authorities also shut down blockchain conferences (although the Central Government would later mention blockchain technology in its Five-Year Plan as a key pillar of the digitalization of its economy), and in Hong Kong the regional government announced that "token sales would be a regulated activity under Hong Kong law." Meanwhile, back on the Mainland, by April 2018 Baidu, Tencent, and Weibo had all banned ICO advertising.

Japan accepts Bitcoin as legal tender (2017)

In stark contrast to China and the U.S., where regulators were cracking down on the crypto market by enforcing securities law, Japan passed a law that recognized Bitcoin as a legal tender from April 1 2017 onwards. This brought Bitcoin under anti-money laundering (AML) and know-your-customer (KYC) compliance rules while recognizing Bitcoin as a kind of prepaid payment instrument. Several retailers supported the law.

In the meantime the Japanese National Diet, the official legislator in Japan, had passed a series of tax reform bills in March 2017 which effectively exempted Bitcoin from the consumption tax starting on July 1 2017, while Japan's Financial Services Agency (FSA) had put in place capital requirements for crypto exchanges, as well as cybersecurity and operational stipulations. All exchanges, for example, were required to submit annual audits. By September 2017 the FSA had approved eleven companies as operators of crypto exchanges.

During the same month Bitcoin trading in Japanese yen accounted for forty-eight percent of the country's overall volume, followed by US dollars (thirty-one percent), Chinese yuan (eight percent), Korean won (five percent), and Euros (four percent). Thanks to the Japanese government's favorable stance and regulatory support, demand was extremely strong, resulting in Bitcoin prices trading on Japanese crypto exchanges at a premium of up to six percent compared with their value on other global exchanges. As in the time of the Mt. Gox exchange, Japan had once again become the world's largest Bitcoin market.

China closes onshore Bitcoin exchanges (2017)

Earlier in September 2017 the Chinese government, local authorities, and financial regulators officially requested Chinese Bitcoin exchanges and trading platforms to halt their services by the end of September. The two largest exchanges, OKcoin and Huobi, were allowed to operate until October 30 as they had not been involved in any ICOs.

Some prominent crypto professionals expressed their optimism over the shutdown of the Chinese Bitcoin exchange market. Charlie Lee, for example, the inventor of Litecoin, emphasized that the Chinese government would no longer be able to manipulate the market as it had done since 2013. "Cryptocurrency cannot be killed by any country," he stated. "One solution to centralized exchanges is decentralized ones."[119]

Lee was right. Despite the ban on Chinese crypto exchanges, traders started to trade Bitcoin directly with each other on peer-to-peer (P2P) marketplaces, messenger apps, or at over-the-counter (OTC) venues. To avoid regulatory scrutiny, Chinese crypto players were also moving away from Tencent's WeChat app to the encrypted messenger app Telegram.

But the lack of local crypto exchanges resulted in Bitcoin prices trading at a premium in China relative to the global benchmarks. As a result overseas traders could buy Bitcoin in the U.S. and sell it for sometimes thirty to forty percent more on Chinese P2P marketplaces. CoinCola—founded by Allan Zhang, who had previously been a director at Tencent, became a popular P2P venue for exchanging Bitcoins.

Data obtained by Chainalysis showed constant one-hundred million dollar monthly inflows of cash onto ten OTC trading platforms from April 2018 onwards.[120] Often these OTC platforms were run by the crypto trading exchanges themselves, prompting WeChat to update its user policy in May 2018 so that cryptocurrency could no longer be used to pay merchants on the app.

Chinese crypto traders could also buy the stablecoin Tether, which traded at a 2.5–3.5-percent premium in China, even rising temporarily to ten percent as demand became exceptionally strong in January 2018. The elevated Bitcoin premiums of thirty to forty percent in China allowed Tether to become popular among Chinese traders, who could buy the stablecoin for a much smaller premium and then buy Bitcoin on global crypto exchanges by using a VPN.

Figure 7: Tether slowly starts to gain traction (US billion dollars)

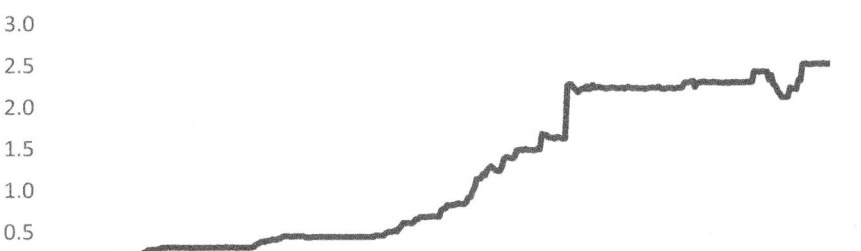

In September 2017 Tether's market capitalization was just 320 million dollars. But it started to increase rapidly from October 30, when OKcoin and Huobi stopped serving customers in Mainland China. By December 31 Tether's market capitalization had increased to 1.4 billion dollars, and by the end of January 2018 it had reached 2.2 billion dollars. When Tether announced on January 28 that it had parted ways with its auditor Friedman as it "took too long with its audit," 600 million additional dollars in Tether were quickly minted over the weekend. Some have questioned how Tether could have received dollars for minting Tethers over the weekend when U.S. banks were closed.

When China banned its citizens from trading Chinese yuan for cryptocurrency in September 2017, trading volume first moved from BTC-CNY (Bitcoin to yuan) to BTC-USD (Bitcoin to dollars), and then to BTC-USDT (Bitcoin to Tether) by January 2018. The most convenient way to buy crypto in China was to purchase stablecoins like Tether through OTC platforms and then trade it into any other cryptos on exchanges around the world. Fiat was normally wired through banks to OTC brokers or escrow accounts held by a legal firm—a process that could take up to three days, depending on banking restrictions. Traders would then use VPN solutions to enter crypto exchanges.

Bravecoin has speculated that OTC volumes could have been three times the size of those on China's exchanges,[121] while TABB Group estimated the OTC market to be valued at twelve billion dollars per day, with Digital Asset Research quoting 250 million in 2018.[122] But nobody could really grasp the full picture of the OTC trading activities.

In addition to anonymity OTC platforms offered more liquidity, as they could settle transactions in fiat—something that most crypto exchanges could not do. OTC platforms could also avoid price slippage, as an agreed price would be executed, and they helped to avoid prohibitive crypto exchange limits. The U.S. crypto exchange Coinbase, for example, limited daily purchases to twenty-five thousand dollars, while the U.S.'s second-largest exchange, Kraken, let its users withdraw only twenty thousand dollars per month.

Tether was often used to circumvent exchange limits, and was heavily utilized by OTC trading desks. However Dan Matuszewski, the cofounder of CMS Holdings who, as former head of Circle's OTC desk, had created and redeemed billions of Tethers, has another theory. He points to the large spread between Bitcoin prices on Bitfinex and Coinbase, which led to a unique investment opportunity in 2017 that caused the explosive creation of Tethers. At the time Coinbase was onboarding lots of retail investors, and prices were materially cheaper on Bitfinex. So traders minted large volumes of Tether to buy cheap Bitcoin on Bitfinex and then sell on Coinbase. Matuszewski also believes that traders in Asia dislike Circle's USDC stablecoin because Circle would not push back against any regulatory issue—contrary to Tether, which has operated mostly outside of the U.S.[123]

Chicago Bitcoin Futures become a major driver of the bull market (2017)

Just as the ICO bubble was about to burst in December 2017 due to regulatory scrutiny, the Chicago Board of Options Exchange (Cboe) and the Chicago Mercantile Exchange (CME) were ready to list the first Bitcoin futures, on December 10 and 18 respectively. On December 10 Bitcoin prices rose to 15,455 dollars, and on December 18 they climbed further to 19,114 dollars. But the top of this third major bull market had already been reached on December 16, when prices rose in anticipation of the CME listing to a high of 19,497 dollars per Bitcoin.

Initially prices traded at a huge premium on both exchanges, as suddenly traditional-finance (TradFi) investors could buy Bitcoin contracts through the normal broker relationships they used to clear stock, bond, commodity, currency futures, and other traditional contracts. But prices would eventually drop by eighty percent from the December 2017 high, before bottoming out in April 2019. As always during bear markets the power then shifted away from projects and protocols to the (derivatives) crypto exchanges.

Bitcoin becomes hugely popular in South Korea (2017)

The Bitcoin premium in South Korea was generally called the "kimchi premium," after the popular side dish. At its peak the premium reached fifty percent as demand increased exponentially during the CME Bitcoin futures launch. With youth unemployment at ten percent and young Koreans burdened with a fiercely competitive employment market and expensive living costs, Bitcoin and crypto represented a rare shot at prosperity for a significant proportion of the population.

Koreans were already familiar with micropayment transactions, as they were early adopters of technology through social networks and video games. Hangame, a Korean gaming company, had revenues of eighty thousand dollars per day on micropayments of just 0.5 dollars by the end of 2001, when online games were mostly free, and by 2004 the company was generating ninety-three million dollars in annual revenues. Crypto also offered an attractive alternative to gambling—most forms of gambling are illegal in South Korea—and as a result the term "Bitcoin zombie" soon started to gain traction, with many Koreans checking crypto prices around the clock.

According to some statistics thirty percent of Koreans had invested in crypto by 2017.[124] In May of that year the Korean fintech company Blockchain OS raised 6,900 Bitcoins through the country's first ICO, which sold out in just nine minutes and attracted a lot of media attention. Other ICOs followed, such as ICON launching its ICX token sale for 150 thousand Ethers (forty-two million dollars), followed by Glosfer raising thirteen million dollars in its ICO.

On May 22 Samsung SDS, an affiliate of Samsung Electronics, joined the Enterprise Ethereum Alliance. Like Shinhan Bank, the company had already started to invest in crypto startups in 2015. In anticipation of the Korean authorities legalizing and regulating cryptocurrencies in 2017 Shinhan Bank had also teamed up with Streami, a blockchain remittance middleware and infrastructure firm, to provide cheaper cross-border remittances.

Korean-based crypto exchange Korbit was the first exchange to offer Bitcoin–Korean won trading. The exchange was founded by Kangmo Kim, Louis Jinhwa Kim, and Tony Lyu in 2013 and received 400 thousand dollars in seed capital from Tim Draper, Naval Ravikant, Digital Currency Group (DCG), and others. On September 28 2017 Nexon, a Korean video game developer with headquarters in Japan, bought sixty-five percent of Korbit for eighty million dollars.

By July 2017 Bithumb, which had launched in 2014, had a seventy-six-percent share of the Korean Bitcoin market, making it the world's fourth-largest crypto exchange. But Bithumb was repeatedly hacked, likely by the North Korean hacker group Lazarus. In February 2017 it was hacked for seven million dollars; in June 2018 the user information of a Bithumb employee's personal computer was stolen, leading to the removal of thirty-two million dollars from the exchange; in March 2019 the company was hacked for another twenty million dollars; and in June 2019 thirty million dollars' worth of crypto was stolen from Bithumb's hot wallet.

By 2017 Korea accounted for as much as forty percent of global Ethereum trading, despite the government not allowing ICOs, with the regulator threatening to issue "stern penalties."[125] As a result Korean companies became actively involved in blockchain projects. In September 2017 Kakao, the maker of the Kakaotalk messenger app, acquired fintech startup Dunamu, which had previously operated Kakao Stock, Korea's popular stock trading app. The following month Kakao launched its own crypto exchange, Upbit, which was developed in partnership with the U.S.-based exchange Bittrex. Upbit listed 110 cryptocurrencies and immediately gained market share due to its broad offering.

In November 2016 the South Korean government had formed a task force to look into crypto trends, and by early September 2017 the Financial Services Commission (FSC) had started to distinguish between securities-type and utility-type tokens, emphasizing that, in line with regulators in the U.S., it would regulate the former. However money kept flooding into South Korean crypto firms from China following the Chinese government's banning of ICOs, and on September 29 the task force announced its intention to propose to the government that ICOs be prohibited.[126]

On December 8 the Ministry of Justice took charge of the FSC's task force, signaling that regulation and potential punishment would be implemented in the case of the crypto industry. Concerns were also raised about asset protection at Bithumb. Within a few days Bitcoin prices had declined by twenty-five percent.

Meanwhile, in July 2017 lawmakers had set in motion a bill to license cryptocurrency exchanges. The bill did not pass, but by December the government was ready to act. On December 13 it rolled out plans to curb speculation, including trade bans for minors and proposed taxes on crypto investment returns.[127] Korean banks that provided bank accounts for crypto traders would also need to provide verified identification of account holders, while financial institutions were barred from investing or obtaining cryptocurrencies.

These measures were followed on December 28 by the announcement of further restrictions from Korean regulators, including a ban on anonymous accounts. Some Korean crypto users criticized the "tyranny of President Moon Jae-in," while others submitted an online petition to the president with over seventeen thousand signatures.[128] Nevertheless, in January 2018 the government announced that crypto exchanges would be required to pay a twenty-two-percent corporate tax as well as local taxes. These extra costs would be passed on to the exchanges' users.

Despite the South Korean government's intervention Bithumb briefly became the world's second-largest crypto exchange in terms of trading volume. But due to the high premium relative to other global exchanges, crypto data provider CoinMarketCap started to exclude Korean exchanges from their average price calculations on January 8 2018.

On January 9 of the same year South Korea's National Tax Service raided the country's largest crypto exchanges.[129] One theory making the rounds at the time was that during their summit in December 2017 China and South Korea had discussed how North Korea was using crypto to pay for its ballistic-missile program, concluding that crypto values needed to be brought down to keep North Korea in check.[130]

On January 18 2018 South Korea's justice minister Park Sang-ki announced that the government was preparing a bill that would ban crypto trading.[131] Bitcoin dropped twelve percent following his remarks, and later in the day the Presidential Office intervened, stating that any potential bill "is not a measure that has been finalized." Nevertheless a public petition to remove the justice and finance ministers gathered over 200 thousand signatures, forcing the government to officially respond, and on January 31 the finance minister, Kim Dong-yeon, confirmed that "Korea had no intention to ban or suppress cryptocurrencies."[132]

In May 2018 South Korea's National Assembly officially proposed legalizing domestic ICOs, on the condition that they were regulated and had received government approval.[133] But as crypto traders could no longer trade anonymously and had their verified bank accounts linked to exchanges, the "kimchi premium" started to disappear. Foreign traders could also no longer take advantage of the exuberance in Korea, as exchanges needed to report transactions above a certain threshold to the tax authorities as gains would be liable to capital gains tax.

As a result Ripple Lab's XRP token saw an immediate twenty billion dollar drop in market capitalization as prices decreased by thirty percent. Ripple Labs, originally named OpenCoin, was founded in 2012 in San Francisco by Chris Larsen and Jed McCaleb (the creator of the Mt. Gox exchange). Its goal was to create a more sustainable digital asset that was built specifically for payments.

After graduating from Stanford Business School, Larsen had cofounded and developed a mortgage lending website called E-Loan, which would later also offer direct home equity and car loans. In 1999 E-Loan filed for IPO, and in 2005 Larsen stepped down as CEO to start Prosper Marketplace, which acted as an eBay-style online auction marketplace with lenders and borrowers.

In 2016 Ripple partnered with Japanese financial services group SBI Holdings to launch SBI Ripple Asia, which served markets in Mainland China, Japan, Korea, Taiwan, and elsewhere in Asia by establishing dedicated sales and engineering groups to provide cross-border bank payments. Rumors began circulating that Coinbase would also soon be supporting Ripple's XRP token, offering buying, selling, and trading on its platform. At the time Coinbase was adding 100 hundred thousand new users per day.

In March 2018 a Japanese consortium comprising sixty-one banks led by SBI Ripple Asia, launched MoneyTap, a Ripple-powered mobile app providing on-demand domestic payments in Japan. However, in 2020 the SEC would launch a lawsuit against Ripple Labs alleging that the firm had raised over 1.3 billion dollars issuing illegal, unregistered digital-asset securities.

Figure 8: Ripple's XRP token price exploded in December 2017, driven by Korean retail traders

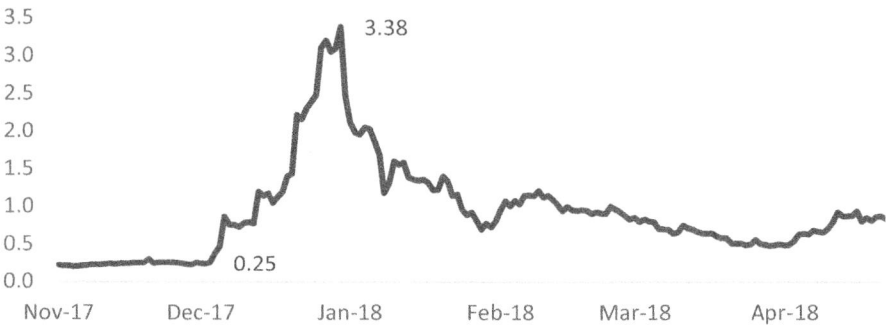

In 2017 the price of Ripple's XRP token had increased by a factor of 360, and from December 1 2017 to January 3 2018 alone the market capitalization of XRP increased from 9.2 billion to 131 billion dollars, making it the world's second-largest cryptocurrency and the first altcoin to reach a 100-billion-dollar market valuation. As a result Larsen's estimated net worth rose to 61.8 billion dollars, making him briefly one of the top five richest people in the U.S.[134]

The South Korean market is often driven by FOMO (fear of missing out) and herd mentality. About fifty percent of Ripple's trading volume was accounted for on the three largest Korean exchanges: Bithumb, Coinone, and Korbit. Despite XRP prices being twenty to thirty percent higher on Korean exchanges than on their global peers, Koreans were driving up the price of Ripple.

According to crypto exchange data for January 2018 Bithumb's twenty-four-hour trading volumes for Bitcoin were 200 million dollars, compared to 210 million dollars for Ethereum and over 830 million for Ripple. But on January 4 Coinbase rejected Ripple's listing on its exchange, resulting in a decrease in XRP's market capitalization from 148 billion to 126 billion dollars.

By mid-January 2018 six of South Korea's largest banks were under surveillance by authorities for money laundering via cryptocurrencies, and by February Ripple's market capitalization had dropped from a peak of 148 billion to thirty billion dollars as demand from Korean crypto traders disappeared. The "kimchi premium" for Bitcoin went from fifty percent on January 8 to a five-percent discount by February. Ethereum and Litecoin followed a similar path.

At its peak South Korea accounted for thirty percent of all crypto trading, and was the largest trading venue for Ethereum and Ripple. While the government never actually banned ICOs, Korean blockchain companies stopped offering ICOs, opting instead to incorporate elsewhere—in Switzerland and predominantly in Singapore—to avoid the risk of shutdown.

8

"It's all fun and games if you're a … $10 billion market cap stablecoin"
(Paolo Ardoino, Bitfinex)

On January 26 2018 Japanese crypto exchange Coincheck disclosed a hack of 534 million dollars. The stolen coins were kept in a hot wallet, and the exchange took eight hours to notice the hack. Once the hackers had managed to steal the private key for the wallet, they were able to transfer the funds to their own wallets.

The Coincheck hack was Japan's second-biggest cryptocurrency hack after the one on Mt. Gox. In 2018 twelve percent of Bitcoin trading was paired against Japanese yen, a sign that Japanese traders were an important part of the crypto trading community.

Coincheck was founded in 2012 and launched its crypto exchange in 2014. The firm was based in Tokyo, with just seventy-one employees. On April 16 2018, less than three months after the hack, Coincheck became a subsidiary of Monex Group, which runs an equity brokerage and stock trading platform in Japan. Monex acquired a hundred percent of Coincheck shares for 33.5 million dollars, with Coincheck founders Koichiro Wada and Yusuke Otsuka stepping down from their positions as CEO and COO respectively, in accordance with the acquisition agreement.

In March 2022 Monex planned to list Coincheck on the Nasdaq in the U.S. through an SPAC (special purpose acquisition company) merger, valuing the company at 1.3 billion dollars—more than thirty-eight times the valuation of 33.5 million dollars just four years earlier. At the time of the planned listing Coincheck had 1.5 million verified customers.

Weeks before the 2018 attack virus-infected emails had been sent to several Coincheck staff. The company's systems began contacting external services without proper authorization, and in the early morning of January 26 NEM tokens started leaving the exchange's wallet. Otsuka later revealed that 523 million NEM tokens had been removed from the exchange's address.[135] Some of the stolen NEM was traced back to a Vancouver crypto exchange, where it had been laundered and sent back to the Japanese crypto exchange Zaif. In the end thirty people would be charged for allegedly exchanging stolen NEM tokens.

NEM tokens had become popular among Japanese crypto traders after Yousuke Sato, the owner of a popular restaurant in Tokyo, the St. Arnould, started to accept the tokens as payment. Other stores, restaurants, and bars in Japan also began accepting cryptocurrency, including retail company Yamada Denki, which introduced Bitcoin payments in two of its stores in Tokyo. By 2017 there were 260 thousand stores in Japan accepting Bitcoins as payment.[136] Bic Camera, which operates massive consumer electronics centers and outlets across Japan, also started to accept Bitcoins, promoting the digital currency with local media, which quickly picked up on the enthusiasm around the cryptocurrency.

Zaif, the exchange that had received the laundered NEM from the Coincheck hack, ranked as the thirty-fifth-largest crypto exchange back in 2018. In September of that year, only a few months after receiving the laundered tokens, Zaif itself was hacked, losing 62.5 million dollars in digital coins. While initially all services were stopped, six months later Zaif resumed its business activities after the investment firm Fisco Cryptocurrency Exchange had acquired the exchange for 44.7 million dollars. The new owners refunded all users who had lost money in the hack.

Another attack occurred the following year in Japan when, in July 2019, the BITPoint exchange was hacked for thirty-two million dollars. As a result shares in Remixpoint, which owned the exchange, dropped nineteen percent—the daily limit on the Tokyo stock exchange. Once again the funds had been stolen from a hot wallet.

But it wasn't only crypto exchanges in Japan that were being targeted by hackers. In fact the main victims of hacks in 2018 were the South Korean exchanges. Coinrail, for example, which was barely a top 90 exchange globally, was hacked for forty million dollars in altcoins in June 2018.

The repeated attacks on crypto exchanges prompted many prominent finance professionals to make negative comments about the crypto industry. Jamie Dimon, for instance, the CEO of J.P. Morgan Chase, told participants at a conference in October 2018 that "I don't really give a sh*t about Bitcoin,"[137] while earlier in the same year legendary investor Warren Buffett had called Bitcoin "probably rat poison squared."[138]

Meanwhile the heads of Bitfinex and Tether had both been subpoenaed by the U.S. Commodity Futures Trading Commission (CFTC) in December 2017, and the U.S. Department of Justice was investigating possible price manipulations with the use of Tether. As a result of such regulatory pressure Bitcoin prices dropped sharply in 2018.

By mid-May, however, some positive stories had started to emerge. Coinbase, for example, began to roll out crypto custody for institutions, with users having to pay a one-hundred-thousand-dollar setup fee and keep a minimum of ten million dollars in deposits.[139] The industry was clearly preparing itself for institutional adoption of cryptocurrencies, and Coinbase's move resulted in other companies pivoting their services to institutions.

A few months later, in October 2018, the investment firm Fidelity, which administered more than 7.2 trillion dollars in client assets, announced a new and separate company called Fidelity Digital Asset Services. Fidelity's president and CEO, Abigail Johnson, is known to be a supporter of Bitcoin, and has even mined Bitcoin in her office.

Also in October 2018 the chief investment officer of Yale's endowment fund, David Swensen, who managed 29.4 billion dollars for the university, told CNBC that he had invested in two dedicated cryptocurrency funds.[140] Twenty years earlier Swensen was a major proponent of endowments allocating funds toward alternative assets, notably private equity. His forward-thinking investment approach is illustrated in the way he mastered the recessions of 2001–02 and 2008–09 with a diversified investment strategy.

But, despite these developments, Bitcoin prices kept falling, and in early December 2018 the SEC postponed its approval of a physical Bitcoin exchange-traded fund (ETF), with an eventual announcement expected on February 27 2019. This caused Bitcoin prices to fall back to nearly three thousand dollars.

North Korean hackers linked to most crypto attacks

State-sponsored North Korean hackers initially targeted South Korean crypto exchanges because they often maintained escrow accounts which were holding Bitcoins in hot wallets connected to the internet. South Korea's largest exchange, Bithumb, was raided at least four times. Usually through the guise of being a trusted business partner, the hackers would plant malware on an exchange employee's computer, before finding ways to gain access to the keys to the exchange's hot wallets.

If the exchanges had adequate know-your-customer (KYC) and anti-money-laundering (AML) procedures in place, it would be very difficult to move large sums of cryptocurrencies around. The preferred method for criminals to conceal a cryptocurrency trace is to use DeFi (decentralized finance) platforms and swap currencies without ever taking custody of the funds, as DeFi does not require any KYC or AML documentation. Based on data from Chainalysis, North Korean hackers used the DeFi protocol Uniswap to launder 275 million dollars of hacked cryptocurrencies from the KuCoin exchange on September 26 2020. This was one of the largest hacks ever.

Eventually hackers need to move stolen coins to an exchange or venue that can help them to turn crypto back into fiat. But to cover their tracks, criminal groups tend to leave sizable amounts of cryptocurrency untouched for many years after hacks.

In 2018 the Hong Kong–based exchange Bitfinex was hacked by the North Korean Lazarus Group for nearly 250 million dollars of cryptocurrencies—including ninety-five million dollars in Bitcoin and 141 million in Ethereum, plus smaller amounts of Zcash, Dogecoin, Ripple, Litecoin, and Ethereum Classic.[141] The stolen coins were moved through other exchanges, with some of the Bitcoins then being transferred into an account held by Tian Yinyin and Li Jiadong, who had successfully opened accounts at other exchanges using fake pictures and names.[142] Tian moved more than thirty-four million dollars to his bank account, while Li used nine different banks to funnel thirty-three million dollars.

Tian and Li are also believed to have laundered other misappropriated cryptocurrencies for North Korea after previous crypto exchange hacks, gaming the KYC process by uploading photoshopped government IDs and cashing out using several Chinese banks (a number of Chinese financial institutions offer accounts to North Koreans or front companies with relationships with the North Korean government). Both Tian and Li remain fugitives at large to this day.

The Lazarus Group is believed to be associated with the North Korean government, and has been linked to cyberattacks and ransomware which fund North Korea's military ambitions. The attacks on South Korea's crypto exchanges were executed in a similar way to the WannaCry hack that targeted Sony Pictures in May 2017, which is why experts have attributed many hacks to the Lazarus Group. Lazarus hackers would impersonate job recruiters and target specific individuals believed to have access to private keys. They would also use token offerings and social media to launch attacks.

Anne Neuberger, U.S. deputy national security advisor for cyber security, said in July 2022 that North Korea uses cybercrimes to gain financing for up to thirty percent of its missile program.[143] North Korean hackers are sent to Shenyang in China for special training, and their hacking apprenticeship puts them through six years of special education. Chainalysis estimates that North Korea stole approximately 1.7 billion dollars in cryptocurrencies in 2022 alone. Thirty million were recovered after analysts traced back the flow of funds that had moved through "crypto mixers"—DeFi protocols that can shuffle holdings of different users to obfuscate the funds' origins. Some analysts believe that North Korea was also behind the Coincheck hack in January 2018.

U.S. officials have also linked the Lazarus Group to the 625-million-dollar theft of crypto game Axie Infinity in March 2022. The Axie Infinity blockchain was hacked via a fake LinkedIn job offer which duped a senior engineer at the company into applying for a job that did not really exist. After multiple rounds of interviews the engineer received a fake job offer delivered in the form of a PDF document that he downloaded. This allowed spyware to infiltrate the Ronin Network, an Ethereum sidechain that Axie Infinity is built on, enabling the hacker to take control of four of the nine validators on the network. Validators create transaction blocks and update the data in crypto oracles (feeds that bring data from off-chain sources and put them on the blockchain for smart-contract use).

Figure 9: The value of the Axie in-game token peaked in November 2021

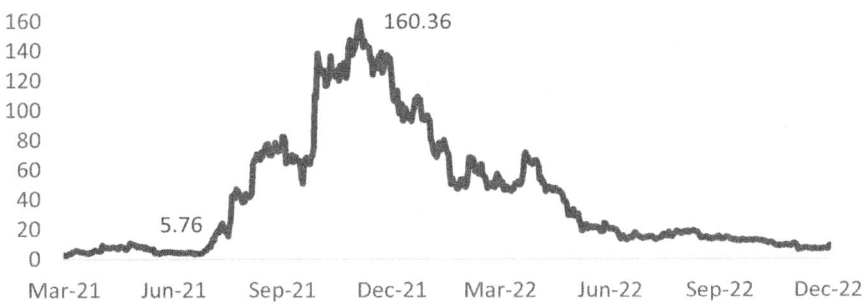

Funds could only be moved out of the Axie Infinity blockchain wallet if the attacker got hold of five of the nine validators, giving him/her majority authorization. The attacker managed to do this by getting the Axie DAO to sign the transaction for moving the funds out. How this happened has not yet been revealed by Sky Mavis, the developer behind Axie Infinity, nor by the firm's CEO Trung Nguyen. The company is based in Vietnam and has been described as a "pyramid scheme that relies on cheap labor from countries like the Philippines to fuel its growth."[144]

In the Axie Infinity game players collect and mint NFTs (non-fungible tokens) which can be won and lost during battles with other players in the game. These NFTs are called Axies (or AXS), and can be traded among players on the Axie Infinity marketplace, with Sky Mavis charging a 4.25-percent fee on each trade.

Axie Infinity became extremely popular, particularly in the Philippines, and was the key game for the play-to-earn movement, where users could make a living by earning in-game items and then reselling them. At its peak Axie Infinity had 2.7 million active users and a weekly trading volume in Axies of 214 million dollars. In June 2021 Axies had a market capitalization of 180 million dollars, and at its peak on November 8 2021 the value had reached 10.5 billion dollars.

Crypto money laundering in Russia

North Korean cybercriminals tend to prefer to cash out through bank accounts in either China or Russia. Chainalysis has named several exchanges in Russia, notably OTC brokerage SUEX, as "making a concerted effort to serve a cybercriminal clientele."[145]

Nearly fifty percent of all Russian crypto exchanges are based in the Federation Tower, a skyscraper in Moscow. Bloomberg has called the building "Ransomeware HQ" and a "Cybercriminal Cash Machine".[146] At least a dozen companies with offices in the skyscraper are known to convert cryptocurrencies into cash, while at least four companies have been linked to money laundering with the ransomware industry. SUEX operates out of Suite Q on the thirty-first floor and has been linked to processing Bitcoin from illicit sources. EggChange, on the twenty-second floor, is under investigation in the U.S. and Europe on allegations of money laundering according to Bloomberg sources. CashBank, another of the building's occupants, has also been linked to illicit transactions, while a fourth occupant, Buy-Bitcoin.pro, has been accused of processing transactions from ransomware cases and darknet markets.[147]

The MMM Bitcoin Ponzi Pyramid (2014–17)

Russia also became home to some of the most notorious scams and Ponzi schemes. Most of these were exposed during bear markets, when prices stopped going up. This was the case with MMM Bitcoin, a scheme that defrauded millions of people around the globe.

The MMM Bitcoin scheme was run by the organization MMM China, which was founded by Russian fraudster Sergei Mavrodi. MMM promised thirty-percent profit per month as new fund investors sent Bitcoins as a means of "mutual assistance" to those who had become members of the pyramid scheme before them. These members could get help for up to ten thousand dollars in Bitcoin by means of MMM's virtual currency, the Mavro, which was pegged to Bitcoin one-to-one. The members would "pay in" Bitcoin and receive the equivalent of 1.3 Mavros.

Mavrodi claimed that the doubling of the Bitcoin price in October 2015 was due to his Ponzi scheme. While the scheme operated in many countries, members in Indonesia received twelve times more money than those in India—a sign that Indonesia may have been a central hub for the MMM organization, which is known to have withdrawn a significant amount of money through an Indonesian Bitcoin exchange.

At its peak the MMM Bitcoin Ponzi scheme circulated more than 150 million dollars a day.[148] It appears to have been active in eighty countries and seems to have impacted nearly sixteen thousand people, who collectively made a total of 422 thousand transactions. The scheme was especially popular in Africa and Asia, largely due to poverty, a lack of regulations or law enforcement, and limited access to financial institutions. While the scheme was in operation for almost six years, ninety-eight percent of all transactions occurred between September 2014 and August 2017.

The Bitfinex hack eventually worth 4.5 billion dollars (2016)

The Bitfinex crypto exchange was decentralized from the beginning, with senior people spread around the world and the team using the latest communications channels—first Skype, then Slack, and then Telegram. While this had its advantages, it also set up vulnerabilities as all communication happened online between the executives.

When Bitfinex was hacked on August 2 2016, it was not using a traditional hot-and-cold-wallet system. Instead it was working on a custom integration with BitGo which aimed to create segregated wallets for all the exchange's customers. Bitfinex stored its coins in segregated user accounts, and each account was protected by three keys—one for the user, one for the exchange, and one for BitGo—with two out of the three keys sufficient to move the funds. Bitfinex also had a special API key that allowed it to instruct BitGo to provide a signature programmatically.

When the CFTC fined Bitfinex in June 2016, the company agreed not to offer margin trading to its customers anymore.[149] But the exchange found a way around this by planning to offer physical delivery for its crypto futures, which would not be considered margin trading under the Commodity Exchange Act.[150] But instead of creating segregated accounts, the automation that was involved in this process created a huge hot wallet that could easily be drained by a hacker.

When the hack came in 2016, more than two thousand unauthorized transactions were made, and it took Paolo Ardoino, Bitfinex's CTO, seven days to get the platform back up and running. "I had to install old servers in a new environment," he explained.[151]

The seventy-two million dollars that were hacked from the Bitfinex accounts, as well as some price impact from collapsing the margin and peer-to-peer loaned positions on the exchange, resulted in every customer balance being marked down by thirty-six percent—an average "haircut" on all assets on the platform, with losses from the theft "generalized" across all clients and assets. "This is the closest approximation to what would happen in a liquidation context," the exchange commented.[152]

All Bitfinex users impacted by the hack received one BFX token for every dollar of value that had received a haircut. The idea was that these tokens could be converted into equity in iFinex, Bitfinex's parent company. The holding company for iFinex is DigFinex, which was set up on December 1 2015 in the Cayman Islands, with the listed shareholders being Giancarlo Devasini (thirty-five percent), Jan Ludovicus van der Velde (thirty-four percent), Raphael Nicolle (twenty-six percent), and Rodolfo Fracassi (five percent).[153] To facilitate the conversion of BTX tokens, Simon Dixon from BnkToTheFuture created an SPV (special purpose vehicle) where small traders could convert their tokens into iFinex equity, while Alistair Milne created the BFX Trust, which was another vehicle for smaller investors.

Bitfinex users could also use their BFX tokens as collateral for margin trading. When the market for BFX opened, it quickly dropped in value, trading at ten cents on the dollar, but then started to stabilize at around thirty to thirty-five cents. Christopher Harbone, a businessman with dual citizenship in the United Kingdom and Thailand who had received some BFX tokens as his funds on the exchange had been impacted by the hack, started buying large amounts of tokens at steep discounts. When these tokens were later converted into equity in iFinex, his stake was roughly twelve percent. Harbone would subsequently become a major donor in British politics, contributing £14.8 million mainly to Nigel Farage's Brexit Party.

Bitfinex deliberately overissued tokens, creating eighty million BFX to give the exchange a buffer for working capital and a defense against a potential lawsuit. The company also created Recovery Right Tokens, which allowed users to get paid back first if funds were ever recovered. This created a lot of goodwill toward the exchange, which has always valued the privacy of its traders, and user buy-in incentivized traders to keep supporting the platform.

Initially users were skeptical about BFX tokens, with rumors circulating that they were just a scam to buy more time. But Bitfinex kept reassuring token holders that its plan would work, and on September 1 2016 the exchange started to buy back tokens from the market. As a result trading volumes increased, and by December the value of the tokens had climbed to sixty cents to the dollar. By March 2017 the tokens were trading at ninety cents, and after March 31 the conversion ratio was increased to 1.25 per dollar to incentivize faster conversions.

Then, on April 3, Bitfinex stopped all trading of BFX tokens and started allowing users to cash them out for their full value of one dollar per token. The exchange explained that the redemption was possible due to a dramatic uptick in equity conversions and record operating results in March 2017.

None of the victims of the 2016 Bitfinex hack ever got their original funds back. But two individuals were eventually arrested on February 8 2022 for "alleged conspiracy to launder cryptocurrency" from the hack.[154] The two individuals were Ilya Lichtenstein and his wife, Heather Morgan, both from New York City. Lichtenstein, who has dual Russian-American citizenship, described himself on Medium as a "tech entrepreneur, explorer, and occasional magician." His Twitter feed (@unrealdutch) is a stream of cryptocurrency, Web 3.0 and NFT posts. Morgan, meanwhile, was initially a journalist for *Forbes* magazine.

Lichtenstein and Morgan are accused of laundering the proceeds of the 119,754 Bitcoins stolen from the Bitfinex platform. Over the previous five years twenty-five thousand of these Bitcoins had been transferred out of

Lichtenstein's wallet via complicated money-laundering transactions into accounts controlled by Lichtenstein and Morgan. The rest of the stolen coins had not been moved, and law enforcement officers were able to seize 3.6 billion dollars of the approximately 4.5 billion dollars that had been stolen.

Investigators from Washington D.C., New York, Chicago, and Germany all collaborated on the lengthy probe. They have not accused either Lichtenstein or Morgan of hacking Bitfinex; the couple are charged only with laundering the stolen coins.[155] If found guilty, they could each serve up to twenty-five years in prison.

In January 2017 small amounts of money began to move out of Lichtenstein's single wallet through the darknet marketplace AlphaBay, where transactions were moved through a mixer, with only the site being able to link incoming and outgoing transactions. AlphaBay was eventually seized and shut down in July 2017, giving law enforcement agencies access to the site's internal transaction logs, which enabled them to link the stolen funds to the person behind them.[156]

In early 2018 and late 2020 more of the stolen Bitcoins were moved through the Russian darknet site Hydra, before the remaining Bitcoins were moved a week prior to the couple's arrest. Hydra was a Russian-language darknet marketplace that launched in 2015 selling illicit items such as drugs, hacked materials, forged documents, and illegal digital services such as Bitcoin-mixing to break the blockchain trace. The site had seventeen million user accounts and nineteen thousand seller accounts, and a lifetime revenue of five billion dollars before it was seized by U.S. and German law enforcement agencies on April 5 2022. The agencies had had been tipped off that the website's infrastructure was hosted in Germany. A week after the seizure Russian national Dmitry Pavlov was arrested as one of the administrators behind Hydra.

9

"Intelligent people keep voting with their money"
(Giancarlo Devasini, Tether)

The concept for Tether, a USD-linked stablecoin, was formulated by the people behind Mastercoin, notably Craig Sellars, Brock Pierce, Reeve Collins, Jonathan Yantis, and William Quigley. Together they decided to start Realcoin, which was advertised as a token backed by U. S. dollars and used on the Mastercoin blockchain, a second-layer protocol which was later rebranded as the Omni Layer.

The origins of Tether (2014)

When Mastercoin was trying to raise capital, its cofounders came across Giancarlo Devasini, Jan Ludovicus van der Velde, and Phil Potter, who ran the Bitfinex crypto exchange. Devasini, van der Velde, and Potter had themselves started working on a concept that would separate Bitfinex's fiat operations from its crypto operations, as either one on its own would have a higher chance of receiving regulatory approval.

In early 2014, as the government in China was regulating crypto activities, Chinese banks were told to cut off banking relationships with crypto exchanges. This made the flow from fiat currencies into crypto more difficult. A few months later the U.S. government pushed through enforcement actions that removed any incentive for reputable banks to deal with dollar flows from crypto firms.[157] Then, in July 2014, France's largest bank, BNP Paribas, agreed to pay a record nine billion dollars for breaking U.S. sanctions against trade with Sudan, Iran, and Cuba.[158] "Between 2004 and 2012 BNP engaged in a complex and pervasive scheme to illegally move billions through the U.S. financial system," the Attorney General, Eric Holder, stated during a press conference.

Crypto exchanges with banking relationships now had a huge problem. For banks the risk of doing business with crypto exchanges, which had notoriously careless know-your-customer (KYC) and anti-money-laundering (AML) compliance requirements, was just too great for the small fees they could make on Swift and wire transactions. But with Tether, rather than setting up all the necessary bank accounts and banking relationships, crypto exchanges and firms could just accept the stablecoin to attract flows to their platform. Tether would handle the banking relationships, and other industry players could use these banking relationships to convert fiat into crypto.

Bitfinex, for its part, would simply handle the crypto exchange, while Tether would handle the fiat on- and offramp. The Tether concept was just like PayPal—which initially also had no KYC requirements, unless users wanted to cash out their funds.

As revealed in the Paradise Papers leak in 2017, Appleby, an offshore law firm, assisted Bitfinex in setting up Tether Holdings Limited in early September 2014 in the British Virgin Islands. A few days later, on September 8, Tether Limited registered in Hong Kong. When the first Tethers were issued, it was under the control of the Bitfinex management, as the same senior executives that run the Bitfinex crypto exchange also run Tether, the stablecoin that is now widely used in the industry. Bitfinex CFO Giancarlo Devasini is Tether's controlling shareholder, with an estimated forty percent of Tether's parent company, while Tether's CEO Jan Ludovicus van der Velde owns twenty percent of the combined entities. The COO of both Bitfinex and Tether is the wife of Bitfinex CTO Paolo Ardoino, although she is not listed as a shareholder.

The very first Tethers (USTD) were minted on October 6 2014. On November 20 Realcoin rebranded as Tether, without disclosing its full relationship with Bitfinex,[159] and on January 15 2015 Bitfinex enabled the trading of Tethers on its platform.

But people were initially hesitant to deal with Tether as its origins were not well known. The inflection point came when a small crypto exchange called Poloniex integrated Tether as its "fiat option," as it did not handle any fiat itself. Craig Sellars had sold them on the idea. On February 26 2015, while still in private beta, Tether was integrated with the Poloniex exchange.

Poloniex was founded by Tristan D'Agosta in 2014 and traded in over 120 altcoin markets. The exchange was one of the first to list Ethereum in 2016. The peer-to-peer payments company (and subsequent stablecoin issuer) Circle bought the exchange in early 2018 for 400 million dollars, appearing to have lost 156 million dollars on the transaction as the SEC investigated Poloniex in December 2017. Circle thought that it could transform Poloniex into a Nasdaq-type exchange, but when it tried to enforce straight compliance rules, asking users for government-issued IDs, trading plummeted. Circle sold Poloniex two years later to a consortium of initially unidentified Asian investors. The sale was the first sign that Circle would concentrate on a stablecoin-focused business model in the future. In 2021 the SEC charged Poloniex with operating an unregistered digital exchange, and the firm agreed to pay more than ten million dollars to settle the charges.[160]

When Ethereum took off in 2016, altcoins followed, and Poloniex was perfectly positioned to benefit. People had started doing cross-exchange arbitrage with Tether in 2015 and other exchanges started integrating Tether as well. Several exchanges that had tried to copy Poloniex's success with altcoins also started copying the Tether integration, as banking had become the most difficult problem for exchanges and Tether provided a solution.

In 2016 Tether issued six million USDTs—six times the number it had issued the previous year. But in 2017 it ran into problems with its banking relationships. Part of these relationships were with the Taiwanese banks HwaTai Commercial Bank, KGI Bank, First Commercial Bank, and Taishin International Bank, many of which relied on the banking giant Wells Fargo as their U.S. banking correspondence. When Wells Fargo cut off these relationships at the end of March 2017,[161] Tether turned to Noble Bank in Puerto Rico, a one-hundred-percent reserve bank with all its money custodied with the Bank of New York. One of the cofounders of Noble Bank was Brock Pierce, who was also a cofounder of Tether's predecessor, Realcoin.

On September 15 2017 Tether opened an account with Noble Bank, transferring 382 million dollars from Bitfinex's account with Noble into the new account. Later that day Friedman LLP did a brief audit, verifying that Tether was fully backed. But instead of an audit report it issued an "attestation" that included sixty-one million dollars held at the Bank of Montreal in a trust account controlled by Tether and Bitfinex's general counsel, Stuart Hoegner. The report was issued without disclosing either the names or the locations of Tether's banking relationships.

Tether gets hacked for thirty-one million dollars (2017)

On November 21 2017 Tether revealed that a malicious attacker had swiped thirty-one million dollars in tokens from its "Tether Treasury Wallet" two days earlier. As Tether was the issuer of these assets, it announced that it would not redeem the stolen USDT.

Emin Gün Sirer, the Cornell University professor who would later launch Ava Labs, criticized the Tether team for its handling of the hack. "Tether quietly did a hard fork to blacklist a specific address and freeze funds," he observed.[162] Others criticized the lack of transparency, as software updates, fixes, and hard forks had been carried out in an opaque manner.

In April 2017 Tether had announced that its access to U.S. dollar wire exchanges of funds had been blocked by its corresponding bank, Wells Fargo.[163] Tether and Bitfinex sued the U.S. bank, but the lawsuit was dismissed, causing the market to worry that Tethers might not be fully backed by fiat. So Tether hired Friedman LLP to perform an audit showing that users' assets were indeed backed one-to-one by U.S. dollars. With a market capitalization of just 675 million dollars, Tether was the twentieth-most-valuable cryptocurrency at the time.

On the legal section of Tether's website the company explicitly states that it is not obligated to let customers exchange their tokens for dollars.[164] "Tethers are not money and are not monetary instruments," it states.[165] "There is no contractual right or other right or legal claim against us to redeem or exchange your Tether for money. We do not guarantee any right of redemption or exchange of Tethers by us for money."[166]

In 2017 Bitcoin prices rose from one thousand to almost twenty thousand dollars. Half of the gain was associated with coordinated price manipulation, according to University of Texas finance professor John Griffin, a leading expert in uncovering fraud in financial markets.[167] Griffin claims that Tether was used to buy Bitcoin when the cryptocurrency was losing momentum and prices needed to be stabilized. Using data that tracked public ledgers of Bitfinex transactions, he found that fifty percent of all the Bitcoin rallies could be traced back to one percent of trading activity in Tether. The impact for other major cryptocurrencies was even higher, at sixty-four percent. In 2016 the CFTC had fined Bitfinex seventy-five thousand dollars for failing to register with the agency and for offering "illegal" cryptocurrency transactions.

Bitfinex suffers an 850 million dollar loss (2018)

In a press release on April 25 2019 the office of the New York Attorney General revealed that it had obtained a court order against iFinex Inc., the parent company of Bitfinex and Tether, for engaging in a cover-up to hide the apparent loss of almost one billion dollars of comingled client and corporate funds.

Tether did not have access to banking services in large parts of 2017, and at one point eighty-five percent of its cash was in the Bitfinex bank account, marked as "receivable" from its sister company. The remaining fifteen percent was in an account under the name of Stuart Hoegner, Tether and Bitfinex's general counsel.

Tether had published a "verification" of its cash reserves in 2017, which it characterized as "a good faith effort on our behalf [that] provides an interim analysis of our cash position."[168] However the cash backing the Tether had only been placed in its account the very morning of the "verification," before the auditor Friedman LLP issued its report.

When Noble Bank was audited by Puerto Rico's bank regulator in 2017, concerns were raised as the bank relied on two crypto firms which caused Bitfinex and Tether to look for a new banking relationship. Noble Bank closed the following year with several of its employees joining James "Bo" Collins who was previously the president of New York Mercantile Exchange. After twenty-five years trading commodities Collins went all-in on Bitcoin and set up the crypto firm Mercantile Global Holdings in Puerto Rico.

In October 2018 Tether started banking with the Bahamas–based Deltec Bank & Trust.[169] The following month it published another "verification" of its cash reserves, claiming that Tether was fully backed by cash at one dollar for every Tether. The next day, however, the company moved hundreds of millions of dollars from its bank account to Bitfinex's account.

Deltec Bank is a financial services institution that at the time of writing is headed by Jean Chalopin, a cocreator of the cartoon *Inspector Gadget*. Deltec was the only bank willing to work with cryptocurrency firms in 2018, when Bitfinex and Tether were desperately looking for a banking relationship.

In 2017 and 2018 Bitfinex began to rely increasingly on third-party payment processors to handle customer deposits and withdrawals from its trading platform. One of these was Panama-based Crypto Capital Corporation (CCC), which also counted BitMEX, Kraken, and the now defunct Canadian crypto exchange QuadrigaCX among its clients.

CCC was founded in 2013 by Ivan Lee, a Canadian Panamanian with expertise in offshore incorporation who had come up with the idea of setting up a shadow bank for cryptocurrency companies. CCC used links to banks in Poland and Portugal, and was later accused of having dealings with South American drug cartels.

In late 2017 Lee bought in former American football player Reginald Fowler and Israeli entrepreneur Oz Yosef (also known as Joseph Oz) to help run CCC. Oz's sister, Ravid Yosef, joined shortly after. Fowler ran several entities in Panama, but the biggest was CCC, where he was briefly the alleged shadow banker for Tether and Bitfinex.

A former football player for the Northern Arizona Wranglers and a former minority owner of the Minnesota Vikings NFL (National Football League) team, Fowler led an attempted investment in the Alliance of American Football (AAF) in 2019, allegedly using funds from CCC accounts. He was first indicted in 2019 for running a shadow banking ring catering to crypto firms that were getting rejected by mainstream banks.

In September 2018 Bitfinex appeared to be banking with HSBC through a private account of Global Trading Solutions—a company registered under Fowler. But four days after the account became public, Bitfinex temporarily suspended all cash deposits. This suggested that the company was once again looking for a new reserve bank as its sub-account with HSBC appeared to have been closed.

In October 2018 rumors started circulating that Bitfinex was insolvent. On October 7 the company claimed to "not entirely understand the arguments that purport to show us insolvent." [170] But correspondence between Bitfinex and CCC indicated that the exchange was under immense pressure, as a spike in client withdrawal requests was threatening its existence. "Please understand all this could be extremely dangerous for everybody, the entire crypto community," one Bitfinex executive wrote, according to the attorney general.[171] "BTC could tank to below 1,000 if we don't act quickly." Bitcoin was trading at 6,500 dollars at the time.

Despite the vast amounts of money that it handed over to CCC, Bitfinex never signed a contract or other agreements with the payments company. Then, in November 2018, Bitfinex suffered a loss of 850 million dollars from its CCC account. Bitfinex executives suspected that CCC had either lost or stolen the money. However they did not reveal the loss, which only became public in April 2019 as a result of the court action initiated by the New York Attorney General.

After the loss of the 850 million dollars Giancarlo Devasini pleaded for months with Oz Yosef for the return of the missing cash. In the meantime he and his fellow executives at Bitfinex and Tether cooked up a series of "conflicted corporate transactions", according to New York Attorney General Letitia James.[172] This allowed Bitfinex to access 900 million dollars of Tether's cash reserves, with Devasini effectively transferring the funds to himself on November 5.[173] The credit facility obligated Bitfinex to repay Tether the amount held in Tether's CCC account on "commercially reasonable terms over 3-years and an annual interest rate of 6.5 percent."[174] Sixty million shares in iFinex were pledged to Tether as collateral, although this was initially unknown to the market.

The New York Attorney General saw this as an illusory credit, and accused the executives of "fraudulently shifting most or all Bitfinex's risk of loss of several hundred million dollars onto Tether's balance sheet but continued to represent to the market that Tethers were fully backed by U.S. dollars sitting safely in a bank account."[175]

In May 2019 Bitfinex launched a utility token, UNUS SED LEO, to raise cash to help keep the exchange afloat. The company promised to buy back the tokens eventually. Bitfinex and Tether's parent company, iFinex, intended to create a subsidiary under the name Unus Sed Leo Ltd. to make available up to one billion dollars of "LEO" tokens for purchase. LEO holders would receive benefits such as ten-to-fifteen-percent taker fee reductions, a 0.5-percent discount for lending fee reductions, twenty-five-percent withdrawal and deposit fee discounts, and one-basis-point taker fee reductions for derivatives.

All LEO tokens would be bought back with twenty-seven percent of the firm's profits from the previous month. According to iFinex's financial statements the company made 333 million dollars in gross profit in 2017, and had only 6.8 million dollars in expenses with a team of thirty-five to sixty employees. For the financial year 2018 the company made 418 million dollars in gross profit, with fourteen million dollars in expenses as the team grew from sixty to ninety employees.[176]

Zhao Dong, the founder of RenrenBit (one of China's biggest OTC traders) and a Bitfinex shareholder, published the iFinex document on May 4 2019.[177] He revealed that sixty percent of the tokens had already been sold, stating that a sum of 600 million dollars had been raised by the firm in private through verbal commitments. If the remaining tokens were not sold through the private sale, they would be released for a public offering around May 10.

A year after the loss of the 850 million dollars two people were charged with the CCC bank fraud. Initially Reginald Fowler was charged with the "disappearance" of the money from the Bitfinex account. Fowler was offered a plea deal that would have meant spending five years in prison, but he rejected this and was eventually slapped with more charges, ranging from bank fraud and money laundering to operating an unlicensed money transmitting business.[178] He could be facing eighty years in prison for his crimes.

Oz Yosef, meanwhile, has been indicted by a grand jury in New York on charges of conspiracy to commit bank fraud, bank fraud, and conspiracy to operate an unlicensed money transmitting business. Yosef allegedly took part in a scheme from February to October 2018 to open numerous accounts in the U.S. at different banks under the pretense that they would be used for real-estate investments, while they were actually used to send funds on behalf of an unlicensed money transmitting business related to the operation of crypto exchanges.[179]

On February 23 2021 the New York Attorney General fined Bitfinex 18.5 million dollars.[180] Bitfinex was also required to increase transparency, and to cease any further trading activity with New York residents as Bitfinex and Tether had deceived clients by overstating reserves and hiding approximately 850 million dollars in losses around the globe.

Tether confesses to using only fractional reserves (2019)

On February 26 2019 Tether admitted for the first time that it was operating a fractional reserve, and that Tethers were no longer backed by cash alone.[181] Instead "every Tether is always backed by our reserves, which include traditional currency and cash equivalents and may include other assets and receivables from loans made by Tether to third parties." The company also disclosed that, "Tether has cash and cash equivalents (short term securities) on hand totalling approximately 2.1 billion percent, representing approximately seventy-four percent of the current outstanding Tethers."

In other words, instead of being backed one-to-one Tethers were only backed 1:0.74. The remaining 0.26 could have been backed by the pledged iFinex shares for the 900 million dollar credit facility after the CCC incident. Later Tether would confirm that Bitfinex had fully repaid the amount, including interest rate payments.

Tether would later reveal that it was holding large amounts of commercial paper that was paying higher interest rates. At one point Tether was the seventh-largest holder of U.S. commercial paper. But nobody seemed to know who Tether was dealing with on the commercial-paper side. Investigative journalists have called the largest brokers for commercial paper, but nobody seems to have traded with Tether.

Rumors have circulated that Tether bought commercial paper from Chinese property developers, as the company accepted Chinese yuan for its USDT-yuan onramp but was likely unable to move the yuan outside of China. When the Chinese property market tanked in 2021–22, rumors circulated again that these property bonds were deep in the red and that Tether was carrying a huge mark-to-market loss on its reserves as bond prices declined. If this was true, then the money that was backing the stablecoin might have been much less than one-to-one.

Under corporate licenses Tether is obligated to be a profitable business, and its CTO, Paolo Ardoino, expected the company to generate 600 million dollars in profits in 2022. By this time Tether had increased its reserves in cash and cash equivalents to 82.45 percent, leaving only 17.55 percent of its sixty billion dollars of assets (nearly ten billion dollars) for riskier investments.

Tether had loaned 841 million dollars, collaterized in Bitcoin, to crypto lender Celsius Network. But Ardoino stated that these loans had been paid back in full before Celsius filed for bankruptcy in 2022. Tether also stated that around four percent of its assets were invested in the tokens and equity of private crypto companies, including Blockstream, Dusk Network, and RenrenBit. Tether had also made investments in ShapeShift, OWNR Wallet, STORK, Lightning Network (LN) Wallets, and Exordium Limited.

Tether itself can make huge returns by buying higher-yielding dollar debt and pocketing the yield, as USDTs do not pay interest to their holders. When interest rates were near zero, there was no opportunity cost for holders, but by 2022 the U.S. Federal Reserve had raised interest rates to four percent. Normally Tether takes a 0.1-percent creation and redemption fee and requires minimum orders of 100 thousand dollars. Tether has easily generated 110 million dollars in creation and redemption fees since its inception in 2014.

Tether also revealed that it was loaning USDT to various entities at nine percent annual yields. But in light of the bankruptcies of several crypto lending companies in 2022, the company stopped new loans. When Tether deviates far enough from the 1.00 USDT-USD peg, large trading desks can arbitrage the spread—as was the case in 2017, when Tether traded at a 2.5-percent premium in China.

Tether has also used funds to invest in other companies, becoming one of the largest supporters of the crypto ecosystem. In 2020 Tether was the lead investor in Celsius's Series A round. This was effectively a contribution to bail out Celsius through secured loans that were then extended. Tether also stepped in to bail out Hong Kong–based Babel Finance.

Tether's market capitalization does not seem to expand and contract in time with the rest of the crypto industry or other stablecoins. Rather Tether tends to be slower to decrease when the industry contracts. Tether creates inventory without issuing it, and it also redeems USDTs without destroying them immediately, keeping them as inventory for future use. Many of Tether's users are Chinese OTC desks and Chinese Bitcoin miners that do not necessarily have U.S. bank accounts, where they can move Tethers into dollars, so their Tethers are stuck in the system and might never be redeemed. Any shortfall on Tether's balance sheet might therefore have a limited impact.

In the U.S. both Circle and the blockchain company Paxos have started the process of trying to acquire banks or apply for bank charters, presumably anticipating that at some point legislation will be passed that is going to move stablecoins into the broader banking regulatory framework. When Binance launched its collateralized futures products, the easiest way to collateralize them was with Tethers, and traders who wanted to trade these collateralized futures—for example Alameda and Cumberland—needed Tethers to engage in trading. This was a major driver for USDT demand. However once Binance switched to cross-asset collateralization, favoring its own Binance stablecoin (BUSD) for these assets, Tether's dominance started to decline.

During the de-pegging of the Terra stablecoin Sam Bankman-Fried's trading firm Alameda Research was actively arbitraging the Tether peg, buying up USDT at 99.30 and selling it back to Tether at 99.90. These market makers had direct relationships with Tether's Treasury, where they could mint and redeem USDT. If market makers like these have confidence in the peg and have balance sheet capacity and risk appetite, they will maintain the peg.

In August 2022 Tether switched auditors once again, dropping MHA Cayman for BDO Italia, which planned regular "attestation" reports once a quarter. Auditors that take on crypto firms potentially have a lot to lose. For a few hundred thousand dollars in auditing fees the company could lose its reputation, so the risk-reward ratio is not very favorable.

Other stablecoins had their issues too. Gemini, the crypto exchange and custodian founded by the Winklevoss twins, offered a "printing bonus" where people could buy BUSDs for ninety-nine cents and sell them at a dollar. But Gemini did not allow the discounted stablecoins to be redeemed for six months to a year. Meanwhile, when Huobi allowed convertibility of certain stablecoins at face value, traders tried to arbitrage the difference.

Tether became particularly popular for OTC trading in Asia and as collateral position management, as U.S. banks are closed during Asian hours and traders wanted to move positions around quickly. Moving money around through international banks sometimes takes days as funds and sources of funds need to be cleared. Tethers, on the other hand, can be moved around instantly at near-zero cost and without institutional oversight.

The first step in the issuance of Tethers is the authorization. This leads to the creation of Tethers on a blockchain, which are then available to the public. When they are sold to customers, these authorized Tethers are added to the actual circulation. Each Tether has multiple private keys held by different signers in various geographical locations. They can subsequently be redeemed in return for fiat, and are then either held in inventory for future purchases, added to Tether's treasury, or destroyed. In the last case they are destroyed forever, leading to a reduction in the overall number of Tethers in circulation.

Bitcoin moves in ten-minute increments because that is how long it takes to produce one block on the Bitcoin blockchain—much faster than dollar transfers. To close the price discrepancies between different exchanges, market participants need to have trading pairs with both legs using the same underlying blockchain. But Tether could eventually outgrow the crypto market, as it could be used for remittances. In the future Tether Limited aims to become the payment solution for the world's two billion unbanked people. As Paolo Ardoino has explained, if Tether's clients also have an account at Deltec Bank in the Bahamas, the bank personnel can make an internal transfer between the accounts, allowing Tethers to be issued and redeemed on weekends and during public holidays as well.[182]

Some have argued that the Bitfinex debt was paid by the dollars earned from simply minting Tethers. Tether's Terms of Service state that, "There is no contractual right or other right or legal claim against us to redeem or exchange your Tethers for money." Anybody who wants to redeem Tethers for dollars is therefore basically restricted at the company's discretion.

Tether and Bitfinex agreed to pay sixty million dollars in fines across two settlements in which neither admitted nor denied wrongdoing. Paolo Ardoino has stated that, "Tether has strong banking relationship with more than seven, eight banks across the world," but without revealing who these banks are.[183]

Tether issued another attestation showing excess reserves of 960 million dollars and more than 700 million dollars in net profit for the last quarter of 2022. This equates to a 4.1-percent return on assets for Tether Limited, with fifty-eight percent of these assets allocated to U.S. Treasury Bills. In late 2021 Tether had reached a settlement with the U.S. regulator allowing Tether Holdings Ltd. to work with an entity of Cantor Fitzgerald to gain access to the treasury market. Cantor Fitzgerald helped to convert Tether's commercial paper assets into Treasury Bills and served as custodian of the bonds. Cantor's sister company, BGC Partners, had existing relationships with Tether, its trading desk having bought and sold large volumes of USDT.

In 2021 Tether had moved thirty-seven billion dollars of its reserves to the Bahamian Capital Union Bank, which maintains trading relationships with multiple U.S. banks and is located across the street from Deltec Bank in Nassau. Capital Union was founded in 2013 and had assets of only one billion dollars as of the end of 2020. Tether was also able to hold some of its reserves with the Bahamian private bank Ansbacher (Bahamas) Limited, which was acquired by Deltec in January 2022.

10

"The best is yet to come"
(Justin Sun, TRON)

I n the aftermath of the bull market of 2017 the U.S. share of global crypto trading volume declined from fifty percent in the second quarter of 2017 to just seven percent by the end of the fourth quarter of 2018.[184] The driving force behind this decline was the dramatic growth in the use of Tethers (USDT), which outstripped the use of dollars in crypto trading pairs. In fact crypto-USDT trading pairs increased 2.5 times faster than crypto-fiat trading pairs during this period.

The leaderboard for crypto exchanges with the most volume also changed dramatically between 2016 and 2018. In 2016 the top five exchanges globally were all based in Mainland China, with the U.S.-based Poloniex number six, whereas from the third quarter of 2017 to the second quarter of 2018 Hong Kong–based Bitfinex was the most dominant exchange, with South Korea's Bithumb gaining market share. Over the course of 2018 Hong Kong–based BitMEX was the number one exchange, followed by OKEx (now OKX), Binance, Huobi, and Bitfinex, with the two Korean exchanges Upbit and Bithumb as number six and seven. The rise of Hong Kong's crypto-trading market share was dramatic, growing from 305 million dollars per day in the third quarter of 2017 to 1.2 billion in the fourth quarter of 2017 and nearly two billion in the first quarter of 2018, making Hong Kong the most liquid crypto market in the world.

While Bitcoin tended to be the most actively traded crypto asset in most countries, in South Korea every quarter saw a new cryptocurrency becoming the most popular. In the fourth quarter of 2017 it was Bitcoin

Cash; in the first quarter of 2018 it was Ripple; in the second quarter of 2018 it was EOS; and in the fourth quarter of 2018 it was Zcash and Monero.

China zero-fee Bitcoin trading ends (2017)

Three Chinese crypto exchanges—Huobi, BTC China, and OKcoin—entered into a zero-fee war on September 20 2013, when Huobi began offering "no fee trading." This meant that the exchanges had to make their money from withdrawal fees, which decreased as clients started trading higher volumes. The result was "wash trading," which boosted volumes as it gave traders the impression that the crypto assets were in high demand.

While the zero-fee incentive was supposed to be only temporary, it lasted until January 23 2017, when regulatory pressure from the People's Bank of China (PBC) caused it to be withdrawn. The central bank, which was concerned about prices rising "too high, too fast," stated that both Huobi and OKcoin had violated guidelines by getting into the margin financing business without having proper anti-money-laundering (AML) controls, thereby causing abnormal market volatility. On January 19 both exchanges halted all margin trading.[185]

Chinese Bitcoin miners take control of the Bitcoin network (2016)

By 2016 over seventy percent of transactions on the Bitcoin network were going through just four Chinese Bitcoin mining pools. Bitcoin miners generally join mining pools to smooth financial returns. Since running a mining pool confers the right to vote on changes to Bitcoin's software, as the pools control most of the network, the four Chinese mining pools effectively had veto power over any changes to Bitcoin software and technology. With Chinese crypto exchanges accounting for forty-two percent of all Bitcoin transactions at the time, this started to raise questions about Bitcoin's independence and centralization.

In April 2016 executives from American Bitcoin-related firms, notably Brian Armstrong from Coinbase, were trying to convince the Chinese Bitcoin miners that the Bitcoin software should be upgraded so that the network capacity and transaction processing power could increase to compete with payment processing companies like PayPal and Visa. This new software proposal would later be known as Bitcoin Classic.

Bitcoin's structure consists of software, hardware, and energy resources, while its governance is managed entirely by code. Without any central authority the Bitcoin community can decide on future core protocol changes through a process called Bitcoin Improvement Proposals (BIPs), which can cover bug fixes to the algorithm, simplification of the code to provide more efficiency, consensus rules, and so on. A BIP must be approved by ninety-five percent of Bitcoin miners. The first BIP was submitted in 2011 by Amir Taaki, one of the people accused of leaking the source code for Bitcoinica, which was used to set up the Bitfinex exchange.

The amount of data that could run through the Bitcoin network was capped at seven transactions per second. As Bitcoin became more popular, this caused severe network congestion and transaction delays, which is why the American executives wanted to upgrade the software. But the Chinese miners wanted to keep Bitcoin smaller and more secure. Some argued that the miners were only motivated by high profits, as users needed to pay higher fees to have their transactions processed within the mined blocks. The miners also wanted to keep the status quo to avoid taking risks with their investments.

The most powerful mining pool in 2016 was F2Pool, which had twenty-seven percent of the network's computational power. But the most important player at the meeting between the American and Chinese Bitcoin executives was Jihan Wu, who had cofounded Bitmain in 2013 and built computers designed specifically for Bitcoin mining. Bitmain also ran the second-most-important Bitcoin pool, Antpool, which accounted for twenty percent of the network's computational power at the time. Bitmain itself had secured ten percent of the global Bitcoin network, producing Bitcoins with a market value of 230 thousand dollars every day in 2016.

A group of China-based miners was unhappy with the proposed improvement plans for the Bitcoin network, and worked on alternative plans which would increase the block size limit. Wu agreed with some of his Chinese counterparts but was also looking for ways to expand the Bitcoin network. He became a vocal proponent of increasing Bitcoin's transaction capacity, and in June 2017 Bitmain drew up a contingency plan should the Bitcoin community decide to upgrade the network.

On July 21 2017 Bitcoin miners locked in a software upgrade referred to as BIP 91, which enabled second-layer solutions on Bitcoin. Ten days later a Shenzhen-based mining company called ViaBTC orchestrated a hard fork of Bitcoin, creating Bitcoin Cash (BCH). ViaBTC created the first BCH block five hours after the fork, mining the second block just five hours later. The third block was mined by a then unknown miner with the coinbase message "Genesis Block 269–273 Hennessy Road Wan Chai Hong Kong."

"Bitcoin Jesus" Roger Ver and others felt that BIP 91 favored Bitcoin as a digital investment while the BCH hard fork would favor Bitcoin as a transactional currency. At the time of the fork anyone who owned Bitcoin came into possession of the same number of BCH units. The original price for Bitcoin Cash was 240 dollars, or nine percent of Bitcoin, although it reached an intraday high of 4,355 dollars when Bitcoin rallied, or twenty-six percent of the price of Bitcoin. Asia-based traders were euphoric about the hard fork, and many borrowed significant amounts of Bitcoin from U.S. investors so they could receive the BCH units.

China's ICO ban pushes crypto trading to Hong Kong

On January 11 2017 the PBC launched spot checks on Huobi, OKcoin, and BTC China covering a range of possible rule violations, amid increasing government efforts to stem capital outflows and relieve pressure on the yuan.[186] The following April OKcoin joined Bitfinex in freezing wire transfers, citing issues with intermediate banks,[187] only to be accused in May of using idle clients' funds to make investments in wealth management products, which are often high-yielding but risky.[188]

Then, on September 2 2017 China banned raising funds via ICOs.[189] Later that month the government prohibited crypto exchanges based in Mainland China from offering fiat-to-crypto trading for customers. While these new rules still allowed Chinese citizens to trade, use, and invest in cryptocurrencies, traders had to use peer-to-peer (P2P) or over-the-counter (OTC) marketplaces outside of China to gain onramp access. As a result the funds of many Chinese crypto traders left for other jurisdictions.

In response to the government's measures OKcoin split into two entities, with one (OKEx) moving to Hong Kong on September 4 2017 while the original OKcoin relocated to San Francisco, where it set up a regulated exchange focusing on fiat-to-crypto onramp spot trading. While OKEx was headquartered in Hong Kong, the exchange was officially based in Malta from April 12 2018. Nevertheless, in an effort to legitimize its presence in the former British territory OKEx bought a controlling stake in a Hong Kong publicly listed company, LEAP Holdings, in a reverse takeover on January 24 2019.[190] To finalize the backdoor listing, OKEx's founder and majority shareholder, Mingxing "Star" Xu, needed access to sixty million dollars, and the source of these funds remains a mystery.

Mingxing Xu studied applied physics in Beijing, graduating in 2006. He worked at Yahoo, and prior to founding OKcoin in 2013, he was the technical officer at docln. Despite the Bitcoin crackdown in early 2014 and plummeting crypto exchange volumes, in March 2014 OKcoin announced a ten million dollar funding round from numerous venture and angel investors.[191]

In a speech at The North American Bitcoin Conference (TNABC) in Miami in January 2015 Xu explained that while the price of a stock is based on the company's profits or revenue, people buy Bitcoin because they believe that it will be used in the future.[192] Xu aimed to encourage his listeners to focus on building projects that enhance the adoption of "a new use case." He also stressed that more consumers and merchants should be encouraged to use Bitcoin.

OKcoin's senior officials were prohibited from leaving the country in 2017 as investigations into the exchange continued, and in September 2018 Xu was detained by Chinese police after a dispute with investors who had suffered huge losses on the OKcoin platform. In October 2020 he was detained again by the Chinese authorities, with OKEx temporarily halting withdrawals on October 16 due to "its inability to contact one of its private key holders."[193]

Xu's detention in 2020 coincided with a crackdown on money laundering activities on various crypto OTC trading platforms in China. Immediately after news of the detention became public twenty-six thousand Bitcoins, or 350 million dollars, left the OKEx exchange, prompting OKEx to transfer 400 million dollars in USDT onto the exchange to provide liquidity and prevent a bank run. Xu reappeared a few days later.

Meanwhile, on October 9 2017 Huobi, which was headquartered in the Seychelles, had incorporated its presence in Singapore, before subsequently moving its business there.[194] The following year, on September 7, the company acquired sixty-six percent of Pantronics Holdings, a publicly listed company in Hong Kong, for seventy million dollars.

Like their counterparts in OKcoin, however, senior officials from Huobi were prohibited from leaving the country in 2017, and on November 2 2020 the company's COO, Robin (Jiawei) Zhu, was placed under police investigation after being invited for "tea" with the Chinese authorities. Zhu had joined Huobi in 2015 and was initially an assistant to the founder, Li (Leon) Lin. He would step down five months after the start of the police investigation. In a message sent to Huobi's users over WeChat at the time Li suggested that even if clients could not access Huobi, "exchanges like Binance and OKEx would be options for them to migrate to."[195] The result was a record number of Bitcoins being moved from Huobi to Binance, which is known for being decentralized and operating out of unspecified physical locations.

In October 2022 Lin sold Huobi to Justin (Yuchen) Sun through a Hong Kong–based investment fund for a rumored one billion dollars. Sun had graduated from Peking University in 2012, founded the smartphone audio communication app Peiwo, and by the end of 2013 was the chief representative of Ripple in China. In 2015 Sun was also in the inaugural class at Hupan University, a business school launched by Jack Ma, the founder of Alibaba. Hupan offers a three-year course dedicated to teaching and mentoring entrepreneurs, and Sun—the youngest of his cohort—is believed by some to be Ma's protégé.

Sun's contacts in high places might explain why he has been able to time policy and market decisions so accurately. His company TRON, for example, raised seventy million dollars during the 2017 ICO boom, with the ICO finishing the day before the Chinese government banned the capital-raising process. Rumor has it that Sun was tipped off by Binance's Changpeng "CZ" Zhao, who had learned about the ban from his own sources.[196]

In 2019 Sun acquired BitTorrent—a peer-to-peer protocol for file sharing with 100 million active users—for 140 million dollars. BitTorrent's files had tended to be pirated, and the solution was to make the site decentralized, spreading the burden of bandwidth and liability across users. Earlier in 2019 BitTorrent had issued the BTT token, which raised 7.2 million dollars and sold out within fifteen minutes. BTT was expected to be used as a tool to either reward file sharing or be spent by users who wanted faster downloads.

In 2020 Sun placed the winning, 4.6 million dollar bid for a charity lunch with Warren Buffet. Leaders from Litecoin, Binance Charity, Huobi, and eToro all accompanied him to the lunch. Sun was also the underbidder on the historic sixty-nine million-dollar Beeple NFT auction in 2021. In December that year he retired as CEO of TRON to become a diplomat for Grenada, acting as the island country's permanent representative to the World Trade Organization (WTO) in Geneva.

TRON wants to create a decentralized internet, and while its TRON tokens were initially issued on the Ethereum blockchain, the company would have its own network by 2018. On April 16 2019 Tether started issuing its stablecoin USDTs on TRON, and as TRON was paying the 0.1-percent issuance and redemption fees, demand grew quickly. In the following weeks Huobi and Poloniex also announced support for USDT on TRON.

In October 2019 Sun bought the Poloniex exchange, which had been instrumental in the initial growth of Tether. This caused Tether issuance on TRON to pick up exponentially. Despite Ethereum's head start and initially broader usage, Tether issuance on TRON had eclipsed that on Ethereum by April 2021, as TRON was cheaper to issue, transact in, and redeem. This made the TRON blockchain more attractive for gaming applications as well. By February 2023 thirty-seven billion dollars of Tether were outstanding on TRON, while twenty-nine billion were outstanding on Ethereum. According to Tether CTO Paolo Ardoino TRON has "good adoption across crypto exchanges and is extremely cheap compared to Ethereum."[197] When high-frequency traders started entering the crypto market, the cost advantage of USTD issued on TRON really began to play out.

A month after buying Poloniex Sun moved its headquarters to the Seychelles, which had very few regulations in place for cryptocurrency exchanges. Poloniex's architecture was poorly programmed, and when users had accidentally deposited Bitcoin to wallets only designed to accept Tether, the Bitcoins had been irretrievably lost. Poloniex's engineers later discovered these irretrievable funds, which they referred to as "crypto dust."

By the time Sun took over the exchange, this "dust" had a value of twenty million dollars.

But unlike on Ethereum, a lot of transactions on TRON appeared to be purely linked to stablecoin transactions, as TRON was offering U.S.-dollar exposure, giving it the appearance of a store of value. Out of the fifty billion dollars of USDT that were minted on the TRON blockchain, fifteen billion dollars were burned, while FTX / Alameda received thirty-five billion dollars. The USDTs issued on Ethereum, by contrast, were largely transferred to Binance and the Cumberland crypto asset trading company.

Some commentators argued that TRON / FTX and Tether / Binance had divided up the world, with TRON focusing on offering U.S.-dollar-type exposure for Asia-based users while Binance offered U.S.-dollar exposure for users everywhere else—from the Middle East to Africa and South America. FTX had started to support USDT on TRON on July 18 2020, when Tether's outstanding market capitalization was only ten billion dollars.

Figure 10: Tether outstanding balance (in billion dollars) on TRON (thick line) vs Ethereum (thin line)

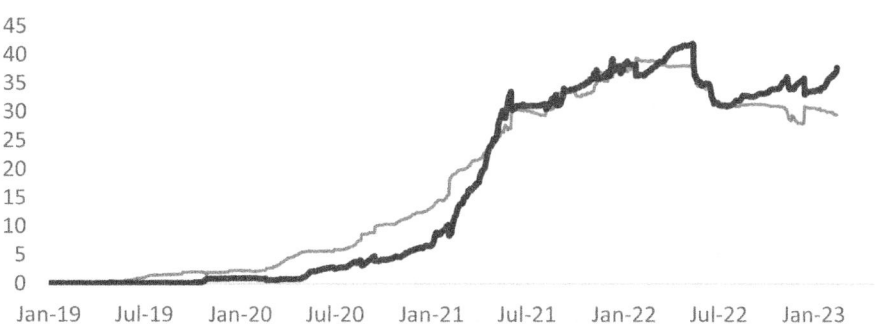

When Hong Kong announced a more pro-crypto stance in late 2022, Sun was the first crypto personality planning to relocate there from Singapore. He argued that Chinese regulators were using Hong Kong as a policy test for the Mainland, suggesting the city's embracing of crypto was an "opening up overall of all crypto policy in China."[198] He also wrote that "experts predict that China will dominate the next crypto bull market."[199]

Sun's timing has been praised by CMS Holdings' Dan Matuszewski. The announcement that he had acquired the Huobi crypto exchange on October 7 2022 was followed just days later by news that Hong Kong planned to legalize retail crypto trading to become a crypto hub, once again showing how well informed he was.[200]

But the 2017 China ban had forced many Chinese crypto exchanges to find a new domicile for their headquarters. BTC China had changed its name to BTCC and become a U.K.-based exchange, after being sold to a Hong Kong–listed company on January 29 2018. In February of the same year the Chinese government banned all exchanges serving Chinese citizens and blocked all websites offering crypto trading. According to data from Statista crypto trading in China accounted for just 0.1 percent of global crypto trading in 2018, down from ninety-three percent in August 2016.[201]

Binance, which was founded in July 2017, quickly moved its servers out of China as well, relocating to Japan in September 2017. Just three months after launch the new exchange had been processing five hundred million dollars in daily trading volumes. In March 2018 Binance announced that it was moving its operations to Malta, a move which OKEx also made the following month. Meanwhile, on March 28 2018 Bitfinex had revealed plans to move its exchange from Hong Kong to Switzerland, although the company was still considering its relocation the following August.

After the China crypto exchange ban Tether became the most important instrument for OTC trading desks. Traders were bidding 7.00 yuan when the real Tether price was just 6.70—a premium of 4.4 percent. China-based OTC broker BitKan—which had been cofounded in December 2012 by Liu Yang, head of the Huawei Wireless Technology Research & Development department at the time—had suspended services on September 14 2017 because of the ICO ban and moved its OTC business to Singapore. Other OTC brokers had moved to Hong Kong.

Genesis Block: a physical shop accepting cash for crypto (2017–22)

When Bitcoin Cash started to trade on August 1 2017, a miner from Hong Kong, who had initiated the first BCH block after the Chinese pool ViaBTC, decided to leave a local address on each block he processed. The address belonged to a hostel in Wan Chai called Check Inn HK, and the miner was Wincent Hung Ka-hoa former Ernst & Young auditor who had started to accept Bitcoin for payments at the hostel, making him one of the earliest merchants in Hong Kong to accept digital assets as an alternative to fiat.

Next to his hostel Hung was setting up a Bitcoin education and trading center called Genesis Block, having established a significant mining business in China in 2016 and formed relationships with Chinese OTC traders. Genesis Block had also started trading the "kimchi premium" in 2017, as well as engaging in arbitrage opportunities in Japan. Hung was originally mining BCH to promote his business, but Genesis Block quickly accounted for seventy-five percent of the network processing power.

Genesis Block had a physical storefront in Hong Kong, where people could come in with cash and buy cryptocurrencies. Often customers' identities were only loosely checked, and when fiat-to-crypto onramp was made illegal in Mainland China, people could travel across the internal border to Hong Kong and buy crypto at the store.

Genesis Block also ran a network of Bitcoin ATMs across Asia. The firm had good partnerships with money exchanges and a network of fifty to a hundred linked bank accounts. The firm was even active in "grey-area" places such as Cambodia according to Charles Yang, Genesis Block's former head of trading. Yang, who had joined the company in January 2018, explained that Tether was finding immense popularity in Asia as hundreds of millions of dollars were being traded every day with OTC trading desks. Despite previous concerns about Tether's reserves confidence among traders remained high, especially within short holding periods when timeframes are measured in hours or days.

Genesis Block attended the Sora Summit blockchain conference on November 13 and 14 2018 in Macau. There Hung met Sam Bankman-Fried (SBF), who the previous year had launched Alameda Research, a crypto quant-trading hedge fund in San Francisco. SBF was trying to get some insights into the crypto industry in Asia. Genesis Block and Alameda would eventually become intertwined in their money flows, with Genesis collecting money from people who wanted to invest in crypto and transferring the funds to Alameda for trading purposes. Alameda may also have gained access to banking services and various liquidity channels that Genesis was able to tap into with its extensive network of high-net-worth individuals and family offices in Hong Kong.

Shortly after his encounter with Hung SBF started establishing his crypto trading business in Hong Kong. FTX Co. Limited had been set up on June 28 2018, and on December 14 2018 Cottonwood Grove Limited was registered in Hong Kong. Cottonwood Grove was wholly owned by Alameda Research, which was registered in the British Virgin Islands (BVI). The original directors of Cottonwood Grove were SBF, Jen Chan Luk-wai, Clement Ip (a cofounder and board member of Genesis Block), and Charis Law Wing-man, with Ip Tak-yan joining as a director in January 2022. Jen Chan, who is also the sole shareholder and director of the Hong Kong–registered Salameda Limited, was the CFO of FTX when SBF launched his cryptocurrency exchange.

Alameda, FTX, and Genesis Block would continue to be closely intertwined.[202] While FTX moved to The Bahamas in 2020, it registered a Hong Kong subsidiary on September 29 2022, with SBF and Clement Ip both serving as directors. The registered addresses of both FTX Hong Kong and Salameda were secretarial companies in a commercial building in Sheung Wan, right next to Hong Kong's financial district.

Immediately before and after the FTX implosion at the end of 2022 the Hong Kong directors of two FTX-affiliated companies registered in Hong Kong, Jen Chan and Clement Ip, resigned. On November 9 2022—the same day that Binance announced the cancellation of its planned acquisition of FTX—Chan, Ip Tak-yan and Charis Law all resigned as directors of Cottonwood Grove, while Chan and Ip Tak-yan also resigned as directors of FTX Hong Kong on November 14. Genesis Block shut down shortly after FTX filed for bankruptcy.

11

"It's just the beginning"

(Changpeng "CZ" Zhao, Binance)

Sam Bankman-Fried (SBF) was born in 1992 into a family of professors at Stanford Law School. His father, Joseph Bankman, is a professor of law and business, while his mother, Barbara Fried, is a professor of law. SBF attended the Crystal Springs Uplands School in Hillsborough, California, where he attended summer programs for mathematically gifted high-school students. He spent his childhood playing strategy games like chess and bridge.

During college SBF became interested in effective altruism, a philosophical movement that uses calculations to understand how people can use their time, money, and resources to help others best. His mother has written about effective altruism and is a cofounder of Mind the Gap, a political fundraising organization that advocates for candidates running for the Democratic Party.

SBF graduated from the Massachusetts Institute of Technology (MIT) with a degree in physics in 2014. He joined the quant-trading firm Jane Street Capital, where he had interned the previous summer. During his three years at Jane Street he gave away half his salary to animal welfare groups and effective-altruism charities. He left the company to work for William MacAskill, one of the leaders of the effective-altruism movement.[203]

SBF has often referred to the Kelly criterion, which assumes a decreasing marginal utility of money.[204] To do well in the world, he felt, you needed to donate money. When the backdrop was to donate trillions of dollars every year for everything from disease prevention, global warming, animal welfare, etc., there should be no tendency to avoid risk.[205]

From an altruistic perspective, SBF felt, people should take risks in their careers so that they could give back with both hands. "Kelly tells you that when the backdrop is trillions of dollars, there's essentially no risk aversion on the scale of thousands or millions,"[206] he affirmed. "Seek out the opportunities with the biggest upside, not the ones which are the safest, and hone in on that vision."[207] When it came to scales of money, the greater the better. "If you bet $100k (everything) and lose, you can never bet again," he cautioned.[208] "You should bet an amount that you can always start again if you lose the bet."

The start of Alameda Research (2017)

On November 27 2017 SBF set up Alameda Research in Berkeley, California with his friend and fellow altruist Tara MacAulay. MacAulay had been trading cryptocurrencies on her own, and it was her idea to set up a firm like Alameda as the quickest way to raise money for the effective-altruism movement. "Cryptocurrency gains?" she had written on Twitter earlier that year. "Give appreciated assets to charity instead of cash. Give more and avoid CGT [capital gains taxes]."[209]

MacAulay had been the CEO of the Centre for Effective Altruism (CEA), the charity founded by William MacAskill and his fellow Oxford University philosopher Toby Ord. MacAskill had convinced SBF to join the CEA in 2013. As an MIT undergraduate SBF was viewed as "someone likely to make a lot of money."[210] Some have voiced that SBF is "a creation of the Effective Altruism movement and not, as has often been written, the other way around."[211] BitMEX cofounder Ben Delo, another Oxford University graduate, was also a donor at the CEA.

According to Naia Bouscal, an early software engineer at Alameda, the effective-altruism movement was Alameda's pitch.[212] The initial funding came from two effective-altruistic donors: Luke Ding, an Oxford University graduate and currency trader at the hedge fund Brevan Howard, who loaned the firm six million dollars; and Jaan Tallinn, who had sold Skype to eBay for 2.6 billion dollars in 2005, and who loaned 110 million dollars' worth of Ethereum.[213] The loans charged an interest rate of forty-three percent.[214] Ding visited the Alameda offices on March 22 2018 and demanded his and Tallinn's money back after an intense meeting.

MacAulay repeatedly warned MacAskill about SBF, but he often took the side of his protégé. But after the CEA had conducted an internal investigation, SBF resigned from the board in 2019. Nevertheless, in 2022 SBF gave 160 million dollars to effective-altruist causes, including thirty-three million dollars to organizations linked to MacAskill, who had previously introduced SBF to Elon Musk as his "collaborator."

Alameda Research was named after the California city Alameda, where SBF's apartment had been back then. SBF's former MIT roommate and childhood friend Gary Wang joined the company as CTO. After majoring in math and computer science, Wang had initially pursued a career as a software developer at Google. SBF owned ninety percent of Alameda, and Wang ten percent.

Andy Croghan, Alameda's COO, had previously led operations for Susquehanna's crypto desk, while its software engineer, Nishad Singh, knew Gabe Bankman-Fried, SBF's younger brother, from high school. Singh had been a software engineer on the Applied Machine Learning team at Facebook, having graduated from Berkeley with a degree in Electrical Engineering and Computer Science.

In January 2018 SBF started to take advantage of higher Bitcoin prices in Japan compared to those on other international exchanges—the classic arbitrage trade. The year before China had shut down its local cryptocurrency exchanges, and this had caused market distortions, with prices trading higher on some exchanges. As the Chinese currency weakened, crypto helped to facilitate capital flight out of China. With the government investigating crypto exchanges' foreign-exchange management and anti-money-laundering (AML) approach, Chinese crypto trading gravitated to other Asian crypto markets, but due to their inaccessibility and capital controls, crypto prices traded at a premium there.

By January 2018 the price of Bitcoin had almost jumped to twenty thousand dollars, with prices in South Korea carrying a thirty-to-fifty-percent "kimchi premium." Over-the-counter (OTC) venues sprang up in and around China on messaging platforms like WeChat and peer-to-peer platforms such as CoinCola, Alipay, and Taobao. These "kimchi premiums" only existed briefly, as banks offered banking services to crypto firms on a sporadic basis. But the spreads existed on paper, and they existed for a reason.

SBF teamed up with a Japanese local named Takashi Hidaka, who he had met through the effective-altruism network in Japan. Takashi, who had started working for Alameda in March 2018, had been head of compliance at TransferWise and was familiar with anti-money-laundering procedures from his days at the Japanese banking giant Mizuho. He would also be the local representative director for FTX Japan when it acquired a local crypto exchange in 2022.

In March 2018 SBF also approached Caroline Ellison at Jane Street, pitching her Alameda as a crypto hedge fund that would exploit price discrepancies between different countries. Alameda's goal, he explained, was maximizing wealth, which meant taking excessive risks.

Ellison was born in 1994 and grew up outside of Boston. Her father, Glenn Ellison, is the head of economics at MIT, while her mother, Sara Fisher Ellison, is an economics department lecturer, also at MIT. A Harry Potter superfan, Ellison also had an affinity for altruism, joining the Effective Altruism Club at Stanford and becoming its vice president. Ellison graduated from Stanford with a bachelor's degree in mathematics in 2016, and at Jane Street was part of the team responsible for equity index rebalances. She was seen as a quiet, risk-averse person who doubted herself.[215]

Alameda develops creative ways to raise funds (2017–19)

Despite SBF's inexperience Alameda Research received one million dollars in seed capital from several wealthy investors in 2017, some of whom SBF had met through the San Francisco Effective Altruism community.[216] But the firm was very secretive about disclosing Alameda's performance. The "kimchi premium" did not last long, and banks were not willing to deal with regular flows from crypto exchanges as the regulator could impose hundreds of millions of dollars of fines if a bank was found not to have followed strict AML and compliance procedures. So instead of making blockbuster returns to attract capital, SBF was particularly good at marketing and telling a good story.

SBF became very focused and creative in his money-raising efforts. He continually tried to borrow cash and crypto assets. That way he could pay out disappointed investors with the new investors' money that was coming in. Instead of audited performance numbers investors were shown a letter signed by Daniel Friedberg from the law firm Fenwick & West LLP stating that "we know the owner of Alameda and consider him of the highest reputation in the industry."[217] Friedberg, who SBF's father had introduced to his son, would join FTX as chief regulatory officer in early 2020.[218]

SBF borrowed crypto from many wealthy investors, promising to return the crypto plus an agreed-upon interest rate. Some reports claim that Alameda made between ten and thirty million dollars in profits by buying Bitcoin on international exchanges and selling it in Japan at higher prices. However there was no audited track record.

In early 2018 arbitrage opportunities suddenly closed, and Alameda started experimenting with automated algorithmic trading and high-volatility trading with esoteric crypto assets. Alexander Pack, a venture capital (VC) investor, recalls when Alameda lost more than ten million dollars in the early days on a trade error.[219] The loss, which caused the company to lose two thirds of its assets in April 2018, was known internally as the "April fiasco." It occurred when Alameda was betting on

Ripple's XRP token, which Korean investors had become actively engaged in by December 2017, only for XRP prices to then crash in January on news that the South Korean government was restricting crypto trading and Ripple was facing an SEC lawsuit. The spectacular crash prompted Jaan Tallinn to recall his loan, causing Alameda's assets to drop back to thirty million dollars.

After the "April fiasco" four Alameda executives, including Tara MacAulay, offered SBF a buyout on the grounds that he was "unethical, failed to update investors on poor performance and will lie and distort the truth for his gain."[220] But SBF refused to resign, and half of Alameda's thirty employees, including the four executives, resigned shortly afterward. MacAulay's U.S. work visa was tied to Alameda, and she left the country.

MacAulay and a few other early Alameda employees started Lantern Ventures and the affiliated Pharos Capital Group. Lantern Ventures is an investment firm with 400 million dollars under management and Luke Ding listed as an investor, while Pharos Capital was listed as the biggest creditor of Celsius when the crypto lender went under in 2022. The Lantern Ventures website says that the company was founded on philanthropic principles and aims to donate fifty percent of the founder's profits in line with her altruistic beliefs.[221] These words also resonated with people who had seen a modern version of Robin Hood in SBF and his firm.

While Bitcoin prices dropped by seventy-four percent in 2018, Alameda claimed it was making steady returns through its market-neutral arbitrage trading. At the Sora Summit blockchain conference in Macau in November 2018 the company bought a booth and distributed flyers advertising its arbitrage trading strategy as generating "high returns with no risk."[222] Several Hong Kong family offices were interested in this "debt with no downside risk" strategy with "twenty percent guaranteed returns, enforceable by U.S. law," as the flyer stated.

The company's pitch deck from November 2018 claimed that Alameda was the best crypto trading firm in the U.S. and among the most serious firms globally. The marketing material stated that its assets under management (AUM) were fifty-five million dollars in 2018, and that the firm traded up to 300 million dollars daily across major coins, altcoins, and derivatives. It also stated that the company had already established a presence in the U.S., Japan, and the British Virgin Islands. This was true, as Alameda was based in the U.S., the LLC was registered in the Virgin Islands, and Takashi Hidaka was operating out of Japan.

According to the pitch book Alameda boasted decades of experience from quant and tech firms, and its OTC quotes were the tightest in the industry. While many were suspicious, Asian family offices loved the proposition of high returns in any regime with "zero downside," as the company's unaudited eight-month track record showed returns of 110.6 percent during a period when Bitcoin had declined 49.8 percent and Ethereum 89.1 percent, and when the U.S. equity market had delivered flat returns.

Alameda claimed that it had outperformed the bear market in 2018 by deploying a strategy that did not depend on the direction of Bitcoin prices, with hundreds of thousands of trades capturing inefficiencies across thousands of markets and exchanges. According to the company the strategy was so promising that it did not have a losing week in six months.

Alameda avoided making directional bets and had only ten percent of its assets under management in unhedged positions. Returns were juiced up with fee rebates by providing liquidity to exchanges. Investors could sign up for only one investment product if they wished, with the company initially offering a fifteen percent annualized fixed-rate loan without any lock up and with a capacity of 200 million dollars—a compelling debt instrument offering. Later this promissory return would increase to twenty percent.

Alameda's competitive edge was built on four pillars: idiosyncratic trading advantages, best-in-class technology, a solid operational framework, and maintaining flexibility across market regimes—all according to its unaudited prospectus. At the time the company appeared to have only five million dollars in capital, which it levered up to sixty million dollars. But the company talked a big game, and it worked.

Alameda moves to Hong Kong (2018)

Hong Kong is known for its accessible business environment and favorable corporate tax rate. Alameda "moved its headquarters from California to Hong Kong due to the difficulty of establishing and maintaining relationships with banks in the U.S. as a cryptocurrency trading firm".[223] One of his colleagues recalled him saying "I think we're losing fifty thousand dollars a day by not working out of Hong Kong instead of Berkeley".[224] And when SBF met Wincent Hung from Genesis Block at the Sora Summit in Macau, he realized that Hung could help him raise a lot of capital in Asia.

Alameda would work closer and closer with Genesis Block as it set up a base in Hong Kong. Genesis Block had made its name during the 2017 Bitcoin Cash fork. A fork occurs when the software of different miners becomes misaligned, and during all forks there is increased price volatility, as the forked versions of the blockchain can become worthless if nobody supports them.

When Bitcoin Cash was forked again on November 15 2018, the forked version was called Bitcoin SV (short for Satoshi's Version). Bitcoin prices dropped by twelve percent into the fork, with crypto trading shops like Alameda on either side of the volatile trades. But despite the increased volatility in the market, SBF continued to take excessive risks.

Alameda trades against other traders

Over time fewer arbitrage opportunities occurred, and Alameda took more short-term market risk by trading against counterparties, either by providing liquidity or trying to influence other traders' decisions. So-called Momentum Ignition Algorithms were used to create a sharp spike in buy or sell orders within a market to deceive traders into placing orders or executing trades they otherwise would not have made.

These so-called "Bart orders"—where prices aggressively spike higher, move sideways and then crash down—are most impactful during low-liquidity periods and most influential during weekends or early morning hours, when other traders are absent from the markets. Alameda was proud to offer crypto market coverage twenty-four hours a day, 365 days a year. The team did not take time off and was always there trading, especially on weekends. So when prices approached levels where other traders might be stopped out and positions could be triggered into cascading liquidations, they tried to force traders to close their positions at unfavorable levels.

Alameda also pursued a strategy of stop-loss hunting—an attempt to artificially move a price to levels where other market participants would automatically be closed out by the exchange's liquidation engine. If a trade triggers many stop losses, auto-liquidation algorithms from the exchanges kick in and sell positions, irrespective of price levels and available volume. The less the volume, the more prices can gap lower. The trader can then buy back the positions after the stop-loss orders have been fully liquidated and prices have adjusted lower, as prices usually reverse once the traders have been stopped out.

As highly leveraged futures trades were prevalent among crypto traders, there tended to be a lot of follow-through once liquidations started, as the exchanges would force traders to close their positions unless they increased their margin balance. Most crypto exchanges set their default futures leverage at twenty times, although some offered as much as 125 times. But even with twenty-times-leveraged positions a drop of only five percent in the futures price would wipe out the initial capital. After regulatory criticism most exchanges would lower their maximum leverage during the summer of 2021, limiting the extreme moves in crypto futures and preventing traders from being liquidated too often.

Sam Trabucco, who joined Alameda as a trader and later became co-CEO, explained that the trading firm had started with strict delta-neutral strategies which were not dependent on the direction of crypto prices.[225] Instead it focused on arbitrage opportunities, such as price discrepancies between different crypto exchanges and mispricing between various contracts. Due to the deep liquidity of the crypto markets and the lack of a unified regulatory setting, arbitrage opportunities offered enough "free money" for them.

While spreads often remained wide for structural reasons, such as market access and liquidity, the Alameda team could move the markets. But smaller traders tended to jump on the Alameda trades, adding momentum and closing the arbitrage opportunities. With a maturing market and the entrance of sophisticated players, the spreads would eventually disappear, so the team needed to find other ways to make money.

In January 2019 Alameda paid 150 thousand dollars to be one of the sponsors of the Binance Blockchain Week. The company used this opportunity to show prospective lenders that the firm had fifty-five million dollars under management. SBF was also thinking about how to copy Binance, as the crypto exchange was onboarding many users, which meant easy access to capital.

In early 2019 Alameda started an over-the-counter (OTC) desk headed by Ryan Salame, who had joined from Circle. By dropping its anonymity in this way, the company hoped to become better known to exchanges and clients. Meanwhile a spin-off from Alameda, FTX, which SBF had started working on during the previous summer, was preparing to launch a crypto derivatives exchange. The exchange debuted in the spring of 2019.

The launch of Binance (2017)

In June 2017 Changpeng Zhao, known by his initials CZ, founded the crypto exchange Binance in Shanghai with a handful of employees from his previous startup, Bijie Tech. Binance was firmly focused on altcoin trading, and now supports six hundred coins. Its trading engine was able to process 1.4 million orders per second.

CZ, a software developer, grew up in China's Jiangsu province and moved with his family to Vancouver when he was just ten. He studied computer science at McGill University in Montreal, and one of his first jobs was working for a trading platform at Bloomberg. During his four years there he worked on developing trading products in Tokyo, New York, Singapore, Hong Kong, and Shanghai. In 2005 he cofounded Shanghai-based Fusion Systems, an IT and business consultancy specializing in ultra-low-latency trading systems for brokers.

In Shanghai CZ was part of a private poker group, where in 2013 he met Bobby Lee, who had just bought the BTC China exchange. CZ's longtime friend, Ron Cao, the managing director of venture capital firm Sky9 Capital, was also part of the group. Cao urged CZ to get into Bitcoin, and in 2014 CZ sold his house in Shanghai and invested all his capital in digital currencies.[226]

CZ left his job at Fusion Systems and became head of development at Blockchain.com. Yi He, the cofounder of OKcoin along with Mingxing "Star" Xu, saw CZ give a presentation about Blockchain and realized that he could explain technology in simple words.[227] She quickly brought him on board, and by 2014 CZ was the CTO at OKcoin, which at the time was China's largest Bitcoin exchange, with a sixty-percent market share. In his role as CTO CZ mentored Zane Tackett, who would move on to Bitfinex in March 2015 and would later be head of institutional sales at FTX.

OKcoin became widely popular, as it enabled derivatives and staking (user-initiated additions to the secure the blockchain). CZ became a community cheerleader for the exchange, driving traffic and bolstering trust through social media. He often posted on Reddit, answering users' questions. And when clients accused OKcoin of artificially inflating token prices and volumes, he denied the exchange was using trading bots to "spoof" volume. However, once he had left OKcoin, he would claim that the exchange had used bots for these purposes.

CZ left OKcoin in February 2015, after just eight months. Xu and CZ then fought on social media to settle their differences, with CZ claiming he had left the exchange because it was "using dubious methods." [228] Xu countered by saying that CZ was "not technologically strong [enough] to bring the exchange forward."[229]

In August 2014 OKcoin had published the crypto industry's first proof-of-reserves audit, written by Stefan Thomas, CTO of Ripple. A well-known entity had also prepared an integrity test at the time on databases supplied by OKcoin to list its assets and liabilities. This test was a sort of checksum of assets, also known as a Merkle root, from which the exchange's on-chain holdings could be verified. But while an exchange can provide the addresses for all the coins in its databases, it is not easy to confirm that it actually owns the coins, rather than them being on loan from the rightful owner.

As the social-media fight between CZ and Xu continued, CZ posted on Reddit that the "OKcoin audit was fake and understated liabilities by hiding its bot accounts," as the bots traded on fractional (or fictional) reserves.[230] OKcoin responded that hiding the bots was done to avoid the double-counting of loaned coins.[231]

Without outside capital CZ launched Shanghai Bijie Network Technology Co., Ltd. in September 2015. Based in Shanghai, Bijie Tech was a provider of cloud-based digital-currency exchange networks that claimed to power thirty exchanges in Asia. Some commentators pointed out, however, that it only supported nine, with most of the websites registered by the same company that also registered the Bijie Tech website.[232]

The Bijie Tech team was also the founding team of Binance, which would later become the world's largest crypto exchange. Roger Wang was the

CTO, and James Hofbauer, who had previously worked at Palantir and Fusion Systems, was the chief architect. Paul Jankunas—who had also worked at Fusion Systems and, before that, Bloomberg—was the VP of engineering, while Allan Yan was the product director and Sunny Li the operations director.

Yi He—the cofounder of OKcoin, who had left the exchange at the end of 2015—also joined Binance as head of marketing, after a few other stints. Yi, a former TV travel show host, was in a romantic relationship with CZ and the two have a son, who was born in the U.S. In August 2022 CZ named Yi the head of Binance's 7.5-billion-dollar venture-capital arm. She also continues to be the company's marketing chief.

The Binance domain was registered by another Bijie Tech employee, Guangying (Heina) Chen, as it was easier for locals to register entities in China than it was for foreigners like CZ, who holds a Canadian passport. Conspiracy theories have surfaced that Binance is actually owned by this mysterious Ms. Chen, who was not listed in the Binance pitch book. Some commentators have even claimed that she is a representative of the Chinese Communist Party who secretly controls the company [233]—something that CZ has denied.[234]

The success of Poloniex, the exchange that had first started to accept Tether instead of fiat dollars and benefited from the rally in altcoins during the ICO bull market, left a positive mark on CZ. "If you do fiat to crypto, you have to have a bank account that can accept money," he commented. "You have to deal with regulatory issues, and usually you're tied to one country".[235] As a result crypto exchanges dealing with crypto as on-ramps, such as initially Binance, would be many times bigger than fiat-based exchanges, CZ concluded in the Binance Whitepaper.[236]

Binance—short for Binary Finance—launched its ICO on July 1 2017, offering 200 million BNB tokens, with fifty percent allocated to ICO investors, forty percent to the founding team, and ten percent to angel investors. Fifteen million dollars were raised in total. Fifty percent of the funds were used for branding and marketing, while thirty percent were used to build the platform and upgrade the ecosystem. Active trading began on July 15 2017. Twenty percent of Binance's quarterly profits were allocated to buying back BNB tokens to reduce supply. *Forbes* magazine compared this to Amway-style multi-level marketing, which creates customer loyalty.[237]

Binance's investors and advisors included Ron Cao and He Yi, as well as Bloq cofounder Matthew Roszak, angel investor Roger Ver, crypto celebrity Chandler Guo, BTC China cofounder Yang Linke, AntShares founder Da Hongfei, Huobi cofounder Jun Du, and RenrenBit founder Zhao Dong, who was one of China's largest OTC brokers.[238]

Within forty-five days Binance had 125 thousand customers. As with BTC-e, the notorious Russian crypto exchange, no identification was initially required to open a Binance account, only an email address. This helped the exchange to trade one billion dollars in the third quarter of 2017, and eighty-two billion in the first quarter of 2018. Within a year the exchange's trading volume had surpassed that of all its competitors, prompting CZ to tell employees that Binance might become the first trillion-dollar company.

CZ was well informed, and moved its servers and headquarters out of China and into Japan in advance of the Chinese government ban on cryptocurrency trading in September 2017.[239] In March 2018 the company announced its intention to move to Malta, and a month later it signed a memorandum of understanding with the government of Bermuda. The fact that Binance did not deal with fiat helped it during the ICO ban and crypto exchange crackdown in China, as being a purely crypto exchange meant that it was not contributing to capital outflows.

Most of Binance's workers are classified as contractors of an entity registered in the Cayman Islands, and they do not enjoy employee benefits. Binance is a super-fast-growing company, and new employees are expected to deliver rapid results, trusting their "good feel" instead of conducting in-depth research or data analysis. Secrecy is highly valued, and staff members are told to keep affiliations to Binance off professional websites such as LinkedIn so that hackers are less likely to identify workers. Employees are also advised not to wear any clothes that could identify them as Binance employees, and they are encouraged to use the fully encrypted messaging service Keybase with "automatic self-erasing messages." Many are paid in Binance's native token BNB instead of fiat currencies.

By 2018 nearly forty percent of Binance's business was in the U.S. Yet the company was not registered with the Securities and Exchange Commission (SEC), the Commodity Futures Trading Commission (CFTC), or the Department of the Treasury. While Bitcoin trading falls largely outside U.S. regulatory jurisdictions, offering derivatives tied to crypto tokens to U.S. residents requires regulatory approval.

On May 7 2019 Binance revealed that it had been hacked for seven thousand Bitcoins, worth around forty million dollars, through a "large scale security breach." In September of the same year it began offering perpetual futures contracts with up to 125-times leverage. And in March 2020 it acquired CoinMarketCap, a price-tracking website for cryptocurrencies founded in 2013, for approximately 400 million dollars.

By 2020 Binance had around 120 million users worldwide and was processing crypto trades worth hundreds of billions of dollars a month. While the company would later become stringent about know-your-customer (KYC) and AML procedures, the early years were dominated by a "move fast and break things" approach.

Binance's "tai chi entity" in the U.S. (2019–)

On June 14 2019 Binance stopped accepting U.S.-based users. Then, on September 24, Binance.US was launched, with BAM Trading Services (BAM) acting as the operator, using Binance.com's wallet and matching engine technologies. Binance.US had strict and lengthy onboarding procedures from the beginning, and all users had to submit identifying documents to open accounts, at least until mid-2021. Developers in China oversaw the software that supported the wallets on the Binance.US platform and also set up Google Sheets for the onboarding of U.S.-based users.[240]

On October 29 2020 *Forbes* published an article claiming that "Binance was using an elaborate scheme to evade regulators."[241] The article was based on a leaked internal document allegedly written by Harry Zhou, the general counsel for Huobi in the U.S. and the founder of Koi Trading Systems—a company known for launching American versions of Chinese companies, which had been backed with three million dollars from Binance in August 2018.

According to the *Forbes* article the leaked Binance document outlined a "tai chi entity" which would be set up to "distract regulators with feigned interest in compliance" while measures were put in place to "move revenue in the form of licensing fees and more to the parent company, Binance." Binance would go on to provide IT licensing, trademark licensing, wallet custody, and exchange operations consultancy for Binance.US.

The leaked document specified that a Cayman Islands holding company would own 100 percent of the "Tai Chi" operating company and pass on service fees to the "Service Company," with only a "contractual relationship" to further "insulate Binance from U.S. [law] enforcement." The "Service Company" would then send revenues to the offshore Binance entity.

The leaked document also explicitly mentioned the need to undermine the ability of "anti-money laundering and U.S. sanctions enforcement" to detect illicit activity. The "tai chi entity" would act as a magnet for regulatory inquiries, engaging the SEC, the CFTC, and the NYDFS (New York State Department for Financial Services) without expecting to gain any approvals from them. Eventually the "tai chi entity" would be absorbed "when it has fulfilled its purpose."

Shortly after *Forbes* published the article, Binance filed a defamation lawsuit against the magazine, which Binance withdrew on February 4 2021. Then, on October 17 2022 Reuters published an article resembling the *Forbes* article, in which it detailed Binance's plan to "insulate" itself from the SEC.[242]

On September 19 2018 the New York Attorney General's Office had stated that Binance, along with Gate.io and Kraken, had been referred to the NYDFS after an investigation into whether they operated in New York.[243] The U.S. Department of Justice (DOJ) had also investigated Binance's compliance with U.S. anti-money-laundering laws and sanctions in 2018.[244] The DOJ addressed the letter to Binance Holdings Ltd., a Cayman Islands–based company, and Binance's chief compliance officer, Samuel Lim.

Meanwhile a Binance employee had noticed that eighteen percent of the page views on Binance.com were based on IP addresses from the U.S.,[245] and in a June 2019 Telegram chat (Binance did not use the Slack messaging app as it believed that the California-based company would obey requests from U.S. agencies) Lim warned about a "nuclear fallout" from any U.S. regulatory lawsuit.

Harry Zhou's proposal on how Binance should handle its U.S. business and clients suggested that Binance should only list utility tokens on its primary exchange, as not offering derivative products in the U.S. would "reduce the attractiveness of enforcement" by the SEC.[246] Making use of virtual private networks (VPNs) would also "offer a loophole and obscure where traders are based." Until 2020 the Binance Academy published a user guide that taught readers how to use a VPN.

In February 2019 BAM, the operator of Binance.US, was incorporated in Delaware, using the same office address as Harry Zhou's crypto trading company in San Francisco.[247] At the same time as Binance was banning U.S.-based users from its platform, BAM registered with the U.S. Treasury as a money services business. Then, shortly after, Binance unveiled its "partnership" with BAM.

BAM appeared to have morphed into Binance.US. Its first CEO, Catherine Coley, reported to the board of Binance.US, which CZ chaired, while custody of the digital wallets of Binance.US customers was kept by Binance's Cayman Islands holding company. This showed how close the business relationships were between the different entities. Over the years Binance has set up at least seventy-three companies worldwide, with CZ owning or partially controlling fifty-nine of them.[248] But it has never revealed which company is behind the Binance entity, or who the shareholders are.

In November 2020 Coley announced that Binance.US had joined Silvergate Bank's proprietary Silvergate Exchange Network (SEN), allowing it to move balances between accounts. Balances could even be transferred on weekends, as they would be treated in a similar way to the bank's internal ledger system. Reuters would later reveal that the Binance.US SEN account was funded with a minimum balance of five million dollars by the trading firm Merit Peak.[249]

On December 23 2020 a "substantial withdrawal" of 7.5 million dollars by Merit Peak from a Binance.US account was flagged to Coley, with Binance.US staff confirming that employees had initiated the withdrawals from Binance.com. Coley wrote to Susan Li, Binance's finance executive, who had access to the Binance.US SEN account, saying that "this transaction is unexpected" as the Binance.US SEN account had hit its daily withdrawal limit of ten million dollars and needed to be lifted to twenty million dollars. "Given we do not have portal access, can we have eyes and ears helping us?" she requested.

According to the Reuters article, from January to March 2021 Merit Peak received transfers from the Binance.US SEN account totaling 404 million dollars. The transfers tended to immediately follow deposits into the Binance.US account by Prime Trust, the Nevada-based crypto custodian firm for Binance.US client funds. Prime Trust made 650 million dollars in wire deposits into the Binance.US account during the first quarter of 2021 alone. But by mid-2021 all Binance.US activity by Merit Peak had stopped.

Merit Peak was incorporated in the British Virgin Islands in January 2019, and in December 2019 it signed a one-million-dollar purchase agreement for shares in BAM. The signed agreement identifies Merit Peak's "Manager" as CZ but does not name the company's owners. Binance.com would send crypto to Binance.US to sell to U.S.-based users and then transfer the funds in U.S. dollars from Binance.US to Merit Peak. Merit Peak would then transfer the funds from its SEN account to the SEN account belonging to a Seychelles-based firm called Key Vision, according to a person with direct knowledge of the transfers.[250] A 2021 corporate filing reveals that one of the directors of Key Vision is CZ.

Binance may have been unwilling or unable to open a U.S. bank account under its name and used the Key Vision entity instead. If Binance customers wanted to move fiat to Binance, they were asked to transfer funds into Key Vision's SEN account.[251] Binance was using the company for U.S.-dollar bank transfers until early 2023.

In December 2020 the U.S. Department of Justice's Money Laundering and Asset Recovery Section (MLARS) sent a letter to Binance requesting any communication involving twelve executives, including CZ, Coley, and Harry Zhou. In the same month the SEC issued a subpoena to BAM, addressed to Coley, regarding the service that Binance provided to Binance.US and asking whether any of the U.S. entity's employees also worked for the main Binance exchange.

By April 2021 Coley had left Binance.US and hired James McDonald, a former CFTC enforcement director and now a partner at law firm Sullivan & Cromwell, as her attorney. Coley was replaced by Brian Brooks, a former banking regulator, who left after three months. In October 2021 Binance.US appointed Brian Shroder as the new CEO. Shroder had worked at Uber Technologies, and his brother worked for the main Binance exchange.

Weak compliance hurdles allow Binance to proliferate (2017–)

By mid-2018 Binance had pivoted its central business registration from Shanghai to Japan and then to Malta. Many regulators were eying the exchange's high-leverage derivatives offerings, which involved high-risk trading for retail investors. Binance offered 125-times leverage—more than its main competitor BitMEX, which offered 101-times leverage. As with the bucket shop strategy, users will eventually lose most of their funds if they trade with high leverage. But importantly, if crypto exchange customers lose more money through leveraged trading than they paid into their accounts, exchanges have tended to socialize these losses.

Binance also launched cryptocurrency-linked versions of stocks like Tesla and Apple. The exchange appended these stock tokens—which also included MicroStrategy, Microsoft, and Coinbase—on July 16 2021, prompting Germany's financial watchdog to warn that Binance had likely violated securities rules. Binance offered the tokens through a partnership with CM-Equity AG, a licensed investment firm based in Germany, which subsequently moved to Switzerland. CM-Equity was also tied to the SBF empire as FTX later tried to issue stock token products as well. Binance faced potential fines for not publishing an investor prospectus for the stock token instruments.

In 2020 the U.K.'s Financial Conduct Authority (FCA) said that Binance Markets Limited "is not permitted to undertake any regulated activity in the UK."[252] By June 2021 the entity was banned from offering regulated services to customers in Britain. Financial regulators had also targeted Binance with warnings or enforcement actions in the Cayman Islands, Hong Kong, Lithuania, Italy, Poland, and Thailand. Binance's chief strategy officer, Patrick Hillmann, disclosed that the company "is working with regulators to figure out what are the remediations we have to go through now to make amends." He added that Binance software engineers were unfamiliar with laws and rules addressing bribery, corruption, money laundering, and economic sanctions.[253]

In November 2018 Binance warned customers in Iran to withdraw their funds as the exchange would "soon" be complying with U.S. sanctions activated on November 5. First the exchange warned users who had provided Iranian passports as part of their KYC compliance process. Then it began warning accounts connected to Iranian IP addresses. [254] Nevertheless Wallex, a money transfer company, and Sarmayex, an Iranian app that allows cryptocurrency transactions, are thought to have moved twenty-nine million dollars through Binance despite U.S. sanctions on Iran, potentially putting Binance at risk of "secondary sanctions."[255] Iran has been an important part of the crypto ecosystem, representing a noteworthy proportion of the Bitcoin mining hash rate and thereby helping to secure the Bitcoin blockchain network, as electricity in Iran is a quarter of the price in most industrialized countries and electricity is the main cost in mining Bitcoins.

Iranian transactions are not the only controversy, however. According to a Chainalysis report from January 2020 more funds tied to illicit activity flowed through Binance than any other crypto exchange. Some commentators have even reported that Binance's user accounts could be bought on the dark web. On June 6 2022 Reuters published an article describing how the exchange had become "a conduit for the laundering of 2.35 billion dollars in illicit funds" from hacks, investment frauds, and illegal drug sales over its five years of existence.[256]

One of the hacks was in September 2020, when North Korea's Lazarus Group stole some 5.4 million dollars from the Slovakian crypto exchange

Eterbase. Within just nine minutes the hackers had opened accounts on Binance, using only encrypted email addresses as identification. They then sent the stolen crypto tokens to the newly opened accounts. A minor part of the Eterbase hack was laundered through the then Seychelles-based Huobi crypto exchange.

Reuters' source for this information was an analysis provided by Crystal Blockchain, a Netherlands-based analysis firm that traces crypto flows. After U.S. and German law enforcement agencies had seized the servers of Hydra Market, a Russian-language site for the darknet drugs market, Crystal estimated that over five years "Binance was used to receive and pay crypto for 780 million dollars from Hydra's users."[257] Not all flows went directly from Hydra's users to Binance or vice versa. Hydra was also used to wash tokens from the 2016 Bitfinex hack.

In January 2023 the U.S. Department of Justice arrested Anatoly Legkodymov, founder and majority owner of the Hong Kong–registered crypto exchange Bitzlato. Bitzlato is marketed as requiring minimal user identification, specifying that "neither selfies nor passports are required," and Hydra was its largest counterparty in anonymous cryptocurrency transactions. The exchange was used in 700 million dollars of illicit transactions directly or through intermediaries until Hydra was shut down in April 2022.[258] The U.S. Department of the Treasury wrote in a court order that Binance had been Bitzlato's top receiving counterparty of Bitcoin between May 2018 and September 2022.[259] However a Binance spokesperson emphasized that Binance had "provided substantial assistance" to international law enforcement partners in support of their investigation.

Chainalysis claims that Binance has received 770 million dollars in illegal flows. Binance has denied this, pointing out that when the Lazarus Group sent it some of the 625 million dollars it had stolen from the crypto game Axie Infinity in 2022, the exchange froze five million dollars and assisted law enforcement officers with their investigation.

Nevertheless CNBC has reviewed messages in Discord servers and Telegram groups where accounts from Binance employees and Binance-trained volunteers known as "Angels" share techniques to evade Binance's KYC and verification systems, including the forging of bank documents.[260] A Binance employee also told users to use a VPN and register as Taiwanese residents, as some Binance products are country- and user-restricted.

Binance also accepts the blockchain-native digital identity offered by the island nation of Palau in the western Pacific Ocean.[261] The Palau Digital Residency, which is available to any world citizen, costs 248 dollars per year and can be used to sidestep Binance's country-specific controls.[262] Users can then pass Binance's European KYC controls and apply for a Binance Visa debit card, which can be used to turn crypto into fiat anywhere in the world. Chinese Mainland users can also obtain proof of address on the Chinese marketplace Taobao.

Over the years Binance has improved its AML requirements and compliance systems, while its onboarding process has become among the most stringent in the industry. The company has also shown signs that it is interested in shaping its narrative in the media. In February 2022, for example, it announced a 200-million-dollar strategic investment in *Forbes*, and although the deal eventually fell through, Binance also pledged 500 million dollars to Elon Musk's forty-four-billion-dollar buyout of Twitter.

As more and more crypto exchanges failed or became victims of hacks over time, Binance was able to win over more users. The exchange ran an aggressive affiliate marketing program, where paid influencers could get up to fifty percent in kickbacks from a recruit's commissions, forever. This compares to twenty percent for Kraken, while Coinbase pays fifty percent for the first three months only. But to keep the Binance kickbacks, the influencer must enlist at least ten new recruits every quarter, and the recruits need to achieve sufficient trading volume.

In a tweet on October 21 2019 it was revealed that Binance's top influencer had made 1,146 Bitcoins (nearly 11.5 million dollars at a Bitcoin price of ten thousand dollars) through the program during the first two years, while the second- and third-best influencers had earned 643 and 573 Bitcoins respectively. [263] In 2022 Binance's top influencers [264] were French entrepreneur Owen Simonin, known as "Hasheur," with over 370 thousand Twitter followers; [265] Ravi Ranjan Singh from India, with 180 thousand YouTube subscribers; [266] Q8Three from Kuwait, who has more than ninety-two thousand Twitter followers: [267] Fisayo Fosudo from Nigeria, who has 467 thousand YouTube subscribers; [268] Kıvanç Özbilgiç from Turkey, who has over 261 thousand Twitter followers; [269] and Deivide Guedes from Portugal, who has 133 thousand YouTube subscribers. [270]

Binance also pursued an aggressive market share strategy by offering zero Bitcoin trading fees from July 8 2022, in the midst of the crypto bear market. This enabled the company to increase its market share from 50.5 percent to 72 percent on March 22 2023, when it stopped the zero-fee offering. Just five days later Binance was charged by the CFTC for conducting certain activities outside the U.S. designed to avoid CFTC regulation, such as intentionally structuring Binance entities and transactions to avoid registration requirements. [271] The civil complaint alleged that Binance had taken a calculated approach to maximise corporate profits by instructing employees and customers to circumvent compliance controls, which are a requirement to prevent and detect terrorist financing and money laundering.

In February 2023, meanwhile, the SEC had issued a Wells notice (notification of a possible enforcement action) to the blockchain company Paxos ordering it to stop issuing the stablecoin Binance USD (BUSD) as it was an unregistered security. [272] Binance and Paxos had announced their partnership to launch the token in 2019. BUSD is owned by Paxos, which only licenses the Binance brand for the stablecoin. Binance had admitted on January 24 that it had mistakenly mixed the crypto exchange's customer funds with BUSD-token collateral, before announcing the suspension of its USD bank transfers from February 8 onwards. [273]

QuadrigaCX: a mysterious death and the disappearance of 190 million dollars (2013–19)

QuadrigaCX, once Canada's largest crypto exchange, was founded by Gerald Cotten and Michael Patryn in November 2013. Cotten was an early crypto evangelist and part of the Vancouver Bitcoin group in 2013, while Patryn would later be identified as Omar Dhanani, who was connected with the online identity-theft ring Shadowcrew.com. Dhanani had been convicted of identity theft in October 2004 and served eighteen months in U.S. federal prison.

Patryn had launched Midas Gold Exchange (M-Gold), a digital-currency exchange site, in April 2008 and started accepting Bitcoin in June 2011. He offered forum members an electronic money-laundering service through the payment processor Western Union for a fee of ten percent of a transaction, which he would filter through accounts in e-gold, an early centralized digital currency.

But Patryn was most active with Liberty Reserve, the Costa Rica–based centralized digital-currency payments service founded by Arthur Budovsky and Vladimir Kats. Liberty Reserve functioned as a "PayPal for criminals," [274] serving 5.5 million users worldwide before the U.S. government shut it down in May 2013. By this time the company had processed more than six billion dollars, most of which were based in the United States.[275]

To fund their Liberty Reserve accounts, users had to go through a third-party exchange such as M-Gold. In fact some 342 of the top five hundred Liberty Reserve accounts by volume were associated to M-Gold, with Cotten's email linked to Patryn, suggesting that they had been working together with Liberty Reserve through M-Gold.

Within a month of the closure of Liberty Reserve Patryn and Cotten launched QuadrigaCX in Vancouver. But by 2016 all the directors had resigned, as there was little volume on the exchange. Cotton stayed on, but QuadrigaCX had no employees, offices, or bank accounts. The exchange experienced a revival during the 2017 Bitcoin rally, when prices increased from one thousand to almost twenty thousand dollars, with about 1.2 billion dollars being exchanged on Quadriga. When Bitcoin prices declined in 2018, however, users wanted to withdraw funds but experienced long delays.

Quadriga was run from Cotten's encrypted laptop from his home, and there was also no formal accounting system. The exchange did not have bank accounts, working instead with external payment processor companies, some of which have since been sued by the SEC and other regulators. One of these companies was WB21, which was run by Michael Gastauer, who has been named by the SEC in a 165-million-dollar fraud case. Another was Crypto Capital Corporation (CCC), which was involved in the 850-million-dollar loss of Bitfinex funds in 2018.

In mid-January 2019 Quadriga announced the death of Gerald Cotten. According to Cotton's new bride, Jennifer Robertson, he died on December 9 while traveling in India. A local municipality in Jaipur issued a death certificate on December 10. Cotten's will, which was signed on November 27, left Robertson the entire eight-million-dollar estate and named her a trustee.

On January 28 Quadriga went offline for "maintenance." No one knew how to access the exchange's reserves or wallets. Quadriga had 363 thousand registered users, with 190 million dollars of user funds on the platform. These assets were held in Quadriga's cold wallet on a laptop which only Cotten had access to. Robertson said that she had no access to passwords and there was no "dead man's switch," which would reveal the private keys of the exchange's reserves. According to Ernst & Young the wallets belonging to Quadriga have been empty since April.[276]

There have been allegations that Cotten faked his death, with customers complaining they could not get their money out of Quadriga in the months leading up to his death.[277] In 2019 it was revealed that Cotten had transferred millions of dollars in crypto out of customer accounts and into other crypto exchanges, which he then used to fund massive crypto trading activities. Cotten lost 115 million dollars under aliases in crypto trading and another twenty-eight million dollars on external exchanges. He also spent twenty-four million dollars on his lifestyle, buying real estate, cars, and other personal belongings.[278] At no point during its transportation from India back to the burial site in Canada was Cotten's body identified.

In June 2020 the Ontario Securities Commission officially concluded that Quadriga was a fraud and a Ponzi scheme.[279] Investigators found that Cotten and Patryn, who were both active in the scheme, had likely met on TalkGold, a popular forum for pushing high-yield investment programs regarded as Ponzi schemes, as early as 2003. They were also both active on BlackHatWorld, a forum where people discuss marketing tactics such as paying someone to promote your product on social media.

So far there has been no proof that Cotten faked his death. However Quadriga had been operating with shady external payment providers, and no secret keys for Quadriga's wallets have ever been found. So, given Patryn's background in identity theft, the suspicion remains.

12

"Bitcoin is the greatest social network of all"
(Tyler Winkelvoss, Gemini)

After the scandals during the 2018 bear market crypto suddenly started to rally on April 1 2019. An April Fool's Day article claimed that the SEC was about to approve a long-awaited Bitcoin exchange-traded fund (ETF) after an emergency meeting over the previous weekend. According to the article Bitwise Asset Management and VanEck would launch Bitcoin ETFs the following month. Traders and journalists started scrambling for reasons why Bitcoin was suddenly spiking. Some claimed a 100-million-dollar order had caused a sudden increase in momentum, while others argued that many shorts had been closed out on Bitfinex. Some forward-looking traders also pointed to the next Bitcoin halving, which was due in May 2020. In return for validating and securing the Bitcoin blockchain, Bitcoin miners receive fixed rewards in Bitcoin for every block they produce. These rewards are cut in half every fourth year, and Bitcoin prices tend to rally as these halvings approach.

In March 2017 the SEC had rejected an application for a Bitcoin ETF from the crypto firm Gemini, claiming that the underlying Bitcoin market was still "too manipulative, volatile, and resistant to surveillance."[280] The SEC has rejected every proposal for an ETF backed by physical Bitcoins since the Winklevoss twins filed the first Bitcoin ETF application on July 1 2013.

The Winklevoss twins, who had famously won a sixty-five million dollar settlement from a lawsuit against Facebook in 2012, led an investment round in BitInstant in 2013. By November of the same year they had also bought one percent of all outstanding Bitcoin, spending eleven million dollars on 100 thousand Bitcoins when the price was only 120 dollars. In 2017 the twins became the first known Bitcoin billionaires. They had launched the crypto exchange Gemini in 2015, and would acquire the NFT marketplace Nifty Gateway in 2019—two years ahead of the NFT market boom in 2021.[281]

In December 2017 Cameron Winklevoss predicted that Bitcoin would become a multi-trillion-dollar asset. He compared Bitcoin's 300 billion dollar market capitalization with the six-trillion-dollar market value for gold, which would justify a twentyfold price appreciation, and concluded that Bitcoin was "gold 2.0."[282] By December 2018 Bitcoin had declined eighty percent from its all-time high, but the Winklevoss twins urged investors to "ignore crypto winter."[283]

In early 2019 Binance held several crowdfunding initial exchange offerings (IEOs), which were initial coin offerings (ICOs) that were vetted and performed by a crypto exchange. These IEOs sold out within seconds, indicating that the market had become full of positive sentiment. Bitcoin finished the month of April with an impressive twenty-eight-percent return.

IEOs raised 1.7 billion dollars in 2019, with Bitfinex's parent company iFinex alone raising one billion dollars for its LEO tokens in May. The exchange had launched the tokens to raise money when U.S. authorities seized funds from Crypto Capital Corporation (CCC), where Bitfinex had kept most of its money after its banking relationships had deteriorated. Twenty-seven percent of the consolidated gross monthly revenues of iFinex were promised to buy back and "burn" LEO tokens. Bitfinex also pledged to use ninety-five percent of any funds recovered from CCC and eighty percent from the 2016 hack to burn LEO tokens. As of October 2022, however, iFinex had only purchased and burned seven percent of the overall LEO supply.

By April 2020 only four out of the top fifteen IEOs had a positive return on investment, with average losses to investors as high as fifty-three percent. IEOs were more a public-relations and marketing tool than a fundraising option. Most of the money raised—sometimes up to eighty-five percent—was used for marketing and market-making activities to support the token price.

Alameda raises its profile (2019)

By studying BitMEX's order book and monitoring how it changed during liquidations, the traders at Alameda Research started to get an intuitive feel for how the market was affected when a large number of liquidations occurred. Alameda worked on models that would predict liquidations, with signals that were a combination of open interest and the premium / discount of the perpetual futures funding rate.

In spring 2019 Alameda needed to attract volume for its crypto exchange FTX, and the company came to the realization that sacrificing anonymity could be traded in for marketing purposes.[284] One of Alameda's first trades was to buy Litecoin and sell it on the U.S.-based Coinbase exchange, where prices were thirty percent higher than on other exchanges.

BitMEX, which was among the largest crypto exchanges in 2019, published a leaderboard of its most successful traders, and two Alameda accounts were listed among the top ten traders by lifetime profits, boasting earnings of more than sixty million dollars cumulatively. But while BitMEX only showed the winners, Bitfinex also showed the losers. And on February 27 2020 Zhao Dong from RenrenBit asked Sam Bankman-Fried (SBF) on Twitter if he was using FTX user funds to trade, as SBF's account on Bitfinex was showing a fourteen million dollar loss—twice as much as the second-worst trader.[285] SBF responded that it was a unique position and a "hedge against shorts elsewhere." Other traders noticed that SBF was short on BitMEX while simultaneously being long on Bitfinex. He was gaming the leaderboards on different exchanges.

Alameda launches the FTX crypto exchange (2019)

In April 2019 Alameda was preparing the ICO for its crypto exchange, FTX. Some market participants were suspicious, as Alameda had tried to raise funds just a few months before by offering fifteen- and even twenty-percent annualized fixed-rate loans with no lockups. Su Zhu from the crypto hedge fund Three Arrows Capital (3AC) said that Alameda could not find "greater fools to borrow from even at 20%+." So Alameda had come up with the idea to set up a "BitMEX competitor" to raise funds for trading. Zhu also criticized the market for not calling out scams early enough as the "risk of exclusion" for future investment opportunities was higher than the "return from exposing" scams.[286]

According to an informal term sheet from April 10 2019 FTX issued 350 million FTT tokens for its ICO. Like Binance's BNB tokens, the FTT tokens would be the backbone of the exchange's ecosystem. Of the 350 million tokens minted, fifty percent were allocated as company tokens to FTX and were set to "unlock" (i.e. become available for trading) over three years. The seventy-three million FTT tokens sold during the ICO became unlocked after between one and three months. During the periodic unlocks SBF directed Caroline Ellison to support the FTT token price as he was concerned that early investors would take profit from their investments.[287] The earliest and cheapest FTT token offering was priced at 0.10 dollars, implying a direct market capitalization of thirty-five million dollars for the FTX exchange. To create FOMO (fear of missing out), each subsequent batch of tokens was sold at a higher price, driving up the token's market cap.

The FTX derivatives exchange had originally planned to launch on April 15 2019, under the web address *ftexchange.com*. In the end it launched in May, after four months of coding. The platform, which later changed to the site name *ftx.com*, offered low trading fees and allowed traders to swap cash as collateral for coins.

In the FTX token white paper, which was issued on June 25 2019, FTX said that it would offer futures, leveraged tokens, and over-the-counter (OTC) trading services.[288] By then average daily trading volumes had already reached 100 million dollars, with OTC adding another thirty million dollars. The affiliate trading firm Alameda was the primary source of volume and liquidity on FTX. According to the white paper Alameda had 100 million dollars under management and was a backer of FTX. No other affiliation between the two firms was mentioned. Alameda claimed it traded between 600 million and one billion dollars daily, which accounted for five percent of the global crypto trading volume. With these high trading volumes from Alameda being passed through to FTX, the exchange was able to attract venture capital investors and sell its FTT tokens.

Later BMA (Bitcoin Manipulation Abatement LLC) sued FTX, accusing it of organizing an illegal token sale on the grounds that FTT tokens were a security offering that had been promoted to U.S. citizens without prior approval from the SEC.[289] In its lawsuit BMA alleged that the token sales had been at a per-token price of 0.16 dollars—a steep discount on the public sale of 0.80 dollars for the fifty million FTT tokens that had initially been issued. It also argued that the exemptions for private offerings did not apply to the sale as it was aimed at U.S.-based investors who "intended to resell and did in fact resell" the tokens.

Security token offerings have different disclosure and marketing requirements from those for commodities, which are more loosely regulated. This is an ongoing overhang from a regulatory perspective. In July 2022 the SEC classified nine tokens as securities, notably Ripple's native token XRP. However, in this case the court dismissed the lawsuit, although it did lead to SBF seemingly resigning from Alameda to focus on FTX.

BMA calculated that the FTT token sale had raised fifteen million dollars, with the U.S. entities and people that had bought the tokens including Proof of Capital, Chris McCann, Edith Yeung, Consensus Lab, FBG, and Galois Capital. Galois was a San Francisco–based crypto hedge fund founded in 2018 by Kevin Zhou. Zhou had previously worked at Buttercoin, a U.S.-based exchange that went under in 2015. He had then become the head trader at Kraken, an exchange backed by Google Ventures and Y Combinator.

Zhou recalls that Bitcoin bid-offer spreads at Buttercoin were sometimes one percent wide, allowing the firm to pocket one thousand dollars in profit instantly by simply matching buy and sell orders on a 100-thousand-dollar trade. Over time spreads tightened as the market matured, narrowing to just forty basis points two years later (which was still wide for traditional markets).

While Galois started with a relatively small number of assets under management (AUM), they would later increase to twenty million dollars in April 2020, before jumping to thirty-five million dollars in April 2021. By that time the fund's trading volume had increased to 1.4 billion dollars—up from 671 million dollars in 2018—meaning that it was turning over its entire assets roughly once every ten days.

Galois engaged in high-frequency trading as its primary trading strategy. Although it was a quantitatively focused hedge fund, Zhou admitted that sophisticated trading models and technologies, such as machine learning, tended to be overkill in the crypto markets.[290]

The fund mainly focused on liquidity provision and matching assets with bidders' quoted prices. This meant that positions were no longer held for more than thirty seconds. Crypto exchanges tend to pay liquidity providers fees to provide volume, and sometimes negative trading costs are implemented to increase exchange trading volumes. Higher volumes attract retail traders as there is a perception that other traders are active on the exchange. But it also means that venture capital and other investors are more likely to fund the expansion plans of the exchange.

Galois bought its FTT tokens at 0.10 dollars in April 2019. Zhou believed that crypto-hedge-fund redemptions would be less impactful on the market, and he expected that by the second quarter of 2019 the market in token prices would be bottoming out. FTT tokens launched on May 8 2019 and traded quickly up to 1.20 dollars. Galois rapidly exited most of its FTT positions when the price reached 0.80 to 1.94 dollars. In 2021 FTT soared to about sixty-one dollars, before hitting an all-time high of eighty-five dollars on September 9 2021.[291]

Despite being credited for predicting the collapse of the Luna crypto exchange in 2022, Galois was caught off guard by the demise of FTX later that year. Half of its assets were stuck on the bankrupt crypto exchange, and the expectation was that it would take years to recover them.[292] At the time the fund had roughly eight million dollars under management, down from 200 million, and Zhou eventually closed it down. Instead of going through a lengthy legal process to recover funds from the FTX exchange, he sold his creditor claims for approximately sixteen cents on the dollar.[293]

FTX claims to provide a superior risk liquidation system

FTX claimed that it had managed to reinvent the risk management approach, reducing the likelihood of clawbacks occurring during liquidations. The exchange's liquidation system was designed to close positions carefully with limited liquidation orders, a unique backstop liquidity provider (BLP), and leverage from FTX's insurance fund to prevent customer losses. All these features were designed to avoid the socialization of losses.

FTX also employed an aggregated portfolio margin methodology, where the exchange could evaluate a user's leverage exposure within one account. Users could take margin positions if they had acceptable collateral in any cryptocurrency in their account. Contrary to futures on BitMEX, the futures on FTX were non-inverted, making it easier for traders to understand.

FTX promised that one third of all the fees generated on the exchange would be used for FTT token repurchases, with the repurchased tokens burned to limit the overall circulation. This strategy was designed to create upward pressure on FTT token prices, as the inflationary pressure from future tokens would be diminished, making the tokens an attractive value proposition and encouraging token holders to keep them if trading volumes kept increasing on FTX.

How FTX's liquidation engine was supposed to work

Crypto exchanges are poorly capitalized, as there are no minimum capital requirements and no clearing firms between the exchange and the customer positions that guarantee an orderly settlement if one side defaults. On September 7 2021 3.5 billion dollars of crypto derivatives contracts were liquidated in just one hour during a flash crash. The trigger was a spike in the funding rate when sentiment was excessively bullish, making it more expensive to hold long positions.

By then FTX was already a leading exchange, and while its competitors Bybit and Huobi recorded liquidations of 1.2 billion and 0.9 billion dollars respectively, the total value of liquidations at FTX was only 123 million dollars.[294] Despite prices trading below users' stop-loss levels on FTX, they were not liquidated. The exchange's liquidation engine did not seem to work, and some traders saw this as a red flag.

FTX attributed its lower liquidations to a "special process" that used a "backstop liquidation provider."[295] During liquidations the exchange could execute trades through an algorithm or hand over the positions to market makers willing to provide liquidity and effectively take the other side of the positions. Alameda was FTX's leading liquidity provider and likely warehoused these positions.

On September 8, the day after the flash crash, users started to complain about a slow withdrawal process on FTX, while the exchange introduced USD lending rates of twenty-five percent (compared with USDT rates of twenty percent). FTX appeared to need money to process withdrawals and was offering excessively high lending rates to attract deposits.[296] Some traders started to believe that the exchange was absorbing the liquidation risk to attract traders to its platform.

Exchanges such as BitMEX and Bybit had a lousy reputation for snowballing liquidations. Crypto exchanges tend to have proprietary trading groups that aim to create volatility and liquidate the exchange's customer accounts. But instead of market orders indifferent to price and volume, FTX claimed to use limit orders, enabling it to start selling positions partially at more favorable prices for its clients.

Alameda, among others, was a backstop liquidity provider (BLP) for FTX, absorbing leveraged positions before they were liquidated. BLPs are exchange customers that take over positions and "catch a falling knife" from other customers for a fee. But when an exchange does not liquidate client orders, it essentially internalizes the risk. And if prices continue to fall and gap lower, the exchange could go bankrupt in one big liquidity crunch.

There was always a gap risk when prices moved unexpectedly during liquidations. FTX customer terms stated that if a leveraged user account went bankrupt and the backstop liquidity fund was empty, the remaining funds would be taken from positions with positive unrealized profits. But under no circumstances did FTX want to make the same mistake as OKEx in 2018, when the exchange socialized trading losses and subsequently lost market share.

On July 31 2018 OKEx had opted to socialize losses when a customer refused to close a position or add more margin. The user had a substantial long position of 400 million dollars in BTC futures. As a result OKEx injected 2,500 Bitcoins, or about eighteen million dollars, to capitalize its insurance fund. But if the fund could not cover the total margin call losses, the investors with short positions would have to make up for the shortfall, and in the end there was a clawback of 8.8 million dollars. According to an OKEx spokesperson this was "split proportionately by all profited traders' realized and unrealized gains."[297] Most of the traders were furious and started trading on other exchanges instead.

FTX launches more exotic derivatives (2019)

FTX was known to issue contracts quickly on tokens that traded elsewhere. This attracted the attention of newly launched protocols, which were keen to hand over free tokens to FTX or Alameda in return for FTX listing them or Alameda providing liquidity in the tokens. This would mean free money without much effort when token prices went up.

Exchanges have a chicken-and-egg problem. Without liquidity there will not be retail users, and without retail users there will not be liquidity. So exchanges pay fees to market makers on the exchange, as higher volumes attract retail traders. The result is excessive volumes relative to the market capitalization of the whole crypto industry.

On September 13 2019 FTX launched a range of leverage tokens which would "allow traders to utilize capital effectively." [298] These exotic derivatives were leverage from a perpetual futures contract contained within a spot token. But the tokens were never at their proper leverage, and FTX rolled them out without having expert market makers update prices around the clock. Instead the exchange only rebalanced the prices once a day at 00:02 UTC (Coordinated Universal Time). To rebalance the prices, FTX would simply inject capital into the respective perpetual futures contract to repeg the leveraged token. For example, if TRON (TRX) moved five percent but the TRX three-times-leveraged token only moved seven percent, FTX would push the token up by eight percent to align with the fifteen percent expected leveraged-token move.

It would take ten minutes to rebalance the prices, and the process was almost always in favor of the leveraged token holders, as the derivatives tended to underperform their expected leverage. It could also be figured out quite quickly which tokens deviated from their actual leverage, and one trader kept up this strategy for eighteen months without being noticed. The company behind those tokens—an Antigua-based company called LT Baskets Ltd.—would file for bankruptcy protection together with FTX.[299]

... and even more exotic derivatives (2019)

FTX invented MOVE contracts, which represent the absolute value of the amount a product moves in a period. If, for example, the daily Bitcoin (BTC) price range was 125 dollars from the beginning to the end of the day, the BTC-MOVE contract would expire at 125 dollars whether BTC went up or down. These contracts were an option strategy known as "straddles," with a strike price equal to the time-weighted average price (TWAP) of the first and last hours of their expiration period.

Alameda, which provided the liquidity on FTX, quoted MOVE contracts in giant sizes at narrow spreads to attract interest from traders. Often it did not adjust its prices after trades were executed, as the company did not have the staff to monitor all contracts and its system was not automated enough. This meant that smart traders could arbitrage FTX, as prices for its exotic derivatives often did not match market prices.

FTX also had option RFQ (request for quote) markets, which needed to be more coordinated and updated. Traders could arbitrage the options against other exchanges—for example the Panama-based Deribit derivatives exchange, which handled ninety percent of all the crypto option volumes.

FTX gave market makers extremely favorable incentives to attract liquidity, including lower trading fees and monthly rebates for reaching a certain monthly trading volume. Some market makers were even paid up to twenty-five thousand dollars per month to provide liquidity. So even if Alameda made money trading its book, it was bleeding money on FTX to attract users. This likely caused losses over time that the exchange could not reclaim.

Alameda and FTX are accused of market manipulation (2019)

On November 2 2019 FTX Trading Limited, Alameda Research, SBF, Gary Wang, Andy Croghan, Constance Wang, Darren Wong, and Caroline Ellison were hit with lawsuits by BMA in California, which accused them of manipulating Bitcoin spot and derivatives markets. The defendants were charged with making illicit profits and misappropriating 150 million dollars from numerous cryptocurrency traders.[300]

The Alameda team was accused of dumping 255 Bitcoins, valued at approximately 2.6 million dollars, at market prices within two minutes on September 15 2019. The alleged aim of the intervention was to lower prices artificially and set off cascading liquidations, triggering Binance's SAFU (Secure Asset Fund for Users). SAFU is an emergency insurance fund that Binance established in July 2018, committing a percentage of trading fees to grow the fund to a sufficient level to safeguard users' funds. The Alameda team was accused of selecting the lowest liquidity window at 9 p.m. EDT (eastern daylight time) on Sunday to maximize the impact of the attack. Binance had just launched perpetual futures trading, and liquidity was often thin.

The trades were caught by Binance's market surveillance team, and on the same day Binance's CEO, Changpeng "CZ" Zhao confirmed the attempted price manipulation on social media, stating that a "well-known account that traded with [Binance], and started their own futures exchange a few months ago" had tried to "attack" the Binance platform.[301] Instead of relying on a potentially manipulated price from only one exchange in the short term Binance uses an index (a basket of reference prices) to liquidate users. So to set off the liquidations on the Binance exchange, the Alameda team would have needed to influence the basket price instead of just the price on Binance.

Binance invests in FTT tokens (2019)

The issue between Binance and Alameda was resolved in a phone call between Binance and FTX. Alameda claimed that the trading behavior had been caused by a problem with its algorithm. Three months later, in December 2019, Binance bought five percent of FTX and became a long-term FTT token holder. In return FTX was expected to help develop Binance's products and OTC business. In September Binance had acquired JEX, a Seychelles-registered futures and options exchange, to boost its derivatives offerings.

While Binance proliferated, BitMEX was still among the largest crypto exchanges in early 2020. FTX was still comparatively small, although in August 6 2019 its official seed round had netted eight million dollars in funding to build the business. So while many traders were still suspicious that the FTX liquidation engine did not really work and its derivatives pricing could easily be arbitraged, causing losses for Alameda, by early 2022 everybody thought that FTX had successfully entered the big league.

13

"Insane theory of the day: there was no ... issue"
(Sam Bankman-Fried, FTX)

On March 12 2020, in the midst of the COVID crash, Bitcoin prices dropped fifty percent in a matter of hours. The decline was the biggest loss in Bitcoin's history. Due to the aggressive price moves the day became known in the crypto industry as Black Thursday—in remembrance of the October 19 1987 stock market crash, when prices fell twenty percent in a single day referred to as Black Monday.

Figure 11: Bitcoin prices crash during the Black Thursday panic

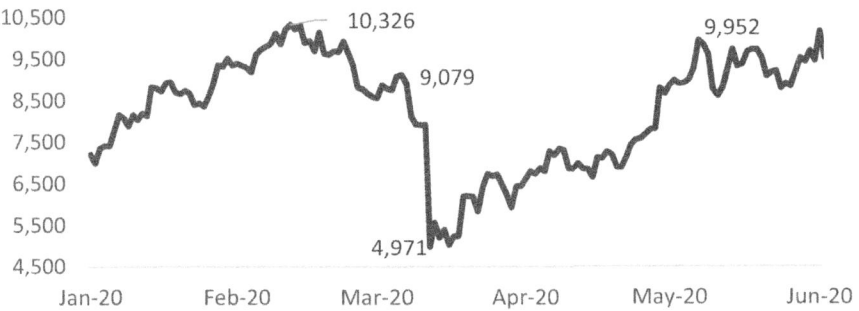

After the 1987 crash most major stock exchanges set up circuit breakers, which would temporarily halt trading to curb panic-selling. There are three circuit breakers in place for U.S. stocks. Prices are halted for fifteen minutes when the benchmark index, the S&P 500, drops by seven percent and thirteen percent, while trading is stopped for the day when prices decline by twenty percent compared to the previous closing day.

Large declines rarely occurred after circuit breakers were implemented. The next major incident was on May 6 2010, when a flash crash caused trading to be halted for fifteen minutes after a seven-percent decline. When stocks started trading again, the S&P 500 rallied and a V-shaped rebound occurred. Traders who had panicked and cut their positions suffered huge losses, while those who had not reacted to the declining prices were not impacted. Then, in March 2020, when equity markets crashed due to the COVID pandemic, circuit breakers were triggered on four different days: March 9, 12, 16, and 18.

While Bitcoin prices dropped by fifty percent on March 12 2020, some smaller altcoins dropped by seventy percent. In fact two large Bitcoin drops occurred during that day. The first was a twenty-three-percent decline that occurred within one hour, and the second a decline of thirty-three percent that occurred within three hours.

BitMEX suffers a DDoS attack on Black Thursday (2020)

BitMEX was the largest crypto exchange at the time, handling billions of dollars of trading transactions daily. The exchange could no longer control its liquidation engine, and this caused a cascading effect as prices collapsed across the whole crypto sector. Traders held 280 thousand Bitcoins on BitMEX, and they deposited another forty thousand to fulfill margin requirements to avoid liquidations. The exchange's flagship perpetual futures contract was critical to Bitcoin's price discovery on other exchanges due to its massive volume.

During the second Bitcoin drop BitMEX experienced an intentional DDoS (distributed denial of service) attack, which made it impossible to trade during that time. As soon as BitMEX was "attacked" and the exchange stopped its liquidation engine, the Bitcoin price surged back from 3,900 to

5,300 dollars. This demonstrated how important BitMEX was for the price discovery of Bitcoins, and how one exchange could influence the crypto market. As the liquidation engine took over customer positions, the clients had no ability to access their trading books.

One billion dollars' worth of perpetual futures contracts were liquidated during the two Bitcoin declines. BitMEX offers leveraged trading and no trader can lose more than their margin position. If positions get close to the liquidation level, the automated system takes over and liquidates the positions at a favorable level. The difference between filled position and the remaining margin of the perpetual futures contract gets added to the insurance fund. If the position gets liquidated below the customer's margin, then the insurance fund deducts this amount to make the exchange whole. BitMEX's insurance fund was around thirty thousand Bitcoins, or 150 million dollars, at the time.[302]

Many have speculated that BitMEX turned off trading to stop the vicious cycle of ever more longs being liquidated at a time when the insurance fund might have run low on capital.[303] This would have put the exchange at risk of bankruptcy.

During the crash bid-ask spreads widened materially as market makers withdrew liquidity, making it more likely that cascading liquidations would be set off. The bid-offer spreads stayed wide for several days, as some market makers stopped providing liquidity during these uncertain times, when they might also have taken large losses. When market makers take over positions, they speculate on a mean-reversion in prices. So when prices continue in one direction, their positions suffer huge losses. Only the well-capitalized market makers can survive these periods.

The fifty percent decline in the market would have wiped out any long positions as well as the collateral that borrowers offered. Many traders and crypto firms hedged their spot positions with futures on BitMEX, while others shorted futures on BitMEX to profit from the decline. But with the exchange being taken offline, traders were unable to hedge their positions, and this caused a huge mismatch in users' profit-and-loss expectations.

BitMEX's proprietary trading desk had likely taken over many trades from the exchange's liquidation engine and was potentially sitting on hundreds of millions of dollars of paper losses that day—for as long as prices continued to decline.

BitMEX's decision, if that is what it was, set the stage for Binance to become the largest crypto trading exchange. This is because traders thought that, rather than suffering a DDoS attack, BitMEX had switched off its liquidation engine, and that was seen as an unfair move. For this reason many traders moved away from BitMEX after the incident, withdrawing forty percent of their Bitcoin holdings on the exchange. As a result Binance was able to increase its market share, which rose from just ten percent to more than twenty-five percent in the aftermath of Black Thursday. "Traders were confronting how BitMEX's liquidation engine really worked after it auto-liquidated their futures contracts and those traders were looking for alternatives," Su Zhu, the CEO of Three Arrows Capital (3AC) stated.[304]

By the end of March 2020 expectations grew for fiscal and monetary government stimulus around the world to buffer the effects of the COVID crisis. This helped stocks and crypto prices to recover. Governments responded by providing free stimulus checks and loans to support their citizens and business owners. The U.S. increased its money supply exponentially, printing in just the two years following the outbreak of the COVID pandemic an amount equal to forty percent of all the U.S. dollars that had ever been printed before. Governments circumvented central banks in creating liquidity and issued loan guarantees to backstop any economic downturn. In the aftermath of the crash and the subsequent aggressive rebound in prices the perception developed that prices would follow a V-shape rebound.

During the crash crypto prices had moved wildly. Crypto market makers had demanded non-liquidation terms due to unreliable cross-exchange basis spreads that traded unpredictably wide as a result of a lack of liquidity. Crypto lenders and borrowers had negotiated not to margin-call each other, as sharp price moves were seen as temporary. Stop-loss signals were ignored, as they might have set off a cascading liquidation effect. Nobody expected thirty-percent declines in a single day, and nobody wanted to jeopardize their business relationships or push others into bankruptcy. Surprisingly no major exchanges or trading firms went under after March 2020. The perception that crypto exchanges were able to manage clients' leveraged exposure through their liquidation engines without going bust was seen positively.

In the aftermath of Black Thursday Huobi, which had 5.7 billion dollars in daily trading volume, implemented a liquidation circuit breaker on all its derivatives products. But its liquidation engine would not stop trading; instead it would "help users hedge against liquidation risk, providing partial liquidation and gradually reducing a user's positions rather than liquidating them in full in a single event."[305] Huobi's new liquidation engine appeared to work in a similar way to FTX's.

The growth of stablecoins explodes after Black Thursday (2020)

Investors had only two choices to protect themselves from falling prices: they could short futures on derivatives exchanges like BitMEX, or they could move their crypto positions into stablecoins. Moving money from crypto to fiat is costly for some, and for others without U.S.-dollar-denominated bank accounts often impossible. So demand for stablecoins started to increase in the aftermath of the March 2020 crash.

As investors looked for stability, money poured into stablecoins. The market capitalization of Circle's stablecoin, USDC, increased by fifty-seven percent from February to March 2020, while the overall stablecoin market capitalization relative to Bitcoin doubled during the first two weeks of March from 3.5 to 7.0 percent. USDC was mainly used on Coinbase, but also started to be used as collateral on MakerDAO and other decentralized finance (DeFi) applications.

MakerDAO made the decision to add USDC as collateral—in addition to Ethereum and the Basic Attention Token (BAT)—after its own stablecoin, DAI, increased in value far above the peg, rising to 1.06 dollars on March 12 2020. The increase was caused by a mass MakerDAO collateral liquidation. Meanwhile Tether issued on Ethereum (USDT-ETH) increased from 660 million dollars on March 10 to 3.7 billion dollars on March 22. Tether's market capitalization rose to eighty-three billion dollars over the next two years, fueling the liquidity which was necessary to lift crypto prices higher as more investors became willing to move their fiat currencies into cryptocurrencies.

Figure 12: Tether's USDT market capitalization exploded after the March 2020 crash

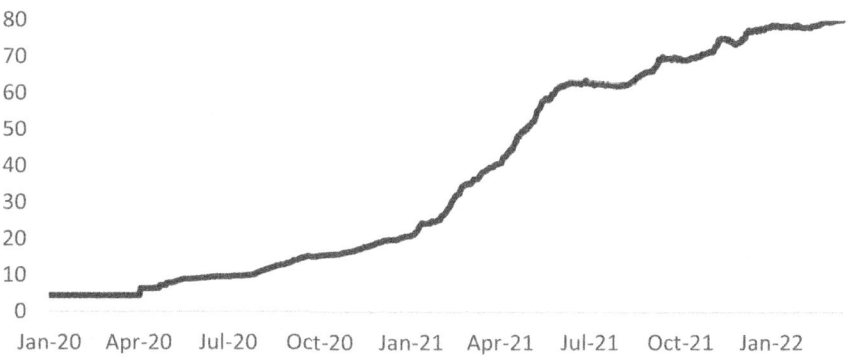

A speculative phase starts with stimulus checks and lockdowns (2020)

Social-distancing rules suddenly made DeFi a lot more attractive, as less human-to-human contact was the norm. The COVID crash set off the DeFi summer of 2020, where financial products that resembled banks without intermediaries became tremendously popular. At the same time the trust in experts and institutions was low, as the truth was overrun by the desire to control the pandemic. This was the time when expectations for peer-to-peer transactions started to become widespread, with most of the activity going through the Ethereum network.

The U.S. government announced three rounds of stimulus checks to support the U.S. economy through subsidized spending. Eligible tax-paying adults received a check of up to 1,200 dollars, while eligible dependents under sixteen each received five hundred dollars. The very first stimulus checks were paid into people's bank accounts over the weekend of April 11 and 12 2020.[306] In anticipation of these checks stock and crypto prices started to rise.

The second stimulus checks, consisting of six hundred dollars plus extra claims for child dependents, were paid out between December 29 2020 and January 15 2021. Almost immediately retail meme-stock trading exploded, with shares in the bankrupt GameStop Corporation rallying 2,166 percent in a matter of days. It was the time of the little guy on the street taking on the establishment.[307] The notion of democratizing access to finance, which in many ways crypto embodies, also applied to these meme stocks, as hedge funds that were betting that GameStop would go bankrupt were overrun by the herd mentality of YOLO (you only live once) traders. It all became a game.

During the GameStop short squeeze of January 2021 Gabriel Plotkin's hedge fund Melvin Capital lost fifty-three percent, or 6.8 billion dollars, of its capital. GameStop shares rallied from fifty to 350 dollars in just one week, as the community of small retail traders united to force the funds that shorted the stocks to buy them back at huge losses. Once a star trader at Ken Griffin's hedge fund Citadel and Steve Cohen's S.A.C. Capital Advisors, Plotkin was overrun by users of the social-media platform Reddit and the r/WallStreetBets community, who saw betting against the economy and profiting when people lost their jobs as companies went bankrupt as unethical behavior. This coalition of predominantly retail investors coordinated the squeeze by buying short-dated call options on GameStop.[308] Up until that point Plotkin had been one of the most successful long/short hedge fund managers, generating sixty-seven-percent returns in some years, with the majority coming from shorting stocks. But in May 2022 he announced the closure of his fund. The WallStreetBets crowd had won.

Figure 13: GameStop shares increased twentyfold in a matter of days in January 2021

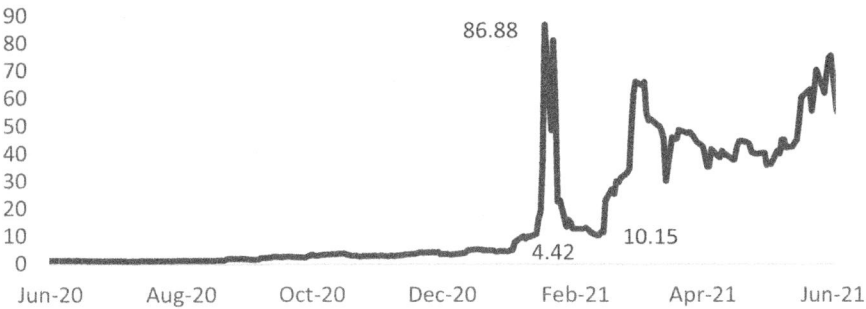

The free COVID stimulus checks provided everybody with extra cash to speculate with. Either become rich or die trying was the ethos of the day. The speculative craze was intensified by FOMO (fear of missing out), a phenomenon commonly observed on social-media sites. Young people displaying their perceived wealth on Instagram sucked in more new traders, while influencers started to push penny stocks and dubious crypto projects. By November 2021 the stock market was back to record highs, while the crypto market capitalization had reached three trillion dollars, driven by Bitcoin, Ethereum, and meme coins such as Shiba Inu.

Meanwhile the stock market had become a video game simulation, where stock buy orders were greeted with confetti effects on the Robinhood trading app. "It felt like the Candy Crush game," Peter van Dooijeweert, a managing director at the world's largest hedge fund, Man Group, observed.[309]

During the social-distancing restrictions people were encouraged to stay home, where they could trade stocks on retail trading apps from their basement. People's risk tolerance skyrocketed, and the volume of stock call options traded (a bet on higher prices) tripled from ten million contracts per day to thirty million contracts. Another bearish hedge fund manager, Russell Clark, threw in the towel and closed his fund. The WallStreetBets crowd had won again.

When U.S. President Joe Biden signed the 1.9-trillion-dollar American Rescue Plan into law on March 11 2021, GameStop shares rallied 130 percent as the third government handout provided eligible taxpayers with a check of up to 1,400 dollars. But the successive rounds of stimulus checks did more than just invigorate the stock market; combined with easy monetary policy from the central banks and the perception that social-distancing rules required the financial system to be rebuilt, they also set off the next crypto bull market.

PART FOUR: THE FOURTH CRYPTO BULL MARKET (2021)

14

"I knew I was not the only one"
(Hayden Adams, Uniswap)

The DeFi (decentralized finance) summer officially started on June 15 2020, when the lending protocol Compound transitioned from being controlled by a company to being owned by its vastly decentralized token holders.[310] Compound distributed ownership of the project to its community by issuing the COMP token, which allowed holders to "debate, propose, and vote on all changes to Compound." This was the beginning of "DAO community governance," where the protocol's authority would be governed by the DAO (Decentralized Autonomous Organization). It was a watershed moment for DeFi.

Figure 14: The fourth crypto bull market peaked in November 2021

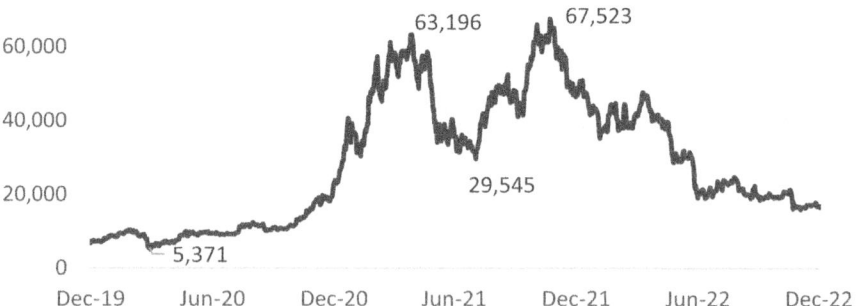

From April 2020 COMP tokens were allocated according to users' on-chain activity within the Compound ecosystem, with users receiving tokens over four years. The more a user lent or borrowed on Compound, the more tokens he/she would receive. Ten million COMP tokens were distributed, half to users and the other half to founders, team members, and investors in the protocol.

Compound was initially launched on September 27 2018 as a money market on the Ethereum blockchain, allowing users to earn interest on or borrow crypto assets without negotiating lending and borrowing rates with a counterparty.[311] Distributing ownership greatly impacted the borrowing and lending protocol and set off the DeFi summer yield-farming craze. Compound's total locked value (TVL), a measure of user funds on the platform for transactional, lending and borrowing, went from seventy million dollars in June 2020 to twelve billion dollars in May 2021. The COMP token price increased from seventy to 855 dollars during that period.

Compound was not, in fact, the first company to offer token rewards for on-chain activity; that was Synthetix, a protocol enabling synthetic assets issuance on the Ethereum blockchain. Balancer, an automated market maker (AMM) that allows users to create liquidity pools, followed a week later with a similar approach. The project's TVL went from fifty million dollars to 3.6 billion dollars as a result, while the price of its BAL token increased from fifteen to seventy dollars.

On September 16 2020 Uniswap, a decentralized exchange (DEX), began its own decentralization process. Retroactively everybody who had interacted with the Uniswap protocol received four hundred UNI tokens through an airdrop (new crypto projects usually use airdrops to generate social-media buzz or reward early community members by sending free token assets directly to their wallets). The value of the tokens was more than one thousand dollars. Some 150 million UNI governance tokens were also distributed. Eventually the UNI token rallied from three to forty-three dollars by May 2021, by which time the market cap had nearly reached twenty-three billion dollars.

A DEX is a peer-to-peer network for swapping tokens. At their peak in May 2021 DEXs traded 211 billion dollars, with Uniswap alone accounting for eighty-two billion dollars. The first version of Uniswap was built in 2018 by Hayden Adams, a twenty-seven-year-old native of New York, after he was fired from his job as an engineer at Siemens. Adams had been introduced to AMMs via a 2016 post on Reddit by Vitalik Buterin, the founder of Ethereum. The post had been sent to him by Karl Floersch, a friend from Stony Brook University who worked for the Ethereum Foundation.

Floersch told Adams that Ethereum needed more contract developers, so Adams started to learn JavaScript and Solidity. He also flew to a blockchain conference in Seoul, where he met Buterin. Then, with a sixty-five-thousand-dollar grant from the Ethereum Foundation, he built an AMM similar to Bancor, which had raised 150 million dollars in a 2017 ICO. Buterin advised Adams to change the name of the AMM from Unipeg to Uniswap, and the new exchange was launched in November 2018.

Uniswap is open-source, so anybody can launch a clone or modified version. And when a pseudonymous competitor, SushiSwap, offered a token reward for Uniswap users to move their liquidity over to the Sushi AMM in a so-called vampire mining attack, Adams reacted by offering the UNI tokens. Shortly afterward the company's trading volume had eclipsed that of even Coinbase, the largest U.S.-based centralized exchange.

As with eBay anybody can list a token on Uniswap, and in exchange for posting tokens into its liquidity pools, where users can exchange their tokens, users received a small percentage of the value of every trade, effectively letting them earn a yield from their crypto assets. But the process had no safeguards against money laundering there were no KYC (know your customer) forms to be filled out. So when 281 million dollars were stolen from the KuCoin exchange in 2021, it came as no surprise that part of the money was traded through Uniswap, which has no central set of servers and cannot be shut down. While Adams has led the team that developed Uniswap, it has handed the protocol's governance to a broad community of users that can vote to make policy changes.

Figure 15: Uniswap's UNI token was one of the early DeFi summer tokens

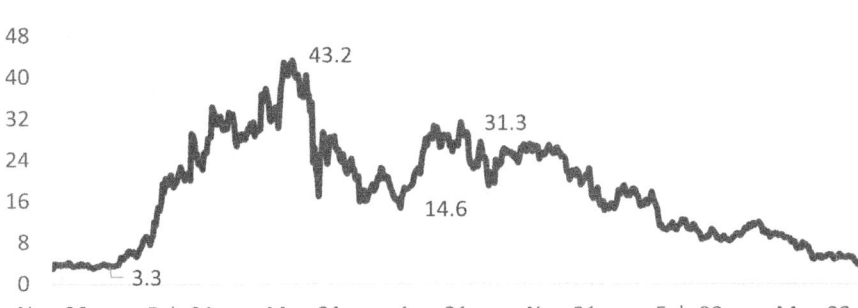

At its peak in May 2021 Uniswap generated more monthly fees than the rest of the Bitcoin mining network put together. It recorded a trading volume of eighty-five billion dollars for the month, with the UNI governance tokens valued at thirty-three billion dollars. The Uniswap team held twenty-one percent of these tokens, and the protocol's treasury was fourteen billion dollars strong. Uniswap's three million users had locked up nearly ten billion dollars on the exchange that month, with the AMM making 250 million dollars from the 0.30-percent fee it charged for swapping tokens on the platform.

The following year, four years after Adams had first programmed Uniswap, the firm behind the protocol raised 165 million dollars from venture capital (VC) funds at a 1.66-billion-dollar valuation.

In addition to Uniswap many other new protocols issued tokens to users, who would then stake the tokens and generate more yield as the tokens continued to receive rewards. These staked tokens were not used for the borrowing or lending of exchange assets but rather as a proof of asset.

New projects would piggyback on other communities by offering free money from staking to get their community off the ground. Some offered staking yields of one thousand percent APY (annual percentage yield) to attract users. This diluted the value of the tokens. But if token prices rose fast enough as more users bought them, the high annual yields could offer high returns. So marketing new projects excessively through social media became the norm. If the new project had some success, however, the yields quickly dropped lower—which meant that users who wanted to generate the highest returns and receive the most free tokens had to find new projects and move tokens around quickly.

Figure 16: TVL (total value locked) increased 362 times from June 2020 to January 2022

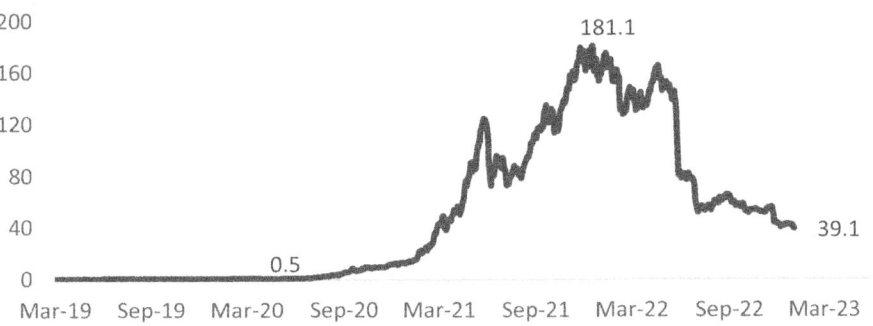

The bull markets in previous crypto cycles never lasted more than eighteen months, as frauds ran rampant and government regulation eventually changed the direction of prices. Blinded by promises of great returns and hip-looking protocols, the community put trust and money into them, only to be often disappointed when the project's developers were just after some quick cash. Some DeFi teams even stayed anonymous so the team could focus on building. This, of course, caused many tokens to be "rug-pulled."

Rug pulls, or "pump-and-dump" schemes, are scams in which a fraudster uses misleading information to inflate the price of a new token before taking the money and running away, leaving the investors with a worthless asset. For example users swap Ethereum for SakeSwap tokens, only to be left with the worthless tokens. Meanwhile the developer sends the acquired Ethereum to Tornado Cash, where his/her identity and the destination of the acquired Ethereum remain fully anonymous.

Rug pulls have been relatively common in DeFi, as protocols are mainly open-source. This is especially the case for copycat DEXs, where developers can simply amend the code and launch the new projects effortlessly. SakeSwap, KwikSwap, and PancakeSwap, for example, are all copies of SushiSwap, itself a clone of Uniswap.

Despite being a forked or copied version of Uniswap, SushiSwap went from a fifty-million-dollar market capitalization in November 2020 to 3.6 billion dollars in May 2021. At its heart were tokens distributed to the project's founders before they had any value. A few tokens were then sold to users, and the funds were used for influencer marketing to attract more users. For example CryptoCoin.News charges between thirty thousand and seventy-five thousand dollars for its direct email marketing campaigns, with 4.5 million crypto investors on the distribution list. Influencers on YouTube and Instagram have also participated extensively in pump-and-dump schemes.

How the pump-and-dump token flywheel works

During an interview with Bloomberg's *Odd Lots* hosts on April 26 2022 SBF was remarkably open when he described how the classic pump-and-dump token flywheel works.[312] During the interview he admitted that yield farming had become a more significant source of income than trading for his firm, and as he described the yield farming process, he seemingly realized he was detailing a classic Ponzi scheme, where investors are lured in to pay off earlier investors.

Unenthusiastically SBF described the process of a company "building a box which is dressed up as this life-changing or world-altering protocol that would replace all the big banks in 38 days." His uninterested description made the listeners understand that he was not a real believer in DeFi. The audience was supposed to ignore what this company or box would do. Instead what mattered was that the box could receive funds in the form of Ethereum or other assets, and that it could issue IOUs (promissory notes) which could then be redeemed for a token that the protocol issued, so users could take out their funds.

SBF continued describing the process half-heartedly, stating that anything cool that happened to the box would ultimately benefit the governance vote of holders of the tokens. Then the protocol would mint more tokens and give them to the users through an airdrop, thereby incentivizing them to hold the tokens if the story sounded legitimate.

With only a low free float of these tokens the market capitalization could easily reach high levels, even if it was a mark-to-market valuation that could not be readily cashed out due to the small free float. If the box paid the token holders a return, they would be incentivized to keep their tokens in the box to receive a high yield, while new users would also be attracted to buy the tokens. Other users might feel even more confident and put more money into the box as the valuation of the tokens and the valuation of the cash inside the box started to rise. The more money that was put into the box, the more the concept was validated, and the easier it would be for the box to pay the yields.

In reality SBF's crypto exchange FTX raised its own FTT tokens, which rose in value and allowed the firm to use them as collateral. Similar to the box in his description the exchange's tokens had little intrinsic value. Nevertheless a small float of tradeable tokens allowed the value of the collateral to be manipulated, giving the impression of real value.

To return to SBF's analogy, the more money the box attracts, the easier it is for the team behind the project to raise funds from VC firms. This lifts the value of the box and the tokens even more. The box's competitors will likely become demotivated when they see the company building up its business and gaining even more credibility with VC funds. Eventually they might give up, and the company with the box will get the actual business. According to SBF this seemed like the "standard operating procedure, frankly, for startups right now." It was, he concluded, "very similar to what we're talking about in some ways with these [protocols]."

An interesting way to monetize artificially inflated tokens is to place them into a "borrow and lending" protocol that accepts them as collateral. Often two thirds of the tokens can be used to borrow a more stable cryptocurrency like Ethereum. If the token falls back by fifty percent or more, the protocol will unwind the borrowed amount, or what is left of it. But since it is an automated protocol, it cannot claim what has already left its ecosystem. So the user can exchange tokens at artificially inflated prices for higher quality and less volatile crypto holdings. This is exactly what the crypto trader Avraham Eisenberg did in October 2022 when he drained 116 million dollars from the Mango Markets DeFi trading platform.

How the token flywheel gains traction

Several companies, such as the IBC Group, run project and token advisory services in the form of "social engineering campaigns" to help pump token prices.[313] Carefully curated email distribution lists from crypto websites are used for power marketing, along with social-media channels on Discord, Twitter, Instagram, and YouTube.

These advisory companies design giveaways, with unique viral gifts boosted by growth. The aim is to implement marketing strategies to spread the word rapidly, generate hype around projects, and grow the number of active, engaged, and real followers across numerous sources and channels.

The companies also promise "a significant increase in community engagement and lots of emails to use in future campaigns," and offer specialized token design suggestions to make projects more appealing than competitor projects.[314] According to the IBC Group Twitter is the virtual front door to every project, where most viral marketing begins.

The token flywheel starts to come into full swing after the pumping of the price through marketing with influencers and the publishing of "thought pieces" by crypto exchanges. With a small free float and a rising token price the protocol can mark the gains on its balance sheet and show them to investors. The inflated valuation allows the firm to raise cash by selling stakes in the company or taking out loans, as the lender will be confident due to the company's valuation. These steps, in turn, pump the price even more.

With the help of respectable market makers such as Alameda, Cumberland, Jump Capital, and Wintermute the token prices can then be inflated, as market makers tend to receive free tokens to provide liquidity. This incentivizes them to lift token prices higher, as the tokens can then be offloaded to others when the price and liquidity are highest. The market maker will work with exchanges to list the token and promote it to even more users.

The protocol can now mark these additional "gains" and approach a reputable VC firm for significant funding. Some VC firms publish detailed articles about the companies they have financed and try to build momentum by showing their support. This can also be seen as pushing the flywheel and legitimizing the project.

But with higher prices the incentives for token holders start to diminish, as unless the protocol begins to generate revenue, it must adjust down the yield it pays to its token holders. As less money starts to come in and the protocol's treasury reserve gets slowly depleted, handing out free tokens for the market makers also becomes costly from an engineering perspective. Slowly but surely the project collapses under its own weight.

The token's internal stakeholders are the first to notice; the last are the less informed retail investors.

The most money to be made in the process is just before the new tokens are listed on popular crypto exchanges such as Coinbase, Binance, and FTX. Ahead of the listings token prices tend to rise, and while "front running" (insider trading) is illegal, many trades have been detected. A study by researchers at the University of Technology Sydney estimates that insider trading occurred on ten to twenty-five percent of new crypto listings on Coinbase between September 2018 and May 2022.[315]

Figure 17: Token prices ahead of exchange listings

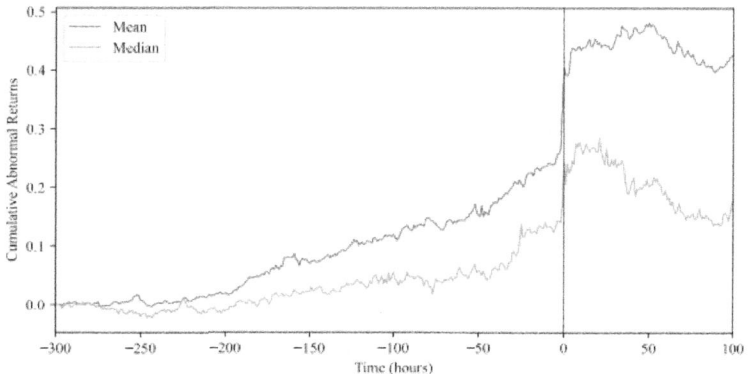

In July 2022 the U.S. Department of Justice charged a product manager at Coinbase, Ishan Wahi, for insider trading. Wahi was accused of sharing confidential information with his brother, Nikhil, and a friend, Sameer Ramani, tipping them off at least fourteen times from June 2021 through April 2022 of listings for upcoming tokens, which they then acquired ahead of the dates and sold for profits of more than 1.5 million dollars. Nikhil Wahi pleaded guilty to one charge of wire fraud in September 2022 and was sentenced to ten months in prison, while on

February 7 2023 Ishan Wahi pleaded guilty to two counts of conspiracy to commit wire fraud.

A similar situation occurred on the online marketplace OpenSea, a noncustodial platform where users can buy, sell, and create non-fungible tokens (NFTs). In the first ever case of digital-asset insider trading Nate Chastain, an OpenSea employee who was responsible for selecting NFTs to be featured on the platform's homepage, is accused of front-running the listings. Chastain has protested his innocence, as the charges necessitate "the existence of trading in securities or commodities," which currently do not include NFTs. However the judge denied the dismissal motion, and Chastain awaits his day in court.[316]

Flywheel collaboration between market makers and exchanges

If traders can invest in a project, receive tokens in return, offer market-making services which provide even more tokens for free, and then list the tokens on an affiliated exchange, and if they are also entirely in control of the process, including its exact timing, then the financial returns are almost guaranteed. This was the case with the VC funds Alameda Ventures and, later, FTX Ventures, both of which were highly incentivized to inflate token prices, spread the word, and sell tokens to other users.

Alameda / FTX Ventures would invest in a project that was little known at that point and receive tokens in return. They would ask the token's treasury to deposit the tokens at FTX and draw down only needed balances for the token's operating expenses. FTX would then send the treasury balances back to Alameda / FTX Ventures so that they could invest in more projects without the token project being aware of it. That way FTX would still control the assets while having limited actual investment fund outflows as it engaged in the token investments.

In return Alameda / FTX Ventures would offer market-making services and receive more tokens, primarily for free, or borrow these tokens and commit to paying back the token loan in USDT. FTX would then list the tokens on its exchange, opening up the token to its user base, while Sam Bankman-Fried (SBF) promoted the tokens on Twitter. This offered Alameda / FTX Ventures a way to liquidate the tokens, convert them into USDT, and repay the loan.

Each step in the process legitimized the protocol through the FTX / Alameda brand name, maximizing the firms' bargaining power to receive attractively valued deals. The key was to find protocols with a small float that could easily be manipulated. Any upside was for Alameda / FTX Ventures, as the money was paid back in stablecoins.

FTX / Alameda amassed a portfolio of 474 companies with mostly token warrant incentives. The portfolio was valued at 5.3 billion dollars in late 2022 and was undoubtedly much higher—perhaps forty billion dollars— at the peak of the 2021 bull market, before most altcoins declined by eighty percent or more. For two companies that had been in business for less than four years, that was an amazingly fast deal flow, with 150 investments signed up every year—or two to three deals every week—on average.

Alameda front-runs eighteen different tokens (2021–22)

According to an analysis done by crypto compliance firm Argus, between February 2021 and March 2022 Alameda held sixty million dollars' worth of eighteen tokens that were eventually listed on FTX.[317] The eighteen assets were IndiGG, LooksRare, Guild of Guardians, Render Token, Boba Token, Gala, Immutable X, Gods Unchained, BitDAO, Spell Token, Eden, RAMP, Orbs, DODO, Convergence, SAND, Linear, and BAO. Alameda had almost always bought the tokens just one month before their listing.

For example three weeks before Eden tokens started trading on FTX, Alameda received 2.5 million tokens from the Eden Network private investment distribution wallet. The tokens were moved to the liquidity pool on the SushiSwap DEX, where Alameda received enough incentives during those three weeks to increase their allocation to 5.8 million tokens. On the listing day Alameda then sent 4.8 million tokens to FTX and 1.0 million to another wallet, which slowly liquidated the position on FTX. After the listing the token value increased 170 percent to 9.27 dollars, as Eden announced a well-timed seventeen-million-dollar funding raise from Multicoin Capital, with participation from Alameda and Jump Capital.

In the case of BitDAO Alameda accumulated 377 thousand BIT tokens on October 17 2021 and sent them the next day to FTX, where they started trading. There was a lot of controversy around these BIT tokens as they were a swap with FTT tokens. A year later, when the FTX exchange was imploding, the BitDAO community asked Alameda for proof of funds after the BIT tokens suddenly declined by twenty percent, fearing that Alameda was dumping its tokens to raise cash to defend the FTX liquidity crunch.

Serum: manipulating tokens to multi-billion market capitalizations (2020–22)

In 2020 SBF created Serum, a DEX built on Solana, a platform well-known for its fast speed compared to other blockchains, including Ethereum. According to Solana cofounder Anatoly Yokovenko DeFi 1.0 had been focused on innovation in money markets, including lending and borrowing, while DeFi 2.0 would bring "high-speed trading and derivatives."[318]

Serum was intended to rival AMMs such as Uniswap, SushiSwap, and Bancor. Eleven business advisors were behind the project, including SBF; Robert Leshner, the founder of the Compound protocol; and Long Vuong, the founder and CEO of TomoChain.

Serum raised twenty million dollars in venture capital over six funding rounds. The fundraising was set up in tranches so that investors who committed a few hours later would have to pay higher prices. Serum's utility token, SRM, enabled holders to receive a discount of up to fifty percent on their trading fees, while stakers could vote and participate in the platform's governance mechanism. Ninety percent of the Serum tokens were locked up for the long term, including all the seed sales and all the team tokens. The seed tokens would only unlock after seven years, while the team tokens were mainly reserved for Serum's founders, including SBF.

FTX launched multiple projects within the Serum / Solana ecosystem, such as the Oxygen Protocol and the FIDA and MAPS tokens. SBF even tweeted that "MAPS would be the product with the largest user base in crypto."[319] For all these projects the business model was the same: to create value out of nearly thin air by issuing lots of tokens for almost zero cost, selling several tokens to finance some development and marketing, and then starting to buy from the open market to bring the value of the overall holding up and to use it for collateral and financing rounds.

Before the FTX bankruptcy filing in November 2022 FTX held 2.2 billion dollars of Serum tokens. The Serum protocol stopped working on the main network after the collapse of the exchange. As the authority to update the platform belonged to FTX, other protocols refused to work with the DeFi protocol for security reasons.

Previously the news of SBF's ever-increasing net wealth had started making the rounds. When hardly anybody outside crypto had heard of him, Bloomberg began to run stories that he was worth ten billion dollars. This gifted young guy, the son of two Stanford professors, who slept in the office and worked twenty-four seven, seemed to only care about providing a great user experience and eventually giving all his money away to charity. The media loved him, or so it appeared before it became known that he was paying off the press.

SBF gave money to Vox, the progressive news website founded by Ezra Klein, Melissa Bell, and Matthew Yglesias. He also made a 3.25-million-dollar grant to the left-wing U.S. news website The Intercept, while also loaning, through Alameda, twenty-seven million dollars to Michael McCaffrey, the CEO of the crypto news site The Block. Having publications like these in his pocket helped to drive the narrative of SBF's wunderkind image.

Meanwhile the significant funding rounds for FTX had legitimized SBF within the VC and finance circles. SBF understood that mainstream adoption required a significant marketing expense. Having seen how Elon Musk had influenced the price of Dogecoin, he went on TV and spoke at conferences almost every week.

15

"Doge is e-god spelled backwards"
(Vitalik Buterin, Ethereum)

B y April 2020 the legendary hedge fund manager Paul Tudor Jones was warning about the coming inflationary consequences of the U.S. central bank's excessive money printing, combined with stimulus checks issued by the U.S. government.[320] He claimed that Wall Street could be witnessing the historic "birthing of a store of value" and that Bitcoin would be the "fastest horse" during the next hyperinflation cycle.

Jones said that he had been left speechless by the magnitude of government support, as 3.9 trillion dollars were "magically created through quantitative easing" as an initial response to the COVID pandemic. Acknowledging that a lack of demand would prevent inflation from rising in the near term, he warned that inflation could increase significantly after that. He described Bitcoin as his preferred inflation hedge, thereby legitimizing Bitcoin as an asset class for institutional investors.

Rather than being an inflation hedge, however, Bitcoin was actually a hedge against money printing and the deviation of purchasing power with U.S. dollars. So when the Federal Reserve indicated its intention to raise interest rates and tighten excess liquidity in December 2021, crypto asset prices started declining meaningfully.

Jones's backing of Bitcoin was supported by other major financiers. In a CNBC interview in November 2020 Jones's friend and fellow billionaire hedge fund manager Stanley Druckenmiller stated that Bitcoin could outperform gold.[321] A month later the family office of billionaire George Soros confirmed that the firm was holding Bitcoins, while Rick Rieder, Chief Investment Officer of Fixed Income at investment giant BlackRock, told investors that, "Bitcoin and cryptocurrencies are here to stay."[322] Rieder also said that Bitcoin could "take the place of gold."

Based on the comments made by all these billionaires, Bitcoin could replace gold as an inflation hedge. In that case it could increase its market capitalization of one trillion dollars by a multiple of three, as gold is estimated to account for three trillion dollars in private investments.

MicroStrategy promotes Bitcoin as a treasury investment for companies (2020)

On August 11 2020 the Virginia-based business and intelligence software firm MicroStrategy started to buy 250 million dollars' worth of Bitcoins (21,454 BTC) as part of its capital allocation strategy for the company's treasury reserve.[323] The NASDAQ-listed company went on to buy 130 thousand Bitcoins, with an aggregate purchase price of 3.98 billion dollars and an average purchase price of 30,639 dollars per Bitcoin. MicroStrategy funded the purchases by issuing secured notes and sales of its common stock in 2021 and early 2022, and used retained earnings in the second and third quarters of 2022 for additional purchases.[324]

Phong Le, MicroStrategy's CFO, gave three reasons why the company had started buying Bitcoin. First the money that MicroStrategy spent on sales and marketing fell to zero as the world went into lockdown in March 2020, causing the company's cash flow to increase dramatically. Second, in response to the COVID downturn U.S. interest rates fell to zero, which meant that the 550 million dollars the company had in short-term treasury bills were providing no interest. And third, as the U.S. central bank printed twenty-five percent more dollar bills to provide stimulus, it devalued the purchasing power of these dollars. Phong summarized MicroStrategy's position as having more cash flow that was earning no interest but was worth twenty-five percent less.

Michael Saylor, the founder and CEO of MicroStrategy, became an advocate for other corporate treasuries to buy into Bitcoin as well. The company set up webinars for corporations interested in diversifying their treasury function into Bitcoin, while Saylor, who had studied at the Massachusetts Institute of Technology (MIT) and worked as a consultant for corporations such as Exxon and DuPont before building MicroStrategy in 1989, became a vocal promoter of Bitcoin on social media, with 2.7 million followers. But with Bitcoin prices at seventeen thousand in January 2023 MicroStrategy was by then carrying a loss on paper of 1.3 billion dollars on its Bitcoin holdings.

COVID stimulus checks drive a speculative frenzy (2020)

As the COVID downturn hit, almost eighteen trillion dollars of negative-yielding debt forced investors to hide in assets that could beat inflation expectations. The demand for yield was so strong that emerging markets, which were prone to inflation and defaults, raised 730 billion dollars in fresh capital at less than four-percent annual interest rates. Ten years of near-zero interest rates had pushed investors out of the risk curve, with long-duration assets such as investments in technology companies attracting the most interest. Access to the most promising Silicon Valley startups was seen as yielding the highest returns.

By November 2020 animal spirits were running wild across Wall Street. Special purpose acquisition companies (SPACs) that raised money for blank-check companies to buy whatever they wanted raised over sixty billion dollars in 2020—more than during the previous ten years combined. Meanwhile initial public offerings (IPOs) raised 175 billion dollars, with first-day returns of IPOs averaging forty-percent gains—the highest ever during the current millennium.

Facebook and Uber stayed private for much longer, causing investors to have a fear of missing out (FOMO) on significant returns. Investors focused more on who was leading the funding rounds, as high-net-worth individuals benefited from privileged access to pre-IPO shares and could always lead in the next round, guaranteeing that the company was large enough to qualify as an IPO.

Just as there was FOMO in the stock market, there was FOMO among the venture capital (VC) community, where everybody wanted to be part of the hottest cap table (a table showing the equity ownership capitalization for a company). VC firms had unprecedented access to capital, and several non–Silicon Valley supersized players, such as Softbank and Tiger Global, entered the market deploying sizable tickets and vast amounts of money. This was a sellers' market, where founders could dictate which VC firm was privileged to invest with them.

But COVID lockdowns and travel restrictions prevented many VC teams from meeting face-to-face with founders and doing due diligence on their investments. As a result the crypto exchange FTX managed to raise four billion dollars in VC money without sacrificing a board seat or undergoing the due diligence which might have exposed some of the conflicts of interest and the lack of adequate accounting protocols that came to light during the FTX bankruptcy filing.

As technology shares became the most important segment in the equity market, Tesla, founded by Elon Musk, justified much higher valuations than other car companies as it was seen as a technology company. Tesla, which designs and manufactures electric vehicles, battery energy storage, and solar panels, was also an advocate for a greener future. It had a market capitalization of 555 billion dollars, compared to 196 billion dollars for the second-largest car manufacturer, Japan's Toyota, and 94 billion dollars for Germany's Volkswagen. At its peak in November 2021 Musk's net worth was 340 billion dollars.

Tesla buys Bitcoin (2021)

In an SEC filing on February 8 2021 Tesla announced that it had purchased 1.5 billion dollars of Bitcoin. The announcement caused the price of Bitcoin to skyrocket, as crypto fanatics expected other corporations to follow Tesla and put Bitcoin on their balance sheets. Tesla bought Bitcoins when prices were between thirty-six thousand and thirty-eight thousand dollars, and sold 272 million dollars' worth when prices ran higher, to "proof the liquidity."

In a Reddit post on January 2 a user named "TSLAinsider," who claimed to be a "software dev working at R&D at Tesla in California" had revealed that "our Company just bought 800 million worth of Bitcoin." Major news outlets reported on this "insider leak," but it turned out the post had been written by a twenty-four-year-old political-science student from Germany, who had been high on acid at the time.[325]

On April 26 Tesla reported a ten-million dollar "positive impact" toward profitability from its Bitcoin investment. The company went on to sell seventy-five percent of its Bitcoin holding by the second quarter of 2022, when coins were trading at around twenty-nine thousand dollars.

Tesla recorded 101 million dollars in impairment losses in 2021 from its Bitcoin investment, but also realized gains of 128 million dollars after selling some of its holdings in March to test Bitcoin's liquidity. In 2022 Tesla reported an impairment loss of 170 million dollars, resulting in a net loss of forty million dollars for its venture into Bitcoin. However this was likely a more than acceptable marketing expense.

Elon Musk pumps Dogecoin to the moon (2020)

Dogecoin was created in 2013 by Jackson Palmer and Billy Markus as the first meme coin alternative to traditional cryptocurrencies such as Bitcoin.

Unlike Bitcoin, which was designed to be scarce, Dogecoin was intentionally created to be abundant, with ten thousand new coins mined every minute and no maximum supply.

The Dogecoin meme typically consists of a picture of Kabosu, a Shiba Inu dog, accompanied by colorful text representing a kind of internal monologue, which is deliberately written in broken English. Over 2020 and the first months of 2021 Elon Musk's humorous tweets about Dogecoin often caused its price to surge.

On April 2 2019 Dogecoin had run a community survey on Twitter, with forty-nine percent of respondents indicating that they would prefer Elon Musk as the CEO of Dogecoin—ahead of Vitalik Buterin from Ethereum, Charlie Lee from Litecoin, and Marshall Hayner from Metal Pay. Musk responded, "Dogecoin might be my favorite cryptocurrency. It's pretty cool."[326]

Musk would speculate—often ironically, it seemed—about the integration of Dogecoin into significant companies. For example he would say that SpaceX, like Tesla, would soon accept Dogecoin as a merchandise payment. He also said that he would eat a "happy meal on TV if McDonald's accepted Dogecoin" as a payment method, and floated the idea that Twitter would allow Dogecoin as a transaction scheme.[327]

Musk started to influence the price of Dogecoin on July 18 2020, when he tweeted that Dogecoin was "inevitable."[328] Dogecoin's diehard fan base, the Dogecoin Army, had stated that its goal was to send the token's price "over the moon" (i.e. above one dollar) when it was trading at only 0.003 dollars. As a result the term "to the moon" had become hugely popular in the crypto community.

The price of Dogecoin frequently skyrocketed on the back of Musk's bullish comments. Traders that shorted were often liquidated, which caused prices to rally even more. Crypto trading teams started to follow Musk, as he greatly impacted prices and the retail crypto trading community. Traders bought when he tweeted about Dogecoin, and prices tended to spike higher afterward. Musk was seen as fighting the establishment, sitting with the little guy. Despite his immense wealth he was seen as one of the ordinary people.

Suddenly the crypto trading team at Alameda, which had previously only focused on low-risk arbitrage trading, became very confident about taking directional bets and started to bet on Musk's market-moving tweets. Sam Trabucco, an Alameda trader, gave credit to the company's 24/7/365 news flow digestion of market information, as he called it. Understanding market structure, notably how open interest and futures liquidations were handled, had been Alameda's bread and butter during the sharp-down moves in previous years. But now the game had changed.

Crypto was in a new bull market, and many small crypto investors followed the signals of influencers. They acted in herds, looking for free "alpha" from opinion leaders that would enable them to outperform the market. As the bull market during the DeFi (decentralized finance) summer progressed, crypto trading was all about making directional bets. Arbitrage trading did not offer the returns that traders could make by finding the next hot protocol. Some crypto tokens went up ten times, others even 100 times. Trading teams focused on the best idea with the highest expected value and then bet big. "When there is a reasonable chance of being right, it's crucial to bet huge early on in games, and when the odds are low, the bets should be small,"[329] Trabucco concluded.

When Musk tweeted on December 20 2020, "One word: Doge,"[330] trading volume increased by 125 times in minutes. He could clearly move prices around with billions of dollars of impact.

On January 14 2021 Musk tweeted that the Tesla merchandise shop would start accepting Dogecoin as a payment option, resulting in a three-hundred-percent increase in the price of DOGE in four hours.[331] The price dropped to nearly half its new high in the following couple of hours, but every tweet from Musk would cause a sharp move in prices.

On January 26 Musk tweeted "Gamestonk" about the GameStop shares,[332] and the meme "stonks" became popular among the YOLO (you only live once) retail crowd, who were trading meme stocks that had no value and were flirting with bankruptcy. The next day GameStop reached its closing high of 347.51 dollars, before falling back to fifty dollars in a few days.

As the bull market progressed, investors who followed Musk's tweeting leads could make a lot of money. On January 29 Musk added "#bitcoin" to his Twitter bio, which lifted the Bitcoin price by fourteen percent. Over the next two weeks Dogecoin's market capitalization also increased, from one billion to ten billion dollars.

A few days later, on February 4, Musk tweeted, "Dogecoin is the people's crypto, and I am become meme, Destroyer of shorts," with a picture of him as Rafki, from the film *The Lion King*, holding the Shiba dog instead of Simba.[333] Dogecoin rallied by more than sixty percent.

On February 10 Musk announced that he had bought Dogecoin for his son so that "he can be a toddler hodler"[334]—a reference to the crypto term "hodl," which stands for "hold on for dear life." The term originated from a 2013 online post where "hold" had been misspelled by someone referencing never selling his Bitcoin, even when prices dropped.

Figure 18: The price of Dogecoin was primarily influenced by Elon Musk's comments

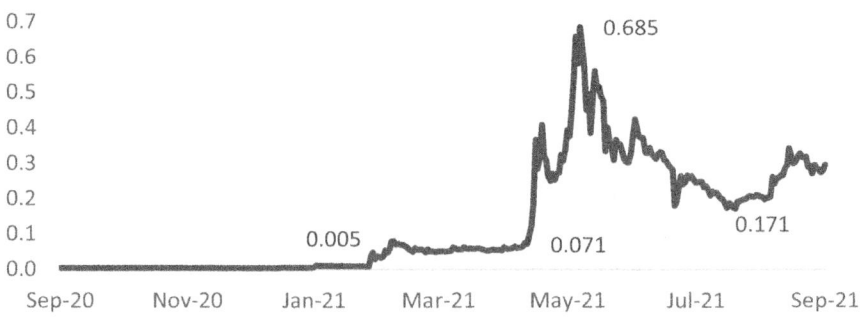

On April 15, when Dogecoin's market capitalization was ten billion dollars, Musk posted another tweet, "Doge Barking at the Moon."[335] A few days later, on April 25, *Saturday Night Live* (*SNL*) announced that Musk would be in the cast for its May 8 show. In the run-up to the show Dogecoin's market capitalization rose from thirty-five billion to over eighty-eight billion dollars. Within four months Dogecoin had rallied by 8,800 percent.

Expectations that Musk would say something positive about Dogecoin on national TV ran high. But in the end he disappointed his audience. Many investors had bought Dogecoin ahead of Musk's *SNL* appearance, but the show became a "buy the rumor, sell the news" event. His TV performance flopped because he did not write the script himself.[336] Dogecoin fell by thirty percent during the show, with the retail stock trading platform Robinhood experiencing an outage in crypto trading during airtime. Two years after Musk's *SNL* appearance Dogecoin had declined by over ninety percent.

While this was not the end of the DeFi summer bull market, Bitcoin prices crashed later in May. On May 12 Musk announced that Tesla would no longer accept Bitcoin due to the vast amounts of fossil fuel used in its production. "We are concerned about the rapidly increasing use of fossil fuels for Bitcoin mining and transactions," he wrote.[337] "Energy usage trend over past few months is insane." By then it had been calculated that the Bitcoin proof-of-work network consumed more energy than a country like the Netherlands. Bitcoin prices dropped seventeen percent on Musk's comments.

On May 18 China started to ban financial and payment institutions from providing services related to cryptocurrency transactions. It also warned investors against speculative crypto trading.[338] On June 4 Musk tweeted "#Bitcoin," a broken heart emoji, and a picture of a couple discussing a break.[339] Bitcoin prices fell by more than seven percent. Musk's tweets had undoubtedly provided great entertainment, but many had come late to the "party" and lost money.

But on July 21, when Bitcoin prices had fallen from an all-time high of sixty-three thousand to thirty thousand dollars, Musk started to walk back his comments about Bitcoin's environmental footprint, saying that Tesla might start accepting Bitcoin for vehicle purchases again.[340] Crypto traders were short, and on June 23 liquidations of perpetual crypto futures contracts had spiked again—a sign that the downtrend would end. The market just needed some positive news to turn sentiment around again. Open interest declined, showing that even bearish traders were unwilling to bet aggressively on lower prices. Alameda's Sam Trabucco was there, predicting the market to rally. Quietly he thought about how to turn Alameda into a long-only fund.

The Coinbase stock market listing (2021)

The first significant crypto firm to be listed on the stock market was Coinbase. The company was founded in 2012 by Brian Armstrong and emerged as one of the most popular crypto exchanges in the U.S. The firm had fifty-six million users when Coinbase started trading on the New York Stock Exchange (NYSE) in 2021. In its last private financing round in 2018 investors had valued the company at eight billion dollars.

Armstrong had been a developer for IBM and a consultant at Deloitte. He had also worked for Airbnb as a software engineer before founding Coinbase with Fred Ehrsam, who went on to launch the crypto investment firm Paradigm.

Instead of going through the standard initial public offering (IPO) route Coinbase used the direct listing method. In an IPO the company hires an investment bank to manage the process and ultimately sells stock to the public. In a direct listing, on the other hand, the company's insiders, early investors, or shareholders are looking to sell out. So going into the listing, there was a concerted effort to push the valuation of crypto and, indirectly, Coinbase higher to achieve the greatest possible value for the insiders.

CNBC stock commentator Jim Cramer told his viewers to buy the shares at the opening price, saying that any price below 475 dollars per share should be used to start building a position, as "Coinbase is the real deal –

the numbers are incredible … If you, like me, [are] a big believer in cryptocurrency … you'll want to own Coinbase for the long-haul."[341] Other commentators even argued that Coinbase would be the Goldman Sachs of crypto. Since Goldman Sachs has a market capitalization of around 120 billion dollars, Coinbase shares offered a lot more upside.

The media hype caused significant initial demand and set high price expectations. After Coinbase had provided a reference price for the listing of 250 dollars per share, many retail investors put in orders to buy "at market." When the company began publicly trading, the share price surged past its initial reference price, opening at 380 dollars per share. The intraday high was 429 dollars, with the shares closing at 328 dollars, giving the company a value of 85.8 billion dollars. Coinbase's valuation was almost fifty-three times its revenue in 2020, compared to eleven times for the NYSE's parent company Intercontinental Exchange (ICE).

As with token projects with a small float in circulation, where the value can be engineered higher, Coinbase insiders and early investors sold about five billion dollars in shares through the direct listing. Coinbase also went public with a dual-class share structure, giving insiders more than sixty percent of voting control—enough power for them to manage the company directly.

Of the five billion dollars' worth of Coinbase shares offloaded, venture capitalist Fred Wilson sold almost two billion dollars, while his VC firm Union Square Ventures sold another two billion dollars. Marc Andreessen and his firm Andreessen Horowitz, meanwhile, sold 450 million dollars, with Armstrong, Coinbase's CEO, selling nearly 300 million dollars and Coinbase CFO Alesia Haas selling 100 million dollars. Armstrong used the money to buy one of the most expensive single-family homes in Los Angeles: a 133-million-dollar property in Bel Air.

Celebrities start to endorse FTX and SBF (2021)

With crypto sentiment exceptionally strong and media coverage at an all-time high with the Coinbase listing, investors started lining up after FTX signed endorsement deals with NFL (National Football League) quarterback legend Tom Brady and his wife, ex-supermodel Gisele Bündchen. In May 2021, near the peak of the crypto bull market, Brady changed his Twitter profile to a picture that showed him with red laser eyes, signaling that he was bullish on Bitcoin (a picture with blue laser eyes would have indicated bullishness for Bitcoin's competitor, Ethereum).

FTX also forged deals with the Washington Wizards and Golden State Warriors basketball teams, and signed up individual players like Steph Curry. In addition FTX agreed to pay 135 million dollars over nineteen years to acquire the naming rights for the Miami Heat basketball arena.

In June 2021 FTX announced a deal with the MLB (Major League Baseball), which placed its logo on all the umpires' uniforms. The same month it also acquired the naming rights for Team SoloMid (TSM) for 210 million dollars. Founded in 2009, TSM is the world's most valuable esports organization, fielding players in competitions for games like *League of Legends* and *Fortnite*. FTX also signed a sponsorship deal with the Formula One racing team Mercedes, and spent thirty million dollars airing an ad featuring the comedian Larry David during the 2022 Super Bowl.

In July 2021 FTX had raised another 900 million dollars from VC firms and hedge funds to expand its operations. Notable investors included SoftBank, Sequoia Capital, and Third Point. FTX continued to spend money on partnerships and endorsement deals until its implosion in November 2022.

Well before then Kevin O'Leary had become one of the biggest cheerleaders for Sam Bankman-Fried (SBF). O'Leary—who had made a name for himself as an angel investor on the TV show *Shark Tank*, where aspiring entrepreneurs pitch their startup ideas—had called Bitcoin "garbage" and "worthless" in 2019.[342] But after signing an endorsement deal with FTX paying him fifteen million dollars (which was kept secret until FTX went bankrupt), he became a major promoter of FTX and SBF. He claimed his change of heart was due to Canada allowing the first physically settled Bitcoin ETF (exchange-traded fund)—something that the U.S. Securities and Exchange Commission (SEC) had blocked for several years.

Purpose Bitcoin ETF had started trading on the Toronto Stock Exchange on February 18 2021. Its launch coincided with the twenty-six-billion-dollar closed-end fund Grayscale Bitcoin Trust (GBTC) trading at a discount of its net asset value (NAV). Investors now had a cheaper alternative to GBTC's two-percent annual management fee. Unlike closed-end funds ETFs can freely create and redeem shares according to investor demand, so the price of an ETF tends to track the underlying NAV closely.

O'Leary wanted to invest in the infrastructure of the crypto industry, and besides Coinbase there was also no sizable U.S. crypto exchange to invest in. Even after it became apparent in mid-November 2022 that SBF had engaged in a massive fraud with customer funds, O'Leary still defended him, endorsing him as an entrepreneur until it became known that O'Leary had been paid by FTX.

16

"Been a long time. Just bought more Bitcoin"
(Jesse Powell, Kraken)

On May 21 2021 China's State Council's Financial Stability and Development Committee cracked down on Bitcoin mining and trading activities "due to concerns around financial risk."[343] China's state broadcaster CCTV also warned against the "systematic risks" of cryptocurrency trading, calling Bitcoin a speculative instrument. The Chinese government was worried that crypto was being used to move money out of China, as Bitcoin miners paid electricity bills in Chinese yuan while they could sell Bitcoin for U.S. dollars. It was the first time that China's influential State Council had explicitly targeted crypto mining activities. Bitcoin prices fell sharply on the news, and 1.5 billion dollars of Bitcoin positions were liquidated.

The Bitcoin hash rate, an estimate of the computational power generated by Bitcoin miners trying to solve the current Bitcoin block, declined from 176 terahashes per second (TH/s) to fifty-eight TH/s a month later. Before the Bitcoin mining ban seventy percent of the Bitcoin hash power had operated out of China.

In response to the Bitcoin mining ban Chinese miners moved their machines to nearby Kazakhstan or the U.S., which became the country with the highest Bitcoin mining hash rate. As the U.S. stock market was still in a bull market and the IPO frenzy was in full swing, many Bitcoin mining companies filed for IPO in the U.S. and Canada, subsequently using the capital raised to expand their mining operations. But there was a year's waiting period for the newest Bitcoin mining machines and several newly listed miners did not have enough devices to deploy their capital.

They had also bought Bitcoin from the open market at higher prices than it would cost them to mine, which set them up for massive losses and bankruptcy proceedings when Bitcoin prices crashed in 2022.

Hong Kong requires crypto exchanges to be licensed (2021)

On the same day as the announcement from China's State Council Hong Kong declared that cryptocurrency exchanges in the city would have to be licensed by the Hong Kong Securities and Futures Commission (HK SFC) and would only be allowed to provide services to professional investors.[344] According to Hong Kong law an individual must have a liquid portfolio of at least eight million Hong Kong dollars (1.03 million U.S. dollars) to qualify as a professional investor.

The expectation was that the HK SEC's announcement would become law during the 2021–22 legislative session, which ran from October 2021 onward. As the crypto exchange licensing regime started to gain traction, FTX began to move to the Bahamas, where regulation was more relaxed.

In July 2021 the HK SFC announced that Binance was prohibited from conducting regulated activity in Hong Kong, explicitly referring to trading in stock tokens, which were likely to be considered securities under the Securities and Futures Ordinance. Binance responded by ceasing to offer support for stock tokens in companies such as Tesla, Coinbase, and Apple.

On July 23 a *New York Times* article criticizing high-risk crypto trading hinted that high-leverage margin trading would also run into regulatory scrutiny.[345] As a result exchanges such as Binance and FTX started to lower users' futures leverage from 100 to twenty times. While 100-times leverage was a headline-grabbing feature, traders rarely used the maximum leverage. For FTX, for example, it represented less than one percent of its trading volume, with the average leverage being closer to two times, according to SBF.[346]

On June 9 the U.S.-based crypto exchange Kraken had already informed its users that it would no longer be offering margin trading for U.S. investors that did not meet specific requirements.[347] The exchange cited regulatory guidance about leveraged digital-asset transactions as the reason behind the change of policy.

Kraken had officially launched in 2013 in San Francisco, although cofounder Jesse Powell had begun developing the exchange immediately after the Mt. Gox security breach in June 2011. But when Powell started to raise venture capital in 2013, it took him until January of the following year to close the investment round. He later called for more commitment from Silicon Valley venture capitalists. Kraken's first investor was Hummingbird Ventures, based in Belgium, although investment from Barry Silbert and Blockchain Capital followed. Powell also experienced difficulties securing a banking relationship for Kraken, receiving rejections from thirty banks before eventually landing the Berlin-based Fidor Bank.

While Kraken initially had operations in New York, it left the state in 2015 after a BitLicense was introduced by the New York State Department of Financial Services (NYDFS). The BitLicense, which required all crypto businesses that held customer funds to be registered as money transmitters, was aimed at protecting consumers from fraud and preventing money laundering and the funding of terrorism. It had twenty pages of rules to follow, requiring companies to disclose information about their operations and to implement KYC (know your customer) requirements.[348] While the cost of the BitLicense itself was manageable, at five thousand dollars, the extensive paperwork and legal costs rounded costs up to fifty thousand dollars for Coinsetter's application, while Bitstamp's BitLicense cost the company 100 thousand dollars.[349] As a result companies such as Bitfinex, Bitquick, BTCGuild, Genesis Mining, GoCoin, Paxful, Poloniex, and ShapeShift all left New York as well.

According to Powell, to comply with all the rules for the BitLicense, Kraken would have had to "disclose all the information about our entire global client base to the state of New York," which was "potentially illegal" under privacy laws of other countries.[350] During a 2018 panel discussion Powell cited Japan's Virtual Currency Act as a more reasonable regulation.

Powell had been part of the San Francisco crypto meetups, which Jed McCaleb of Mt. Gox (and Ripple Labs) and Brian Armstrong of Coinbase frequented as well. He was also a high-school friend of the early Bitcoin enthusiast Roger Ver, who had traded cards with him on *Magic: The Gathering Online*, the predecessor of the Mt. Gox site. Ver had moved to Japan after serving ten months in U.S. prison and was living down the street from Mt. Gox when the 2011 security breach took place. Powell and Ver helped Mt. Gox out, and both became seriously involved in Bitcoin.

When Kraken stopped offering margin trading for U.S. customers, many U.S.-based crypto traders moved their margin trading accounts to FTX, which would acquire the U.S.-licensed derivatives exchange LedgerX on August 31 2021. While margin trading is not illegal per se, it is strictly controlled, with crypto exchanges needing to register with the Commodity Futures Trading Commission (CFTC).

On the same day as Kraken's announcement about margin trading El Salvador passed its Bitcoin adoption bill, with a supermajority of sixty-two out of eighty-four votes in Congress. But by the following May the tokens that had driven the DeFi summer bull market had all peaked out, although the fourth crypto bull market was still not over, as non-fungible tokens (NFTs) suddenly became a craze.

17

"Things take time for everyone to recognize"

(Vignesh Sundaresan, Metapurse)

The tokens that started the DeFi (decentralized finance) summer in May 2020, such as Compound and Aave, never regained their May 2021 peaks. While the fourth crypto bull market continued for a few more months, the sentiment shifted from DeFi to NFTs (non-fungible tokens) as the critical driver. NFTs are unique identifiers that cannot be copied, substituted, or subdivided and which are recorded on the blockchain and used to certify authenticity and ownership. Proponents have said that NFTs cannot be exchanged like-for-like with other NFTs, making them scarce and justifying higher values. NFTs are linked to physical collectible items like rare trading cards and works of art.

The craze for NFTs really took over in July 2021, when an Ethereum "whale" spent six million dollars to purchase a limited series of CryptoPunks (24x24-pixel images).[351] In 2017 CryptoPunks creators Matt Hall and John Watkinson had handed them away for free, but suddenly they achieved prices of fifty thousand dollars or more. By the end of August 2021 CryptoPunks saw massive turnover, with 2,800 transactions recorded and the top CryptoPunks selling at over 2.5 million dollars. The payment network Visa bought a CryptoPunk for 150 thousand dollars.

It is not entirely clear what drove the sudden interest in NFTs, as seventy-five percent of the market was driven by transactions smaller than ten thousand dollars.[352] NFTs are concentrated in the hands of a few whales, with 360 thousand owners holding 2.7 million NFTs between them but just 32,400 wallets owning eighty percent of the market. In addition the market was likely inflated by wash trading. NFTs were also seen as social capital, acting as a status symbol like a Rolex or Lamborghini.

Figure 19: Monthly NFT transaction values increased nearly ten times during August 2021 (billion dollars)

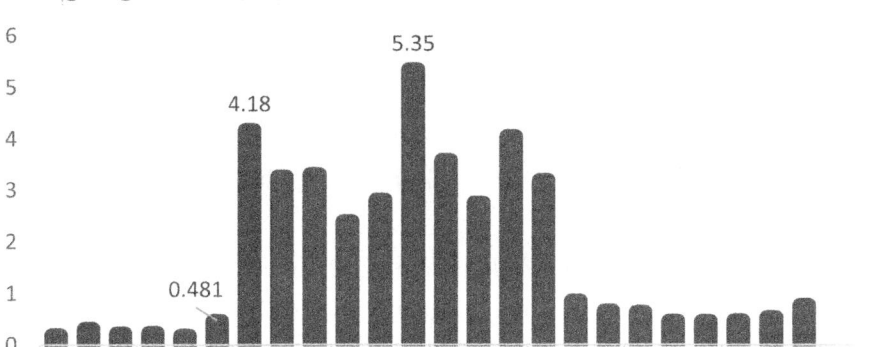

NBA Top Shot collectibles tip off the NFT craze (2020)

In 2020 the owner of the Dallas Mavericks basketball team, Mark Cuban, became a major proponent of NFTs, participating in the NBA Top Shot marketplace—a blockchain-based trading system where users can buy and sell "moments" of NBA history. The platform, a partnership between the NBA and the blockchain company Dapper Labs, has generated over one billion dollars in gross sales, with sellers charged five percent for every transaction. Fifty percent of all the transactions were in the first quarter of 2021, with prices dropping by ninety-four percent since then.[353]

Dapper Labs was started in March 2018 by Stanford University graduate Roham Gharegozlou, and launched the NBA Top Shot collection in 2020. In March 2021 the company raised 305 million dollars in funding, and another 250 million dollars later the same year at a 7.6-billion-dollar valuation.

The hype around NBA Top Shot coincided with demand for digital ownership as people became bored during COVID lockdowns. To meet skyrocketing demand and ease queue waiting times, the Top Shot marketplace dramatically increased supply into the market. As the platform reached its technological capacity, resellers also needed to wait weeks and even months to withdraw their money. These oversupply and transaction problems led to losses for anyone holding onto their "moments" of NBA history.

Beeple NFT sells for sixty-nine million dollars (2021)

On 16 February 2021 Mike Winkelmann, a digital artist known as Beeple, sold a collection of NFTs at the Christie's auction for sixty-nine million dollars. The artwork, called *Everydays: The First 5000 Days*, found a new owner after going through a two-week bidding process. The buyer did not get much—just a digital file plus the vaguest rights to present the image. As in most cases with digital-art NFTs, the new owner did not receive the copyright for the artwork either.

Six months earlier Beeple's artwork had been selling for only 100 dollars. Then, in October 2020 one of the pieces had sold for sixty-six thousand dollars, before being resold for 3.5 million dollars in December. Another piece sold for 6.6 million dollars in January 2021.

For the *Everydays* auction both the buyer (Vignesh Sundaresan, the Singapore-based founder of the Metapurse crypto investment firm) and the seller (Winkelmann) had a vested interest in driving up the price, as it also drove up the price of twenty other Beeple NFT artworks that Sundaresan owned. The cost of all the Beeble artwork peaked with the *Everydays* sale and then collapsed.

Reuters has written that Sundaresan "represents a new generation of investors who have created fortunes out of sight of financial regulators."[354] In May 2013 he quit his job as a developer at a newspaper in India and launched an online crypto exchange called Coins-e, where users could buy and sell cryptocurrencies. He worked on the exchange while pursuing a master's degree in Canada. But a year later traders started complaining that Coins-e would not return the money they had deposited into the exchange, with around fifty complaining in public forums. Sundaresan sold Coins-e a year later for 315 Bitcoins (about 180 thousand dollars). The exchange held 456 Bitcoins from customers, with the new owner claiming that Sundaresan had "honored all transactions made by users."[355]

Subsequently Sundaresan launched Bitaccess with two other founders. The company made Bitcoin ATMs, which were becoming popular in 2014. Its first customer was Anthony Di Iorio, one of the cofounders of Ethereum, which was raising capital through an ICO at the time. Sundaresan bought twenty thousand Ethereum during the ICO.

In December 2017 Sundaresan was trying to raise three million dollars for Lendroid, a company he was setting up in Singapore that would offer peer-to-peer lending and borrowing—an early version of the DeFi protocols. By the time of the fundraising launch in February 2018 demand for ICOs was so strong that he ended up raising fifty thousand Ethereum—the equivalent of forty-eight million dollars—within just two days. Reuters discovered that most of the Ethereum from the ICO was sold or transferred by Lendroid to unknown entities. The project did not go anywhere, and people started to leave. By the end of 2019 the firm had only 650 Ethereum left on its books. Lendroid's cofounder, Paul Martens, went on to file a whistleblower report with the Ontario Securities Commission in Canada, accusing Sundaresan of fraud.

In 2019 Sundaresan started to buy NFTs, and in December 2020 he paid 2.2 million dollars in Ethereum for twenty artworks by Mike Winkelmann, aka Beeple. When Sundaresan opened the Metapalooza party at his virtual art gallery, attendees could buy a digital token called B20 to get a stake in his Beeple collection. Ten million B20 tokens were initially priced at 0.36 dollars each, with 2.5 million tokens allocated for public sale—keeping the float relatively small. Sundaresan held fifty-nine percent of the tokens through his company Metapurse, while Winkelmann held two percent. This effectively made Beeple a business partner of Sundaresan.

By the time of the auction for *Everydays* the B20 token price had hit twenty-nine dollars—an eighty-times return for early B20 buyers. Two months later the price had declined to 1.2 dollars, and two years later it had dropped to 0.04 dollars—far below the initial launch price.

Figure 20: B20-USD token price – the Everydays auction ran from 25 February to 11 March 2021

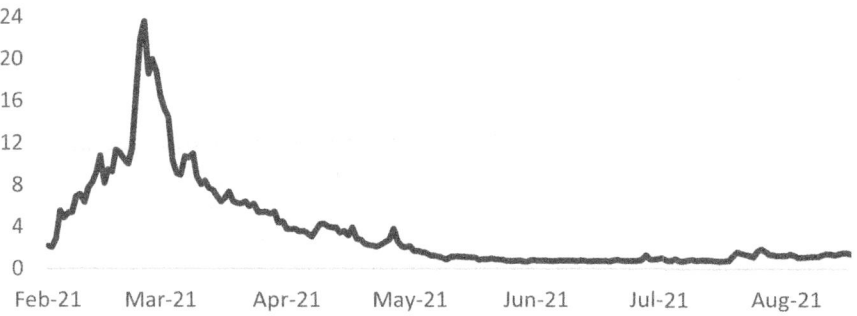

Plenty of works of questionable artistic value were also sold at hype-driven NFT auctions during this period. Artists' works have also allegedly been stolen and auctioned off as authentic pieces at auctions for NFTs.

Yuga Labs launches the Bored Ape Yacht Club (2021)

On April 28 2021 Yuga Labs, a company founded in late 2020, launched the Bored Ape Yacht Club (BAYC). The BAYC collection comprises ten thousand unique NFTs derived from 172 individual assets that center on images of apes. It was created by four friends hiding behind the pseudonyms Gargamal, Gordon Goner, No Sass, and EmperorTomatoKetchup. In February 2022 the identities of Gargamel and

Gordon Goner were revealed as Greg Solano and Wylie Aronow respectively.

Along with CryptoPunks BAYC spearheaded the NFT craze. The BAYC mint price, which was initially only 0.08 Ethers (or 210 dollars), reached a floor price of 150 Ethers (or 450 thousand dollars) at its peak—an increase of 1,875 times. The floor price is the lowest price for any NFT in a given collection.

Bored Apes became a status symbol for owners who regularly used the animated creatures as avatars on social media. Many owners also bought them due to the potential marketing and branding projects they could launch by owning the intellectual property rights of a BAYC NFT. The sports apparel company Adidas, for example, bought a Bored Ape in September 2021, while *Rolling Stone* magazine released a BAYC cover feature the following November. Many celebrities also bought Bored Apes, notably Eminem, Neymar, Snoop Dogg, Mark Cuban, Post Malone, Steph Curry, and Serena Williams.

Subsequently Yuga Labs launched a copy version of BAYC called Mutant Ape Yacht Club, which achieved a market capitalization of 1.4 billion dollars. BAYC itself reached 3.65 billion dollars, while CryptoPunks were still valued at a respectable 2.4 billion dollars.

On March 13 2022 Yuga Labs acquired the intellectual property rights to the 432 CryptoPunks and Meebits collections. The company announced that holders of these NFTs would soon have the same commercial rights as BAYC owners. As a result the floor price for BAYC increased temporarily by twenty-five percent.

Four days later, on March 17, the BAYC governance and utility token, APECoin, was airdropped to BAYC NFT holders. Some complained about the unfair distribution, as only fifteen percent of the airdropped tokens went to NFT holders. Thirty-seven percent went to the BAYC partners (including venture capital [VC] firms), Yuga Labs, and Yuga Labs' founders, while the remaining forty-seven percent went to the APECoin

DAO (Decentralized Autonomous Organization) treasury, which had been formed to embody the APE ecosystem.

Later that month Yuga Labs announced a 450-million-dollar financing round by VC firms, which valued the company at four billion dollars. By the end of April the APECoin market capitalization had increased to seven billion dollars. All this value had been created out of thin air through an airdrop from a company that in early 2022 still had only eleven employees.

The Yuga Labs ecosystem became a dominant force in Web3, accounting for forty-three percent of the market capitalization of Ethereum's NFT collections. But in October 2022 it was reported that the U.S. Securities and Exchange Commission (SEC) was investigating Yuga Labs amid concerns that its NFTs are unregistered security offerings.[356]

Leaked data has shown that Yuga Labs made 137 million dollars from its NFT creations, reaping net revenue of eighty-four percent at a profit margin of 95.5 percent in 2021, with profit margins expected to rise to 98.8 percent in 2022. The company also raised 15.9 million dollars for community building and 28.2 million dollars for game development. In addition it sold more than 300 million dollars' worth of metaverse land (the Otherside), which had cost just 4.6 million dollars to build and sell.[357]

OpenSea becomes the largest NFT marketplace (2021)

In the NFT market OpenSea was the dominant exchange with an eighty-percent share.[358] OpenSea company was founded in 2018 by Alex Atallah, a computer science graduate from Stanford University, and Devin Finzer, and went on to raise 100 million dollars at a 1.5-billion-dollar valuation on July 20 2021.[359]

The OpenSea platform had 250 thousand active users buying and selling NFTs. In January 2022 the monthly trading volume soared to five billion dollars, surpassing the previous peak of three billion dollars in August

2021 and earning the platform 125 million dollars on a 2.5-percent transaction fee. The same month OpenSea raised 300 million dollars at a 13.3-billion-dollar valuation.

OpenSea's daily trading volume reached a record 2.7 billion dollars on May 1 2022, but four months later it had dropped by ninety-nine percent. NFTs had proven to be highly profitable for those who had bought them early on, and even more beneficial for those who had created them.

18

"Our risk framework combines counterparty analysis"
(Zac Prince, BlockFi)

On March 2021 the Grayscale Bitcoin Trust (GBTC) reached a peak market capitalization of 34.6 billion dollars. For many institutional and high-net-worth investors GBTC was the easiest way to buy Bitcoin into their brokerage accounts.

The comprehensive discussion paper issued by the U.S. Department of the Treasury's Financial Crimes Enforcement Network (FinCEN) in 2013 had pushed Bitcoin trading activity mainly offshore to Asia,[360] but Grayscale Investments was able to issue a passive investment trust which gained investors' interest during the bull market of 2013.

Grayscale Investments was launched by Barry Silbert, an early crypto investor who was CEO of Restricted Stock Partners. Silbert later launched the Digital Currency Group (DCG), which provides seed funding for blockchain startups as well as owning and operating Grayscale and Genesis Global Trading, another subsidiary that provides lending, borrowing, and trading services for crypto companies. Silbert was also an early investor in Coinbase and Ripple Labs.

The GBTC debuted as the Bitcoin Investment Trust on September 25 2013. Positioned as a private placement to accredited investors,[361] it later received approval from FINRA (the Financial Industry Regulatory Authority) for eligible shares to trade publicly. This meant that investors could buy and sell public shares in the trust under the symbol GBTC, with the trust trading at a significant premium to its net asset value (NAV). The premium existed because the GBTC can only create new shares through private placements to accredited investors and the shares are not tradable until six months after they have been created.

As there were no Bitcoin ETFs (exchange-traded funds) at the time, the GBTC offered investors a convenient way to gain exposure to Bitcoin. The trust started trading on public markets on May 5 2015.[362] It trades on the OTCQX, an over-the-counter (OTC) marketplace, under the Alternative Reporting Standard for companies not required to register with the U.S. Securities and Exchange Commission (SEC). GBTC shares can be bought and sold through a brokerage firm and are available within tax-advantaged accounts like IRAs (individual retirement accounts) and 401(k) workplace retirement plans. While investors can purchase shares in the trust, the shares are not common stock under the regulatory and consumer protection laws set out in the Investment Company Act of 1940.

For large parts of 2018 the GBTC NAV traded at a sixty-percent premium, as access to Bitcoin was more challenging than buying OTC shares in the trust through a brokerage account. But over the years the premium shrank as investors set up dedicated crypto trading accounts and some institutional investors started to arbitrage the premium. In 2019 the premium shrank to twenty percent, and then to fifteen percent in 2020.

Many traditional finance investors who wanted quick exposure to Bitcoin during the 2021 panic-buying period could easily buy GBTC shares from the OTCQX marketplace. Setting up crypto trading accounts with reputable investment platforms, by contrast, sometimes took months, as there was a long backlog of KYC (know your customer) onboarding processes. But since GBTC shares are trust shares, they can only be created, not destroyed or redeemed for Bitcoin. This means that the outstanding number of shares does not decline, and when investors want to exchange them back to fiat dollar, they can only sell them at the OTCQX marketplace to another buyer.

The extensive marketing surrounding the Coinbase listing caused investors to set up trading accounts at crypto exchanges. As a result, on March 2 2021 GBTC shares started to trade at a discount to the trust's NAV. This had enormous implications for the crypto industry, with a time lag of about a year.

BlockFi: leveraging the GBTC trade (2020–21)

In 2020 GBTC shares traded at an average premium of fifteen to twenty percent. An accredited investor could subscribe to the Grayscale trust and hold onto the shares for six months before disposing of them on the OTCQX marketplace. To hedge the underlying Bitcoin risk, an institutional investor could then borrow Bitcoins from one of the crypto lenders for three-to-five-percent lending fees for six months and sell them on the open market. At the end of the six-month lockup period the investor could then sell the GBTC shares, buy back the Bitcoin, and close the loan. This would result in at least twenty-to-thirty-percent annualized returns for as long as the GBTC shares traded far above the cost of borrowing Bitcoin.

Figure 21: GBTC shares essentially traded at a premium until March 2021

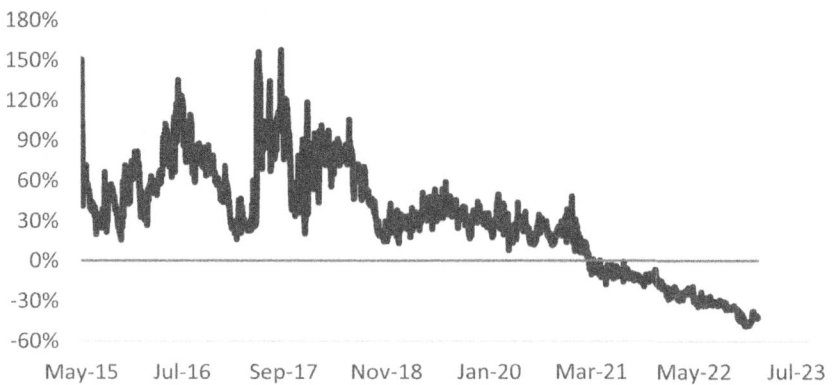

By the end of 2020 crypto lender BlockFi held five percent of the overall GBTC shares for trading, with clients pledging the shares as collateral. This helped to increase the company's loan book. As BlockFi CEO Zac Prince commented, "There are lending markets alongside investment opportunities related to the product and our significant participation enables us to add value for our clients."[363]

Singapore-based investment firm Three Arrows Capital (3AC) was BlockFi's most important client, and in April 2020 it became a strategic investor in the company. In return BlockFi offered six to eight times the leverage on collateral that 3AC provided to BlockFi. Genesis Asia Pacific Ltd., a subsidiary of Genesis Global Trading, lent 2.4 billion dollars to 3AC.

Since both Genesis (previously run by Michael Moro) and Grayscale (run by Michael Sonnenshein) are subsidiaries of DCG, there was an incentive for 3AC to borrow more and more capital from Genesis and subscribe to shares in Grayscale's GBTC, as this would increase the revenue that Grayscale received through the two-percent management fee that GBTC shares generated per year, ultimately benefiting DCG's subsidiaries as the number of outstanding shares charged a management fee was not allowed to decline.

Three Arrows Capital: from zero to ten billion to minus three billion dollars (2012–22)

Three Arrows Capital (3AC) would become the largest holder of GBTC shares. The investment firm disclosed a 1.2-billion-dollar position—or six percent of the outstanding shares—which had likely increased to two billion dollars by the end of the first quarter of 2021.

Founded by Su Zhu and Kyle Davies, 3AC was incorporated on May 3 2012. Zhu and Davies had first met at the prestigious prep school Phillips Academy in Andover, Massachusetts, where annual tuition fees run to seventy thousand dollars per student. They both studied at Columbia University, before briefly working for Credit Suisse. Initially 3AC was set up to focus on arbitrage opportunities in emerging-market currency derivatives, where the firm tried to take advantage of mispricings between market makers and banks.

While the founders often claimed they had no outside investors, they had gigantic loans from different counterparties. By April 2022 the company had three billion dollars' worth of cryptocurrency under management and controlled assets of ten billion dollars through various loan agreements with crypto lending platforms.

When 3AC filed for bankruptcy after its overleveraged crypto hedge fund had suffered during the bear market in July 2022, the crypto lender Voyager Digital had to file for chapter 11 bankruptcy protection as 3AC owed it 650 million dollars. Genesis Global Trading and Blockchain.com, one of the earliest crypto firms, also had unpaid loans from 3AC of 2.4 billion dollars and 270 million dollars respectively.

Crypto lenders often provide loans without requiring any form of collateral. A third of BlockFi's 1.8-billion-dollar loan book, for example, was unsecured. Crypto lending involves lending cryptocurrencies and cash in return for a yield, and by waiving any collateral requirements, lenders can charge higher interest rates. This practice of unsecured borrowing had become the standard in the industry. Crypto lenders were the de facto banks of the crypto industry, attracting retail customers with promises of high single-digit yields in return for their cryptocurrency deposits, and lending the deposits out for higher interest rates to trading firms such as 3AC, Alameda, and others. As crypto lenders are not regulated, they are not required to hold capital or liquidity buffers, and during periods of bank runs they can see their business implode as depositors lose trust in the enterprise and withdraw their funds.

Voyager Digital's crypto loan book grew from 380 million dollars in March 2021 to around two billion dollars in March 2022, and it took collateral for just eleven percent of the funds.[364] When 3AC filed for bankruptcy after failing to repay the 650-million-dollar loan, Voyager collapsed.

The DeFi (decentralized finance) lending protocol Maple Finance launched at the market's peak in May 2021 with a business model that did not require cryptocurrencies to be deposited as collateral, which could be seized or quickly liquidated in the event of a default. Underwriters evaluated the borrower's ability to pay based on creditworthiness alone. By the end of 2022 sixty-six percent of the debt representing Maple's loan pools had been classified as defaulted or distressed.[365]

After its launch Maple became popular among trading firms and market makers ready to provide liquidity to borrowers. Depositors included retail investors and institutional players who were seeking yield on their crypto holdings. By May 2022 the protocol's loan book had reached 900 million dollars, with the native MPL token reaching a valuation of 300 million dollars.

Unsecured lending has been estimated at between twenty billion and fifty billion dollars. If the growth of the Voyager loan book is representative of the industry, it would easily explain how crypto funds were able to deploy so much capital in November 2021 as leverage increased exponentially. As central banks kept interest rates near zero percent and crypto investment firms were willing to borrow money at ten to fifteen percent per annum, many institutions were ready to provide financing at these attractive rates.

Three Arrows also owned seventeen percent of the Panama-based crypto derivatives exchange Deribit, which handles most crypto options volume. The trading firm could borrow crypto assets like Bitcoin from Deribit at only 2.5-percent annual interest rates.

Su Zhu, the cofounder of 3AC, traded according to his "supercycle" theory that the "odds of a bear market would become significantly lower as institutional and mainstream capital [would] come into the space."[366] The "supercycle price thesis was regrettably wrong".[367] Three Arrows might have borrowed ten billion dollars from firms taking in retail deposits, paying fees of ten to fourteen percent while the firms passed on six to eight percent to their retail depositors.

Zhu's theory was based on the 1997 book *The Sovereign Individual*, in which the authors predicted the emergence of the cyber economy, non-state digital money, personalized media, and the record level of public distrust in established institutions.[368] The real message of the book is that incentives guide human action, so if we are aware of the incentives, we can forecast human activity. The book also describes the logic of violence, and how throughout human history taking has been easier than making. Working hard only means something if possessions are protected. But the emergence of cryptography in conjunction with the borderless jurisdictions of cyberspace would drastically alter the logic of violence and shift power away from institutions and the state to the individual. Wealth would be stored and protected by unbreakable cryptography instead of through state-owned armies. The book describes ownership of wealth as a zero-sum game between the state and the individual, with citizens continuing to take advantage of new technological innovations while institutions fight to reclaim control.

Sam Trabucco: Alameda's trader and future co-CEO (2019–22)

Sam Trabucco joined Alameda Research as a trader in March 2019. Before that he had been a bond ETF trader at Susquehanna for two years. Like Sam Bankman-Fried (SBF) he graduated from the Massachusetts Institute of Technology (MIT), with a degree in math and computer science.

Trabucco, who was the son of a Wellesley College campus police officer and a preschool teacher, attended a private boys' high school, the Roxbury Latin School. There he participated in math competitions, sometimes competing against Caroline Ellison, who attended Newton North High School in Boston. For two summers he attended a highly selective math camp, also attended in 2008 by Gary Wang, who would later be FTX's

CTO. Trabucco first met SBF in 2010, when the math camp was held at Mount Holyoke College.

Trabucco was in the same class as Wang at MIT, and both were one year behind SBF. But Trabucco was not interested in effective altruism and did not seem to fit into SBF's inner circle. The fact that he was later picked to be co-CEO of Alameda probably had more to do with his willingness to take risks and his determination to make money.

In 2017 Trabucco left Susquehanna and moved to San Francisco, before eventually joining Alameda. In 2020 he bought a four-bedroom house in Maine for 500 thousand dollars, and in 2021 he purchased a luxury condo in San Francisco with a view of the Golden Gate Bridge for nearly nine million dollars. He also bought a fifty-two-foot boat named "Soak My Deck."[369]

19

"Well. Crypto's crashed quite a bit"
(Sam Trabucco, Alameda Research)

By March 2019, when Sam Trabucco joined Alameda Research, Bitcoin had dropped to just four thousand dollars from nearly twenty thousand in December 2017. The crypto trading firm had just relocated from San Francisco to Hong Kong and was looking for other ways to make money during the bear market after the almost complete disappearance of the "kimchi premium" in South Korea.

When China blocked access to all domestic and foreign crypto exchanges and ICO (initial coin offering) websites in June 2019, crypto trading went underground. During the anti-government protests in Hong Kong that year Bitcoin prices tended to trade four percent higher in the city than on international exchanges. As a result Tether often sold at a two-to-three-percent premium, and Alameda could take advantage of those spreads.

Trabucco would sell Bitcoin for U.S. dollars and then send the dollars to Tether Limited's account at Deltec Bank in the Bahamas, which would mint USDT tokens for a 0.1-percent fee. After deducting some execution costs, Trabucco would then be able to sell the USDTs at nearly the two-to-three-percent premium against Bitcoin, and keep repeating the process. Each time USDT traded above the 0.20-percent minting and execution costs, he could just pocket the arbitrage spreads.

At first there was a trial-and-error process. Trabucco was too conservative, as the creation and redemption of Tether went faster than he had estimated and the cost of locking up the capital during the minting process had been overstated. But things changed quickly, and Alameda was very active in recycling capital. Between 2014 and 2021 108.5 billion dollars of Tether were minted, with Alameda and Cumberland accounting for at least sixty billion dollars (fifty-five percent). In 2020 alone sixty percent of Tether's total supply was created.

Figure 22: The market capitalization of Tether (billion dollars)

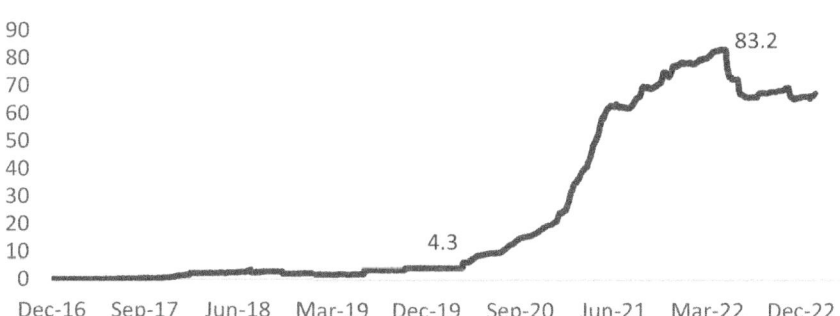

Institutional money starts to flow into crypto (2020)

The crypto market rallied around Thanksgiving 2020 (November 26) and was squeezed higher by aggressive buying of levered-long futures. The sentiment was bullish, and shorts were getting liquidated, contributing to rising prices. The market had suddenly turned from a bear market, where arbitrage trading was favored, to a bull market, where active trading would become most lucrative.

Smaller altcoins also started to rebound, because once the Bitcoin price had stopped rallying, traders immediately started looking around for other coins that could catch up. The altcoins that followed the Bitcoin rally were quality cryptocurrencies with a U.S. bias—such as Nano (XRB), a coin which addressed the Bitcoin scalability problem, and Stellar (XLM), a cross-border transaction protocol founded in the U.S.

But the trade only worked sometimes, and Alameda gained a competitive advantage by analyzing who was buying Bitcoin in the first place, as this determined possible spillover effects into altcoins. The Thanksgiving Bitcoin rally was driven by U.S. institutional buyers—not a rotation out of Ethereum into Bitcoin, for example. Traditional investors had entered the crypto space, and this was a game changer for the market.

Alameda's trading systems made a thunderclap sound when liquidations happened, and as the market was short on altcoins, it thundered all night as positions were liquidated. Since crypto traders tend to move in herds, there were usually more liquidations once one trader had been liquidated. The thunder alerted the Alameda team of a possible trend of order books searching for liquidity.

The liquidation cascade overpowered order books as altcoins such as Ripple (XRP) rallied ten percent during the Thanksgiving weekend, when liquidity was low. It is a common feature in crypto markets that periods of low trading activity, such as holidays and weekends, are used to push positions into specific directions and force liquidations. Crypto exchanges tend to have proprietary trading teams that often have visibility over where the exchange's customers have their stops and margin liquidation levels. Liquidation models also frequently failed to adjust for low volumes during weekends, and many traders were levered short going into the quiet, low-liquidity Thanksgiving weekend. Based on historical data futures open positions were high, indicating that speculative short positions were at risk of liquidation.

The Bitcoin rally sucked in momentum from other traders, and overall positioning changed to levered-long positions. When the last buyer bought and no one else was there to buy, prices collapsed as short-term traders were liquidated when the market suddenly went on a down leg. As many traders used twenty-times leverage, a four-percent downturn would cause large cascading liquidations. Bitcoin was easily moved higher or lower during low-liquidity periods on weekends, and the trading teams with weekend staff could take advantage of retail traders.

The pattern of organic buying in Bitcoin from U.S. institutions continued with the second-order effect that blue-chip altcoins went up later. But once the buying stopped, everything sold off again, and the pattern continued due to the high leverage and the cascading effect of liquidations. The increased influence that crypto exchanges provided further exacerbated the moves up and down.

When liquidations ended, the market tended to revert quickly to the mean, which made it profitable for large market makers to provide liquidity and take the other side of the trades. But Alameda started to lose money when prices did not reverse as expected, and the trend continued. While its trading approach had been quantitatively driven and initially market-neutral without directional views, the firm realized it needed to be better informed about the latest news driving crypto prices. As institutions started to enter the market and the buying continued, the money was made by predicting when institutional flows would enter the market and how long it would take for the order book to fill those positions. Alameda needed access to exchange flow data.

Alameda's staff engaged with other traders on social media and were encouraged to share market-moving news. Being informed about market news helped build conviction, and Alameda switched from being a purely market-neutral, non-directional trading shop to a trading firm that would take directional bets.

Making directional bets around SEC's Ripple lawsuit (2020)

When rumors surfaced that the U.S. Securities and Exchange Commission (SEC) was investigating Ripple Labs, its native token XRP reacted negatively. At the peak of the 2018 bull market XRP had a market capitalization of 120 billion dollars, with Korean retail traders being the biggest buyers. But by November 2020 XRP's market cap had been stagnating at twelve billion dollars for eighteen months. Then, in

December 2020 the price of XRP suddenly doubled as institutions started to allocate funds toward crypto, only to drop by fifty percent in a matter of days when the SEC filed a lawsuit against Ripple Labs at the end of the same month.

Ripple Labs had been founded to provide financial institutions with a low-cost and speedy clearance of cross-border money transfers. Transactions were settled and cleared on the RippleNet network with the XRP token. But as Ripple Labs had also used the XRP token to raise funds, the SEC alleged that the fundraising was an "unregistered securities" offering to investors in the U.S. (and elsewhere), which should have had SEC approval.[370]

While Sam Trabucco was no legal expert, he judged that futures open interest was high enough to set off cascading liquidations. He made a list of other potentially destructive news items that might also occur, and each time the news came out as he had predicted, prices dropped further. It was easy money.

There were many second-order effects arising from the Ripple lawsuit, with exchanges announcing the delisting of XRP tokens, OTC desks declaring they would stop making markets in XRP, and investment funds liquidating their XRP holdings. From December 28 2020 Coinbase only allowed limited trading in XRP, and from January 19 2021 it delisted the token entirely.[371]

Trading the U.S. election through esoteric products listed on FTX (2020)

In February 2020 FTX listed futures where traders could bet on the outcome of the U.S. presidential election in November, with Alameda, as the exchange's leading liquidity provider, making markets in these esoteric derivatives contracts. Joe Biden had been declared the winner of the election, but the market had started to get nervous that Trump might not vacate the White House after Biden's inauguration on January 20 2021. Trabucco was confident that Trump would eventually give in, and the futures contract priced a fifteen-to-twenty-percent probability that Trump would remain in office after losing the election—great odds that would likely get compressed to zero or one percent.

For Trabucco this was like free money. He understood his edge, and when the time was right to bet big, he maximized the PnL (profit and loss) outcome and sold as many contracts as possible. But controversies started arising later, when Alameda began to engage directly with protocols.

Bitcoin breaks the 2017 high (2020)

By December 2020 Bitcoin prices were back to their 2017 high, after trading in a volatile range for nearly three years. Many traders expected Bitcoin to fail at the previous high, as those prices were seen as resistance. But after some brief back-and-forth, prices exploded higher. By studying the trading flow from institutional investors in the U.S., Trabucco gained confidence to bet on higher prices. This was a new bull market.

When Bitcoin prices traded above twenty thousand dollars for the first time since 2017, the rally continued as forced liquidations lifted prices higher. The momentum kept going, and Trabucco got as long as he could. When Bitcoin approached thirty thousand dollars, he became less convinced about higher prices because the market had never traded above that level. But in the first four months of 2021 Bitcoin prices tripled from twenty thousand to sixty thousand dollars, driven by Tesla's purchase of 1.5 billion dollars of Bitcoin and the listing of the Coinbase exchange.

Alameda manipulates protocols for profit (2021)

On March 8 2021 the blockchain company Reef Finance agreed to a deal with Alameda to offer an initial twenty million dollars' worth of Reef tokens at a twenty-percent discount to create long-term synergies with the Serum decentralized exchange (DEX) and the Solana blockchain.[372] The Reef protocol was a blockchain that tried to make "Web3 accessible for the next billion users."[373] But Alameda immediately sold the tokens for a quick four-million-dollar profit.

Alameda claimed that both parties had agreed to a deal of eighty million dollars without any endorsement or synergies. When Reef refused to send the remaining sixty million dollars' worth of tokens, which it had sold for a considerable profit, Trabucco threatened Reef. And in an apparently coordinated response between Alameda and its affiliated exchange, FTX launched a poll on its official Twitter page, asking the community if it should delist coins that had been "rug-pulled," specifically naming Reef.

Denko Mancheski, Reef's CEO, later claimed that this was collusion and market manipulation.[374] And many traders agreed, believing that Trabucco was manipulating the market during Hong Kong trading hours when U.S. traders were asleep, as the lower liquidity made it easier to move prices.

Alameda pumps up the price and FTX lists the tokens (2021)

Crypto projects often made only a tiny fraction of their token supply available to the market, allocating the remaining tokens to the founders and early investors. These remaining tokens would remain unlocked for months or even years, and like the shares that a traditional company continues to issue into the market, would eventually dilute the ownership structure of the existing token holders.

Token prices with a small float could easily be manipulated to have a higher price—an approach that Alameda provided in return for free or discounted tokens. Alameda would promote a project by running its marketing machine on Twitter or Discord channels, and when the token listed on FTX, the token price tended to rise even more. Alameda could then use the liquidity to offload the tokens for a considerable profit. This was called "dumping on retail."[375]

Alameda became the poster child for these fake "fully diluted valuations." Industry insiders called them "S[c]am coins," as the tokens that Sam Bankman-Fried (SBF) was personally involved with all had the same playbook: thinly traded volume and a small float that could easily be manipulated, and ideally used as collateral to borrow stablecoins that could then be converted into other crypto holdings.

One of the tokens that Alameda promoted was Serum (SRM), which was the product of a consortium formed in August 2020 including the Solana Foundation, FTX, and Alameda. Serum had a market capitalization of 105 million dollars but a fully diluted valuation of only three million dollars. The circulating supply stood at 372 million tokens, as opposed to a complete collection of 10.2 billion tokens to be released through unlocks over time. The goal was to create awareness, "pump" the token price, and keep selling once the tokens were gradually unlocked. Crypto users who ignored the unlock periods, when the supply suddenly increased, would see their token price frequently devalued.

After *Forbes Magazine* had included SBF in its billionaire's list in January 2021, he periodically sent them a Google Sheet detailing his token holdings. He marked his wealth at twenty-nine billion dollars, with Alameda having funds under management of 8.6 billion dollars. Both numbers included unlocked tokens that had been reserved for him. SBF valued his stake in FTX at 15.9 billion dollars, FTX.US at 4.2 billion, the FTT tokens at 4.6 billion, Serum tokens at 2.4 billion, and Solana tokens at 1.7 billion.

A few months later SBF sent *Forbes* an update. This time he valued himself at forty-seven billion dollars and Alameda funds under management at 37 billion dollars. The most interesting part was that his Serum holdings had increased to twenty-two billion dollars, and that he had sold Solana tokens to buy more FTT tokens.[376] As would become evident after the FTX implosion in November 2022, SBF and Alameda had borrowed billions of dollars by pledging FTT and Serum tokens as collateral.

Embracing the bull market (2021)

After reading *Reminiscences of a Stock Operator*, Edwin Lefèvre's classic novel inspired by the life of legendary stock trader Jessy Livermore,[377] Caroline Ellison started to echo Sam Trabucco's view that "trading back and forth for a few points of profit was a waste of time."[378] Both realized that crypto markets had changed again, and instead of trying to make quick trading profits, they needed to understand which news was driving positions. They needed to bet on higher prices to benefit from the bull market.

The Kelly criterion is a probabilistic formula that determines the optimal theoretical size for a bet. For example if there were a ninety-percent chance that Dogecoin would decline by seventy-five percent when Elon Musk tweeted about it but a ten-percent chance that it would go up ten times, then the expected value would be 32.5 percent—(0.1 x 1,000) – (0.9 x 75). This would mean that it was worth betting, because even though the chance of winning was small, the upside was much more significant than the downside. The high-risk reward of cryptocurrencies was the prototypical best thing for young people to invest in, the Kelly criterion assured them. Either you become rich, or you die trying. You only live once, as the WallStreetBets group was preaching.

But the new ecosystem of DeFi (decentralized finance) required more market insights, as the trades were less driven by investment theses. Crypto traders needed to know which protocols offered the highest yields to attract funds. It was more about soaking up high annual percentage yield (APY) with new DeFi protocols being launched and then quickly moving on to the next launch to receive the high incentive yields paid to attract depositors. There was no need to run quantitative models, nor was there time to think about the long-term investment case for crypto.

Alameda was trading five billion dollars daily, and part of its trading activities was financed by money from DeFi lending protocols.[379] The firm borrowed 750 million dollars from the uncollateralized DeFi lending platform TrueFi, and invested 12.5 million dollars in TrueFi's parent TrustToken when the company raised funds in August 2021. Alameda also borrowed funds from Maple Finance and other DeFi lending protocols, and from anybody else that was willing to lend.

TrueFi, an institution-focused DeFi lender and borrower that launched in November 2020, had lifetime loans of 1.26 billion dollars. The protocol does not require borrowers to put up collateral. Alameda did a "double-digit percentage" of its trading through DeFi apps, and borrowing from TrueFi became a significant part of its balance sheet.[380] Alameda paid 7.5 percent in interest on its stablecoin borrowings from TrueFi, compared to the 8.5 percent that FTX charged its customers—a one-percent spread that could easily be pocketed.

In some cases crypto traders could juice up their returns by taking out multiple loans against the same collateral, a process called recursive borrowing. This allowed them to engineer the highest yields possible. Lennix Lai, a director at the crypto exchange OKX, explained that "it's something appealing in terms of yield, and it looks like and is packaged like a risk-free financial product to ordinary people."[381] Leverage worked well during the bull market. But the DeFi lending market declined from 150 billion dollars in early 2022 to fifty billion dollars a year later.[382]

Preparing for the supercycle (2021)

By June 2021 the market was starting to get concerned about the negative net asset value (NAV) of Grayscale's Bitcoin Trust (GBTC). Investors had stopped subscribing to new shares when the trust's premium vanished. New inflows now depended on the SEC approving the GBTC's conversion into an ETF (exchange-traded fund). The newly issued shares were locked up for six months, and the NAV went negative in March. Previously issued shares could only be sold on the secondary market. By then the trust had twenty-four billion dollars in Bitcoin. Some predicted that a large sell order of sixty thousand Bitcoins (or 627 million dollars) could hit the market by July 19 as expectations increased that holders would sell their positions. As a result Bitcoin prices continued to decline during the summer.

But the market regained its bullish sentiment after Amazon's payment team advertised on July 23 that it was looking to hire a digital-currency and blockchain expert, [383] signaling to the market that Amazon was seriously considering adding cryptocurrencies as payment options for its products. A few days later a bipartisan infrastructure bill limiting a proposal to increase federal regulation of cryptocurrencies was amended. This was also good news for crypto prices. [384]

Then, on September 8 Bitcoin dropped suddenly by seventeen percent without any specific reason. Positioning was exuberant based on the premium that perpetual futures were trading relative to physical Bitcoin prices. Weak longs were liquidated in a thinly traded market, as the crypto exchanges that offered the most leverage had seen the most significant inflows. Since there was no fundamental reason for the drop, Sam Trabucco concluded that "the best and most predictably great thing is to buy the HUGE dip -- buying right here has just never not been awesome." [385]

Alameda uses FTX customer money to push prices higher (2021)

According to an analysis by Coin Metrics, Alameda deployed an extra twenty-two billion dollars near the market peak between September, October, and November 2021. The trading firm sent 7.8 billion dollars from its company wallet addresses to DeFi lending protocols, 4.6 billion dollars to yield-farming protocols, and 4.4 billion dollars to crypto exchanges other than FTX. Cross-chain outflows reached 9.5 billion dollars, with the most significant Ethereum outflows going to Avalanche, Fantom, and Polygon.

On-chain flows indicate that in the week of August 30 Alameda had received four billion dollars from FTX, and another four billion dollars a month later. As a benchmark Ethereum prices were approximately 3,500 dollars at the time. SBF later claimed that FTX had only loaned the money to Alameda, but even FTX's user terms specifically said that user funds would not be lent out unless users agreed.

Alameda deployed the funds it received from FTX in risky protocols that would see their values deteriorate when the bear market came. The firm was also active in bridges prone to security breaches—such as the Wormhole Bridge, which was hacked for 325 million dollars in February 2022.

Alameda's loans were in stablecoins, but the firm bought illiquid assets that would crash in 2022. By April of that year Ethereum had fallen back to 2,700 dollars—roughly twenty percent lower than when Alameda had received the eight billion dollars from FTX. The firm's wallets started to show considerably less activity after December 2021. Positions could have been underwater, with the team hoping prices would rally. The directional long-only strategy appeared to have taken a hit.

Toward the end of November 2022 the FTX bankruptcy managers filed a motion in the Delaware district court showing that Alameda and FTX had posted a net operating loss carryover of 3.7 billion dollars in the entities' combined 2021 tax returns.[386] So Alameda could have been bankrupt before the UST / LUNA implosion happened in May 2022.

PART FIVE: THE CRYPTO BEAR MARKET (2022)

20

"A long-time friend"
(Jean Chalopin, Deltec Bank)

On November 30 2021 Jerome Powell, chair of the U.S. Federal Reserve, avoided using the term "transitory" when describing inflation. Fed officials had previously been assuring the public that year-on-year inflation comparisons were only due to supply chain bottlenecks, and that inflation would only rise temporarily. The Fed, it seemed, was no longer expecting higher inflation to be transitory, which meant that it would need to fight it with interest rate hikes.

Powell also floated the idea that the Fed would stop its asset purchase program, which had primarily been a backstop for markets during the COVID period. Two years on from the outbreak of the pandemic, the Fed was preparing the market for a hawkish central bank that would restrict liquidity. Ethereum was trading at 4,500 dollars at the time, while Bitcoin was trading at sixty thousand dollars.

The minutes of the mid-December 2021 meeting of the Federal Open Market Committee (FOMC), which were released in early January 2022, confirmed that the central bankers had contemplated the idea that "inflation would remain higher for longer,"[387] with several Fed members preferring faster rate hikes to fight inflation.

On March 9 the Fed conducted its final open market purchase, effectively ending the fourth quantitative easing (QE) program, which had started in March 2020. The Fed operated QE by purchasing treasuries, mortgage-backed securities (MBS), and agency debt, injecting nearly six trillion dollars into the markets over two years. During the fourth QE program stocks had rallied by twenty-two percent per year, far outpacing the average eight-percent per annum that stocks had averaged over the previous 100 years.

While the crypto markets were shaken by the UST / LUNA and FTX implosions in 2022, crypto assets also corrected lower whenever the Fed turned more hawkish on inflation, rallying whenever the Fed became tactically dovish to smooth the transition. While DeFi (decentralized finance) lending protocols offered yields of seven to ten percent—or in some cases even higher—once the Fed started raising interest rates sufficiently, it became uneconomical to hunt for yields in DeFi protocols when similar yields could be achieved in traditional financial markets. There needed to be an incentive for companies that could access treasury markets; otherwise they would not deploy capital in DeFi protocols. And in the absence of an incentive the demand for DeFi yields gradually collapsed. Subsequently DeFi yields continued to tumble as traditional finance yields were rising sharply.

Holders of Tether (USDT), meanwhile, could not receive any interest unless they deployed their stablecoins into lending protocols. By contrast Tether Limited, the issuer of the stablecoins, was able to deposit nearly eighty billion dollars in outstanding USDTs into treasury bonds that paid four-percent yields. Tether had struggled in the past to access the traditional banking system. In the Bahamas it had relationships with Deltec Bank, which held around fifteen billion dollars of its reserves, and also a boutique bank called Capital Union Bank, which had one billion dollars in assets at the end of 2020. The chair of Capital Union Bank, Lonnie Howell, had previously cofounded EFG International, a publicly traded Swiss bank. But most conventional crypto-related firms had by this time started using California-based Silvergate Bank for their U.S.-dollar fiat on- and offramp.

Biden's stimulus goals are blocked (2022)

Not only was the central bank restricting liquidity in 2022, but fiscal stimulus also ended. On February 3 swing voter Joe Manchin, the Democrat senator from West Virginia, announced that President Biden's Build Back Better (BBB) plan was "dead."[388] BBB was another 1.7-trillion-dollar package to fund various social investments. But according to Manchin the plan was too costly and would have added too great a burden to the national debt as interest rates were rising. Higher interest rates caused liquidity to tighten, and the reversal in easy-money policies caused funding for low-quality tech investments and crypto to disappear gradually.

Crypto prices peak (2021)

Although eighty percent of China's crypto mining capacity had already moved overseas, mainly to Kazakhstan and the U.S., China's top economic planner, the National Development and Reform Commission (NDRC), reasserted its influence on November 10 2021, vowing to "We will focus on cleaning out state-owned units involved in virtual currency and bitcoin mining, reiterating that all virtual currency-related activities are illegal. Virtual currency does not have the same legal status as legal currency".[389] As part of the new regulations electricity prices were raised for any institution that abused its access to subsidized power to participate in crypto mining.

Before the NDRC meeting Bitcoin had been trading near sixty-eight thousand dollars, but after the meeting prices fell seven percent, before dropping below sixty thousand dollars shortly afterward. Despite China's clampdown on Bitcoin mining in May 2021, twenty percent of the global Bitcoin mining hash rate was still believed to originate in China. An estimated 220 billion dollars in total cryptocurrency transactions were also recorded in China between June 2021 and July 2022, as Chinese traders used VPNs (virtual private networks) to circumvent the Great Firewall.

While market sentiment was bullish coming into November 2021, the U.S. Securities and Exchange Commission (SEC) rejected another proposal for a spot Bitcoin exchange-traded fund (ETF) on December 2. This time it was the ETF provider WisdomTree that had been hoping to offer retail investors easy access to Bitcoin. As with the December 2017 listing of Bitcoin futures at the Chicago Mercantile Exchange many traders had bought Bitcoin in anticipation of an approval for the Bitcoin ETF.

On December 4 Bitcoin suddenly dropped by twenty percent as stop losses were triggered during poor weekend liquidity. The cascading liquidations were a sign of overleverage—a bubble that would be popped by expectations that interest rates would be higher in the future. By this time Bitcoin prices had dropped below fifty thousand dollars, and large Bitcoin holders—the so-called whales—were moving coins onto crypto exchanges, indicating their willingness to liquidate them.

On December 8 six crypto executives testified in front of the U.S. House Financial Services Committee, with lawmakers weighing in on how to best regulate the industry. This was the first time that crypto executives had faced tough questions from lawmakers about risk and regulations.[390] Executives from Coinbase, Paxos, Bitfury, Stellar, FTX, and Circle all urged for a light touch regarding regulation, as overly tight oversight, they argued, would shift innovation overseas.[391]

During the previous crypto-related hearing in front of the House in 2018 some Congress members had expressed deep skepticism around digital currencies, warning retail investors that they would lose money when the crypto bubble burst.[392] The subcommittee had called for a hearing on March 14 to discuss initial coin offerings (ICOs), as the SEC had begun regulating these fundraising efforts. But in 2021 regulation was still lagging behind crypto adoption, and retail participation remained high, with institutions keen to get involved in digital assets as crypto prices rose, creating more value for early adopters.

FTX relocates to the Bahamas (2021)

The FTX executive who testified before the House in December 2021 was Sam Bankman-Fried (SBF), who supported regulation of the crypto industry. During the hearing SBF explained that FTX was primarily regulated in the U.S. and other jurisdictions.[393] He had just flown in from the Bahamas, where the exchange had recently relocated its headquarters from Hong Kong, where financial regulators had indicated that crypto exchanges would be subject to more stringent controls.

SBF also criticized Hong Kong's COVID quarantine policies, which made traveling very difficult. But while Hong Kong had become more stringently regulated for crypto firms, other jurisdictions were providing more favorable terms. In the Bahamas, for example, the Digital Assets and Registered Exchanges (DARE) Act had come into effect on December 14 2020. The act regulates the issuance, sale, and trade of digital assets in (or from within) the jurisdiction.

The Bahamas became known as an essential base for piracy in the Caribbean in the seventeenth century. During the Prohibition era in the 1920s and early 1930s, when the production and sale of alcohol was banned in the U.S., the islands' Bay Street Boys would smuggle rum to the U.S. Then, from 1933 to 1939, during Franklin D. Roosevelt's New Deal the Bahamas established insurance companies to help wealthy Americans evade higher taxes. And when Fidel Castro's revolution was gathering steam in the 1950s, famed Mafia accountant Meyer Lansky moved his casino operations from Cuba to the Bahamas, forging close ties with one of the Bay Street Boys and also Wallace Groves, a former Wall Street speculator.[394] The casinos that Lansky and his associates opened brought more money onto the islands and a growing presence of organized crime.

From the 1980s onward the Bahamas were a place where foreign nationals could park their money and evade taxes. The Organization for Economic Co-operation and Development (OECD) has criticized the Bahamian government for failing to cooperate and share information. But the country has always managed to reinvent itself and cater to the needs of a specific group of people. When it passed the DARE Act in 2020, FTX became the first significant crypto company to register there. Other crypto firms and crypto hedge funds would soon follow.

The Bahamas are just a forty-five-minute flight from Miami but still outside the SEC's purview. FTX needed to keep some distance from the U.S., as it was offering crypto derivatives that under U.S. regulations could not be provided to U.S.-based clients. The FTX subsidiary registered in the Bahamas was called FTX Digital Markets, and was run by Ryan Salame, who had previously been head of OTC (over the counter) markets at Alameda Research.

Deltec Bank's chairman, Jean Chalopin, had assisted the Bahamian government in drafting the country's crypto legislation. Deltec's parent company, the Cayman Islands–based Deltec International Group, had dreams of a potential U.S. public offering. Yet, in October 2021 it accepted a fifty-million-dollar loan from Norton Hall Ltd., an entity controlled by Ryan Salame.[395]

By this time SBF had distanced himself from his trading firm Alameda, as he was increasingly in the spotlight of the media and U.S. regulators. In August 2021 he ostensibly delegated power to two of his lieutenants, Sam Trabucco and Caroline Ellison. Alameda remained registered in Hong Kong, while the firm's personnel increasingly traded out of the Bahamas. Trabucco and Ellison were co-CEOs until Trabucco unexpectedly resigned in August 2022. Ellison oversaw the trading firm's systems, while Trabucco led the trading strategy.

Silvergate becomes the primary bank for all crypto firms (2013–23)

The U.S.-based Silvergate Bank was initially founded as an industrial loan company. For thirty years it was a tiny community lender focused on real-estate deals in Southern California. The bank had less than one billion dollars in assets and had desperately tried to increase its deposit base.

But in late 2013 Silvergate's CEO, Alan Lane, started to get the bank involved with crypto firms, after noticing that no lenders wanted to deal with companies like Coinbase. Lane went to the Federal Reserve Bank of San Francisco and requested that Silvergate be allowed to service crypto firms. After gaining approval, Silvergate set up relationships with crypto firms such as Xapo, Paxos, and Bitfury. Over the years its real-estate group was slimmed down as the bank focused increasingly on crypto firms, growing its client base to more than two thousand companies.

In 2017 Silvergate launched the Silvergate Exchange Network (SEN), a platform that allowed crypto investors to transfer U.S. dollars from their bank accounts onto crypto exchanges twenty-four seven if the sender and receiver banked with Silvergate. The SEN platform made the bank an effective clearinghouse for crypto firms.

Figure 23: The stock price for Silvergate Bank, one of the few banks serving the crypto industry

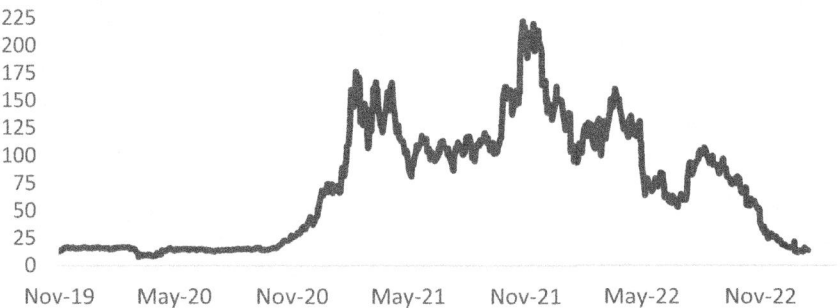

By 2019 Silvergate had built relationships with an astonishing 1,600 crypto firms and was offering an onramp for crypto hedge funds, lenders, and exchanges, among others. In mid-2019 the bank sold its small-business lending division "to increase its focus on its digital currency initiative and specialty lending competencies."[396]

Deposits surged from two billion dollars in 2020 to over ten billion in 2021. The bank was listed on the New York Stock Exchange (NYSE) at the end of 2019 at twelve dollars per share. By early 2022 share prices had reached over 220 dollars as net profits increased from 7.6 million to 75.5 million dollars. The shares would subsequently decline by ninety percent by the end of the year.

Initially when FTX customers wanted to send money into their user accounts, they were asked to wire the deposits through an account named Alameda Research Ltd. Unlike FTX Alameda had a banking partnership with Silvergate. The collusion between Alameda and FTX over customer funds would later become their main point of failure.

On December 14 2022 a class action complaint was filed against Silvergate due to its involvement with FTX and its allowance of direct transfers between FTX and Alameda accounts. According to the complaint FTX had diverted customer funds in two ways. First Alameda was allowed to draw down limitless credit. Second the bank had directed FTX customers to deposit fiat currency into bank accounts controlled by Alameda. According to the complaint this made Silvergate complicit in the actions of FTX and Alameda.

Since Silvergate had accepted funds from FTX customers that were intended for trading on the FTX exchange but had deposited them into Alameda accounts, its internal monitoring system should have brought this to the attention of the bank's compliance and risk management personnel, as the comingled funds could have had severe implications for its anti-money-laundering (AML) procedures. In 2022 around ten percent of Silvergate's total assets belonged to FTX, which by then had managed to open twenty different accounts at the bank. The allegations around the misuse of banking loopholes would intensify when FTX imploded.

On February 2 2023 U.S. federal prosecutors opened a probe into Silvergate Capital Corporation and its dealings with FTX and Alameda. This caused a bank run, resulting in a deterioration in the bank's capital and liquidity ratios. To address large deposit withdrawal requests,

Silvergate was forced to liquidate debt securities that it had invested in at a loss, as interest rates had climbed in the aftermath of the COVID stimulus support packages. On March 4 the bank closed the SEN platform, which had become instrumental in providing transactional services to crypto firms and exchanges around the clock. A few days later Silvergate entered into liquidation.

Alameda uses Moonstone to gain access to the U.S. banking system (2022)

The collapse of Silvergate Bank was a scenario that FTX had tried to diversify away from with the purchase, via its sister company Alameda, of a stake in a small rural bank from Washington State called Moonstone. Jean Chalopin, the chairman of Deltec Bank, had originally pitched FTX and Alameda the idea of an investment in Moonstone, a bank he owned and hoped to transform into a U.S.-based crypto fiat service provider. Many suspect that the investment in Moonstone was made to bypass the requirement of getting a banking license.

In January 2022 Alameda invested 11.5 million dollars to buy a ten-percent equity stake in Moonstone's parent company FBH, a deal that was publicly announced on March 7. According to the Federal Deposit Insurance Corporation (FDIC), the investment was more than double the bank's net worth. Buying a stake in a U.S.-licensed bank typically requires approval from federal regulators.

The investment from FTX Ventures was led by Ramnik Arora, who was also responsible for the funding rounds that FTX received from venture capital firms such as Silicon Valley–based Sequoia Capital. A week before the investment Moonstone had changed its name from Farmington State Bank to reflect the two industries the bank intended to focus on as part of "the evolution of next-generation finance:" crypto (with "moon" referring to the popular crypto expression "to the moon") and cannabis (with "stone" alluding to the effects of the drug). At the time the bank held only ten million dollars in customer deposits, and until early 2022 had only three employees.[397]

While Moonstone recorded a six-hundred-percent increase in customer deposits—from thirteen million to eighty-four million dollars—in the third quarter of 2022, the increase came from only four accounts according to FDIC data. In January 2023 prosecutors seized nearly fifty million dollars from the bank's FTX Digital Markets account.

Jean Chalopin's son, Janvier Chalopin, is Moonstone's chief digital officer, while his father is chairman of its parent company FBH. "We pitched [Alameda] the whole roadmap," Janvier would later explain.[398] The idea was to replace Silvergate Bank as the primary on- and offramp for fiat money. FTX and Alameda had long been one of the largest trading partners of Tether, minting billions of the stablecoin, so owning a regulated U.S. bank could also have given them a way to issue stablecoins.

Daniel Friedberg, FTX's chief regulatory officer, is believed to have been the mastermind behind the Moonstone investment. In late 2022 he would cooperate with U.S. prosecutors to build a case against SBF. Friedberg had close relationships with Stuart Hoegner, the general counsel for Bitfinex and Tether. Hoegner was the head of compliance at Excapsa Software, the parent company of the *Ultimate Bet* website. The online poker site had allegedly had a back door where some of the executives' friends could see other poker players' cards.

Rumors started circulating that Alameda owned more than ten percent of Moonstone, as it had overpaid for the investment. But SBF had a clear vision to acquire a bank with a U.S. banking license and acquire more retail customers through the stock trading app Robinhood. Shortly after the Moonstone investment it became public knowledge that SBF had also bought a stake in the trading app.

SBF had also talked with angel investor Kevin O'Leary and TRON founder Justin Sun about creating a Layer 2 secondary payment system where transactions would not need to be settled on-chain. This was effectively a proposal for a liquidity pool for central bank–denominated currencies. It would have created a bank for international settlements for CBDCs (central bank digital currencies), establishing a stablecoin system across multiple jurisdictions.

But things were turned upside down. When the Terra stablecoin started to de-peg, Alameda was caught off guard. And when FTX clients started to liquidate their Terra and LUNA positions, the trading firm was left holding tokens on its balance sheet that quickly became worthless.

21

"Deploying more capital – steady lads"
(Do Kwon, Terraform Labs)

Kwon Do-hyung (Do Kwon), the son of a pharmaceutical and medical equipment distributor from South Korea, spent many years in Canada and graduated with a bachelor's degree in computer science from Stanford University. After working as a software engineer at Microsoft, in 2016 he launched his first company, Anyfi, with a million dollars in grants from angel investors and the South Korean government. The company used a mesh network to relay bandwidth to those without internet access.

With his university friend Nicholas Platias Kwon wrote a white paper for a decentralized payment system that the average person could use. The idea was to create a stablecoin pegged to fiat. When Kwon met Daniel Shin, everything went very quickly. Shin had founded the e-commerce site Ticket Monster and cofounded Fast Track Asia, and was a legendary entrepreneur in South Korea.

Terraform Labs is formed with a great vision (2018)

In 2018 Terraform Labs was launched to oversee the development of a new e-commerce platform called Chai. Unlike the Stripe payment app Chai was built entirely using crypto infrastructure. It was like a neobank, where consumers could plug into their existing accounts, including accounts for debit and credit cards, digital wallets, wires, and PayPal, to make the online shopping experience easier. The idea was for merchants to settle payments quickly without the fees that traditional credit card services required.

Shin helped with his e-commerce industry contacts, and when Terraform raised capital, it already had fifteen established firms using its payment system. The company marketed the system as Alipay on the blockchain, referencing China's leading digital payment network.[399] By the end of 2018 Terraform had raised thirty-two million dollars from Binance, OKEx, Huobi, TechCrunch founder Michael Arrington, and others. Binance's stake eventually reached a market value of 1.6 billion dollars. Later Chai would spin out of Terra, but both entities kept working together.

In April 2019 Kwon and several coauthors released the Terra white paper, which described the plan to create Terra Money as an algorithmic stablecoin that, when pegged to the U.S. dollar, would become Terra (UST). In September 2020 Kwon announced the launch of UST through the crypto exchange Bittrex Global. The central feature of the stablecoin was an algorithm that guaranteed exchangeability with another digital asset, the LUNA token, and its corresponding supply control.

The Terra economy is best understood when visualizing the entire ecosystem as a pool, with the size of the collection being determined by the total supply of UST. If more people want UST, the tide rises, and vice versa. The pool height represents each UST's value. If the height increases, it can be brought down by expanding the water level to one dollar by increasing the supply of UST.

When the Terra economy grew, demand for UST would pick up, the water level would rise, and the size of the pool would need to be increased by selling UST and buying LUNA to bring the water level down. As LUNA became scarce, its price would rise, while the cost of UST stayed stable, pegged at 1.0 to the dollar. When the demand for UST decreased, causing the price to go below 1.0 dollar, holders of UST would be incentivized to arbitrage and mint 1.0 dollars of LUNA (which increased its supply) in exchange for UST.

The white paper, which was released in June 2020, concluded that "investors who hold LUNA would see its value rise during [the Terra ecosystem] expansion, and if they choose to stake, they will earn transaction fees in UST. Even when demand for UST is low, Terra's algorithm automatically increases fees so that validators are always rewarded with a steady cash flow of UST."[400]

Subsequently Terra launched the Anchor Protocol, a DeFi (decentralized finance) saving and lending protocol, to provide a passive profit-making incentive to UST holders. Nicholas Platias, head of research at Terraform Labs, called it the "gold standard for passive income on the blockchain." Other protocols tied into the Terra ecosystem followed, with Terraform incentivizing the adoption of its stablecoin by building and connecting a suite of use cases. Every Terra-related protocol that was made was helping to develop the Terra ecosystem as a whole.

Users could buy UST directly from the Anchor Protocol via Transak or on KuCoin, Coinbase, Uniswap, or Terraswap. Traders could also buy LUNA on most exchanges for other cryptocurrencies, or onramp via fiat currencies and then send LUNA to their Terra wallets and convert it to UST.

How the UST peg and LUNA relationship worked

In the Terra ecosystem UST is the stablecoin and LUNA the governance token. LUNA is valued according to the fees from UST usage over time, while recognizing that UST is 100-percent uncollateralized and algorithmically targeted via incentives. To mint UST, users must deposit LUNA, which is subsequently burned, shrinking the overall supply and increasing the value of the tokens. This mechanism caused a parabolic UST adoption over time.

In December 2021 five percent of the circulating supply of LUNA tokens (380 million) was burned. Ninety percent of UST adoption was based on the Anchor Protocol, which was Terra's money market. This made the success of the UST stablecoin and LUNA tokens heavily dependent on an incentivized yield farming protocol instead of actual adoption.

In a balanced scenario the Anchor Protocol charged borrowers fees and paid out the fees to depositors. But for most of 2021 Anchor financially incentivized borrowing, as demand for UST was lackluster. Subsequently many LUNA tokens were burned, and a decreasing supply caused the LUNA token to rally. A higher price allowed borrowers to lever up even more as their collateral became more valuable.

The high annual percentage yield (APY) of 18.5 percent incentivized borrowers, but it depleted the Anchor Protocol's reserves over time, as users were only interested in receiving high yields. Either Anchor needed to decrease its deposit rate or find ways to close the gap between borrowing and lending. By early January 2022 Anchor's reserves could only cover the next eighty days. The protocol needed to lower its incentive (staking) yield.

But lowering the staking yield would risk losing depositors, as they could start withdrawing capital and move on to other DeFi yield platforms which paid higher rates. In that case users would sell UST, which required minting LUNA tokens. An increase in LUNA supply would cause the token price to drop to a level that might liquidate borrowers as their collateral became less valuable. This would trigger stop-loss levels. A decrease in borrowers could also mean fewer resources to fund the high-paying deposit rates. This was the risk that everybody knew the UST / LUNA relationship would eventually face.

When users borrow UST, they deposit "bLUNA," which is LUNA staked and routed through the Lido staking system. The ratio of bLUNA to LUNA was an important signal, given how unreliable the peg was. The LUNA system was critically vulnerable to forced position unwinding if the price of LUNA dropped below the fifty-five-dollar level, given the leverage and maximum loan-to-value (LTV) threshold at Anchor.

To disincentivize traders from swapping large amounts of UST and LUNA at one time, there was a 100-million-dollar UST-LUNA swap cap at 0.5 percent. While more significant redemptions would have been possible, the spread would have gapped even wider.

During the May 2021 decline, a year before the eventual implosion of the Terra ecosystem in May 2022, there were eighty million UST-LUNA unwinds at their peak, and the redemption cap was set at twenty million dollars.[401] On May 19 2021 UST briefly de-pegged as Bitcoin prices fell, and UST dropped to 0.85 dollars. The next day UST recovered to 0.96–0.99 dollars, before reaching parity on May 25. Market makers could make easy money by buying briefly de-pegged tokens that traded back to par shortly afterward.

It has been reported that Chicago-based crypto liquidity provider Jump Crypto agreed to stabilize the UST peg in May 2021, deploying sixty-two million dollars. In return the firm received heavily discounted LUNA tokens, earning 1.28 billion dollars selling them later, when the peg was reestablished.[402] According to the terms of the agreement between Jump and the Luna Foundation Guard (LFG) LUNA tokens changed ownership for as little as 0.40 dollars while LUNA was trading at ninety dollars on exchanges. The existence of Jump Crypto, a subsidiary of the secretive quantitative trading firm the Jump Trading Group, was only revealed in September 2021. According to the U.S. Securities and Exchange Commission (SEC) Jump Trading had worked with LFG since November 2019.

The president of Jump Crypto is Kanav Kariya, who also served on the LFG board. Originally from Mumbai in India, Kariya only joined Jump Trading as an intern in 2017, becoming a full-time employee the following year. Within five years he had risen to head a company of more than 170 employees.

When volatility rose in the market, notably during sell-offs, LUNA prices tended to decline as people started to risk-manage their positions. The drop in LUNA prices would drive an increase in liquidations on the Anchor Protocol as the LTV ratio fell below a key threshold amid declining collateral. When redemptions exceeded the 100-million-dollar swap cap and spreads widened significantly, there would be a temporary break in the peg.

Traders could always redeem LUNA for UST, dollar-for-dollar and vice versa. If LUNA traded at fifty dollars, traders could exchange it for fifty UST. Similarly they could exchange one UST for one dollar of LUNA. LUNA would be burned to create more UST, making the token deflationary. The UST demand change determined the amount of LUNA that needed to be burned, while the LUNA burn reduced supply and drove up the price of LUNA. This flywheel kept increasing the value of the Terra ecosystem, and specifically the price of LUNA.

By using their current UST as collateral, traders could effectively be paid to borrow UST, borrowing more and depositing the extra coins on top of their original holdings. That way annual yields of even thirty percent could be achieved.

In December 2020 Terraform launched securities called "mAssets," which were designed to mirror the price of stocks of U.S. companies. But in September 2021, just as he was about to walk on stage at Messari's Mainnet conference in New York, Do Kwon was served an SEC subpoena, which had already been emailed to him in May that year.[403] As a South Korean citizen Kwon believed that the U.S. regulators had no jurisdiction over him.

The Col-5 upgrade helps UST / LUNA to explosive growth (2021)

The Terra ecosystem got its most significant upgrade on September 29 2021, when the Columbus-5 (Col-5) version was deployed to the mainnet, allowing Terra to integrate with the Inter Blockchain Communication (IBC) protocol. This cross-chain communication protocol bridges the Cosmos, Solana, and Polkadot ecosystems and connects Terra with over 250 decentralized applications (dApps). The upgrade also created a seamless UST connection to the Solana ecosystem, through a wormhole bridge where digital assets could be swapped between the blockchains.

After the upgrade Terra's TVL (total value locked) started to increase sharply, and the market capitalization for LUNA exploded. By November 2021 there was extreme demand for UST, raising its market capitalization from 2.5 billion to ten billion dollars within two months and lifting the price of LUNA from forty to 103 dollars. In December the leveraged yield farming protocol Abracadabra Degenbox was launched, allowing users to earn even higher yields. Terra added 1.4 billion UST and instantly sold out. There were allegations that Do Kwon used the DegenBox protocol to cash out of 2.7 billion dollars from Terra.[404]

TVL represents the number of assets deposited by liquidity providers, and during the DeFi bull market it became an essential metric for investors who wanted to assess whether a protocol was worth investing in. Terra's development team fueled the fire by predicting that throughput capabilities would increase by 100 times.[405]

But after the Col-5 upgrade all LUNA tokens in the community pool (4.5 billion dollars' worth) were burned, creating downward pressure on LUNA supply and boosting its price. Meanwhile fees for swapping UST to LUNA and vice versa were allocated to community pools and distributed to LUNA stakers, which incentivized the holding of LUNA tokens.

How the Anchor Protocol provided 18.5-percent annual yields for stakers

There were several risks with the Anchor Protocol. Firstly the people behind the protocol could one day just withdraw the money from Anchor and delete all the evidence of user deposits, as when users send their crypto to someone, they effectively lose ownership. As the saying goes, "not your keys, not your coins."[406] There was also the risk of a UST de-peg. In theory, if UST traded below parity, market makers like Alameda, Jump, Cumberland, and Wintermute could buy UST at a discount and wait until prices climbed back to 1.0 dollar. The Terra protocol was the effective market maker for the UST / LUNA mechanism, offsetting demand for UST by decreasing demand for LUNA and vice versa.

The Terra protocol was designed to manage twenty million dollars of redemptions with a two-percent spread. But an aggressive sell-off in LUNA combined with liquidations on the Anchor Protocol could cause redemptions from LUNA to UST to exceed the eighty-million-dollar cap. This would cause UST to trade at a significant discount to its peg, and every time the peg was in jeopardy, confidence in the stability of the algorithm was at risk.

By the end of February 2022 Anchor's reserve fund was nearly depleted. It asked LFG for an extra 450 million dollars to shore up confidence. This would have allowed it to maintain the 18.5-percent yields based on the existing borrow / lending spread until November 2022. Unless the ratio of borrowers to lenders increased, yields still needed to be subsidized to keep users from depositing their UST into the pool and draining the reserves.

In March 2022 a community proposal to lower the incentive yield was voted down as the incentive yield structure became unsustainable. Eventually Terra's founders realized that UST could enter a death spiral in the event of rapidly declining demand for LUNA. They decided to depart from the white paper's promise to back UST by LUNA, and to rely instead on a mix of Bitcoin and other non-LUNA reserves as a stabilizing mechanism.

LFG raises one billion dollars to diversify the collateral (2022)

On January 19 2022 Do Kwon announced the launch of the Luna Foundation Guard (LFG) to support the Terra ecosystem.[407] LFG received an initial gift of fifty million dollars' worth of LUNA tokens from Terraform Labs. The funds would be used to launch initiatives such as driving awareness, building educational programs, and continuously supporting peg stability.

By February 22 LFG had raised one billion dollars to form a Bitcoin reserve for the UST stablecoin, with Jump Crypto and Three Arrows Capital (3AC) leading the round and the latter contributing 200 million dollars.[408]

As a market maker and liquidity provider Jump carried out most of the Bitcoin buying for LFG. By early March the foundation had bought 1.3 billion dollars' worth of Bitcoin and expected to hold 2.3 billion dollars by April 6. This linear and predictable buying supported Bitcoin prices, as other traders were front-running the orders and Bitcoin prices rose in anticipation of the purchases. Through on-chain data and the associated wallets traders could spot when USDTs were being sent from LFG to Jump so that the market maker could buy Bitcoins shortly afterward.

Traders start calling UST / LUNA a Ponzi scheme (2022)

Proponents of the UST / LUNA mechanism proudly called themselves LUNAtics.[409] This helped to drive the cult status that had been very common in crypto over the years. But critics of the algorithmic stablecoin started to get louder.

On February 16 2022 a trader with the pseudonym Algod, who had nearly 180 thousand Twitter followers, called LUNA a Ponzi scheme.[410] He explained that demand for LUNA was being engineered by offering twenty-percent fixed APY "printed out of thin air, which is unsustainable."

Meanwhile, on March 18 crypto hedge fund Galois Capital said that LUNA would unlikely succeed, and the later in the process it failed, the worse it would be for the crypto space, as this would present systemic risk and contagion for the entire industry. When LUNA went down, Galois wrote, "an enormous amount of paper wealth will get wiped out ... and regulators will come down so hard that the landscape won't even be recognizable anymore."[411]

On March 14 Do Kwon had accepted a one-million-dollar bet with Algod, who had asserted that LUNA would be trading below eighty-eight dollars in one year's time.[412] The funds were moved into an escrow wallet managed by the crypto personality Jordan Fish, who operates under the alias Cobie and hosts the *UpOnly* podcast.[413] A few hours later another trader, Gigantic Rebirth, wanted to make the same bet but for ten million dollars, and Do Kwon happily agreed.

On March 23 Jump Crypto proposed a mechanism for deploying Bitcoin reserves to prop up UST's price in a crisis. On March 28 LFG purchased twenty-seven thousand Bitcoins, worth 1.3 billion dollars,[414] and on April 5 LUNA reached an all-time high of 119.20 dollars and a market capitalization of 40.9 billion dollars. On April 14 Terra gave LFG ten million LUNA tokens, valued at 820 million dollars, as Do Kwon ultimately wanted to build a reserve of ten billion dollars in Bitcoin to back the UST peg.[415]

Launching 4pool starts the imbalance (2022)

In early 2022 Curve's 3pool, a de facto savings account, held a massive 3.4 billion dollars of liquidity in three stablecoins: Tether's USDT, Circle's USDC, and MakerDAO's DAI. With this deep liquidity 3pool provided the most capital-efficient route for swapping USDT, USDC, and

DAI, with minimal slippage costs. Inclusion among these important stablecoins would certainly add trust and consistent demand for any new stablecoin, as the pool would undoubtedly grow over time.

In 2021 Daniele Sestagalli, head of Abracadabra, wanted to overtake DAI with Abracadabra's stablecoin Magical Internet Money (MIM). On November 1 he tweeted "Bye Bye $DAI," a call which Do Kwon would later echo.[416] In response, on January 4 2022 Rune Christensen, the founder of MakerDAO, called out UST and MIM as "solid Ponzi schemes."[417] This was possibly a reference to Abracadabra's recently launched Degenbox, which provided leveraged yield farming to attract deposits that could then be paid out to existing users in the form of yield.

On November 5 2021 MakerDAO had set its Peg Stability Module (PSM) fees to 0.0 percent, down from 0.1 percent for Paxos (USDP) and 0.2 percent for USD Coin (USDC). This attracted liquidity away from the Curve pool, as traders could now exchange stablecoins for almost no cost.[418] This obviously represented lost value for Curve, and the Curve community started discussing ways to exclude the Terra stablecoin UST.

On April 2 2022 Do Kwon announced 4pool, a new stablecoin pool on Curve that would include USDT, USDC, Terra's UST, and Frax Finance's FRAX. Users could deposit any of the four stablecoins into the pool to earn yield. Liquidity providers would receive rewards as other users traded between the pooled assets for a small fee. The new pool was a direct attack on DAI, which was excluded from 4pool as Do Kwon sought to attract liquidity away from 3pool.

The key to making 4pool function was a significant liquidity increase so that stablecoins could be seamlessly exchanged without impacting the prices. Size mattered, so the two algorithmic stablecoin entities, Terra and Frax, decided to work together to incentivize deposits. The battle to attract stablecoin liquidity came to be known as the "Curve Wars."[419] Do Kwon's plan was to use the large number of Convex Finance CVX tokens that both Frax and Terra were holding as an incentive to users who deposited their stablecoins into 4pool.

Through their partnership Terra and Frax could vote to divert Curve (CRV) tokens away from 3pool toward 4pool, using their combined position in CVX to essentially control the issuing of CRV. The rewards gauge that supplied CRV to 4pool was approved on May 5, and once it went live, it looked as if 3pool's dominance would end. But Do Kwon became overconfident, and made a crucial mistake.

Terra and LUNA start to implode (2022)

The market capitalization of UST reached 18.7 billion dollars on May 5 2022, up from just three billion dollars on October 1 2021. Most of the UST were stored on the Anchor Protocol.

On May 7 2022 Terraform Labs withdrew 150 million dollars in UST from Curve's 3pool in preparation to deploy it to 4pool. A trader believed from Jane Street—the quant trading firm where SBF, Caroline Ellison, and former FTX.US president Brett Harrison had all previously worked, and where longtime traders Thomas Uhm and Turner Batty had been instrumental in building up the firm's crypto desks—then swapped eighty-five million dollars in UST for USDC just thirteen minutes later. A second wallet traded 100 million dollars in UST for USDC in twenty-five-million-dollar increments.

As 3pool then contained too much UST, Terra withdrew a further 100 million dollars in UST to rebalance it. The pool was finally back in balance after fifty thousand Ether and another twenty thousand Ether were sent to Binance. Then rumors started to spread, and two billion dollars of UST were withdrawn from Anchor, with the peg suddenly softening to 0.987–0.995. But Alameda's Sam Trabucco tweeted that he was not selling UST and had no plans to do so.[420] He probably believed that UST would eventually re-peg at 1.0, as had happened so often before.

Some arbitrage traders bought UST at the de-pegged price, and the price started to reverse slightly. But it never recovered to the whole peg level, so investors panicked and many holders who had deposited their UST in Anchor withdrew their funds.

Figure 24: The Terra UST stablecoin starts to de-peg violently

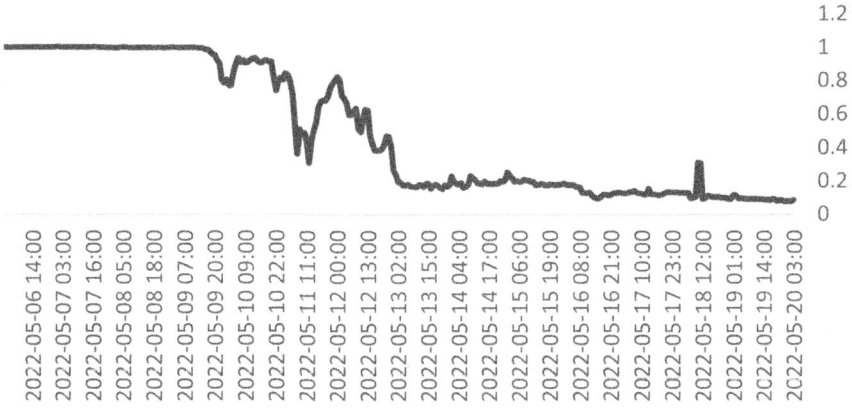

On Monday May 9 LFG said that it would lend out 1.5 billion dollars in Bitcoin and UST to defend the UST peg as the algorithmic stablecoin slipped to 0.9955 dollars against USDT.[421] The LFG Council voted to loan out 750 million dollars' worth of Bitcoin to OTC (over the counter) trading firms and 750 million dollars in UST to accumulate Bitcoin as market conditions normalized.

There were several large withdrawals in UST from the Anchor Protocol, and UST started to de-peg further. Altogether UST holders withdrew five billion dollars in UST from Anchor, and UST fell to just 0.35 dollar. But Do Kwon expressed calmness, tweeting "Deploying more capital - steady lads."[422]

How the Terra de-peg started to impact its sister token, LUNA

One rumor that started to gain traction was that Gemini, the crypto exchange and custodian platform set up by the Winklevoss twins, had jointly lent 100 thousand Bitcoins (three billion dollars) in an OTC transaction to BlackRock and Citadel or another attacker. These Bitcoins were then partially swapped for UST (twenty-five thousand Bitcoins), before both the Bitcoins and the UST were dumped onto the market.

As LFG removed 150 million dollars in UST from the Curve 3pool in preparation for the new 4pool, an attacker used 350 million dollars of the UST bought OTC to drain the 3pool, creating a small de-peg. Liquidity crashed, and market panic started when seventy-five thousand Bitcoins were sold.

Combined with weakness in the stock market, which was occurring coincidently, Bitcoin prices came under pressure. The peg kept moving lower to 0.97 dollars, and LUNA prices crashed. The attackers had 650 million dollars in UST left, which they started to sell on Binance.[423] LFG stepped in and sold Bitcoins to buy UST to try to restore the peg. But the death spiral started gaining momentum, and Bitcoin prices dropped further.

This Bitcoin selling pressure pushed the whole crypto market lower and increased the panic in UST, causing it to de-peg even more. As a result users wanted to withdraw more money from Anchor, creating new sell pressure on UST. LUNA prices collapsed because of fear of how the UST / LUNA burn worked. When UST was sold off, there was more LUNA in circulation, which lowered the LUNA price.

Momentum traders started to short LUNA, which further tanked the LUNA price. They also shorted UST through perpetual futures. Mass congestion hit the chains, and centralized exchanges started to ban UST withdrawals.[424] There was a bank run on the Anchor Protocol, and users could not get their money out. There was a minimum twenty-four-hour time limit to stake LUNA, so users who had just deposited LUNA could not withdraw their tokens on time.

Figure 25: The LUNA token price during the Terra de-peg

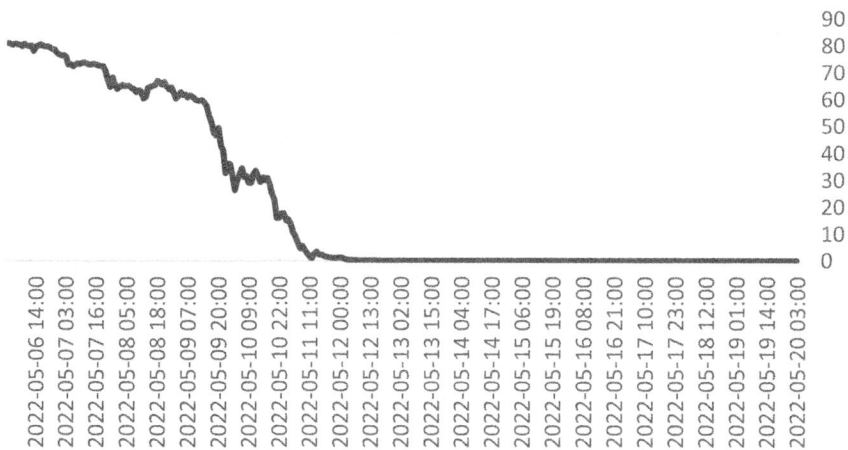

Terra even loaned millions of UST to market makers and liquidity providers to support liquidity during the decline.[425] But while Do Kwon had hoped that providing this funding would make the market for UST more liquid, the market makers turned around and sold UST, receiving LUNA tokens through the burn mechanism and selling those too. LUNA prices kept falling, and the lower the borrowed UST went, the less the market makers needed to repay. There was a lot of money to be made at the expense of LFG and UST / LUNA holders.

The failed LUNA rescue plan (2022)

On May 10 Do Kwon tweeted that LFG was close to announcing a recovery plan for UST.[426] Then, after several hours of silence he indicated that LFG would let the peg digest the flows first and then see how to restore the peg after the flows had subsided. But the pressure was so significant that the foundation decided to stay put and save its bullets with its investor and liquidity provider Jump Capital. This caused the peg to drop from 0.92 to 0.4 dollars.

When the UST peg dropped further to 0.25 dollars, the LUNA price moved from thirty-five dollars to fifteen dollars over the next four hours. LFG's plan did not look credible, and traders started questioning the foundation's financial strength. At this point Do Kwon indicated a move away from the algorithmic model to another version of the stablecoin. This caused a drop in the price of LUNA from five dollars to below one dollar over the next few hours. The priority was to save the UST peg, and as a result LUNA was devalued in hyperinflation as billions of LUNA tokens were issued.

Later that day LFG reached out to large crypto investors to raise one billion dollars to recapitalize the UST stablecoin.[427] The deal offered LUNA spot tokens at a fifty-percent discount with one-year and two-year lockups plus monthly linear vesting over that time. As a result UST recovered from 0.61 to 0.91 dollars.

On May 11 Jump Capital, Celsius, and Jane Street committed 700 million dollars to shore up the UST peg. Despite being a large liquidity provider and proprietary trader, Alameda still needed confirmation before committing capital. Some interpreted this as a sign that it wanted the peg to break and was profiting from the decline.

But the rescue plan had come too late. LUNA kept tumbling. By then its market capitalization was just 541 million dollars, and its price had declined to 0.004 dollars. A few days later LFG confirmed that it had depleted its eighty-thousand-Bitcoin reserve. When it sold Bitcoin to buy more UST, the whole crypto market declined on the weight of the Bitcoin selling. This had a cascading effect on UST and LUNA, which reinforced itself on Bitcoin and the broader market. Within less than three days UST / LUNA had imploded. Once trust is shattered, crypto traders move to new protocols and exchanges. Rarely are entities able to recover.

When Terra withdrew the initial 150 million dollars from the Curve 3pool, it had been too eager, as 4pool was not ready yet. The three billion dollars from 3pool would have likely moved to 4pool, as the latter would have provided more incentives for liquidity providers. In that case it would have required several billion dollars to break the liquidity in the pool, not just 350 million dollars. As it was, the attacker potentially made 800 million dollars in profits on the UST decline, and maybe even more if the LUNA tokens had been shorted.

In crypto rarely does anything happen that is entirely anonymous. So the question arises, who borrowed three billion dollars of Bitcoin from Gemini, and who dumped 650 million dollars of UST on Binance? Both these firms would know through their KYC (know your customer) process which client had broken the market. Matching OTC dealing relationships and checking wallets to users would also likely reveal who the attacker was.

Some thought that Alameda was behind the attack, as it was believed to have viewing access to FTX client positions and could therefore have seen where significant crypto hedge funds like 3AC which were large holders of LUNA tokens might start to get liquidated if collateral prices dropped to the auto-liquidation levels. This would then have allowed Alameda to trade against 3AC.

Months later—after the FTX implosion and revelations by Binance's CEO "CZ"—3AC cofounder Kyle Davies tweeted, "We now understand that FTX/Alameda hunted our positions."[428] Davies believes that 3AC messed up the thesis behind the LUNA / UST relationship. The quality of the backers, the builders, and the team behind Terraform Labs had attracted them, in spite of numerous warnings that the UST / LUNA constellation was a Ponzi scheme. The company should have spent more time on the mechanics, notably the potential contagion effect of a de-peg.

UST was once the third-largest stablecoin, and at one time LUNA had a market capitalization of forty-one billion dollars. All this vanished within three days. While other stablecoins also briefly de-pegged during the UST / LUNA crash, Tether processed over sixteen billion dollars of withdrawals as the USDT peg dropped to 0.95 dollars. But the fiat-backed peg quickly recovered.

Do Kwon becomes a crypto fugitive (2022–23)

In September 2022 South Korean prosecutors issued an INTERPOL warrant for Do Kwon's arrest on charges of fraud and breaches of capital markets law. South Korea has no extradition treaty with Serbia, where Do Kwon was hiding until his arrest.[429] Warrant arrests have also been issued for five other people linked to the UST / LUNA implosion.

On February 16 2023 the SEC charged Singapore-based Terraform Labs PTE. LTD. and Do Kwon with selling unregistered securities and running a fraudulent scheme that led to losses of at least forty billion dollars.[430] According to the SEC Do Kwon and Terraform Labs had "misled, deceived and defrauded investors." Contrary to Do Kwon's claims, for example, market forces had not been responsible for restoring the UST peg in May 2021. The restoration of the peg had actually resulted from a secret deal with a market maker, Jump Crypto.

Kwon had also made inaccurate statements about the e-commerce platform Chai using the Terra blockchain to transact. Despite Kwon's assertions there had been no breakthrough in the "real world" use of crypto as a payment method. Instead payments had been "deceptively replicated" and were purely sham transactions. Chai has written to its investors explaining that the use of blockchain to process payments is not legal in South Korea.

Kwon—the sole director of Terraform Labs, with ninety-two percent of its shares—is also believed to have transferred ten thousand Bitcoins from Terraform and LFG to a cold wallet used to transfer Bitcoin periodically to Sygnum Bank, a financial institution in Switzerland, which then converted the proceeds into cash. Over 100 million dollars is thought to have been converted into fiat in this way.

The SEC also investigated Do Kwon for money laundering.[431] According to Terra employees Kwon had withdrawn eighty million dollars per month for operating expenses a few months before the collapse. The SEC has seen an internal statement confirming that the funds were moved to dozens of virtual wallets. In addition Terraform might have violated the Securities Act, as Terra made it possible to buy U.S. stocks with LUNA tokens.

Just before the UST / LUNA crash Do Kwon had started sending money to South Korea's top law firm Kim & Chang. The sums involved—seven million dollars over the subsequent months—suggest that he was aware of rising legal problems.[432]

On April 25 2023 the South Korean authorities also indicted Daniel Shin and nine others on multiple charges related to the Terra cryptocurrency, including infringements of capital markets law such as illegal trading. The nine individuals worked in marketing, systems development, and management.[433]

The aftermath of the UST / LUNA implosion

In the weeks and months after the UST / LUNA implosion SBF projected strength to the public, leading many market participants to suspect that Alameda / FTX had made enormous sums of money during the crash. Some believed that Alameda had borrowed the three billion dollars of Bitcoin from Gemini to break the UST peg. Others believed that Alameda had been shorting LUNA.

But Alameda likely lost billions during the UST / LUNA crash. According to the latest evidence SBF sent Alameda four billion dollars of FTX customer money to bail it out.[434] Alameda was due to receive four billion dollars' worth of FTT tokens during the next unlock cycle on September 28 2022, but it needed a bridge loan until then. Nobody would notice. It could just be treated as a loan between friends.

22

"Supercycle thesis was regrettably wrong"
(Su Zhu, Three Arrows Capital)

Although FTX claimed that its liquidation engine was superior to that of other crypto exchanges, the opposite appears to have been the case. In fact liquidations on FTX were so infrequent, relatively speaking, that some suspected Alameda Research of subsidizing losses on FTX to attract trading volumes.[435]

As came to light in December 2022, Alameda could take unlimited risk on FTX without any danger of being liquidated.[436] The trading firm could run up substantial negative balances, which would be covered by FTX client funds and which were the backstop when the FTX liquidation engine failed or the insurance fund was depleted. But not only had Alameda deployed billions of dollars of capital near the peak of 2021 that subsequently went underwater; it was also handed the selling flow that customers could not execute on FTX when volumes were thin.

In early March 2021 MobileCoin completed an eleven-million-dollar funding round after receiving technical guidance from Moxie Marlinspike, the creator of the messaging app Signal.[437] MobileCoin, which focused on privacy-protecting payments, had launched an MOB token, which FTX had listed in December 2020. A trader on FTX used perpetual futures contracts to build a leveraged short position of 100 million dollars—equivalent to twenty-five percent of the overall MOB supply.[438] A large sell order then caused the token price to decline by twenty percent within minutes, and as liquidity was minimal on FTX for this contract, the exchange offered MOB holders three-thousand-percent yields if they loaned their tokens. But then the token price rallied, and the crypto investment firm CMS Holdings tweeted that "All Bears Will Die," a sign that it would squeeze the short seller of the MOB tokens.[439] Other traders started to buy too, and the price rebounded from seven dollars to sixty-seven dollars within ten days. Halfway through the rally the short seller stopped closing his/her position, letting the negative position run larger. The losses were likely so significant that the short seller walked away from his/her account on FTX. As the exchange was slow in liquidating accounts, it was stuck with the losses.

While one trader lost, another made enormous returns. This trader used his/her MOB tokens as collateral and borrowed against it on FTX,[440] extracting hundreds of millions of dollars from the platform. As MOB crashed back to six dollars shortly after, the borrower had no incentive to pay back the funds he had borrowed from the exchange, forfeiting his now nearly worthless MOB collateral in the process.

FTX is believed to have suffered nearly one billion dollars in losses from these MOB trades,[441] with the exchange and related entities carrying over a net operating loss of 3.7 billion dollars at the end of 2021.[442] This was a sign that FTX and Alameda had become financially unsound months before the UST / LUNA implosion.

FTX stated in its user terms, "the thing that causes socialized losses, and clawbacks, and auto-delevering, is when an account goes *beyond bankrupt.* If a user has a leveraged futures position on and markets move against their account enough that their net asset value is negative, then someone has to pay for that loss; and in crypto you can't reposses assets from the bankrupt account's owner from outside the system, so you're stuck with other users — the users who aren't getting liquidated — footing the bill."[443]

FTX had special agreements with market makers and liquidity providers. Third-party market makers were protected by the liquidation engine in case of "toxic flow," where market makers are providing liquidity at a loss to informed traders. Market makers adjust spreads according to the order flow of uninformed participants versus the order flow that materially impacts the midpoint between bid and offer prices. Uninformed order flow is usually random and distributed in nature. At the same time toxic flows such as arbitrage transactions and liquidations directly impact the midpoint.

As toxic flow is part of daily trading, market makers tend to widen the bid-offer spreads to compensate for the losses and price jump risk during liquidations. Alameda often posted stale quotes, luring in arbitrage activity and thus volume, thereby attracting retail interest and higher trading volumes.

To make up for these market-making losses, Alameda took over every liquidation and managed the risk discretionary based on internal models, instead of letting the algorithms execute it automatically. This allowed third-party market makers to quote much tighter prices on FTX, as toxic flows were removed entirely and instead sent to Alameda. As a result FTX could provide users with the best quotes and deepest liquidity. But the liquidation cascades subsequently came with the UST / LUNA crash, as positions could not be sold fast enough when FTX clients dumped them on the exchange. Alameda had to warehouse the position until prices recovered. But they never recovered.

If FTX had acknowledged its liquidation engine breakdown, it would have lost the third-party market makers, leading to a drop in flows, which would have made spreads more expensive. FTX would also have lost its competitive edge, jeopardizing its success. As BitMEX had already learned, once users lose trust in an exchange, their liquidity moves to other exchanges. So FTX needed to prevent any negative news from getting out.

During the LUNA collapse prices sometimes gapped up and down by thirty percent, and the way the FTX risk engine was designed made it impossible to liquidate customer positions during those wide swings. Quant trading firms usually switch off their algorithmic trading during extreme volatility. But Alameda was forced to take these positions onto its books.

Only a tiny group of SBF's inner circle had access to the data around the FTX liquidation engine, so only a few people knew about the actual losses that Alameda was accruing. Alameda had borrowed billions of dollars from crypto lending firms, and these firms had recalled their loans after the UST / LUNA incident. But as this was money that Alameda did not have anymore, there were only two ways out: declare bankruptcy or use FTX customer funds to fill the hole. SBF chose the latter option, even though it was against FTX's customer agreement terms. As a result he needed to move the media's attention away from any doubt about the financial strength of his firms which might have arisen from the crash.

FTX aims to increase its user base through acquisitions (2022)

During the week that UST / LUNA went under, a filing with the U.S. Securities and Exchange Commission (SEC) revealed that SBF had taken a 7.6-percent stake in the retail stock-trading platform Robinhood. A year earlier Robinhood had announced that its crypto wallet service had received one million waitlist requests.[444]

There was also speculation that FTX was trying to integrate stock trading and crypto trading. But to grow FTX, SBF needed more users, and trading volumes were dropping off as crypto entered a bear market. The pie was getting smaller, so SBF needed to get his hands on more slices to achieve growth.

3AC fails to meet margin calls (2022)

On June 17 2022 Three Arrows Capital (3AC) failed to make margin calls to crypto lender BlockFi.[445] The three-billion-dollar crypto hedge fund had potentially borrowed several billion dollars, pledging its two-billion-dollar stake in the Grayscale Bitcoin Trust (GBTC) as collateral. Its 200-million-dollar investment in Terraform Labs and another 600 million dollars' worth of LUNA tokens had evaporated over the course of the previous month.

Three Arrows, along with Alameda, was one of the most significant DeFi (decentralized finance) users. DeFi's total value locked (TVL) peaked at 255 billion dollars in December 2021, dropping to just forty-five billion dollars during the summer of 2022. But despite the bear market both trading firms continued to take risky DeFi bets.

Shortly before the news became public that 3AC could not make margin calls, thirty-two million dollars were transferred to a crypto wallet that belonged to a Cayman Islands–based entity controlled by the 3AC founders. At least another eleven million dollars were moved to an unknown address.

Three Arrows had strategic investments in crypto lenders such as the Panama-based Deribit crypto exchange, which offered it preferential lending rates. In 2020 3AC could take out Bitcoin loans from Deribit at just 2.5-percent annual fees. It also had a non-liquidating account agreement, giving it two more business days before collateral positions were liquidated.

On June 27 3AC defaulted on a 350-million-dollar USDC and 305-million-dollar Bitcoin loan to the crypto lender Voyager Digital. [446] Stephen Ehrlich, the CEO of Voyager, assured clients and customers that his firm was operating normally and also had a 300-million-dollar line of credit in Bitcoin and 200 million dollars in cash and USDC from Alameda Ventures. Less than two weeks later Voyager filed for bankruptcy.

On June 29 a court in the British Virgin Islands ordered 3AC to liquidate.[447] As recently as March 2022 3AC had managed ten billion dollars. Three months later it owed 3.5 billion dollars to twenty-seven different creditors, including 2.4 billion dollars to Genesis Global Trading. The parent company of Genesis, the Digital Currency Group (DCG), also owned the Grayscale business, the value of which 3AC had helped to drive up by buying GBTC shares.

In addition to Voyager Digital the crypto lenders Celsius Network and BlockFi both went bankrupt. All three firms took in deposits from primarily retail investors, promising yields of eight percent when fiat interest rates were near zero, before handing the funds over to 3AC for speculative trading. "People may call us stupid. They may call us stupid or delusional. And, I'll accept that. Maybe," 3AC's cofounder Su Zhu stated during an interview in July 2022.[448] When 3AC blew up, a domino credit event started to take down nearly all the firms that had lent excessively to the hedge fund.

Although it was initially reported that BlockFi had a net loan versus collateral mismatch of 600 million dollars at the end of the second quarter of 2022, BlockFi signed a deal with FTX to be acquired for up to 240 million dollars. The FTX credit line would wipe out all existing shareholders from previous equity rounds, but it was the only financial offer that CEO Zac Prince had received that would not subordinate client assets to the rescuer. A year earlier, in June 2021, BlockFi had been looking to raise 500 million dollars at a five-billion-dollar valuation.

23

"All funds are safe"
(Alex Mashinsky, Celsius Network)

C elsius Network was a crypto asset borrowing and lending platform facilitating various crypto loans. Celsius's business model, like many others, resembles that of a depository lender, which accepts monetary deposits from consumers and then uses those funds to provide liquidity to the market via loans and investments.

Crypto lenders are meant to invest funds responsibly, earn a return, and pay the depositors the interest they make and their principal back. The lender keeps the spread as a profit. Unlike traditional depository institutions crypto lending firms are generally uninsured against losses of customer funds. Also the loans are not made based on the borrowers' creditworthiness, but on collateral or business relationships. Borrowers must stay within an agreed-upon loan-to-collateral (LTC) ratio or the lender will liquidate the collateral to secure the loan.

Voyager Digital: promising high yields and engaging in speculative trading (2018–22)

Voyager Digital, a crypto brokerage, was a popular digital-asset lender offering customers high-yielding products through its app. The Toronto-based company was founded in 2018 by Steve Ehrlich, and its lending platform had more than 100 thousand creditors, with billions in liabilities.

Voyager promised high returns on entrusted crypto holdings, and allowed its users to trade over sixty crypto assets.

Voyager was listed on the Canadian stock exchange, where its shares rallied from 0.07 dollars in October 2020 to twenty-six dollars in March 2021, before peaking at nearly thirty dollars on April 5. Near the peak Ehrlich reportedly sold almost thirty-one million dollars of Voyager shares, although a complex and opaque corporate structure—including a reverse takeover of a defunct Canadian mining company and the acquisition and disposition of a Delaware limited-liability company—made it difficult to determine exactly how much he had sold. Some people believe it was a lot more than the thirty-one million dollars.[449]

In late 2021 and the first half of 2022 Alameda Research acquired two stakes in Voyager for a combined valuation of 11.6 percent and an overall cost of around 110 million dollars. But to avoid reporting requirements, Alameda surrendered 4.5 million shares, bringing its equity down to 9.5 percent—below the ten-percent reporting level.[450]

The playbook for the Alameda acquisition appeared familiar: the investment arm of a crypto trading firm buys a stake in a lender, and in return takes out a big loan from the firm. In September 2021 Alameda had taken out a 380-million-dollar loan from Voyager, split between Bitcoin and Ethereum. Voyager had collateral in the form of 4.65 million FTT tokens and 63.75 million Serum tokens. A year later prices had dropped fifty percent, and a bankruptcy judge had ordered Alameda to return the two-hundred-million-dollar loan to Voyager. While Alameda indicated its willingness to repay the loan on July 8, the firm only transferred the money on September 30.[451]

In March 2022 Voyager also lent crypto hedge fund Three Arrow Capital (3AC) nearly one billion dollars in users' crypto assets, with very little financial disclosure from the fund. Then, in June Voyager announced that 3AC had not repaid the loan plus interest, which was now worth 666 million dollars.

Also in June Alameda offered a 500-million-dollar bailout for Voyager,[452] which the crypto lender rejected as it could "harm customers." [453] According to Voyager's books the company had loaned 1.6 billion dollars in crypto to an entity based in the British Virgin Islands, where Alameda is registered.[454] On July 1 the company suspended "trading, deposits and withdrawals," before filing for bankruptcy on July 5.[455]

In September 2022 Binance and FTX bid fifty million dollars for Voyager's assets. FTX won the bid, causing Binance to feel increasingly disadvantaged when competing for U.S. assets and U.S.-based clients.

Later in 2022 *Shark Tank* cast member Mark Cuban faced a class-action lawsuit for his promotion of Voyager. In the previous October Cuban, who also owns the NBA (National Basketball Association) team the Dallas Mavericks, had announced a five-year partnership between the Mavericks and Voyager.[456] The lawsuit against Cuban claimed that he and Voyager's CEO Steve Ehrlich had used their influence to mispresent the brokerage and defraud users of five billion dollars.[457] The suit described Voyager as a Ponzi scheme that "targeted young and inexperienced investors." Cuban had endorsed Voyager, saying "it's easy, cheap, fast, and the pricing is good."

In September 2022 FTX.US won a 1.4-billion-dollar auction for Voyager. At the time the value of all Voyager's crypto assets on hand was only 1.3 billion dollars, making the winning bid an eight-percent-premium on the market value of the assets. Just fifty-one million dollars were paid for Voyager's assets, intellectual property and user base. An additional sixty-million dollars consisted of an accumulated fifty dollars account credit for each of Voyager's users successfully onboarding with FTX and a twenty-million dollars "earn out" allowance.[458] Voyager claimed to have had 3.5 million customers before filing for bankruptcy.

Genesis Global Trading: the backbone of OTC crypto trading (2013–23)

Genesis Global Trading launched in 2013 as one of the five subsidiaries of the Digital Currency Group (DCG). Genesis was a crypto trading, lending, and asset custody platform which targeted institutional clients and high-net-worth individuals. In early 2020 it acquired the London-based crypto custodian Volt.

Figure 26: Genesis Global Trading's loan book (billion dollars)

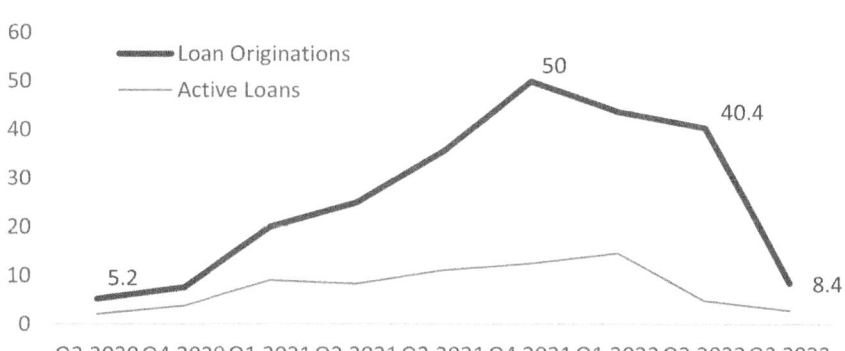

Genesis was the largest crypto lender, with a quarterly fifty-billion-dollar loan origination book. In the second and third quarters of 2022 the company unwound ten billion dollars of loans, causing many defaults in the industry and forcing borrowers to liquidate assets.[459] In late June and early July Genesis publicly revealed that it had been exposed to hundreds of millions of dollars in losses from loans to Hong Kong–based Babel Finance as well as 3AC, and that its parent company, DCG, had taken on some of its debt to keep the company afloat.

As Alameda was the largest crypto borrower, it had potential business relationships with Genesis. But it appears that neither Alameda nor FTX was a creditor of Genesis when FTX filed for bankruptcy in November 2022. Any loans that had been closed out within ninety days of the bankruptcy filing could be subject to clawbacks. So the question arose if any loans were paid back after August 13 2022, as these loans would have been a long-term liability for Genesis since the FTX bankruptcy proceedings will likely take many years.

On November 10 2022 Genesis revealed that it had lost 175 million dollars in the bankruptcy of FTX. The company subsequently told its clients that it had paused withdrawals while it shored up cash. It had also approached Binance for investment and to bid for its loan book.

Before it suspended withdrawals, Genesis had been seeking a one-billion-dollar emergency loan as it entered a "liquidity crunch due to certain illiquid assets on its balance sheet."[460] DCG owed 575 million dollars to Genesis. These loans, which had funded investment opportunities and the repurchasing of stock from non-employee shareholders, were part of DCG's overall debts to Genesis of just over two billion dollars.

On January 20 2023 in a letter to shareholders DCG's CEO Barry Silbert reminded investors that DCG had stepped in and assumed liabilities from Genesis related to 3AC through a 1.1-billion-dollar promissory note due in June 2032.[461] But on January 19 2023 Genesis Global Holdco and two of its lending business subsidiaries, Genesis Global Capital and Genesis Asia Pacific finally filed for bankruptcy protection.[462]

Babel Finance: speculating with customer funds once and then twice (2018–22)

Founded in 2018, Babel Finance, a Hong Kong–based crypto lending and trading firm, suspended withdrawals on June 17 2022. The firm had become a crypto bank by offering both savings and lending products. Only a year earlier Babel had closed a forty-million-dollar equity round, having provided two billion dollars in crypto loans since its founding. By May 2022 Babel had raised another eighty million dollars from venture capital investors, its lifetime loan book having increased to three billion dollars by the end of 2021.

In July 2022 Babel revealed that it had lost over 280 million dollars in proprietary trading with customer funds.[463] When prices fell from thirty thousand to twenty thousand dollars per Bitcoin in June 2022, its unhedged positions faced liquidation and it could not meet margin calls from counterparties. The firm's proprietary trading had not been mentioned in any venture capital rounds nor officially recorded in its systems. The proprietary trading desk had enjoyed uncapped access to Babel's customer accounts.

In March 2020 Babel had accessed customer accounts to speculate on rising Bitcoin prices, only to be wrong-footed during the Black Thursday crash. An audio conversation between Del Wang, Babel's cofounder, and an unknown person was leaked online, revealing the trades.[464] In the recordings Wang said that Babel had started buying at prices of three thousand dollars per Bitcoin in early 2019. The initial capital had come from 750 thousand dollars raised from NeoGrowth Credit and another four million dollars from NeoGrowth's deposits on the Babel platform. Wang also said that Babel had pledged the purchased Bitcoin to another lender to borrow more when Bitcoin climbed above four thousand dollars. When prices climbed still higher, he levered the position up even more. Only Flex Yang, Babel's cofounder and CEO, and Wang had initially known about this "X Plan" ("X" standing for leverage), although later three other shareholders also became aware of it.

At one point during the Black Thursday crash Babel owed Tether two to three thousand Bitcoins to meet the 100-percent collateral-to-loan (CTL) ratio. If Tether did not choose to liquidate Babel, it meant it had taken a mismatch on its balance sheet. When the crash happened on March 12 2020, Tether agreed to extend Babel's margin call by a month, with Babel asking for additional credit loans from Tether so that it could meet margin calls from other lenders. These Babel debts were transferred over to Tether. In April Bitcoin prices rose above six thousand dollars, and with Babel's new savings products, the firm could gather more assets.

In June 2022 Babel said that the firm had 350 million dollars in outstanding loans, with most of its capital coming from other lenders rather than customers' deposits, which were still relatively small. BlockFi, Genesis Capital, and Tether were the firm's borrowing partners.

Babel's investment strategy was to pledge one million dollars' worth of Bitcoin to borrow one million dollars' worth of USDT, which it would then use to buy another one million dollars' worth of Bitcoin, pledge, and repeat. Babel's customers could only borrow at a CTL rate of 160 percent, with the extra sixty percent sitting on Babel's balance sheet. The firm claimed that Chinese Bitcoin miners were its primary lending customers, as they would always meet their margin calls since they actually mine the Bitcoin.

Although Babel raised capital in May 2022 at a two-billion-dollar valuation, the firm faced bankruptcy one month later. Its favorable lending terms had allowed it to accumulate significant leveraged long positions, and while it got away for a long time with speculating with customer funds, destiny eventually caught up with it.

Singapore crypto exchange Zipmex had offered users a high-yielding lending program that transferred funds to Babel, which subsequently speculated with the money. Zipmex, which also had exposure to Celsius, lent 100 million dollars to Babel, and consequently had to halt customer withdrawals when Babel went under.

FTX uses customer funds to offer credit lines to bankrupt lenders (2022)

On July 2 2022 FTX gained an option to acquire crypto lender BlockFi for up to 240 million dollars.[465] With the acquisition of BlockFi and Voyager Digital by FTX.US, Sam Bankman-Fried (SBF) could now move money from the somewhat regulated FTX.US to the unregulated FTX.com central exchange and then into Alameda by using BlockFi's and Voyager's lending books.

On March 11 2021 BlockFi had raised 350 million dollars at a three-billion-dollar valuation. At the time it had ten billion dollars in outstanding loans and fifteen billion dollars in total assets. User numbers had increased from ten thousand in late 2019 to 225 thousand by 2021, and in early 2021 BlockFi was using the Grayscale Bitcoin Trust (GBTC) premium to make money off arbitrage trades for both its clients and itself.

But by June 30 2022, after the UST / LUNA crash, BlockFi had only 3.9 billion dollars in deployable client assets, with thirty-five percent of them held at third-party custodians. And when Celsius stopped withdrawals in early June, users started removing their funds from the BlockFi platform.[466]

FTX.US made 400 million dollars of credit available to BlockFi. If FTX had drawn down these 400 million dollars, FTX.US customer funds could have been channeled to FTX and Alameda. Some compared FTX's bidding for crypto assets as an exercise on the dating app Tinder,[467] while others thought FTX was buying these assets to prevent it from being "market to zero on their own books."[468]

When FTX imploded in early November, BlockFi had to clarify their business relationship. "We have significant exposure to FTX and associated corporate entities that encompass obligations owned to the U.S. by Alameda, assets held at FTX.com, and undrawn amounts from our credit line with FTX.US."[469]

BlockFi had 650 thousand funded accounts, while Voyager Digital had 1.6 million. Both firms focused on crypto investors based in the U.S., promising yield payments of twelve percent per annum to customers. These yields needed to be generated either through charging borrowers at least that amount on loans or putting the money to work in DeFi (decentralized finance) protocols that were riskier but higher yielding.

BlockFi finally filed for bankruptcy protection on November 28 2022. An accidentally uploaded financial presentation by M3 Partners, which acts as an advisor to the creditor committee, revealed that BlockFi had 415.9 million dollars in exposure to FTX and 831.3 million dollars in loans to Alameda—nearly half of the 2.7 billion dollars in unadjusted assets.[470] BlockFi was heavily exposed and dependent on FTX and its entities. Seventy-three percent of its users had account balances below one thousand dollars, and the firm only generated twenty-one dollars in revenue per user between May and November 2022—just fourteen million dollars.

The Celsius bankruptcy: crypto's Lehman Brothers moment (2023)

Celsius Network was another deposit and lending platform founded during the last crypto boom in 2017. Its bankruptcy has been labeled the crypto industry's Lehman Brothers moment.[471] The company relied on vast retail deposits that it lent to large crypto companies, which subsequently pursued risky bets. Celsius's CEO Alex Mashinsky, who was born in Ukraine and raised in Israel, promised eighteen-percent yields on crypto. As a result the company's assets increased fourfold to twenty-five billion dollars in 2021.

Celsius was a bank for cryptocurrencies without regulation, so federal deposit insurance did not cover deposits. Mashinsky had raised fifty million dollars in 2018 through a Celsius token (CEL) sale, with Tether one of the investors. The company moved from the U.K. to the U.S. in June 2021, when the U.K.'s Financial Conduct Authority (FCA) was rolling out a new registration regime for crypto companies.

Celsius's most common yield products offered three to eight percent in annual interest on Bitcoin, four to seven percent on Ethereum, and nine to eleven percent on Tether. Its highest yield was eighteen percent on Synthetix (SNX tokens). Users could earn an even higher yield if they staked SNX directly on Synthetix, a DeFi protocol for issuing synthetic assets that tracks and provides returns for other assets without requiring the user to hold the asset. The highest interest rates were paid to customers who agreed to receive their yields in CEL. Celsius was the biggest holder of CEL, having spent an estimated 350 million dollars buying back CEL tokens from the market since 2019—a strategy which had driven the price significantly higher. At its peak on June 2021 CEL had a market capitalization of 3.4 billion dollars.

Celsius made it easy for users to earn a yield on its platform. Staking SNX tokens on Synthetix was complicated and involved interacting with an Ethereum-based smart contract. Holders of SNX needed to transfer the tokens to an Ethereum wallet such as MetaMask and then connect it to Synthetix.io to initiate the smart contract. But by staking SNX, the user was incurring a debt to the Synthetix network, issued initially as sUSD (synthetic USD), and once the user paid back the debt, the SNX, held as collateral, was freed up. To prevent the withdrawal of SNX, the rewards were locked up in escrow for a year and could not be transferred during that time. Users also had to claim the rewards every week.

In 2021 various regulators from Alabama, Kentucky, New Jersey, and Texas ordered or threatened Celsius not to sell its products, as the tokens might be unregistered securities according to federal rules. [472] The regulators suggested that Celsius needed to be more transparent with users on how it generated returns. Mashinsky claimed that Celsius could offer such high yields because, unlike other companies, it passed on all generated yields to its users. He came up with the idea to share real-life stories about how Celsius users had gained financial freedom through the yield programs on its platform, often reminding them that they "still have the responsibility to help others" in the crypto community.

From March 2021 until the end of the year Celsius assets under management on the platform increased from ten billion to twenty-five billion dollars. Meanwhile a capital raise of 400 million dollars was upsized to 750 million dollars at a three-billion-dollar valuation, allowing the company to increase its head count from 150 to 550 employees. By this time Celsius claimed to have 1.7 million users. But by January 21 2022 assets had declined to 18.1 billion dollars and the firm's eighteen-percent yields on crypto were starting to draw scrutiny.[473]

Former employees have indicated that, besides lending to institutional investors, Celsius invested hundreds of millions of dollars of customer funds through DeFi protocols, starting in 2020. Employees watched YouTube videos on how to interact with these protocols, with some traders joking that Celsius's money was always involved whenever there was a DeFi blowup. The former employees also claimed that the company did not do enough due diligence when it started to engage with DeFi, although the compliance team did raise red flags as internal controls were insufficient to prevent employees from moving funds around. On May 11 2022 Celsius pulled 463 million dollars from the Anchor Protocol during the UST / LUNA chaos.[474]

In December 2021 Celsius lost fifty-four million dollars when hackers stole 115 million dollars' worth of Wrapped Bitcoin from users of the Bitcoin-focused BadgerDAO protocol. Instead of exploiting the protocol directly, the hackers had gone after the web interface connecting BadgerDAO to the users' wallets. So when its Discord users interacted with BadgerDAO, they received additional permission requests. Then, once they had clicked the approved window, their crypto wallet contents were transferred to the wallets controlled by the hackers.

As demand for loans from institutional investors waned, Celsius began taking more significant risks to generate yield. Its compliance department warned about poor oversight, weak internal systems, and potentially misrepresenting financial information.[475] But even as the price of the native CEL token was dropping, management kept telling users to "hodl" while the company itself was selling large chunks of its CEL holdings.

In early 2023 the State of New York filed a lawsuit against Celsius's by then former CEO Mashinsky for defrauding and misleading investors about the firm's health by making false statements between 2018 and at least June 2022.[476] Mashinsky had resigned as CEO in September 2022, having withdrawn ten million dollars from the company weeks before it halted withdrawals. Since many crypto lending and borrowing firms were trying to prevent a bank run as user funds had been lost, they often claimed publicly that the funds were safe, only to file for bankruptcy protection later.

Celsius did not appear to be too concerned about its missing funds, as its terms of service made it clear that "all digital assets transferred to Celsius as part of the service are owned and held by Celsius for its account."[477] In January 2023 a bankruptcy judge ruled that Celsius would win most of its customer funds, leaving the customers at a lower priority level.[478]

During the summer of 2022 Ethereum had declined to nearly one thousand dollars and the crypto industry needed support. Otherwise it was all over for Alameda and FTX. So SBF went on a market-stabilization buying spree. CNBC market commentator Jim Cramer quipped that SBF was "the new JP Morgan,"[479] alluding to the Panic of 1907, when New York's most famous banker stepped in to support the market when stocks had fallen fifty percent from their peak.

Celsius had also been looking for capital by offering instant access to staking yields while its traders' synthetic-token funds were locked up for a year. SBF, through FTX, was considering a loan to Celsius, but during the due diligence process he realized that Celsius needed a two-billion-dollar bailout. This was too much for FTX, and Celsius halted withdrawals and filed for bankruptcy protection shortly afterward. The day after it froze investor funds Gary Gensler, chair of the U.S. Securities and Exchange Commission (SEC), said that crypto tokens probably meet the definition of securities, and that products that offer incredibly high yields seem "too good to be true."[480]

In 2020, when DeFi took off, Mashinsky and Celsius's cofounder and CTO Nuke Goldstein wanted to get involved. But lacking expertise in yield farming, they invested their money with KeyFi, a software staking and crypto investment firm that profited from crypto protocols. They then made a handshake deal with KeyFi to serve as Celsius's investment manager. Celsius set up a special purpose vehicle (SPV) that KeyFi managed. For its services and expertise KeyFi received 7.5-percent net profits for staking and 20 percent from DeFi trading.

Without a formal agreement Celsius transferred hundreds of millions of dollars in crypto assets to KeyFi founder Jason Stone and his team. It also created a new Ethereum address, the 0xb1 account, which Celsius had complete control over but which could also be accessed by Stone's team by using a VPN to log into a computer controlled by Celsius that was already logged into the 0xb1 account.

The assets under management of the SPV totaled nearly two billion dollars by the end of the partnership in March 2021. Celsius traders were supposed to hedge crypto price fluctuations and protect against impermanent loss (IL), which in DeFi trading is caused by exchange rate volatility in liquidity pools. But the business relationship started to break down when Stone discovered that Celsius was actively using customer funds to manipulate crypto assets and also customer Bitcoin deposits to inflate the value of its own CEL token. According to a complaint filed by KeyFi on July 7 2022 improper accounting had resulted in 200 million dollars in liabilities which the company did not even understand.[481] The complaint also alleged that Celsius had been operating a Ponzi-style investment scheme, and that it had failed to honor its handshake profit-sharing agreement.

But when the firm exited its positions, Celsius allegedly suffered IL, and on August 23 it countersued KeyFi, claiming deceit and incompetency leading to tens of millions of dollars in losses.[482] Celsius declared that KeyFi had mispresented itself and Stone as a DeFi expert. It also claimed that it had stolen millions of dollars in coins from Celsius wallets, bought an interest in other crypto companies, and moved Celsius coins through the DeFi protocol Tornado Cash, where they became undetected.

An independent examiner appointed by the New York bankruptcy court later confirmed that in some instances during the days before Celsius stopped withdrawals, it had directly used new customer deposits to fund customer withdrawal requests. The examiner added that Celsius had also used customer assets since 2020 to fund operational expenses and rewards. By mid-2021 thirty-six percent of Celsius loans were unsecured, and some of the collateral was in unstable assets such as FTX's FTT tokens.

24

"A highly profitable trading strategy"
(Avraham Eisenberg, Fortress DAO)

Tornado Cash is an open-source protocol that mixes together potentially identifiable or tainted cryptocurrency funds with other funds to disconnect the trail back to the source. The funds of many users are pooled together and shuffled in a seemingly random fashion, before they are returned to the user's deposited address or a new address. The funds can also remain in the pool if the user wants them to. Pools exist in Ethereum (ETH), Circle (USDC), Tether (USDT), DAI, Compound DAI (CDAI), and Wrapped Bitcoin (WBTC). The Tornado Cash DAO (Decentralized Autonomous Organization) charges a 0.05-to-0.20-percent fee that accrues in part to the protocol.

Tornado Cash was initially released on December 17 2019 by Roman Semenov, Alexey Pertsev, and Roman Storm. Since then around 7.6 billion dollars in Ethereum has gone through the mixer. Almost thirty percent of these funds have been tied to illicit actors.[483] Political donations have also been moved through Tornado Cash without leaving any trail. Vitalik Buterin has used the protocol for this purpose.[484]

On August 8 2022 the U.S. Treasury's Office of Foreign Assets Control (OFAC) blocked Tornado Cash, making it illegal for U.S. citizens and residents to receive or send money through the protocol.[485] According to the Treasury Department the North Korean Lazarus Group is believed to have been an active user of Tornado Cash, laundering over 455 million dollars' worth of the 625 million dollars' worth of cryptocurrency stolen from Axie Infinity's Ronin Bridge protocol. On August 10 Alex Pertsev was arrested in Amsterdam on suspicion of involvement in concealing criminal flows. He was released after nine months under surveillance, awaiting trial from home.

Hackers were increasingly targeting crypto bridges, which were also called cross-chain bridges. These bridges allowed users to transfer digital assets and information from one blockchain to another, enabling token transfers, smart contracts, and data exchange between independent platforms. Often hackers, and others who had gained possession of crypto assets through illicit activities, would use mixers like Tornado Cash.

Wintermute gets hacked for 160 million dollars (2022)

On September 20 2022 crypto market maker and liquidity provider Wintermute was hacked for about 160 million dollars in DeFi (decentralized finance) operations, with the hacker likely exploiting an old address with administrator access.[486] The hacker funneled 111 million USDT, USDC, and DAI through Curve's 3pool platform.

The Wintermute wallet used a vanity address, which replaced the letters and numbers in a typical Ethereum address with zeros to make it look simpler. Earlier in September a vanity address tool called Profanity had disclosed a critical bug that made its addresses unsafe to use, although it remains unknown whether Wintermute actually used Profanity. Nevertheless Mudit Gupta, chief information officer at Polygon Technology, suspected the hack was due to a hot wallet compromised as a result of the disclosed Profanity bug. Profanity generated an address with a 0x0000000 prefix, which is so simple it can be "brute-forced" in seconds using regular hardware. Through the invalid address the hacker then transferred the funds from Wintermute to Curve's 3pool. Evgeny Gaevoy, the founder and CEO of Wintermute, subsequently offered the hacker a ten-percent bounty on the funds taken.

The hacker avoided moving the funds through Tornado Cash, as it had been sanctioned by the U.S. Treasury. Instead he/she mixed them with other stablecoins in Curve's 3pool, which meant that either Circle or Tether would have had to freeze all the funds in 3pool. This was the first time that a decentralized exchange had been used to obscure funds.

Wintermute was a heavy borrower in the DeFi liquidity marketplace Clearpool, with twenty-two million dollars in USDC outstanding. The trading firm also had an outstanding loan with TrueFi for ninety-two million dollars in USDT, and a seventy-five-million-dollar loan with DeFi protocol Maple Finance. The loan with TrueFi matured on October 15, and the crypto world was monitoring whether Wintermute would be able to repay it. It did.

Wintermute was started by Gaevoy, who grew up in Moscow, along with Yoann Turpin and Harro Mantel. Gaevoy's wife, Marina Gurevich, who was raised in Siberia, is the firm's COO. The two met in college, at the Higher School of Economics in Moscow, where they were both placed in the top ten percent of their class and assigned to the same working group. They got married in 2006, and Gaevoy's first job out of college was in Amsterdam, at the trading firm Optiver. In 2017 Gaevoy started trading crypto with just twenty thousand dollars of his own money.

During the crypto bear market of 2018 Gaevoy teamed up with Turpin and Mantel to found Wintermute. It took them nine months to raise less than a million dollars for their crypto trading startup, which they had named after an artificial intelligence creature from the 1984 science fiction novel *Neuromancer*.

In 2019 Wintermute had just half a million dollars to trade with, bringing in less than one million dollars in revenue. But Gaevoy continued building his arbitrage strategies. His breakthrough came during the Black Thursday crash on May 12 2020, when the firm made 120 thousand dollars in twenty-four hours. The following July Wintermute raised 2.8 million dollars in a venture capital round led by Jeremy Liew of Lightspeed Venture Partners. This is when his wife joined the company to run the operations side, while Mantel left shortly after to spend more time with his family.

Wintermute started market-making on the DeFi protocol SushiSwap and other DeFi tokens that offered huge spreads which could be arbitraged away. In 2020 the firm made fifty-three million dollars in revenue and negotiated contracts with protocols that gave it interest-free loans. Protocols tended to provide market makers with free tokens, with options to buy more tokens at a fixed price in the future. Because of the 2020 DeFi summer bull market these deals turned out to be extremely lucrative. The more Wintermute traded, the more it could borrow from lenders.

In 2021 Wintermute traded 1.5 trillion dollars, generating 1.05 billion dollars in revenue and making 582 million dollars in profit—all with just fifty-three employees.[487] This works out at nearly eleven million dollars in earnings per employee. The firm paid out thirty-five million dollars in dividends, and Gaevoy's thirty-three percent stake in the company netted him a twelve-million-dollar payday.

In 2022 revenues were less than 300 million dollars, and as the firm grew, its profitability changed. Wintermute now had ninety-five employees, and the tokens it received for market-making had dropped significantly. The company also had fifty-nine million dollars locked on FTX when the exchange filed for bankruptcy. But as an influential crypto market maker it gained a seat on the FTX creditor committee, where it could steer decisions about winding up the exchange.[488]

Avraham Eisenberg and the 116-million-dollar Mango Markets exploit

On October 11 2022 Mango Markets, a Solana-based decentralized exchange, tweeted that a hacker had drained over 116 million dollars in crypto assets from the platform. Governed by a DAO comprising holders of its native MNGO token, Mango is a protocol that lets investors lend, borrow, swap, and use leverage to trade crypto.

While Mango tweeted that a hacker had manipulated its price oracle, the perpetrator, Avraham Eisenberg, claimed to have executed "a highly profitable trading strategy."[489] Eisenberg had created two anonymous accounts at Mango and funded each with five million dollars in USDC stablecoins. One account took a leveraged long position of nineteen million dollars in MNGO perpetual futures contracts; the other took an offsetting short position of nineteen million dollars in MGNO perpetual derivatives contracts. This would later be seen as a wash trading transaction.

After establishing his positions, Eisenberg submitted and executed a series of large purchases of the thinly traded MNGO tokens at incrementally higher prices to artificially raise their price. The trading volume was two thousand percent higher on October 11 than the average of the ninety preceding days.

MNGO perpetual futures contracts increased by 1,300 percent, and the increase in value of Eisenberg's long position allowed him to use it as collateral to borrow and ultimately withdraw the 116 million dollars' worth of crypto assets from the platform. The total value of users' assets on Mango at the time was approximately 104 million dollars. The platform used the deposits and investments belonging to other Mango users to loan the assets to Eisenberg. Subsequently the MGNO price dropped by ninety percent.

Two members of Mango's Upgrade Council, a seven-member group of Solana and Mango insiders, negotiated with Eisenberg to return some of the funds. A DAO governance proposal was passed with 9.46 percent of the MNGO token holders voting, 5.17 percent of which were controlled by the two Upgrade Council members. Mango DAO then offered Eisenberg a white-knight forty-seven-million-dollar bug bounty and the promise of not pressing charges if he returned sixty-seven million dollars' worth of tokens. Eisenberg publicly agreed to the terms.

The Commodity Futures Trading Commission (CFTC) and the U.S. Securities and Exchange Commission (SEC) would later charge Eisenberg with fraud, market manipulation, and violating the Commodity Exchange Act.[490] The SEC claimed that the MGNO tokens that Eisenberg had purchased and manipulated were bought and sold as investment contracts and were therefore securities that fell under U.S. federal securities laws. Eisenberg, who operated out of Puerto Rico, fled the territory, but was arrested shortly after his return on December 26. After being hit with a lawsuit, Eisenberg was also sued by Mango Markets for over forty-seven million dollars in damages plus interest, with the agreement between the DAO and Eisenberg rendered "invalid and unenforceable."[491]

On November 22 2022 Eisenberg had attempted to exploit the DeFi protocol Aave, first swapping forty million dollars in USDC on November 13 into Aave to borrow Curve DAO Tokens (CRV), which he intended to dump. He then borrowed fifteen million dollars' worth of CRV and transferred them to the crypto exchange OKX for selling. Many DeFi traders had used CRV as collateral, and a sharp drop in the price could have triggered auto-liquidations, causing the price of CRV to decline further.

At first, it seemed Eisenberg was attempting to liquidate Curve's founder, Michael Egorov, after he took out a forty-eight million dollar CRV loan on AAVE with a liquidation price of 0.259 dollars. But the trade to short CRV tokens on Aave was just a distraction.[492] Because while Aave's users were trying to short-squeeze the attacker by buying CRV to defend its price, Eisenberg was hoping for Aave to buy back his CRV short position, as there was insufficient liquidity to cover more than twenty percent of the position. This would have caused upward slippage of 100 percent due to illiquidity, as liquidations are dependent on the decentralized exchange's available liquidity. As a result Aave's looping system would have had to sell significant tokens from its safety module to cover the loss.

Eisenberg's plan can be seen as an attempt to spectacularly bankrupt the Aave protocol and make the Aave token price drop sharply. However the attack did not work as planned, as Aave had more liquidity than expected.

So before the CRV token could fall to the level where the collateral would automatically have been liquidated, CRV started to rally sharply—largely on the back of a Curve white paper for CRV-USD, the company's version of an over-collateralized crypto stablecoin.[493] As a result Eisenberg lost ten million dollars.

The Aave attack also shed light on the issue of rehypothecation, a feature of Aave's borrowing and lending pools. Users can deposit assets in the pools and then borrow against them, depositing the funds again to borrow even more, thereby enabling a loop-borrow scheme for maximum leverage.

PART SIX: FTX—ONE OF THE BIGGEST FINANCIAL FRAUDS

25

"We won't pretend to make love after divorce"
(Changpeng "CZ" Zhao, Binance)

By September 2022 Sam Bankman-Fried (SBF) was contemplating whether to shut down Alameda Research, as the firm's co-CEO, Sam Trabucco, had left the company on August 25.[494] Trabucco's departure was a surprise to many in the industry, as during his tenure as Alameda's co-leader he had been named in *Forbes Magazine*'s "30 Under 30" list. But in hindsight it seems clear that Trabucco resigned. He was just there for the money, and Alameda was so deep in the red that there was no point in staying any longer.

Despite being Alameda's other co-CEO, Caroline Ellison only made minor trading decisions and mainly consulted with SBF. She was not highly respected in the firm, and with her shy demeanor and childish looks lacked authority. SBF started drafting a document titled "We came, we saw, we researched," positing Alameda's closure.[495] He believed that the firm's lack of hedging had cost it more expected value than all the money it could have made or would ever make, and that generating a return above the current borrowing rate seemed impossible.

Before Trabucco's resignation FTX Ventures had absorbed Alameda's venture capital operations. At the time there was speculation this indicated that FTX needed to bail out Alameda. But Amy Wu, who ran the FTX Ventures fund, said that no payments were made as part of the new arrangement. One of the first deals that FTX Ventures signed after the agreement had been finalized was for a stake in the alternative-asset manager SkyBridge Capital.

FTX Ventures acquires a stake in SkyBridge (2022)

On September 9 2022 FTX Ventures announced the acquisition of a thirty-percent stake in SkyBridge Capital, a well-known hedge fund founded by Anthony Scaramucci. SkyBridge had strong ties to the alternative investment industry in New York and had cultivated access for wealthy clients to the best-known investment managers for years.[496]

In July 2022 Legion Strategies, a hedge fund affiliated with SkyBridge, had halted investor redemptions after steep declines in stocks and cryptocurrencies.[497] As a result private investments, which were harder to value as they were not traded daily on public markets, became twenty percent of the underlying portfolio—an excessive amount which resulted in the firm being unable to access the portfolio's fair value.

In the September 2022 redemption window SkyBridge's largest fund was also hit with redemptions of sixty percent of the fund's value, as it had declined thirty-eight percent. The fund had a fourteen-percent allocation to FTX and had diversified its deposits to almost one third, being heavily exposed to crypto assets. SkyBridge was only able return ten percent of the fund's value at the September redemption window.

SkyBridge was the organizer of the SkyBridge Alternatives (SALT) conference, a capital introduction convention for traditional finance firms, and in April 2022 SALT and FTX had launched the Crypto Bahamas conference, with two thousand delegates. In the lead-up to the conference Scaramucci had opened his Rolodex to leading investment professionals and politicians, and the featured speakers included former U.S. President Bill Clinton and former U.K. Prime Minister Tony Blair, as well as NFL (National Football League) quarterback Tom Brady and his wife, former supermodel Gisele Bündchen—both of whom were investors in FTX. The conference was booked out months ahead, and it was so successful that the SALT / FTX team booked the hotel for Crypto Bahamas 2023 in advance.

In October 2020 SkyBridge had started investing in crypto, and by the following December it had begun to set up a Bitcoin fund.[498] In September

2021 the company then partnered with Algorand, a Layer 1 crypto protocol, to raise 100 million dollars for the SkyBridge Algorand Fund, which declined ninety percent in value over the following twelve months.

In 2021 and 2022 SkyBridge had bought equity stakes in FTX, and as the crypto market declined and SkyBridge struggled, the firm received a forty-five-million-dollar investment from FTX Ventures. Under the terms of the deal SkyBridge was obliged to spend forty million dollars buying cryptocurrencies, ten million dollars of which had to be spent on FTX's native token FTT. The deal helped SBF to support the FTT token, which was crucial for collateral management.

Four billion dollars of FTT are transferred from Alameda to FTX (2022)

On September 27 2022 the president of FTX.US, Brett Harrison, resigned. The next day FTX received four billion dollars' worth of FTT tokens from Alameda. Harrison had been at FTX.US since May 2021, having previously worked for almost eight years as a trading systems technology head at Jane Street Capital, where he had taught a programming-for-traders course which SBF had attended.

A day after Harrison's resignation 173 million tokens, with a market value of four billion dollars, were due to be unlocked according to the FTT initial-coin-offering (ICO) token supply.[499] The recipient of the tokens, which constituted an increase of 124 percent in the overall token supply, was Alameda. And while this was not unusual in itself, it was suspect that the funds were immediately transferred to a wallet controlled by FTX.

According to the ICO contract FTT tokens vest automatically. So if Alameda had filed for bankruptcy in May 2022 after the UST / LUNA implosion, the 173 million FTT tokens would have been liquidated through the bankruptcy process, ultimately hurting FTX as the exchange used the FTT token as collateral. But if, on the other hand, FTX had transferred four billion dollars of (customer) funds in May to Alameda so that the trading firm could fulfill its margin call obligations, and if Alameda had then transferred back four billion dollars in FTT tokens that vested in September, then Alameda could be saved.

Caroline Ellison later told a judge that FTX officials knew the crypto exchange had lent Alameda its customer funds to help meet liabilities.[500] SBF had secretly moved ten billion dollars of customer funds from FTX to Alameda. Ellison told employees in a video meeting that she, SBF, Nishad Singh, and Gary Wang were all aware of the decision to move the funds.[501]

Nishad Singh had joined Alameda in December 2017, after working as an engineer at Facebook for five months. A high-school friend of SBF's younger brother, Gabe, Singh studied at Crystal Springs Uplands School in California where annual tuition fees run to sixty-one thousand dollars per student and graduated from the University of California, Berkeley in 2017 with a degree in electrical engineering and computer science. After seventeen months as an engineer at Alameda, he moved to FTX in April 2019. Singh had a 7.8-percent stake in FTX, received a 543-million-dollar loan from Alameda, and donated eight million dollars to the Democratic Party. His girlfriend, Claire Watanabe, later joined FTX as its head of marketing and human resources.[502]

Singh was part of SBF's inner circle and lived in the forty-million-dollar penthouse in the Albany Bahamas resort where SBF and the others also stayed. The inner circle used a Signal chat group called Wirefraud.[503] Signal is an instant messaging app with end-to-end encryption which stores messages only on users' devices, not on Signal's servers or anywhere else. SBF had asked employees to use Signal and to set it to auto-delete messages after brief periods so that no communication within the app could be used against them at a later date.

SBF's crypto bill and Alameda's balance sheet both get leaked (2022)

During an October 14 2022 interview with Politico, SBF said that he could spend one billion dollars in political funds until the 2024 presidential election, a statement he subsequently backtracked on.[504] Six days later Delphi Labs' general counsel Gabriel Shapiro leaked a bill circulating in Washington, D.C., drafted by FTX / SBF.[505] The proposal outlined SBF's beliefs that every crypto transaction should comply with the U.S. Treasury's Office of Foreign Assets Control (OFAC) sanctions, and that all front-end DeFi protocols should register as brokers.

Industry experts saw this proposal as limiting crypto to speculation instead of focusing on improving peer-to-peer innovation. Some interpreted it as an attack on DeFi, others as an abuse of SBF's regulatory influence in D.C., which he had gained through his father's contacts and his own political donations. While SBF had never been seen as a true believer in the crypto movement, many die-hard crypto proponents still criticized him for circulating the proposed bill.

On the same day as the leak a dispute broke out on Twitter between SBF and Erik Voorhees, the former CEO of ShapeShift, on where to draw the line on DeFi regulation. The dispute continued during a two-hour live-stream debate on YouTube, which marked a real turning point in the public image of SBF within the crypto community. Contrary to the more libertarian view of Voorhees, SBF's lobbying efforts appeared to put DeFi on the same regulatory path as traditional finance, making DeFi ultimately indistinguishable from its competitors.

On October 25 SBF attended the Future Investment Initiative (FII) conference in Saudi Arabia with SkyBridge Capital's Anthony Scaramucci. Attending the conference was part of Scaramucci's Middle East trip to Riyadh, Dubai, and Abu Dhabi, where he had substantial capital-raising relationships. The plan was to raise two billion dollars for FTX at a thirty-two-billion valuation. But in some investor meetings SBF started trash-talking Binance and its outspoken CEO "CZ", and according to Scaramucci this got back to CZ, who then dumped his holdings of the FTT token.[506]

In 2022 SBF was traveling to D.C. every other week to speak to politicians, and he is believed to have used his influence to lobby against Binance and CZ. It is also well known that he criticized CZ during private meetings with regulators and politicians there.

Ryan Salame, co-CEO of FTX Digital Markets, also publicly made fun of CZ, tweeting on October 30 2022 that it had been "an absolute pleasure watching @cz_binance have the challenging but transformative debates on Twitter this past week to ensure the crypto industry moves forward in the best possible way."[507] SBF responded that he was "excited to see him repping the industry in DC going forward," before adding "uh, he is allowed to go to DC, right?"[508]

On October 6 Binance was hacked for 570 million dollars through a cross-chain exploit. The exchange claimed that it had retained eighty to ninety percent of its funds, as it had paused the BNB chain to prevent money from leaving the platform.[509] Meanwhile Reuters ran several investigative articles about how Binance had tried to circumvent regulations worldwide, the timing of which appeared to be deliberate.

Then, on November 2 the crypto news website *CoinDesk* reported that, according to a private document that it had reviewed, Alameda had 14.6 billion dollars of assets as of June 30 2022.[510] But most of these assets appeared to be in FTT tokens, which granted holders a discount on trading fees, adding evidence that Alameda and FTX had closer ties than some had initially expected. Alameda's biggest asset was 3.66 billion dollars of unlocked FTT, while the third-most prominent position was a pile of FTT collateral. Among its liabilities Alameda somehow included 292 million dollars of locked FTT that the company had received for its market-making services but was not yet entitled to trade. A footnote indicated that "locked tokens [were] conservatively treated at 50% of fair value to [the] FTX/USD order book," while other assets were in illiquid tokens. Out of the eight billion dollars of liabilities 7.4 billion were loans, with 2.2 billion dollars collateralized with FTT tokens.

It appears to be no coincidence that Alameda's balance sheet was leaked when SBF was trying to lobby for a crypto bill that would have hurt the industry while he was also lobbying against U.S. access for Binance. An upset industry insider was likely behind the leak, as it was a way of preventing SBF from causing any more perceived damage to the crypto industry.

Exchange-token ownership concentration: the root of the problem

The leaked Alameda balance sheet gave the impression that Alameda's financials were mainly consistent with cheaply self-minted FTT tokens rather than valuable crypto assets such as Bitcoin or Ethereum, which are broadly decentralized. Ninety-three percent of the FTT ownership was concentrated within the top ten holders. This appeared to be a common problem within the crypto industry, especially for crypto exchanges, where ownership for the top ten token holders is exceptionally high: Bitfinex LEO 99.84 percent, Huobi 98.6 percent, KuCoin 98.5 percent, and Cronos 92.59 percent.

As crypto companies tend to collateralize their assets, FTT tokens could be used to borrow assets that the lender might liquidate once the FTT token price fell below a given threshold. The FTT token had a fully diluted valuation of eight billion dollars (with the FTT price at 24.45 dollars) and a market capitalization of 3.266 billion dollars. Alameda stated that it owned unlocked and locked FTT worth 3.66 billion and 2.16 billion dollars respectively—a total of 5.8 billion dollars, or 178 percent of the current outstanding FTT market cap.

FTX had been an active buyer of FTT tokens, as thirty-three percent of trading fees generated on the exchange were reportedly removed from the supply through weekly burns, equating to 2.5 to five million dollars per week. As the flywheel of "tokenomics" has shown, the perception of a lower supply tends to increase token prices.

Binance plans to sell 500 million dollars in FTT tokens (2022)

On November 5 2022 the notification service Whale Alert informed its followers that twenty-three million FTT tokens (585 million dollars with an FTT price of 25.4) had been moved to Binance from an unknown wallet. This was seventeen percent of the FTT circulating supply.

The following day CZ reacted to the Whale Alert tweet, saying that "due to recent revelations that have come to light" Binance was planning to sell 500 million dollars of the FTT tokens that it had received a year before from the buyout of Binance's stake in FTX, which was 2.1 billion dollars at the time (partially in cash and FTT tokens).[511] CZ assured his followers that Binance would make the sale "in a way that minimizes market impact," adding that, "Due to market conditions and limited liquidity, we expect this will take a few months to complete."

CZ followed up the next day by stating that, "Liquidating our FTT is just post-exit risk management, learning from LUNA."[512] But he added that "we won't pretend to make love after divorce ... we won't support people who lobby against other industry players behind their backs."

26

"Alameda will happily buy it all"
(Caroline Ellison, Alameda)

When the price of FTX's FTT tokens dropped to twenty-two dollars on November 7 2022, Caroline Ellison responded by tweeting that, "Alameda will happily buy it all from you today at \$22!"[513] When central bankers or corporate executives come up with fixed target prices in stressful situations, the market tends to test those levels, and this was the case here as well. For a few hours FTT prices stayed firm. Was Alameda buying at twenty-two dollars? Or were other players taking advantage of FTX's margin facility?

FTX margin accounts could borrow against other collateral assets, such as FTT, so those margin balances could easily have been withdrawn to other exchanges. A trader with 100 thousand dollars in his/her FTX margin account, for example, could buy 100 thousand dollars' worth of FTT tokens and then use that amount as collateral to borrow ninety thousand dollars against it. The trader could then swap the ninety thousand dollars for USDT and move them to Binance, where he/she could short FTT perpetual futures for this amount. The net position would then be ten percent net long on FTT (100 percent long FTT on FTX versus ninety percent short FTT on Binance). Then, if FTX started to implode, the FTT tokens would crash, since the trader would have no interest in adding collateral on the FTX account as FTX might go under. FTX would then liquidate the trader's collateral, causing selling pressure on FTT and pushing the FTT token price even lower.

Figure 27: FTX's FTT token price (time scale in hours)

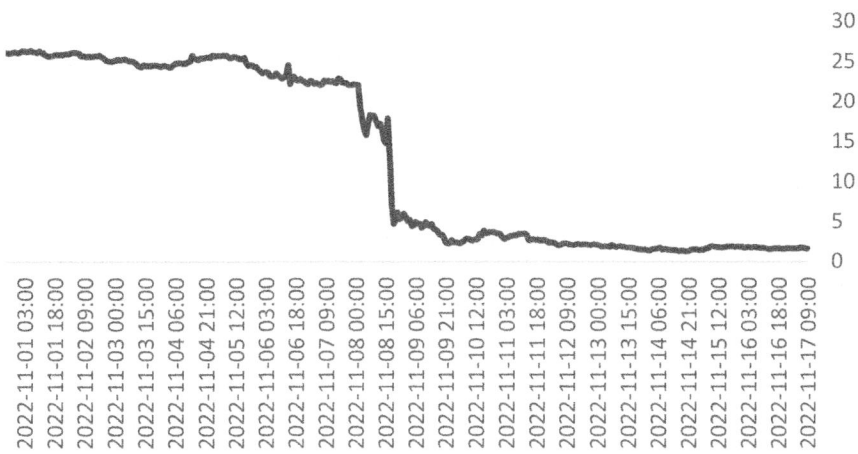

So the trader could effectively put on a ninety-thousand-dollar short with just ten thousand dollars' net exposure. While many assume that Alameda was initially buying FTT at the floor price of twenty-two dollars, intelligent traders could also have joined the FTT buying, at the same time draining the borrowed assets from the FTX platform and shorting them on other exchanges—an approach similar to Avi Eisenberg's emptying of funds on Mango Markets.

If things were fine, the trader would be net long ten percent on FTT. In the worst-case scenario the FTT long position on FTX would go to zero while the FTT short position on Binance would go up ninety percent. Removing balances from margin accounts against FTT collateral could also explain the apparent massive hole in FTX's balance sheet, which was initially estimated to be six billion dollars but later appeared to be around eight billion.

The bank run begins (2022)

The bank run began on November 7 2022, with FTX users complaining about withdrawal complications. FTX assured them that everything was in order, but the situation reminded traders of what had happened at Celsius and other crypto platforms, where halted withdrawals and misled users had come before the eventual collapse. This led SFB to tweet, "FTX is fine. Assets are fine."[514] He also said that a competitor was trying to go after FTX with false rumors, and that FTX did not "invest client assets (even in treasuries)."[515] Tweets that he would delete later.

Alameda had sent large amounts of capital to FTX over the weekend of November 5–6 and earlier to provide enough money for withdrawal requests. Caroline Ellison tweeted on November 6 "that specific balance sheet is for a subset of our corporate entities, we have > $10bn of assets that aren't reflected there."[516]

But the decline in FTT set off a contagion, as the token had been used as collateral for loans that Alameda had taken out. Withdrawals on the Sunday amounted to five billion dollars—twenty-four times Sam Bankman-Fried's estimated average withdrawal level. Caroline Ellison sent a message to SBF saying, "I just had an increasing dread of this day that was weighing on me for a long time, and now that it's happening it just feels great to get it over with one way or another."[517]

On November 7 SBF contacted investors for several billion dollars in bailout money, showing an FTX balance sheet with 9.6 billion dollars in assets versus 8.9 billion in liabilities. But the balance sheet also offered an additional eight-billion-dollar liability in a "hidden, poorly internally labeled 'fiat@' account."[518]

In the middle of the night in Hong Kong SBF called Lennix Lai, his senior contact at the OKX exchange, asking for "a little bit of help." OKX was not prepared to write a billion-dollar check, but before hanging up, Lai gave some advice: "Why not speak to CZ?"[519]

The next day SBF ordered Alameda traders to start selling as much as they could from their investment portfolio as fast as possible, to raise cash and send it to FTX.

In November 2021 the BitDAO community had swapped 100 million BIT tokens for 3.36 million FTT tokens with Alameda. The deal required Alameda to hold the tokens for at least three years. But a sudden dip in BIT token prices raised questions from the BitDAO community, which wanted proof that Alameda was not behind the BIT token sales as the market had realized that Alameda was liquidating positions to pay off its loans from FTX. If no proof was provided within twenty-four hours, the community would vote on a complete sale of its 3.36 million FTT tokens.

Selling pressure on FTT was piling up. But once the twenty-two-dollar FTT level broke, aggregated open interest on stablecoin margined contracts declined by 371 thousand contracts to 5.1 million. Usually open interest—a measure of how many derivatives contracts are outstanding at the end of the trading day—increases on price breaks, as more traders sell into falling prices, increasing their winning short position. The decline in open interest was a sign of capitulation from buyers.

But when Binance CEO CZ tweeted that Binance had eight billion dollars' worth of Ethereum in cold wallets, the market suddenly became concerned about Alameda and FTX's customer holdings being segregated. When an apparent one-billion-dollar liquidity injection failed to find traction among investors, the market grew even more concerned, and traders monitored FTX / Alameda's wallet movements. In the meantime the required liquidity injection had risen to ten billion dollars, because FTX's hole had become more extensive as the value of the FTT token continued to fall and customer funds were leaving the exchange.

Alameda sent large amounts of stablecoins from various exchanges to FTX's hot wallets. But customer withdrawal requests increasingly drained these wallets, and the market started worrying if FTX had any balance in cold wallets. By this time stablecoin reserves on FTX had declined from

500 million dollars in early November to nearly zero. There appeared to be no capital left at either FTX or Alameda.

SBF told investors that FTX had sixteen billion dollars in customer assets and had lent ten billion dollars to Alameda.[520] On November 10 SBF tweeted, "FTX International currently has a total market value of assets/collateral higher than client deposits." He blamed the situation on "a poor internal labeling of bank-related accounts" that meant he was "substantially off on my sense of users' margin."

FTX faces a liquidity crunch, but SBF claims "customers are protected"[521] (2022)

On November 8 2022 FTX faced a liquidity crunch, and SBF announced that he had "come to an agreement on a strategic transaction" with Binance, and that "all assets will be covered 1:1." [522] CZ confirmed that a nonbinding letter of intent to acquire FTX had been signed but was dependent on Binance's due diligence process. Unconfirmed reports circulated that FTX's legal and compliance staff had quit on November 8, while the following day the websites of both FTX Ventures and Alameda were taken offline.

But rumors spread that Binance was not progressing with the acquisition, and SBF texted CZ saying that "we are still extremely excited to work on this with you guys." CZ's response was short: "Sam, we won't be able to continue this deal. Way too many issues."[523]

On November 9 Binance made an official announcement stating the reasons for backing out of the FTX deal. These included "reports regarding mishandled customer funds and U.S. agency investigations." [524] The announcement forced SBF to try to find eight billion dollars of emergency funding to cover the liquidity crunch.

By now FTX and Alameda were both close to going under, and stablecoin pegs started to get tested. Alameda had been Tether's biggest client, and some traders expected it to have inside information about the amount of fiat assets backing the dollar-to-USDT peg. A crypto wallet address associated with Alameda appeared to be trying to break the peg by borrowing USDC from Circle and supplying it to Aave, and then borrowing USDT on Aave and swapping it for USDC on Curve. At the time the 3pool on Curve was holding 75.3 percent USDT, 12.4 percent USDC, and 12.3 percent DAI, and it soon became slightly unstable, with the USDT price falling to 0.9765, below the 1.0 peg level.

But with 675 million dollars of reserves in 3pool Alameda was unlikely to have the firepower to break it. The attempt appeared to be a sign of desperation, and traders thought that Caroline Ellison, under the direction of SBF, had been behind it. If successful, breaking the USDT stablecoin could have made a few million dollars in profit for Alameda, but it would have likely ruined the industry as Tether's USDT has long been an essential backbone for the crypto ecosystem. Alameda did not seem to care. As it was, the attack was unsuccessful, as Alameda no longer had the firepower and nobody else jumped on the trade.

Bahamas regulator learns that Alameda used FTX customer funds (2022)

On November 10 2022, while SBF was busy reassuring FTX customers that their funds would be protected, Christina Rolle, the executive director of the Securities Commission of the Bahamas, filed an urgent affidavit with the Supreme Court of the Bahamas calling for the "winding up" of FTX Digital Markets.[525] FTX Digital was registered with the Commission under the Digital Assets and Registered Exchanges (DARE) Act, with Ryan Salame, SBF, Daniel Friedberg, and Metered Limited as "acting officers."

Rolle was worried about possible "misappropriation and negligence of clients' assets." She had already expressed grave concerns on November 8 about the operations and affairs of FTX Digital when she emailed SBF and Jessica Murray, FTX's compliance officer, requesting a meeting.[526] But neither SBF nor Murray responded immediately, and later that day Murray resigned, while FTX halted all non-fiat customer withdrawals.

SBF waited until 9:27 p.m. on November 9 to reply to Rolle, and then only with vague statements. But during a phone conversation between Rolle and FTX Digital co-CEO Salame, the latter advised her that "clients' assets which may have been held with FTX Digital were transferred to Alameda Research to cover financial losses of Alameda."[527] Salame said that only three people had the necessary codes to transfer clients' assets to Alameda: SBF, Nishad Singh, and Gary Wang. "Given such actions may be deemed criminal, the Commission has requested by way of letter dated November 9 2022, that the Royal Bahamas Police Force carry out an investigation," the affidavit stated.[528]

Rumors subsequently spread that FTX employees were being searched at the airport, with clothing and merchandise that associated them with FTX being thrown away.

Joseph Bankman manages SBF's legal defense

The events surrounding FTX and Alameda on November 8 2022 coincided with the six-month anniversary of the UST / LUNA implosion and also the U.S. Midterm elections, where SBF had donated forty million dollars to the Democratic Party. Along with other FTX executives SBF had donated a total of seventy million dollars to U.S. politicians and fundraising groups in the 2021–22 election cycle. Ryan Salame had given away twenty-four million dollars, primarily to Republican groups. The result was that more than thirty-six percent of the 535 U.S. senators and representatives in the U.S. Congress had received campaign financing support from FTX executives.[529]

Joseph Bankman, SBF's father, had accompanied his son on many of his trips to Washington, D.C., opening numerous doors for him. Since January

2022 Bankman had been on FTX's payroll, frequently traveling to the Bahamas and playing the role of FTX diplomat. FTX funds were used to buy a 16.4-million-dollar property in the Bahamas where Bankman and his wife, Barbara Fried, stayed when they were in Nassau. While the house was intended to be FTX's property, it was held in Bankman and Fried's names.

Through FTX Property Holdings Ltd., an FTX unit, SBF, his parents, and senior executives bought at least thirty-five properties in the Bahamas worth a total of 256 million dollars. The properties—mostly luxury beachfront homes, including seven condominiums—were purchased between 2020 and 2022, although FTX only established its headquarters in the Bahamas in September 2021.[530]

As news emerged that SBF had used FTX client funds to cover losses at Alameda, Joseph Bankman called on fellow Stanford law professor David Mills for advice. A close family friend of the Bankman-Frieds, Mills teaches classes in criminal law and white-collar crime. On hearing what had happened, Mills told Bankman, "Sam needs lawyers, and desperately."[531] Bankman recruited Ronald G. White, a defense lawyer specializing in white-collar crimes, to represent SBF. But lawyers kept resigning on him as the allegations against SBF grew.

Although Barbara Fried, SBF's mother, never worked directly for FTX, SBF had channeled large amounts of money into her political network, primarily making contributions based on the Mind the Gap organization that she had started and was actively involved in. SBF also contributed to Guarding Against Pandemics, a non-profit organization run by his younger brother, Gabe, which was effectively a D.C. lobbying group. In November 2022 Gabe and his mother resigned from their respective organizations. Both would subsequently ignore all requests to work with the FTX creditor team to recover some of the stolen funds.[532]

Fifty million dollars leave FTX through the backdoor (2022)

On Thursday November 10 2022, at 9:27 p.m., SBF sent an email to Ryan Pinder, the Attorney General and Minister of Legal Affairs of the Bahamas, suggesting that "we would be more than happy to open up withdrawals for *all* Bahamian customers on FTX."[533] Joseph Bankman, Ryan Salame, FTX's COO Constance Wang, and FTX's general counsel Can Sun were all cc'd on the email.[534]

At 11:50 a.m. (3:50 p.m. UTC) on the same day, the FTX hot wallet, with a balance of only 469 million dollars, had resumed withdrawals.[535] A Bahamian account holder reportedly withdrew funds for users in other jurisdictions, bypassing the internal balance transfer block by selling NFTs (non-fungible tokens) on FTX's NFT marketplace. The account holder was able to do this by creating an NFT and striking a deal with another user to buy it with his/her total balance, enabling the original account holder to send the money to a decentralized wallet. This was a way for FTX senior employees based in the Bahamas to channel money out of the exchange and circumvent the withdrawal blocks.

FTX stated on its website that "per our Bahamian Headquarters' regulation and regulators, we have begun to facilitate withdrawals of Bahamian funds. The amounts withdrawn comprise a small fraction of the assets we currently hold on hand, and we are actively working on additional routes to enable withdrawals for the rest of our user base."[536]

As a result of this announcement some Bahama-based users were offered steep discounts on the dollar to withdraw funds for international users, while others made deals to buy NFTs from the FTX marketplace in return for kickbacks for removing funds from the platform. Around fifty million dollars were traded on NFTs during the hours after the facilitation of withdrawals.

However the Bahamian authorities had not authorized these withdrawals, and SBF later admitted during a phone interview that he had ordered the reopening of withdrawals as he did not want either himself or the exchange to be in a country "with a lot of angry people in it."[537]

27

"FTX is fine. Assets are fine."
(Sam Bankman-Fried, FTX)

On Friday November 11 2022 SBF filed for chapter 11 bankruptcy proceedings for FTX, FTX.US, Alameda Research, and 134 FTX-related companies. Shortly afterward bankruptcy expert John J. Ray III took over responsibility for the entities. A day earlier SBF had tweeted, "This was about FTX International. FTX US, the US based exchange that accepts Americans, was not financially impacted by this … It's 100% liquid. Every user could fully withdraw."[538] Right until the very end he tried to deceive everybody, making statements that he knew were misleading.

Questionable auditing firms signed off on FTX's financials (2021–22)

The FTX bankruptcy filing raised questions about how a small auditing firm, Prager Metis, with just 139 million dollars in annual revenue, could issue an unqualified audit option for the company's 2021 financial statements despite FTX's vast operations in various jurisdictions. Prager Metis called itself the first accounting firm headquartered in the "metaverse."[539]

Questions were also raised about Armanino, a California-based auditing firm with 458 million dollars in annual revenue, which issued an unqualified opinion for the FTX.US exchange business. Both Prager Metis and Armanino should have noticed the red flags inside FTX, and in the aftermath of the FTX collapse both firms might face lawsuits in the future.

In fact one case has already hit the San Francisco court, where an FTX customer who lost money on the exchange accused both Prager Metis and Armanino of "racketeering conspiracy."[540] According to the lawsuit, in March 2022 both companies had issued certified audit reports giving FTX.US and FTX clean bills of health. Before SBF's Congressional testimony in December 2021 Armanino had even tagged him on a tweet saying, "Let's go buddy," while in June of the following year Prager Metis had posted a photo of Prager Metis and FTX representatives at a baseball game, with the words "Proud to support FTX.US."[541]

Hundreds of millions of dollars are mysteriously removed from FTX (2022)

To gain maximum leverage with law enforcement agencies, the inner circle of FTX senior management appears to have staged a hack on November 12 2022, withdrawing 400 million dollars from the company after it had filed for bankruptcy. When users tried to make withdrawals from the exchange, they noticed that their balances had turned to zero. While the website was down, FTX posted in its official Telegram group that it had been hacked.[542] It advised users not to sign into their accounts on the FTX website, and to delete the FTX app as malware could be uploaded through it onto their phones.[543]

Suspiciously the acting FTX legal counsel Ryne Miller was unaware of the hack, although he later claimed that it was a white-knight move to protect user funds.[544] Miller had joined FTX.US in 2021, and had previously been a partner at Sullivan & Cromwell LLP (S&C). A specialist in matters concerning the Commodity Futures Trading Commission (CFTC) and the U.S. Securities and Exchange Commission (SEC), Miller had also worked under SEC chair Gary Gensler at the CFTC.

On-chain activity showed that 400 million dollars were removed from FTX, and another 200 million were moved to multisignature wallets. As the exchange's API (application programming interface) function had been switched off, it seemed as though FTX personnel were washing the books in what appeared to be a "fog of war" strategy—something that was not expected in standard hacking. The attacker also appeared to have root access to FTX and FTX.US, which suggested it was an inside job. FTX had too many different wallets and products for an attacker to pull off an outside hack. Ryne Miller acknowledged the abnormalities, but said that it was unclear who was moving the funds.

After the alleged hack Solana tokens were swapped into Ether, as the person who had moved the funds seemingly knew that Solana, like USDT, was more likely to be frozen by the issuer. Meanwhile FTX and Alameda assets were actively being pooled, comingled into one address, and then swapped USDT for DAI, which was harder to freeze as Tether was starting to blacklist wallets with funds of suspicious origins. The alleged FTX hacker transferred thirty million dollars of blacklisted USDT, while the DAI was moved to Monero—which, like the DeFi (decentralized finance) mixer Tornado, hides all transaction details. Tom Robinson, cofounder of blockchain analysis provider Elliptic, confirmed that 477 million dollars had been stolen from FTX, and 280 million dollars converted into Ether and then renBTC, which is bridged into Bitcoin.[545]

Some have claimed that FTX's chief technology officer, Gary Wang, was behind the attack, as the hacker needed root access to move the funds quickly and comingle them. Wang's account at GitHub, a code-hosting platform for collaboration, saw abnormal activity shortly before the attack, with three contributions on Thursday November 9 followed by nine on November 10 and another five on November 11. Wang seemed to be testing code before the hack happened. In the following three days there were no more contributions.[546]

Unconfirmed rumors were also spread that an ex-FTX employee was behind the attack. Chief compliance officer Daniel Friedberg had resigned on November 8, and in 2008 had been part of a betting scandal at the online poker site *Ultimate Bet*. During the scandal Friedberg had advised his boss, who had admitted misappropriating fifty million dollars, to "blame a former consultant who took advantage of a server flaw by hacking into the client."[547]

On the same day as the alleged FTX hack Kraken exchange's chief security officer, Nick Percoco, announced that he knew the hacker's identity, as it appeared that the hacker needed to move TRON tokens (TRX) from his/her account at Kraken to FTX to pay for gas fees to move the stolen coins out of the FTX wallet.[548] The hacker had tried to move the USDT twice but did not have funds for the gas fees, so he/she had moved five hundred TRX from Kraken to cover the costs. But the funds could not be transferred, as Tether had blocked the hacker in the meantime.

Also on November 12 the Securities Commission of the Bahamas issued a statement denying that it had directed, authorized, or suggested to FTX Digital Markets the prioritization of withdrawals.[549] Later that day rumors started to surface that SBF was fleeing to Argentina in a private jet belonging to multibillionaire Joe Lewis, the majority owner of the English football club Tottenham Hotspur.[550]

As a successful currency speculator Lewis had teamed up with George Soros to crash the British pound in 1992. Soros is believed to have made one billion dollars in the endeavor, and Lewis might have made even more.[551] A resident of the Bahamas, Lewis jointly owned, along with three other investors, the Albany resort where the penthouse that SBF had bought was located. FTX also owned several other apartments in the same development, which had been purchased with fifty percent FTT and fifty percent FTX stock.

FTX's balance sheet shows a nine-billion-dollar hole (2022)

On November 12 2022 it was revealed that FTX held less than one billion dollars in liquid or efficiently sellable assets against nine billion dollars in liabilities.[552] The most significant portion of these assets was a 470-million-dollar equity stake in the retail trading app Robinhood. To raise capital, SBF tried to offload these shares at a twenty-percent discount to market value in a privately negotiated deal.

The second-biggest liquid asset on FTX's balance sheet was 200 million dollars of cash held with Ledger Prime, a crypto investment firm owned by Alameda. FTX had also issued two billion dollars' worth of Wrapped Bitcoin (WBTC), but these were not on the firm's balance sheet.

The mismatch between assets and liabilities suggested that FTX customers faced massive losses on any user funds they had on the platform. Bankruptcy filings indicated that assets and liability ranged between ten and fifty billion dollars. A negative eight-billion-dollar entry was described as a "hidden, poorly internally labeled 'fiat@' account."[553] FTX Trading, the company behind the exchange, had 9.6 billion dollars in assets. The most significant investment was a 2.2-billion-dollar stake in the Serum cryptocurrency, which had a market value of only eighty-eight million dollars at the time of the filing. Alameda and FTX might have had 5.4 billion dollars of illiquid venture capital investments.

Until November 11 SBF had refused to sign the bankruptcy papers, preferring to lawyer up instead. Besides his father and David Mills, another white-collar criminal defense expert was also acting for SBF personally. Together the three lawyers were contemplating whether a bankruptcy filing in the U.S. would have more punitive consequences for SBF.

Meanwhile a disorderly forced liquidation process could have been set in motion if each regulator globally pushed the FTX entities separately into bankruptcies instead of in one controlled U.S. filing. The Australian FTX entity was forced into insolvency early on Friday morning (November 11), and the unraveling appeared to start. By then the regulator in the Bahamas was close to pushing the FTX entity there into liquidation. So just after 4 a.m. on Friday SBF clicked the automatic signature link on the DocuSign document for John J. Ray III to take over as CEO of the FTX entities.

John J. Ray III becomes FTX's CEO (2022)

John J. Ray III, an attorney specializing in the recovery of funds, took over as CEO of FTX Trading Ltd. on November 11 2022. Previously Ray had overseen the unwinding of other scandal-hit corporations, such as Enron. On December 13 2022 he testified before the House Financial Services Committee.[554]

After a month of leading the investigations into FTX Ray had found that computer infrastructure had given individuals in the company the power to redirect customer assets without security controls. Private keys to move funds around were stored without adequate security controls or encryption, and Alameda could borrow funds held at FTX.com for trading or investments without any practical limits. Customer assets were comingled, and Ray noted the need for more documentation on nearly five hundred investments made with FTX funds and assets. Reliable financial statements were required, and there was a need for more financial and risk management personnel and an independent governance structure. Ray testified that in over forty years of dealing with insolvencies he had never encountered "such a complete failure of corporate controls and such a complete absence of trustworthy financial information as occurred here."[555]

In his testimony Ray clarified why FTX.US was part of the chapter 11 protection. Based on his forensic analysis, there was monumental evidence that FTX.US was not operated independently of FTX.com, and that preventing a "run on the bank" was necessary. Ray also noted that customer assets from FTX.com had been comingled with help from Alameda, with the latter using the funds for margin trading, thereby exposing the customers to massive losses. As a market maker and trading firm Alameda deployed funds to various third-party exchanges which were inherently unsafe.

From late 2021 through 2022 the FTX group had spent five billion dollars on business and investments, with any return on the investments potentially minimal. Insiders had taken out more than 2.5 billion dollars in loans and other payments for their expenses. SBF took out 2.2 billion dollars, Nishad Singh 587 million, Gary Wang 246 million, Ryan Salame eighty-seven million, Sam Trabucco twenty-five million, and Caroline Ellison six million.[556] Analysis from the creditor team on March 17 2023 revealed that the combined entities had a shortfall of 6.8 billion dollars plus customer claims of 11.6 billion dollars. It also showed that Alameda had borrowed fifty-three billion dollars from eighty different counterparties, with the majority collateralized by FTT and other volatile crypto assets, such as SRM (Serum) and SOL (Solana).

FTX mishandled customer funds from day one (2019–22)

At SBF's direction Alameda was essentially allowed to draw down an unlimited line of credit from FTX. Alameda also enjoyed other unfair advantages when transacting on the FTX platform, including quicker execution and an exemption from the auto-liquidation risk management that other trading firms defaulted to.

FTX Trading had numerous employees, including key personnel based in the U.S. who regularly engaged in advertising and promotional activities there, despite the fact that the company was not registered with U.S. regulators in any capacity. Funds were neither segregated nor subject to control or documentation when they flowed between the various FTX / Alameda entities. These entities also shared office space in Berkeley, Hong Kong, and the Bahamas, as well as personnel, technology and hardware, intellectual property, and other resources.

When FTX was launched, the firm directed customer deposits into a Delaware-registered wholly-owned subsidiary of Alameda called North Dimension Inc., because as a crypto exchange FTX could not initially open a bank account in the U.S. Silvergate Bank had clarified that it "would not open an account for customer deposit and withdrawals absent evidence that FTX was licensed and registered."[557] As a result, to further hide the affiliate relationship between FTX and Alameda, SBF directed the incorporation of North Dimension in August 2020, with SBF himself listed as the sole owner. To pass the bank's due diligence process, SBF filled out a false due diligence questionnaire, hiding the true intention of the North Dimension business, which lacked the appropriate money service license. In April 2021 North Dimension's Silvergate bank account was finally opened.

During the early days of FTX customers were asked to wire money to North Dimension to hide the fact that the money was actually being sent to Alameda. North Dimension claimed to sell electronics out of the same address where FTX.US was registered. But its website was full of "misspellings, and product prices were hundreds of dollars above regular priced items,"[558] presumably to discourage anyone who accidentally found the site from purchasing any products.[559] Customers later wired money to North Dimension through Silvergate Bank, where the company held two accounts. The Seattle-based law firm Fenwick & West, where Daniel Friedberg had worked before joining FTX, had set up the incorporation papers for North Dimension, while the website had been created by someone registered in Hong Kong. This turned out to be Nishad Singh,[560] who had paid for the web hosting site with SBF's credit card.[561]

Although customers could see their balances on the FTX website or app, their funds actually remained in Alameda-controlled bank accounts, and were only manually credited to FTX customer accounts. By August 2020 FTX had opened its "for benefit of" (FBO) fiat bank account, but the deposits from Alameda accounts still needed to be transferred to FTX customer accounts. According to the SEC charges filed on December 21 2022 Caroline Ellison was aware that Alameda was receiving FTX customer funds.[562] Alameda was also not required to pay interest on these funds, although when FTX tried to separate Alameda's eight-billion-dollar liability from FTX user funds, the trading firm started to be charged interest on the loan. As a result SBF ordered the Alameda liability to be moved to a new account that would not charge interest.

FTX's terms of service explicitly prohibited the use of customer funds in this way, and the company's senior management consistently emphasized the proper segregation of funds during public statements, on Twitter, and during appearances before the U.S. Congress, the CFTC, and other U.S. federal agencies.

Alameda also helped FTX to maintain an acceptable balance of stablecoins in its wallets. The trading firm was authorized to make large transactions on behalf of FTX Trading, using the latter's assets rather than its own. Alameda could not be auto-liquidated on FTX under any conditions—something that was hard-coded into the FTX system. It also had a unique "allow negative flag" designation, enabling it to engage in transactions even if it did not have funds available. According to the SEC, at the direction of SBF Gary Wang had written software code in August 2019 (which he updated around May 2020) allowing Alameda to maintain a negative balance. Also in May 2020 SBF had directed Wang to exempt Alameda from the auto-liquidation feature on FTX's spot margin trading.

The one time that Alameda reached the limit of how much it could borrow from its FTX account, SBF instructed that the limit be increased to a level that it would unlikely reach in the future—tens of billions of dollars according to the CFTC investigation.[563] The SEC later stated that Alameda's credit limit was sixty-five billion dollars. The funds that Alameda borrowed could also be withdrawn to other platforms.

Alameda also enjoyed trading capabilities on FTX that were several milliseconds faster than its competitors', as its orders did not go through an automated review process for collateral verification like those of other market makers.[564] Alameda did not need to pay for its FTT tokens either. Other firms famously complained about slow latency by API traders on FTX, which may have resulted from an engineered artificial barrier that Alameda could skip.[565]

28

"Clearly we are not done"
(Damian Williams, FTX prosecutor)

On December 13 2022 the Commodity Futures Trading Commission (CFTC) and the U.S. Attorney for the Southern District of New York charged SBF, FTX Trading, and Alameda Research with fraud and material misrepresentations.[566] FTX is accused of comingling, mishandling, and misappropriating customer funds from the moment it was launched.[567] Damian Williams is the prosecutor on the case for the Southern District of New York. A graduate of Harvard, Cambridge, and Yale, Williams was appointed by U.S. President Joe Biden in 2021 after helping to run a special financial-markets crime unit for nearly a decade.[568]

According to the charges against SBF, FTX Trading, and Alameda, SBF was the owner and operator of both FTX and Alameda, running the companies as a joint enterprise under his sole ultimate authority. Despite stepping down from Alameda in October 2021, SBF had remained a signatory on Alameda's bank accounts and was registered for Alameda as a futures commission merchant with the CFTC. He also kept daily communication with senior Alameda personnel.

In 2021 FTX entities held fifteen billion dollars in assets on the platform. In the first quarter of 2022 Alameda had ten billion dollars in notional value of loans to fund directional, unhedged, and illiquid investments from digital lending platforms, traditional bank lines of credit, and FTX customer funds. When these loans were recalled and Alameda faced margin calls, at the direction of SBF Alameda significantly increased its use of FTX customer funds to meet external debt obligations. Alameda's fiat liabilities to FTX were eight billion dollars by mid-2022. As SBF was worried that these liabilities would be discovered, he instructed that a new account be created and the liabilities moved into it. This Alameda sub-account was referred to as "our Korean friend's account" or "the weird Korean account." While the account was not immediately associated with Alameda, it was described as "FTX fiat old." The account received the same "allow negative flag" and liquidation exemptions as Alameda's other accounts.

On November 7 2022, when FTX was processing large amounts of customer withdrawal requests, SBF realized that neither FTX nor Alameda had enough funds to make customer accounts whole. So, through Caroline Ellison, he instructed Alameda traders to liquidate positions and free up capital, and to be "maximally aggressive" in selling everything that could be sold, so that two billion dollars could be moved back to FTX.[569]

But on November 8 FTX executives also noticed a capital shortfall in FTX.US, prompting SBF to direct Alameda traders to prioritize FTX.US's capital requirements. As a result Alameda sent 185 million dollars to FTX.US, while SBF and others within FTX contacted multiple sources in an attempt to raise additional funding to fill the shortfall. But despite good initial discussions, funding sources soon dried up. Yet SBF continued to give interviews on November 9 downplaying his misappropriation of customer funds, saying that he had just expanded too fast and failed to see warning signs.[570]

Meanwhile the U.S. Department of Justice (DOJ) and the U.S. Securities and Exchange Commission (SEC) were examining the relationship between FTX and Alameda. The latter had accumulated a prominent margin position on FTX, essentially borrowing funds from the exchange. "It was substantially larger than I had thought it was," SBF later admitted.[571]

At 10 a.m. on November 9 after the announcement of the then-contemplated Binance acquisition Caroline Ellison held an all-hands meeting, explaining that due to an accounting or bookkeeping problem SBF and other individuals had decided to use FTX customer funds for Alameda.[572] Ellison casually told employees that Alameda "is probably going to wind down; if you don't want to stay or want to take some time off, no pressure; if you want to help with stuff like making sure our lenders get repaid, it's super appreciated."[573]

Ellison also told employees that Alameda had taken out loans and used the money for venture capital investments.[574] When UST / LUNA crashed in May 2022, lenders had recalled these loans, but as Alameda could not pay them back, it had used FTX customer funds. Ellison told her colleagues that four people had known about this arrangement: SBF, her, Nishad Singh, and Gary Wang. Shortly after this meeting most of Alameda's staff resigned. But SBF continued to make widespread false accusations about the depleted customer funds and the relationship between FTX and Alameda.

SBF is arrested in the Bahamas (2022)

On December 12 2022 SBF was arrested in the Bahamas after prosecutors in the U.S. filed criminal charges against him. Prosecutors from the Southern District of New York charged SBF with wire fraud, wire fraud conspiracy, securities fraud, securities fraud conspiracy, and money laundering. The Southern District of New York is one of the most influential courts in the U.S. because of its jurisdiction over New York's major financial centers.

SBF landed in the U.S. on December 21. Shortly afterward he was granted bail on the condition that he surrender his passport and submit to home detention. The bail was guaranteed by an initially anonymously backed 250-million-dollar bond secured by his parents' house. Larry Kramer, a former dean of Stanford Law School, and Andreas Paepcke, a Stanford computer scientist, also signed as guarantors for 500 thousand and 200 thousand dollars respectively.[575] SBF will remain under house arrest at his parents' house in Palo Alto, near Stanford University, until the trial, which is scheduled for October 2 2023.

In the aftermath of the FTX implosion SBF revealed that engaging with regulators had been a public-relations stunt, and that regulations do not protect customers.[576] He also admitted that FTX had not been gambling with customer money, but had rather loaned the cash to Alameda, and that its collateral had not been large enough to cover the loan. He blamed messy accounting and running a derivatives margin exchange with excessive position built up as the causes for losing customer deposits. Filing for chapter 11 bankruptcy protection was a mistake in his view, as it meant that lawyers and distressed investors had taken over.

Caroline Ellison and Gary Wang cooperate with prosecutors (2022)

While SBF was being extradited to the U.S., Damian Williams, the U.S. prosecutor, announced the previously secret guilty pleas from FTX cofounder Gary Wang and Alameda CEO Caroline Ellison. Wang and Ellison were charged with four and seven counts respectively, and the SEC and CFTC released civil complaints against them simultaneously.

Wang pleaded guilty to conspiracy to commit fraud, wire fraud, conspiracy to commit commodities fraud, and conspiracy to commit securities fraud. Ellison pleaded guilty to wire fraud, two counts of conspiracy to commit wire fraud, conspiracy to commit commodities fraud, conspiracy to commit securities fraud, and conspiracy to commit money laundering. She was also singled out in the SEC complaint for engaging in artificial manipulation of FTT tokens as part of a broader effort to boost Alameda's available collateral for lending.

The SEC charges alleged that Ellison and Wang had abetted SBF in defrauding FTX customers. According to the SEC Wang—with the help of Nishad Singh—had created a software backdoor in FTX's platform which allowed Alameda to divert customer funds for its trades.

In early 2023 federal prosecutors accused SBF of witness tampering while under house arrest, as he had contacted FTX's general counsel Ryne Miller through the encrypted messaging app Signal, offering to work closer together in the future. The Southern District of New York charged him with twelve counts. SBF also informed Ellison, who was then cooperating with the prosecutors, that "many legal cases turn on documentation and it is more difficult to build a legal case if the information is not written down or preserved."[577]

By the end of January 2023 FTX bankruptcy lawyers were complaining that Ellison and Wang were no longer cooperating with the ongoing investigation, and that they had declined to give them requested information. But FTX's chief legal counsel, Daniel Friedberg, did cooperate with U.S. prosecutors, without being formally charged. Curiously Friedberg stated that FTX.US's general counsel Ryne Miller was personally interested "to channel a lot of business to S&C [Sullivan & Cromwell] as he wanted to return there as a partner."[578] While FTX.US's customer funds deficit was negligible, Miller wanted to include the entity in the group bankruptcy filing because, as he told Friedberg, FTX.US had the cash to pay S&C its retainer.

Friedberg also accused S&C of overbilling. For the first fifty-one days of work in 2022 lawyers and advisors in the FTX bankruptcy case had billed 19.6 million dollars.[579] S&C assigned nearly two dozen partners and billed 9.5 million dollars after spending 1,900 hours on the case for an hourly rate of 1,452 dollars plus other costs. John J. Ray defended the appointment of S&C, saying that the team had been "essential in bringing order to a chaotic situation."[580] According to Friedberg's statement SBF and Nishad Singh were both represented personally by S&C.

On February 28 2023 Nishad Singh pleaded guilty to one count of wire fraud, three counts of conspiracy to commit fraud, one count of conspiracy to commit money laundering, and one count of conspiracy to defraud the

U.S. by violating campaign finance laws.[581] Shortly after FTX imploded, Singh had started assisting the U.S. law enforcement agencies' investigation. He admitted inflating revenue numbers to raise venture capital funds from investors and lying to auditors about these transactions. He also confirmed that FTX's risk engine in charge of liquidations did not apply to Alameda. In 2021 Singh had borrowed ten million dollars in an undocumented loan from Alameda and handed the money to his friends and family.[582] Even though he knew that Alameda could not repay its debt to FTX, he had withdrawn another six million dollars from FTX for personal use in September and October 2022.

On January 9 2023 SBF pleaded not guilty to eight criminal charges brought against him, while Damian Williams was coming under increasing criticism for granting SBF house arrest at his parents' Stanford home—a deal he had agreed to so that a swift extradition from the Bahamas could be secured. Later the number of charges against SBF increased to twelve and then thirteen, as he was also accused of orchestrating a forty-million-dollar bribe to Chinese officials in November 2021 to unfreeze one billion dollars in funds held on two Mainland China crypto exchanges.[583]

John J. Ray's interim report from April 9 2023 summarized the reasons for the FTX demise as "hubris, incompetence, and greed."[584] The report confirmed that FTX had seven million registered users, while FTX.US had one million—meaning that a total of eight million users had been defrauded. QuickBooks, an accounting software package for small and mid-sized businesses, was used to produce some rudimentary financial statements which relied on Google documents and Excel spreadsheets. Many transactions were entered after months of delay and were mislabeled—for example eighty thousand entries classified as "Ask My Accountant"—while tens of millions of dollars in expenses and invoices were approved with emojis on Slack's internal communication system. Alameda had also transferred tens of millions of dollars to SBF's personal bank account, only for the transfers to be recorded in the QuickBooks ledger as "Investment in Subsidiaries: Investments-Cryptocurrency."

SBF himself described Alameda as "unauditable," saying that the firm's accounting was "hilariously beyond any threshold of any auditor being able to even get partially through an audit." He added that the firm would "sometimes find $50m of assets lying around that we lost track of; such is life."

On July 31 2019—on the same day that SBF said that "Alameda is a liquidity provider on FTX but their account is just like everyone else's"[585]—Nishad Singh altered the code on the FTX site to allow Alameda to borrow up to sixty-five billion dollars. A week earlier he had altered the code to prevent Alameda from auto-liquidation.

FTX also implemented minor cybersecurity controls, with private keys to its crypto assets being stored in Amazon Web Services' cloud computing environment, and nearly all its crypto assets in hot wallets prone to hacking and misappropriation. This was despite the fact that the company had repeatedly signaled to regulators and users that cold wallets were used for any liquidity beyond two days.

Operation Choke Point 2.0 (2023)

In the aftermath of the FTX implosion four influential U.S. senators wrote to Alan Lane, the CEO of Silvergate Bank, to clarify the bank's role in the mishandling of FTX's customer funds.[586] Two days later New York–based Signature Bank, for which twenty-four percent of total deposits came from crypto firms, announced its intention to reduce crypto-related deposits by fifty percent.[587] Then, on January 9 2023 Metropolitan Commercial Bank, which also had banking relationships with crypto firms, announced its withdrawal of services to the crypto community.[588]

Metropolitan Commercial's decision came after the issuing on January 3 of a joint statement by three influential U.S. agencies—the Federal Reserve, the Federal Deposit Insurance Corporation (FDIC), and the Office of the Comptroller of the Currency—warning against the risks of fraud and instability in the banking system due to crypto firms.[589] The joint statement was followed by an announcement from the National Economic Council strongly discouraging banks from transacting with crypto firms.[590] Then, on January 27 the Federal Reserve rejected Wyoming-based crypto-focused Custodia Bank's application to become a member of the Federal Reserve System, due to the lack of a sufficient management framework around the risk associated with crypto, including money laundering and terrorist financing.[591] But Custodia's membership denial was also based on the bank's potential issuance of stablecoins.

On February 8 Binance.com suspended U.S.-dollar transfers for retail clients. The following day crypto exchange Kraken—officially known as Payward Ventures, Inc. or Payward Trading Ltd.—was charged by the SEC for failing to register its crypto-asset staking-as-a-service program. The exchange agreed to pay a thirty-million-dollar fine, and discontinued the program for U.S.-based users.[592]

On February 9 Nic Carter, a partner at Castle Islands Ventures, had a guest post published on *Pirate Wires* arguing that "Operation Choke Point 2.0" was underway.[593] In the post Carter detailed how the Biden administration was quietly trying to ban crypto, and how it was using banking sector regulators to "unbank" crypto companies and shut off exchanges from the banking system entirely.

A week before the publication of Carter's post a criminal investigation had started over Silvergate Bank's handling of its FTX and Alameda accounts. A few days afterward it was reported that Binance.com, Binance's global exchange, had access to Binance.US's Silvergate account and that it had moved hundreds of millions of dollars through this account without the knowledge of the Binance.US CEO.[594]

As a result of the criminal investigation Silvergate faced inquiries from the DOJ, Congress, and bank regulators, and on March 3 it discontinued its Silvergate Exchange Network (SEN) settlement system, which at the height of the fourth quarter of 2021 had facilitated transactions worth 219 billion dollars.[595] A bank run ensued, and on March 8 Silvergate shut down operations.

Silicon Valley Bank (SVB), which also had relationships with crypto firms and other startups, collapsed a few days later, after experiencing a bank run due to interest rate–related losses on its portfolio. SVB had safeguarded 3.3 billion dollars from crypto stablecoin issuer Circle, which some investors feared would not be seen again. As a result the USDC stablecoin lost its peg, trading twelve percent below the peg level until the FDIC moved to support uninsured deposits the following Monday.

The New York State Department of Financial Services (NYSDFS) took advantage of this crisis to shutter Signature Bank, which had relationships with stablecoin issuers, crypto exchanges, and Bitcoin miners. Signature also operated Signet, an internal ledger and real-time payments platform that was launched on January 1 2019. Signet was similar to Silvergate's SEN, allowing customers to move funds any time of the day or week. The platform was designed to move money in thirty seconds by converting U.S. dollars into tokens compliant with Ethereum's ERC-20 standard. These digitized dollars, or Signets, were intended to work exclusively on the Signet platform, and deposits held within the platform were eligible for FDIC insurance.[596]

Signet became even more important for crypto firms than Silvergate's SEN, reporting 275 billion dollars in transaction volumes in the fourth quarter of 2022, compared to 117 billion for SEN. Shutting both these institutions cut off the payment rails for most crypto firms. Tether, for example, had been instructing its clients to send dollars through Signet to its banking partner Capital Union.[597] Barney Frank, one of Signature's board members, accused regulators of looking to send a strong message to crypto firms.[598] As a result of their intervention Circle had to temporarily stop the minting and redemption of its USDC stablecoin, as it needed a new banking partner.[599]

More crypto titans are arrested, while others live to fight another day (2023)

In March 2023 rumors started circulating that Justin Sun, the founder of TRON, had lost his Grenadian citizenship and his position as the island nation's permanent representative to the World Trade Organization (WTO). Sun had acquired the position in December 2021 after making a significant investment in the country,[600] although according to a local source the investment had amounted to only 150 to 300 thousand dollars.[601] The informant also said that Sun's position would not grant him diplomatic immunity outside of Switzerland, where the WTO is based.

Sun has had a history of controversies. Vitalik Buterin, for example, accused him of plagiarism over the TRON white paper, claiming that many parts looked identical to parts of the white papers for the InterPlanetary File System (IPFS) and Filecoin, and that references were not appropriately cited.[602] There were also reports that Sun had been forced to postpone a charity lunch with Warren Buffett in 2019 because he had not been allowed to leave China, as he was under investigation by the Chinese government over accusations of illegal fundraising, gambling, and money laundering.[603]

On March 22 2023 the SEC sued Sun for fraud, unregistered securities sales, manipulative trading, and unlawful touting of assets.[604] According to the lawsuit TRON employees had been instructed to artificially inflate the TRX token price and conduct ten wash trades on average per day over nearly a year. Sun had received a weekly report about these wash trading activities, with one of the accounts opened in his father's name. Celebrities—including singers Akon, Youtuber Austin Mahone, social-media personality Jake Paul, and actress Lindsay Lohan—had been paid ten thousand dollars per promotional tweet about TRON without disclosing that they had been paid for the tweets.[605] Sun was required to register the TRX token with the SEC, as it represented an investment contract actively marketed to U.S.-based persons.

While Justin Sun was being sued by the SEC, on March 23 Do Kwon, the founder of Terraform Labs, was arrested with a forged Costa Rican passport at the airport of the Balkan nation of Montenegro when he attempted to board a private plane to Dubai. The police also found Belgian identification documents hidden in his belongings that were also deemed to have been falsified. Kwon was accompanied by Han Chang-joon, the chief financial officer of Terraform Labs, who was also arrested.

Hours later Do Kwon was charged with fraud by U.S. criminal prosecutors in New York, with the indictment accusing him of deceiving investors about aspects of the Terra blockchain, making misleading purchases of UST and LUNA, engaging in market manipulation with an unidentified U.S. trading firm, and making false and misleading statements about the alleged scheme. If he is extradited to the U.S., Kwon could be facing more than 100 years in prison,[606] as the U.S. adopts the judicial principle of adding up sentences for each individual crime.[607]

The South Korean foreign ministry had already canceled Kwon's passport in October 2022, after he had failed to surrender to authorities the previous month and fled Singapore. Like the U.S. prosecutors, the South Korean authorities officially requested Do Kwon's extradition, having already seized 315 million dollars in assets from eight people connected to Terraform—including 117 million dollars from cofounder and former Chai CEO Daniel Shin—as these properties might be the proceeds of criminal actions.[608] Prior to the seizure Kwon had changed about sixty-nine million dollars of his property in South Korea to Bitcoin, before transferring it to an overseas crypto exchange.[609]

On March 27 2023 the CFTC launched a civil enforcement action against Changpeng Zhao (CZ) and "three entities that operate the Binance platform."[610] The CFTC argued that from July 2019 onward Binance had accepted U.S.-based persons to trade illegally on Binance.com, instructing them to use VPNs to obscure their location.[611] Binance had also left a loophole for withdrawals without know-your-customer (KYC) procedures as long as the withdrawal amount was less than two Bitcoins (twenty to 100 thousand dollars).

Binance's former chief compliance officer, Samuel Lim, was also charged by the CFTC, with the team around him suggesting that a user from the Hydra darknet with five million dollars in transactions had been advised to "make a new account" as "this current one has to go; it's tainted." Lim acknowledged that Hamas, a U.S. government–designated foreign terrorist organization, was also active on the crypto exchange, albeit with small sums.

Lim contended that if Binance was caught with U.S. users on Binance.com, then the CFTC could launch a civil case against it, which might result in a fine. But if a lack of KYC procedures could have allowed money laundering and terrorist financing, then the Bank Secrecy Act (BSA) would kick in, resulting in a criminal case and, potentially, jail time for those held responsible.

The CFTC also argued that Binance.US had been used as a "laboratory" to identify important U.S. customers and bring them to Binance.com through the backdoor. To keep them on the main Binance platform, the U.S. VIPs were instructed to submit "new" KYC documentation. Three VIP clients were identified as quant trading firms the Jane Street Group, Tower Research Capital, and Radix Trading.[612] These three firms could all end up losing their license to operate in the U.S.

In addition to submitting questionable documents, Binance users were also able to operate sub-accounts that Binance only attributed to the primary account holder. This was done without the need for any further identity controls for the sub-accounts.

After the CFTC had charged BitMEX on October 1 2020, Binance had updated all U.S. data in internal meeting documents with the "UNKWN" location classification. BitMEX was charged with a civil enforcement action for operating an unregistered trading platform and violating AML (anti-money-laundering) procedures, among other things, which had allowed U.S.-based users to trade on its platform.[613] The CFTC charge resulted in BitMEX paying 100 million dollars in fines on August 10 2021.[614] On May 23 2022 Arthur Hayes, the former CEO of BitMEX, accepted a ten-million-dollar fine and six months' house arrest plus two years' probation, after pleading guilty to violating the U.S. Bank Secrecy Act. Prosecutors had been seeking a significant prison term for him.[615]

Binance had been trying to settle with the CFTC for two years and was willing to pay a large fine, while the CFTC was seeking to permanently ban the exchange from operating in the U.S. The CFTC also wanted all revenues and fees that had been obtained illegally from U.S. customers to be disgorged, with the regulator estimating this at eighteen to twenty percent of Binance's revenue.[616] According to some sources Binance had traded one trillion dollars in 2019, 1.4 trillion in 2020, thirty-four trillion in 2021, and twenty-three trillion in 2022. A report by CryptoQuant republished on Binance's website estimated that revenues were twelve billion dollars for 2022.[617] After kickbacks and affiliate marketing programs this could still leave Binance making single-digit billions for 2022, a tenfold increase over two years.

The two companies at the center of the CFTC lawsuit, Binance Services Holdings and Binance Holdings IE, are both registered in Ireland, and on April 3 "CZ" quietly stepped down as a director of the companies. He was replaced by Kaiser Ng, a senior vice president in Binance's finance division and the former CFO of the Kraken digital asset exchange.[618]

29

"I don't have time to try to convince you, sorry"
(Satoshi Nakamoto, Bitcoin developer)

Despite the scandals, bankruptcies, and the bear market in 2022—where Bitcoin declined by seventy-seven percent from its peak—the crypto industry recovered in 2023, with Bitcoin rallying seventy-two percent during the first quarter even as a U.S.-focused regulatory crackdown was taking shape. But while the U.S. has started to enforce regulation and securities laws, other jurisdictions are proactively setting the boundaries for crypto trading and innovation in an attempt to attract talent. These jurisdictions include the Bahamas, the U.K., Hong Kong, Singapore, Dubai, and Abu Dhabi, with the latter pledging two billion dollars in February 2023 to back Web3 startups.[619] Coinbase CEO Brian Armstrong has often expressed his frustration with the lack of clarity in the U.S., saying that leaving the U.S. for the U.K., Coinbase's second-largest market in terms of revenue, is "on the table."[620] A geographical divide is shaping up, where regulatory gamesmanship will be front and center in attracting talent and capital and driving innovation.

In their 1997 book *The Sovereign Individual* James Dale Davidson and William Rees-Mogg asserted that taking is often easier than making, and that working hard to acquire possessions means nothing if the possessions cannot be protected.[621] With the emergence of cryptography in conjunction with borderless cyberspace jurisdictions the logic of violence would, they argued, shift from the state to the individual. Whereas expensive armies had traditionally been required to secure wealth, with Bitcoin's invention wealth can now be stored in the human brain by memorizing private key codes. As a result property rights would no longer need to be enforced by the state and institutions, but rather by pure cryptographic mathematics.

The key input to producing Bitcoin and verifying transactions is miners validating and updating the ledger with the help of electricity and an ability to find consensus through a decentralized way of communication. With the spread of computational power and the ability to generate electricity even in remote places, tapping into the consensus mechanism has become the most crucial factor. After the China Bitcoin mining ban in 2021 the Bitcoin network is now decentralized. Although governments and central authorities can restrict the use of the internet through land cables, SpaceX's Starlink has launched over four thousand satellites that freely operate in cyberspace, allowing users to connect to the worldwide web.[622] When Russia turned off the internet in eastern Ukraine in 2022, Starlink was able to provide web services that could also be used in the future to circumvent authorities that aim to restrict cyber communications, including participation in the Bitcoin consensus mechanism. This is why although crypto could be prone to borders, it can also find its connectivity and validation of property rights through space.

Bitcoin was started by the presumedly pseudonymous Satoshi Nakamoto in 2008, when trust in financial institutions was low and debt levels were exploding during the Global Financial Crisis. Bitcoin prices followed a parabolic trajectory when bank depositors were bailed in during the 2013 sovereign debt defaults in Cyprus, and when the financial integrity of the U.S. dollar was eroded by excessive money printing as governments flooded their economies with stimulus checks in 2020 and 2021.

On March 6 2023 Martin Gruenberg, chairman of the Federal Deposit Insurance Corporation (FDIC), which is responsible for ensuring and supervising U.S. banks, revealed that U.S. financial institutions were sitting on 620 billion dollars of unrealized losses.[623] By sending stimulus checks directly to consumers during the COVID pandemic, governments had circumvented the central bank, causing a sharp increase in inflation. This was because, contrary to what happened during the periods of quantitative easing, money was actually spent, ultimately resulting in aggressive rate hikes and the subsequent selling off of bonds. As banks had used customer deposits to buy these bonds, they were sitting on huge losses, and when depositors started to want their money back, it caused bank runs at Silvergate Bank, Silicon Valley Bank, and Signature Bank. Deposits worth 389 billion dollars were withdrawn in March 2023, prompting the FIDC to raise the deposit guarantee from 250 thousand dollars per account to unlimited numbers for all three institutions. At the same time the Treasury Secretary, Janet Yellen, even floated the idea of offering this guarantee to all U.S.-based deposit institutions. This loss in the ability of financial institutions to safeguard customer funds and protect the purchasing power of the world's reserve currency could have significant consequences for Bitcoin adoption as an alternative store of value in the months and years to come—as Satoshi appeared to have predicted.

In 2010 the World Bank released a research paper stating that a country's financial tipping point is reached if its sovereign debt levels are above seventy-seven percent for an extended period.[624] America's debt-to-GDP ratio has increased to 135 percent, which could result in suboptional growth projections and policies that favor higher inflation levels. Lower debt ratios can be achieved through solid growth or excessive inflation, but the latter could result in a significant decline in fiat wealth. In the meantime every major government and central bank is working on its digital currency, and all major financial institutions are building blockchain solutions to streamline the financial system. In July 2023 the U.S. Federal Reserve is launching its real-time payments system FedNow, a precursor to a Central Bank Digital Currency (CBDC).[625] Will this lead to a flight into Bitcoin?

Meanwhile the global monetary system built on the U.S. dollar and its institutions, which have stepped in when trust and confidence have been shaken, appears to be repositioning itself. The swap lines from the Federal Reserve have provided liquidity during crises, while the U.S. dollar and the U.S. Treasury market have offered stability. But countries from China and Russia to Saudi Arabia are now uniting to diminish U.S. monetary influence. Will the world accept the Chinese yuan as a new world reserve currency, or is the divide so significant that a technologically neutral Bitcoin will become the backbone of a new financial order?

Mobile phone applications and web streaming services like Netflix only became viable once the cost and speed of data transmissions had improved significantly. High transaction fees have been a hindrance to mass adoption for crypto so far. But this could change with the introduction of the Ethereum Improvement Proposal (EIP) 4844, as protocol fees could be reduced dramatically while the transaction throughput could increase exponentially through "blobs" of data. [626] EIP-4844 could enable transaction blocks to hold far more data without incurring additional cost[627] and might be introduced before the end of 2023. When transaction costs are near zero with instant settlement and without third-party verification, what viable blockchain applications will we experience?

There are currently 420 million crypto users worldwide, with 260 million in Asia, fifty-four million in North America, thirty-eight million in Africa, thirty-three million in South America, and thirty-one million in Europe.[628] There have also been only twenty-one million Bitcoins mined in the world. This equates to one Bitcoin for each person in megacities like Beijing, Mumbai, Cairo, Mexico City, or Sao Paulo. Bull markets in Bitcoin have tended to coincide with halving cycles, and the next halving is expected in April 2024.[629] While crypto activities may become more regulated, they will not be illegal as three U.S. government agencies have already acknowledged that crypto has become a part of people's lives: in 2014 the U.S. Internal Revenue Service (IRS) issued Notice 2014-21, which states that cryptocurrency is to be treated as property; in 2017 the Commodity Futures Trading Commission (CFTC) approved Bitcoin futures contracts;[630] and in 2021 the U.S. Securities and Exchange Commission (SEC) approved the Coinbase IPO (initial public offering).[631]

It seems likely that the crypto industry will experience another bull market due to monetary debasement, the introduction of CBDCs, clearance of regulatory overhang, or the progress in crypto transaction speed and costs.

Among the smartest computer scientists, engineers, and financial experts from leading universities around the world many are working with blockchain to develop breakthrough technologies and use cases. Each bull market has brought in a new wave of crypto enthusiasts, and crypto will undoubtedly continue to evolve. The history of crypto and the lessons learned in this book show that it will not go away. This is not the end …

Notes

1 Allie Jones, "Former Coworker Regrets Helping Reveal Identity of Bitcoin's Founder" (*The Atlantic*, March 6 2014), https://www.theatlantic.com/technology/archive/2014/03/bitcoin-founders-coworker-regrets-doxxing-him/358878/

2 "The Government sentencing memorandum regarding defendant James Zhong (United States District Court, Southern District of New York, November 4 2022), https://www.docdroid.net/cAA99Gw/123-pdf#page=37

3 Robert McMillan, "The U.S. Cracked a $3.4 Billion Crypto Heist—and Bitcoin's Anonymity", (*The Wall Street Journal*, April 12 2023), https://www.wsj.com/articles/bitcoin-blockchain-hacking-arrests-93a4cb29

4 Loaded, "Re: Wall Observer BTC/USD – Bitcoin price movement tracking & discussion" (*Bitcoin Forum,* March 21 2017), https://bitcointalk.org/index.php?topic=178336.msg18280485#msg18280485

5 David Voreacos, "Theft of Bitcoin that topped $3 billion in value leads to one-year prison sentence for James Zhong: 'I always knew what I did was wrong'" (*Fortune*, April 15 2023) https://fortune.com/2023/04/14/bitcoin-thief-james-zhong-sentenced-to-prison/

6 "Is the Cyprus crisis a boon for Bitcoin?" (*The Conversation*, March 26 2013), https://theconversation.com/is-the-cyprus-crisis-a-boon-for-bitcoin-13081

7 Karolina Tagaris, "Cypriot committee suspends probe into bank transfers list" (*Reuters*, April 9 2013), https://www.reuters.com/article/us-cyprus-list-idUSBRE9380FM20130409

8 "Transcript of secret meeting between Julian Assange and Eric Schmidt" (*Wikileaks*, April 19 2013), https://wikileaks.org/Transcript-Meeting-Assange-Schmidt.html#688

9 Max Raskin, "Meet the Bitcoin Millionaires" (*Bloomberg*, April 13 2013), https://www.bloomberg.com/news/articles/2013-04-10/meet-the-bitcoin-millionaires

10 Timothy B. Lee, "Major Bitcoin exchange shuts down, blaming regulation and loss of funds" (*Ars Technica*, February 15 2012), https://arstechnica.com/tech-policy/2012/02/major-bitcoin-exchange-shuts-down-blaming-regulation-and-loss-of-funds/

11 Application of FinCEN's to Persons Administering, Exchanging, or Using Virtual Currencies" (Department of the Treasury, Financial Crimes Enforcement Network, March 18 2013), https://www.fincen.gov/sites/default/files/shared/FIN-2013-G001.pdf

12 "Application of FinCEN's Regulations to Persons Administering, Exchanging, or Using Virtual Currencies" (Department of the Treasury, Financial Crimes Enforcement Network, March 18 2013), https://www.fincen.gov/sites/default/files/shared/FIN-2013-G001.pdf

13 "Money Transmitter License Cost" (*Faisal Khan*, February 6 2023), https://faisalkhan.com/solutions/licensing-regulatory-coverage/us-money-transmitter-license/money-transmitter-license cost.

14 Max Raskin, "Meet the Bitcoin Millionaires" (*Bloomberg*, April 13 2013), https://www.bloomberg.com/news/articles/2013-04-10/meet-the-bitcoin-millionaires

15 Delton Rhodes, "BitInstant Exchange: Lessons Learned from the Shut Down" (*CoinCentral*, November 29 2018), https://coincentral.com/bitinstant-exchange/

16 Jonathan Stempel, "Liberty Reserve founder must face $6 bln laundering case in U.S." (*Reuters*, September 24 2015), https://www.reuters.com/article/usa-cybersecurity-liberty-reserve-idUKL1N11T2G420150923

17 "The missing MtGox bitcoins" (*WizSec*, April 19 2015), https://blog.wizsec.jp/2015/04/the-missing-mtgox-bitcoins.html.

18 Alexandra Harney, Steve Stecklow, "Special Report: Twice burned - How Mt. Gox's bitcoin customers could lose again" (*Reuters*, November 16 2017), https://jp.reuters.com/article/us-bitcoin-gox-specialreport-idUKKBN1DG1UC.

19 Angela Morris, "This One MtGox Creditor Might Recover $61 Million Dollars" (*Popula*, July 12 2018), https://popula.com/2018/07/12/this-one-mtgox-creditor-might-recover-61-million-dollars/

20 Office of Foreign Asset Control – Sanctions List: https://sanctionssearch.ofac.treas.gov/Details.aspx?id=33151

21 "Chainalysis in Action: OFAC Sanctions Russian Cryptocurrency OTC Suex that Received Over $160 million from Ransomware Attackers, Scammers, and Darknet Markets" (*Chainalysis*, September 22 2021), https://blog.chainalysis.com/reports/ofac-sanction-suex-september-2021/

22 "BTC-e Sends $165 Million Worth of Bitcoin to Personal Wallets, Exchanges, and Other Services" (*Chainalysis*, November 23 2022), https://blog.chainalysis.com/reports/btc-e-bitcoin-transactions-november-2022/

23 Andrey Zakharov, "Bitcoins to the "FSB fund": how $450 million disappeared from the Wex crypto exchange" (*BBC*, November 15 2019) https://www-bbc-com.translate.goog/russian/features-50420738?_x_tr_sl=ru&_x_tr_tl=en&_x_tr_hl=en-GB

24 Dan Goodin, "Bitcoins worth $228,000 stolen from customers of hacked Webhost" (*Ars Technica*, February 3 2012), https://arstechnica.com/information-technology/2012/03/bitcoins-worth-228000-stolen-from-customers-of-hacked-webhost/
25 Bitcoin Forum https://bitcointalk.org/index.php?topic=93109.140
26 Bitcoin Forum https://bitcointalk.org/index.php?topic=93109.140
27 Ofir Beigel, "8 Mind blowing Bitcoin heists" (*99Bitcoins*, January 2 2018), https://99bitcoins.com/8-mind-blowing-bitcoin-heists/
28 Adrianne Jeffries, "Bitcoin woes: users file lawsuit over $460k in missing funds" (*The Verge*, August 11 2012), https://www.theverge.com/2012/8/10/3233711/second-bitcoin-lawsuit-is-filed-in-california
29 Amir Taaki https://en.wikipedia.org/wiki/Amir_Taaki
30 https://bitcointalk.org/index.php?topic=95795.0
31 Adrianne Jeffries, "Bitcoin woes: users file lawsuit over $460k in missing funds" (*The Verge*, August 11 2012) https://www.theverge.com/2012/8/10/3233711/second-bitcoin-lawsuit-is-filed-in-california
32 @TheEndOfMoney interview: Ryan Zhou about Bitcoinica https://www.youtube.com/watch?v=-L-FHB_-qT4
33 Vitalik Buterin, "ICBIT.SE: Bitcoin margin trading reloaded" (*Bitcoin Magazine*, August 23 2012), https://bitcoinmagazine.com/markets/icbit-se-bitcoin-margin-trading-reloaded-1345696813
34 Arthur Hayes, "Comeback" (*The Entrepreneur's Handbook*, October 26 2022), https://entrepreneurshandbook.co/comeback-fda90ba90677
35 Vitalik Buterin, "ICBIT.SE: Bitcoin margin trading reloaded" (*Bitcoin Magazine*, August 23 2012), https://bitcoinmagazine.com/markets/icbit-se-bitcoin-margin-trading-reloaded-1345696813
36 Luke Parker, "Safello acquires ICBIT and appoints founder as new CTO", (*Brave New Coin*, October 21 2016) https://bravenewcoin.com/insights/safello-acquires-icbit-and-appoints-founder-as-new-cto
37 Bitcoin Forum, "Summary – unclescrooge", https://bitcointalk.org/index.php?action=profile;u=4295
38 Bitcoin Forum, "[BETA]Bitfinex.com first Bitcoin P2P lending platform for leverage trading", https://bitcointalk.org/index.php?topic=119745.msg1289419#msg1289419
39 Bitcoin Talk https://bitcointalk.org/index.php?action=profile;u=4295;sa=showPosts;start=340
40 https://bitcointalk.org/index.php?topic=119745.0
41 Vitalik Buterin, "Bitfinex: Bitcoinica rises from the grave" (*Bitcoin Magazine*, November 22 2012) https://bitcoinmagazine.com/markets/bitfinex-bitcoinica-rises-from-the-grave-1353644122
42 "Stock Trading in Bucket Shops" (*Jesse Livermore, Stock Trader Extraordinaire*), https://jesse-livermore.com/bucket-shops.html
43 Nate Raymond, "Texan gets one-and-a-half years in prison for running bitcoin Ponzi scheme" (*Reuters*, July 22 2016), https://www.reuters.com/article/us-bitcoin-fraud-texas-idUSKCN1012W8
44 "Sec. & Exch. Comm'n v. Shavers" (Casetext, August 6 2013), https://casetext.com/case/sec-exch-commn-v-shavers-1
45 binyamin, "Bitfinex's Founder Seemingly Tried to Start a Ponzi Scheme" (*Steemit*, 2016), https://steemit.com/bitcoin/@binyamin/bitfinex-s-founder-seemingly-tried-to-start-a-ponzi-scheme
46 @TheEndOfMoney interview: Ryan Zhou about Bitcoinica https://www.youtube.com/watch?v=-L-FHB_-qT4
47 Redazione Adnkronos, "Computer Pirates: Microsoft's Counterattack" (*AdnKronos*, December 3 1996) https://www1.adnkronos.com/Archivio/AdnAgenzia/1996/12/03/Cronaca/PIRATI-INFORMATICI-MICROSOFT-AL-CONTRATTACCO_130900.php
48 Patent infringement lawsuit filed in Italy due to DVD-related patent infringement (*Toshiba*, December 28 2007) https://www.global.toshiba/jp/news/corporate/2007/12/pr2801.html
49 "Bitfinex now included in the CoinDesk Bitcoin Price Index" (*CoinDesk*, March 14 2014), https://www.coindesk.com/markets/2014/03/13/bitfinex-now-included-in-the-coindesk-bitcoin-price-index/
50 "Data from Paradise Papers: Tether Holdings Limited", (International Consortium of Investigative Journalists), https://offshoreleaks.icij.org/nodes/82024464
51 Kadhim Shubber and Siddharth Venkataramakrishnan), "Tether: the former plastic surgeon behind the crypto reserve currency" (Financial Times, July 15 2021), https://www.ft.com/content/4da3060c-8e1a-439f-a1d7-a6a4688ad6ca
52 Daniel Slotta, "Annual share of Bitcoin trading volume executed in Chinese yuan from 2012 to 2018" (*Statistica*, May 8 2020), https://www.statista.com/statistics/911260/china-annual-share-of-bitcoin-trading-volume-executed-in-chinese-yuan/
53 Geoffrey A. Fowler and Juying Qin, "China's New Coin of the Realm?" (*The Wall Street Journal*, March 30 2007) https://www.wsj.com/articles/SB117519670114653518
54 "Bitcoin Gold Mine or Trap" (*People's Daily Online*) http://finance.people.com.cn/bank/n/2013/0507/c202331-21386427-2.html
55 https://www.reddit.com/r/Bitcoin/comments/1bawmj/i_just_used_bitcoin_to_buy_a_coffee_in_a_beijing/
56 "Bitcoin: a software-based online payment system" (*SourceForge*, July 29 2019), https://sourceforge.net/projects/bitcoin/files/stats/map?dates=2008-11-09+to+2013-01-01

57 Bobby Lee, "Bobby Lee's Bitcoin Awakening" (*CoinDesk*, May 18 2021), https://www.coindesk.com/business/2021/05/18/book-excerpt-bobby-lees-bitcoin-awakening/

58 Matt Clinch, "Baidu division now accepting bitcoins" (*CNBC*, October 16 2013), https://www.cnbc.com/2013/10/16/baidu-division-now-accepting-bitcoins.html

59 Emily Spaven, "Chinese internet giant Baidu starts accepting bitcoin" (*CoinDesk*, October 16 2013), https://www.coindesk.com/markets/2013/10/15/chinese-internet-giant-baidu-starts-accepting-bitcoin/

60 Kashmir Hill, "From Walmart To Bitcoin: The CEO Behind The Chinese Exchange Sending BTC To New Highs" (*Forbes*, November 8 2013), https://www.forbes.com/sites/kashmirhill/2013/11/08/from-walmart-to-bitcoin-the-ceo-behind-the-chinese-exchange-sending-bitcoin-to-new-highs/?sh=6602418d48ac

61 China estimates fake trade invoicing at $75 billion in Jan-April (*Reuters*, June 14 2013), https://www.reuters.com/article/china-economy-fake-trading/china-estimates-fake-trade-invoicing-at-75-billion-in-jan-april-report-idINDEE95D02520130614

62 Trade Summary for Hong Kong, China 2013 https://wits.worldbank.org/CountryProfile/en/Country/HKG/Year/2013/Summarytext

63 Adrianne Jeffries, "FTC shuts down Butterfly Labs, the second-most hated company in Bitcoinland" (*The Verge*, September 24 2014), https://www.theverge.com/2014/9/23/6833047/bitcoin-conspiracy-theorists-vindicated-as-ftc-shuts-down-butterfly-labs

64 https://www.coinwarz.com/mining/bitcoin/hashrate-chart/2012

65 "The miners' giants are listed: the road to transformation is long and long" (Blocking), https://blocking.net/12600/the-miners-giants-are-listed-the-road-to-transformation-is-long-and-long/

66 Qin Xiaofeng, "Jianan past events: floating up and down eight years, or become the first mining machine stocks" https://blocking.net/21148/jianan-past-events-floating-up-and-down-eight-years-or-become-the-first-mining-machine-stocks/

67 The miners' giants are listed: the road to transformation is long and long https://blocking.net/12600/the-miners-giants-are-listed-the-road-to-transformation-is-long-and-long/

68 "ASICME Mining Machine founder Yang Yaorui: The next two years is still the golden period" (*Alibaba Cloud*, March 23 2015), https://topic.alibabacloud.com/article/asicme-mining-machine-founder-yang-yaorui-the-next-two-years-is-still-the-golden-period_2_6_1924226.html

69 Paul Bischoff, "In Depth: Getting Bitcoin into the Hands of China's Average Zhou" (*Tech in Asia*, July 12 2013), https://www.techinasia.com/depth-bitcoin-hands-chinas-average-zhou

70 Wolfie Zhao, "The CoinDesk 50: Bitmain, the Behemoth of Bitcoin Mining" (*CoinDesk*, May 9 2020) https://www.coindesk.com/business/2020/05/09/the-coindesk-50-bitmain-the-behemoth-of-bitcoin-mining/

71 (Singapore Blockchain Technology Foundation, February 2018), https://bcf.sg/2018/05/02/%E7%83%A4%E7%8C%AB%E6%B2%A1%E6%AD%BB/

72 Adrianne Jeffries, "FTC shuts down Butterfly Labs, the second-most hated company in Bitcoinland" (*The Verge*, September 24 2014), https://www.theverge.com/2014/9/23/6833047/bitcoin-conspiracy-theorists-vindicated-as-ftc-shuts-down-butterfly-labs

73 Keira Wright, "In 2013, Wired destroyed the key to 13 BTC now worth $760K" (Cointelegraph, December 2 2021), https://cointelegraph.com/news/in-2013-wired-destroyed-the-key-to-13-bitcoin-now-worth-760k-to-make-a-point

74 Jona Derks, Jaap Gordijn and Arjen Siegmann, "From chaining blocks to breaking even: A study on the profitability of bitcoin mining from 2012 to 2016" (*SpringerLink*, August 23 2018), https://link.springer.com/article/10.1007/s12525-018-0308-3

75 Joon Ian Wong and Johnny Simon, "Inside one of the world's largest bitcoin mines" (*Quartz*, August 17 2017), https://qz.com/1055126/photos-china-has-one-of-worlds-largest-bitcoin-mines

76 Eric Mu, "Chinese Government-Backed TV Program Bashes Bitcoin, Outrages Community" (*CoinDesk*, January 13 2014), https://www.coindesk.com/markets/2014/01/12/chinese-government-backed-tv-program-bashes-bitcoin-outrages-community/

77 Heng Loong Cheong and Fion Law, "Mixed feelings: China censures bitcoin while Hong Kong embraces it" (*DLA Piper*, July 2014), https://www.dlapiper.com/en-sg/insights/publications/2014/07/china-censures-bitcoin-while-hong-kong-embraces-it

78 Danny Lee and Angela Meng, "Hong Kong's first bitcoin shop to open this week in Sai Ying Pun" (*SCMP*, February 23 2014) https://www.scmp.com/business/banking-finance/article/1433555/hong-kongs-first-bitcoin-shop-open-week-sai-ying-pun

79 BitMex Dominates Tech in Asia Singapore Arena, Beating 475 Startups (August 11 2020), https://worldwidetraining.org/bitmex-dominates-tech-in-asia-singapore-arena-beating-475-startups-coin-news-asia/

80 Erik Crouch, "He left a cushy finance job to build the Goldman Sachs of Bitcoin" (*Tech in Asia*, April 7 2016), https://www.techinasia.com/goldman-sachs-bitcoin-bitmex

81 Alex Lielacher, "BitMEX Review" (*Investopedia*, June 1 2022), https://www.investopedia.com/bitmex-review-5216108

82 Yogita Khatri, "Crypto exchanges briefly went out of service as bitcoin crashed by over 50% in one day" (*The Block*, March 13 2020), https://www.theblock.co/post/58675/crypto-exchanges-briefly-went-out-of-service-as-bitcoin-crashed-by-over-50-in-one-day

83 Helen Partz, "BitMEX Reportedly Continues to Lose Market Share to Binance Futures" (*Cointelegraph*, April 21 2020), https://cointelegraph.com/news/bitmex-reportedly-continued-to-lose-market-share-to-binance-futures

84 BitMEX (Twitter March 13 2020), https://twitter.com/BitMEX/status/1238329954967752704

85 SBF @SBF_FTX (Twitter, March 13 2020), https://twitter.com/SBF_FTX/status/1238306306043162625

86 SBF @SBF_FTX (Twitter, March 13 2020),https://twitter.com/SBF_FTX/status/1238306314809303041

87 Arthur Hayes, "BitMEX Market Making Desk" (*BitMEX*, April 30 2018), https://blog.bitmex.com/bitmex-market-making-desk/

88 Matthew Collins, "BitMEX insiders caught in a web of lies" (*Medium*, May 21 2018), https://medium.com/@mattcollburner/bitmex-insiders-caught-in-a-web-of-lies-6d9b90baa693

89 Flood @ThinkingUSD, "Deribit, Bitcoin Options and Volatility" (*Medium*, June 8 2018), https://medium.com/@ThinkingUSD/deribit-bitcoin-options-and-volatility-b370ba276761

90 Cheyenne Ligon, "Former BitMEX CEO Arthur Hayes Sentenced to 2 Years' Probation" (*CoinDesk*, May 21 2022), https://www.coindesk.com/policy/2022/05/20/former-bitmex-ceo-arthur-hayes-sentenced-to-2-years-probation/

91 dacoinmaster (jr.willet@gmail.com), "The Second Bitcoin Whitepaper", https://cryptochainuni.com/wp-content/uploads/Mastercoin-2nd-Bitcoin-Whitepaper.pdf

92 Isiah McCall, "Why Charles Hoskinson Was Shamefully Kicked Out of Ethereum" (*Medium*, May 18 2021), https://medium.com/yardcouch-com/why-charles-hoskinson-was-shamefully-kicked-out-of-ethereum-8b29faa5cd14

93 https://iq.wiki/wiki/charles-hoskinson

94 Pete Rizzo, "Chinese Auto Giant Wanxiang Plans $50 Million Blockchain Fund" (*CoinDesk*, September 30 2015), https://www.coindesk.com/markets/2015/09/29/chinese-auto-giant-wanxiang-plans-50-million-blockchain-fund/

95 EOS Network Foundation (Twitter, May 20 2022), https://twitter.com/EosNFoundation/status/1524023932008939522

96 Brady Dale, "EOS Startup Block.One Is Using Its Billions to Buy Back More Equity" (*CoinDesk*, June 7 2019), https://www.coindesk.com/markets/2019/06/06/eos-startup-blockone-is-using-its-billions-to-buy-back-more-equity/

97 Steven Stradbrooke, "Block.one wash trading? New report puts EOS developer in more jeopardy over controversial ICO" (*CoinGeek*, September 9 2021), https://coingeek.com/block-one-wash-trading-new-report-puts-eos-developer-in-more-jeopardy-over-controversial-ico/

98 Nelson Wang, "Founder of EOS Developer Block. One Buys 9.3% of Crypto Bank Silvergate" (*CoinDesk*, 24 November 2022), https://www.coindesk.com/business/2022/11/23/founder-of-eos-developer-blockone-buys-93-of-crypto-bank-silvergate/

99 Report of Investigation Pursuant to Section 21(a) of the Securities Exchange Act of 1934: The DAO https://www.sec.gov/litigation/investreport/34-81207.pdf

100 "SEC Orders Blockchain Company to Pay $24 Million Penalty for Unregistered ICO" (U.S. Securities and Exchange Commission, September 30 2019), https://www.sec.gov/news/press-release/2019-202

101 Howey Test Definition: What It Means and Implications for Cryptocurrency https://www.investopedia.com/terms/h/howey-test.asp

102 SEC Report on The DAO (*SEC.gov*, July 25 2017), https://www.sec.gov/litigation/investreport/34-81207.pdf

103 "Report of Investigation Pursuant to Section 21(a) of the Securities Exchange Act of 1934: The DAO" (*Securities and Exchange Commission*, July 25 2017) https://www.sec.gov/litigation/investreport/34-81207.pdf

104 https://www.sec.gov/litigation/investreport/34-81207.pdf

105 "What is cryptocurrency Ethereum Classic (ETC) and how does it work?" (*Kriptomat*), https://kriptomat.io/cryptocurrencies/ethereum-classic/what-is-ethereum-classic/

106 "Company Halts ICO After SEC Raises Registration Concerns" (*U.S. Securities and Exchange Commission*, December 11 2017), https://www.sec.gov/news/press-release/2017-227

107 "Securities and Exchange Commission against PlexCorps" (United States District Court, Eastern District of New York) https://www.sec.gov/litigation/complaints/2017/comp-pr2017-219.pdf

108 Aaron Hankin, "Nearly half of all 2017 ICOs have failed", (*MarketWatch*, February 26 2018), https://www.marketwatch.com/story/nearly-half-of-all-2017-icos-have-failed-2018-02-26

109 Chao Deng, "Bitcoin Market Gets a Lift From China" (*The Wall Street Journal*, December 4 2013), https://www.wsj.com/articles/SB10001424052702303997604579237913301162066

110 Eric Mu, "Meet China's Biggest Bitcoin Multi-Millionaire" (*CoinDesk*, December 6 2013), https://www.coindesk.com/markets/2013/12/05/meet-chinas-biggest-bitcoin-multi-millionaire/

111 Eric Mu, "Meet China's Biggest Bitcoin Multi-Millionaire" (*CoinDesk*, December 6 2013), https://www.coindesk.com/markets/2013/12/05/meet-chinas-biggest-bitcoin-multi-millionaire/

112 China Crypto-Whale Li Xiaolai Assaults Binance, TRX, NEO and QTUM in Leaked Audio https://bitcoinexchangeguide.com/china-crypto-whale-li-xiaolai-assaults-binance-trx-neo-and-qtum-in-leaked-audio/

113 Other, "Bitcoin tycoon Li Xiaolai's foul-mouthed rant" (*New Zealand Herald*, July 9 2018), https://www.nzherald.co.nz/business/bitcoin-tycoon-li-xiaolais-foul-mouthed-rant/LEYN3YYBQO5NZYEW4LYA2XIMSM/

114 Bitcoin tycoon Li Xiaolai spills dark secrets in leaked recording https://technode.com/2018/07/06/li-xiaolai-recording/

115 "The Voice of Finance Revolution from Bitcoin Community in Davos" (posted by My Crypto Journey), https://www.youtube.com/watch?v=J7g2JFn68LU

116 The Great Crypto-Wall of China – China Banishes Initial Coin Offerings (September 7 2017), https://www.lockelord.com/newsandevents/publications/2017/09/the-great-crypto-wall

117 Wu Yujian, "Exclusive | ICO included in the special rectification of mutual funds risk No. 99 document to start the clean-up and rectification" (Caixin, September 4 2017), https://finance.caixin.com/2017-09-04/101140069.html

118 China moves to limit activities relating to ICOs and Cryptocurrencies: game over or level up?" (*Hogan Lovells*, September 2017) https://www.jdsupra.com/post/fileServer.aspx?fName=77313e3a-893c-4239-a5cf-73b20199fd34.pdf

119 Joseph Young, "Japan Becomes Largest Bitcoin Market as Traders Leave China" (*Cointelegraph*, September 17 2017), https://cointelegraph.com/news/japan-becomes-largest-bitcoin-market-as-traders-leave-china

120 Why Tether Dominates in China (*Chainalysis*, October 15 2019), https://blog.chainalysis.com/reports/tether-china-apac-report-preview/

121 OTC Crypto Market https://www.capco.com/-/media/CapcoMedia/The-Crypto-OTC-Market-At-A-Glance_v5.ashx

122 Aaron Stanley, "Unchartered Bitcoin OTC Markets" (*Forbes*, October 23 2018), https://www.forbes.com/sites/astanley/2018/10/23/uncharted-bitcoin-otc-markets-gear-up-for-institutional-inflows/?sh=c87dcae7bacd

123 Aislinn Keely, "Former head of Circle OTC says there's more to the Tether narrative" (*The Block*, December 2 2019), https://www.theblock.co/post/48857/former-head-of-circle-otc-says-theres-more-to-the-tether-narrative

124 Hailey Jo, "In a country known for its "bitcoin zombies," one-third of workers are crypto investors" (*Quartz*, December 28 2018), https://qz.com/1166103/a-third-of-south-korean-workers-have-invested-in-cryptocurrencies-like-bitcoin

125 South Korea bans all new cryptocurrency sales (*CNBC*, September 29 2017), https://www.cnbc.com/2017/09/28/south-korea-bans-all-new-cryptocurrency-sales.html

126 South Korea bans all new cryptocurrency sales (*CNBC*, September 29 2017), https://www.cnbc.com/2017/09/28/south-korea-bans-all-new-cryptocurrency-sales.html

127 Son Ji-hyoung, "Korea unveils measures to tame cryptocurrencies (*The Korean Herald*, December 13 2017), http://www.koreaherald.com/view.php?ud=20171213000815

128 Hailey Jo, "In a country known for its "bitcoin zombies," one-third of workers are crypto investors" (*Quartz*, December 28 2018), https://qz.com/1166103/a-third-of-south-korean-workers-have-invested-in-cryptocurrencies-like-bitcoin

129 Reuters, "Authorities raid South Korea's largest cryptocurrency exchanges" (*CNBC*, January 10 2018), https://www.cnbc.com/2018/01/10/police-tax-authorities-raid-south-korea-cryptocurrency-exchanges-for-tax-evasion.html

130 Matthew C Klein, "A theory about the recent crypto price plunge" (*Financial Times*, January 18 2018), https://www.ft.com/content/7c2cd487-1f9a-3530-b88d-ea30c47fdf9f

131 All News, "Gov't mulls shutting down all cryptocurrency exchanges: regulator" (*Yonhap News Agency*, January 18 2018), https://en.yna.co.kr/view/AEN20180118005100320

132 William Suberg, "South Korea Finance Minister Confirms 'No Ban' On Cryptocurrency" (*Cointelegraph*, January 31 2018), https://cointelegraph.com/news/south-korea-finance-minister-confirms-no-ban-on-cryptocurrency

133 Yoon Young-sil, "National Assembly Calls for Measures to Allow ICOs" (*Business Korea*, May 29 2018), http://www.businesskorea.co.kr/news/articleView.html?idxno=22613

134 Noah Kirsch, "Larry Ellison's Net Worth Just Rose $5 Billion In Two Days" (*Forbes*, June 24 2017), https://www.forbes.com/sites/noahkirsch/2017/06/24/larry-ellisons-net-worth-just-rose-5-billion-in-two-days/?sh=3f2cf1d54acd

135 Samantha Cruz, "How to Get Away With $530 Million of Cryptocurrency" (*Horangi*, March 28 2018), https://www.horangi.com/blog/how-to-get-away-with-us-530-million-worth-of-cryptocurrency-the-easy-way

136 "How to Get the Most out of Bitcoin in Tokyo" (*Tokyo Weekender*, December 29 2017), https://www.tokyoweekender.com/2017/12/how-to-get-the-most-out-of-bitcoin-in-tokyo/

137 Aaron Hankin "Jamie Dimon: 'I don't really give a sh*t about bitcoin'" (*Financial News*, November 1 2018), https://www.fnlondon.com/articles/jamie-dimon-i-dont-really-give-a-sht-about-bitcoin-20181101

138 Tae Kim, "Warren Buffett says bitcoin is 'probably rat poison squared'" (*CNBC*, May 6 2018), https://www.cnbc.com/2018/05/05/warren-buffett-says-bitcoin-is-probably-rat-poison-squared.html
139 Nikhilesh De, "Coinbase Rolls Out Crypto Custody Product for Institutions" (*CoinDesk*, May 15 2018), https://sg.news.yahoo.com/coinbase-rolls-crypto-custody-product-120013427.html
140 Kate Rooney and Ari Levy, "The most influential endowment manager just jumped into crypto with bets on two Silicon Valley funds" (*CNBC*, October 5 2018), https://www.cnbc.com/2018/10/05/yale-investment-chief-david-swensen-jumps-into-crypto-with-bets-on-two-silicon-valley-funds.html
141 Daniel Palmer, "North Korean Hacking Group Lazarus Stole $571 Million in Cryptos: Report" (*CoinDesk*, October 19 2019), https://www.coindesk.com/markets/2018/10/19/north-korean-hacking-group-lazarus-stole-571-million-in-cryptos-report/
142 "Treasury Sanctions Individuals Laundering Cryptocurrency for Lazarus Group" (U.S. Department of the Treasury, March 2 2020), https://home.treasury.gov/news/press-releases/sm924
143 "Virtual Event | Cybersecurity Threats and Information Sharing" (Center for a New American Security, July 28 2022), https://www.cnas.org/events/virtual-event-cybersecurity-threats-and-information-sharing-with-anne-neuberger
144 Ethan Gach, "Crypto Gaming 'Landlords' Upset They Can't Keep Exploiting All The Players Quitting" (*Kotaku*, April 16 2022), https://kotaku.com/axie-infinity-nft-crypto-hack-landlord-scholar-pokemon-1848800557
145 Russian Cybercriminals Drive Significant Ransomware and Cryptocurrency-based Money Laundering Activity (*Chainalysis*, February 14 2022), https://blog.chainalysis.com/reports/2022-crypto-crime-report-preview-russia-ransomware-money-laundering/
146 Kartikay Mherotra and Olga Kharif, "Ransomware HQ: Moscow's Tallest Tower Is a Cybercriminal Cash Machine" (*Bloomberg*, November 3 2021), https://www.bloomberg.com/news/articles/2021-11-03/bitcoin-money-laundering-happening-in-moscow-s-vostok-tower-experts-say
147 Kartikay Mehrotra and Olga Kharif, "Ransomware HQ: Moscow's Tallest Tower Is a Cybercriminal Cash Machine" (*Bloomberg*, November 3 2021), https://www.bloomberg.com/news/articles/2021-11-03/bitcoin-money-laundering-happening-in-moscow-s-vostok-tower-experts-say
148 Yazan Boshmaf *et al.*, "Investigating MMM Ponzi scheme on Bitcoin", (December 1 2019) https://arxiv.org/pdf/1910.12244.pdf
149 CFTC vs. Bitfinex (June 2 2016) www.cftc.gov/sites/default/files/idc/groups/public/@lrenforcementactions/documents/legalpleading/enfbfxnaorder060216.pdf
150 "CFTC Orders Bitcoin Exchange Bitfinex to Pay $75,000 for Offering Illegal Off-Exchange Financed Retail Commodity Transactions and Failing to Register as a Futures Commission Merchant" (CFTC), https://www.cftc.gov/PressRoom/PressReleases/7380-16
151 Wesley Messamore, "Tether Has No Plans to Go Public" (*CryptoPotato*, May 4 2022), https://cryptopotato.com/tether-has-no-plans-to-go-public-cto-paolo-ardoino-exclusive-interview/
152 Claire Baldwin, "Bitfinex exchange customers to get 36 percent haircut, debt token" (*Reuters*, August 7 2016), https://www.reuters.com/article/us-bitfinex-hacked-hongkong-idUSKCN10106H
153 Nicola Borzi (*Medium*, February 18 2021), https://nicolaborzi.medium.com/the-lawless-rollercoaster-of-bitcoin-enriches-few-investors-while-many-often-lose-everything-f9b4789444c2
154 "Two Arrested for Alleged Conspiracy to Launder $4.5 Billion in Stolen Cryptocurrency" (The United States Department of Justice, February 8 2022), https://www.justice.gov/opa/pr/two-arrested-alleged-conspiracy-launder-45-billion-stolen-cryptocurrency
155 Ed Caesar, "How a Young Couple Failed to Launder Billions of Dollars in Stolen Bitcoin" (*The New Yorker*, February 14 2022), https://www.newyorker.com/business/currency/how-a-young-couple-failed-to-launder-billions-of-dollars-in-stolen-bitcoin
156 "Elliptic Analysis: New York Husband and Wife Arrested for Allegedly Laundering $5 Billion in Bitcoin Stolen from Bitfinex in 2016" (*Elliptic*, February 8 2022), https://www.elliptic.co/blog/elliptic-analysis-new-york-husband-and-wife-arrested-for-laundering-5-billion-in-bitcoin-stolen-from-bitfinex-in-2016
157 "Virtual Currencies: Emerging Regulatory, Law Enforcement, and Consumer Protection Challenges" (*GAO*, May 29 2014), https://www.gao.gov/products/gao-14-496
158 "BNP Paribas to pay $9bn to settle sanctions violations" (*BBC*, July 1 2014), https://www.bbc.com/news/business-28099694
159 Pete Rizzo, "Realcoin Rebrands as 'Tether' to Avoid Altcoin Association" (*CoinDesk*, November 21 2014), https://www.coindesk.com/markets/2014/11/20/realcoin-rebrands-as-tether-to-avoid-altcoin-association/
160 "SEC Charges Poloniex for Operating Unregistered Digital Asset Exchange" (U. S. Exchange and Securities Commission, 9 August 2021), https://www.sec.gov/news/press-release/2021-147
155 Ben Foldy and Ada Hui, "Crypto Companies Behind Tether Used Falsified Documents and Shell Companies to Get Bank Accounts" (*The Wall Street Journal*, March 3 2023), https://www.wsj.com/articles/crypto-companies-behind-tether-used-falsified-documents-and-shell-companies-to-get-bank-accounts-f798b0a5
162 Emin Guen Sirer (Twitter, November 21 2017), https://twitter.com/el33th4xor/status/932803027207045120

163 Lily Katz, "Tether Theft Isn't the First Controversy for Cryptocurrency Firm" (*Bloomberg*, November 22 2017), https://www.bloomberg.com/news/articles/2017-11-21/tether-theft-isn-t-the-first-controversy-for-cryptocurrency-firm#xj4y7vzkg

164 Legal (Tether, last updated 2 September 2022), https://tether.to/en/legal/

165 David Dinkins, "The Strange Story of Tether, the Digital Money That Claims it Isn't Money" (*Cointelegraph*, August 17 2017), https://cointelegraph.com/news/the-strange-story-of-tether-the-digital-money-that-claims-it-isnt-money

166 Matt Leising, "There's an $814 Million Mystery Near the Heart of the Biggest Bitcoin Exchange" (*Bloomberg*, December 5 2017), https://www.bloomberg.com/news/articles/2017-12-05/mystery-shrouds-tether-and-its-links-to-biggest-bitcoin-exchange#xj4y7vzkg

167 Kate Rooney, "Much of bitcoin's 2017 boom was market manipulation, research says" (*CNBC*, June 13 2018), https://www.cnbc.com/2018/06/13/much-of-bitcoins-2017-boom-was-market-manipulation-researcher-says.html

168 Attorney General James Ends Virtual Currency Trading Platform Bitfinex's Illegal Activities in New York https://ag.ny.gov/press-release/2021/attorney-general-james-ends-virtual-currency-trading-platform-bitfinexs-illegal

169 "Tether Banking Relationship Announced" (Tether, November 1 2018), https://tether.to/en/tether-banking-relationship-announced

170 Josiah Wilmoth, "Fake News? Cryptocurrency Exchange Bitfinex Denies Rumors of Insolvency" (*Yahoo!*, October 8 2018), https://sg.finance.yahoo.com/news/fake-news-cryptocurrency-exchange-bitfinex-152522601.html

171 Amy Castor, "New York Attorney General: Bitfinex is hiding $850 million in losses" (*Amycastor.com*, April 26 2019), https://amycastor.com/2019/04/26/new-york-attorney-general-bitfinex-is-hiding-850-million-in-losses/

172 Erik Larson, Matthew Leising and Olga Kharif, "Crypto Market Roiled by New Allegations Against Tether, Bitfinex" (*Bloomberg*, April 26 2019), https://www.bloomberg.com/news/articles/2019-04-25/bitfinex-operator-accused-by-new-york-of-850-million-coverup#xj4y7vzkg

173 Nicola Borzi (*Medium*, February 18 2018), https://nicolaborzi.medium.com/the-lawless-rollercoaster-of-bitcoin-enriches-few-investors-while-many-often-lose-everything-f9b4789444c2

174 Attorney General of the State of New York v. iFinex Inc. *et al.*, "Affirmation of Stuart Hoegner" (Supreme Court of the State of New York, County of New York), https://amyhcastor.files.wordpress.com/2019/01/408190972-stuart-hoegner-affidavit-4-30.pdf

175 Erik Larson, Matthew Leising and Olga Kharif, "Crypto Market Roiled by New Allegations Against Tether, Bitfinex" (*Bloomberg*, April 26 2019), https://www.bloomberg.com/news/articles/2019-04-25/bitfinex-operator-accused-by-new-york-of-850-million-coverup#xj4y7vzkg

176 "Initial Exchange Offering of Leo Tokens For Use on iFinex Trading Platforms, Products, and Services" (*Bitfinex*, May 8 2019), https://www.bitfinex.com/wp-2019-05.pdf

177 ZhaoDon@RenrenBit.com, "Bitfinex Official document about the LEO token"(Twitter, May 4 2019), https://twitter.com/zhaodong1982/status/1124688103313002497/photo/1

178 "Tether alleged shadow banker Reggie Fowler seeks 6-month sentencing delay" (*CoinGeek*, September 13 2022), https://coingeek.com/tether-alleged-shadow-banker-reggie-fowler-seeks-6-month-sentencing-delay/

179 "Crypto Capital Official Nabbed in Money Laundering Probe" (*Bloomberg*, October 25 2019), https://www.bloomberg.com/news/articles/2019-10-25/crypto-capital-official-nabbed-in-polish-money-laundering-probe

180 "Attorney General James Ends Virtual Currency Trading Platform Bitfinex's Illegal Activities in New York" (New York State Office of the Attorney General, February 23 2021), https://ag.ny.gov/press-release/2021/attorney-general-james-ends-virtual-currency-trading-platform-bitfinexs-illegal

181 Digital Money for a Digital Age (December 20 2014), https://web.archive.org/web/20190304165618/https://tether.to/

182 Amy Castor, "Tether's Paolo Ardoino and Stuart Hoegner do a podcast" (*Amycastor.com*, January 10 2021), https://amycastor.com/2021/01/10/tethers-paolo-ardoino-stuart-hoegner-do-a-podcast-transcript-and-comments/

183 Tether has held some reserves at Bahamas bank Capital Union (*Financial Times*, May 30 2022), https://www.ft.com/content/e4cb9a6e-cb29-4719-b6ee-33a5bf01945e

184 Anton Muehlemann, "The Evolution of the Digital Asset Market in 2018" (*Medium*, January 22 2019), https://medium.com/blockchain-at-berkeley/the-evolution-of-the-digital-asset-market-in-2018-9af4c5de176c

185 Pete Rizzo, "Questions Linger As China's Bitcoin Exchanges Halt Margin Trading" (*CoinDesk*, January 19 2017), https://www.coindesk.com/markets/2017/01/19/questions-linger-as-chinas-bitcoin-exchanges-halt-margin-trading/

186 "PBoC makes spot checks on bitcoin exchanges" (*The Star*, January 12 2017), https://www.thestar.com.my/business/business-news/2017/01/12/pboc-makes-spot-checks-on-bitcoin-exchanges/

187 William Suberg, "OKCoin Follows Bitfinex, Freezes Inbound Wire Transfers" (*Cointelegraph*, April 19 2017), https://cointelegraph.com/news/okcoin-follows-bitfinex-freezes-inbound-wire-transfers

188 "OKCoin" (Golden) https://golden.com/wiki/OKCoin-MKWWBY#:~:text=In%20May%202017%2C%20OKCoin%2C%20were,by%20the%20end%20of%20October.

189 Saheli Roy Choudhury, "China bans companies from raising money through ICOs, asks local regulators to inspect 60 major platforms" (*CNBC*, September 4 2017), https://www.cnbc.com/2017/09/04/chinese-icos-china-bans-fundraising-through-initial-coin-offerings-report-says.html

190 Yogita Khatri, "OKCoin Founder Buys Hong Kong-Listed Firm in $60 Million Deal" (*CoinDesk*, January 24 2019), https://www.coindesk.com/markets/2019/01/24/okcoin-founder-buys-hong-kong-listed-firm-in-60-million-deal/

191 Marc van der Chijs, "OKCoin Raises $10 Million to Become China's 'Largest Exchange'" (*CoinDesk*, March 17 2014), https://www.coindesk.com/markets/2014/03/16/okcoin-raises-10-million-to-become-chinas-largest-exchange/

192 Pete Rizzo, "OKCoin CEO Star Xu: Bitcoin's Price Depends on User Growth" (*CoinDesk*, January 23 2015), https://www.coindesk.com/markets/2015/01/22/okcoin-ceo-star-xu-bitcoins-price-depends-on-user-growth/

193 "OKX official announcement: Reopening of withdrawals and other related updates " (OKX.com), https://www.okx.com/support/hc/en-us/articles/360052758931-OKX-official-announcement-Reopening-of-withdrawals-and-other-related-updates

194 "Huobi Technology PTE. LTD." (OpenGovSG), https://opengovsg.com/corporate/201728801D

195 Stephanie Pearl Li, "Crypto exchange Huobi's COO Jiawei Zhu stepped down in April, five months after reported arrest" (*KrAsia*, October 7 2021), https://kr-asia.com/crypto-exchange-huobis-coo-jiawei-zhu-stepped-down-in-april-five-months-after-reported-arrest

196 Christopher Harland-Dunaway, "The Many Escapes of Justin Sun" (*The Verge*, March 9 2022), https://www.theverge.com/c/22947663/justin-sun-tron-cryptocurrency-poloniex

197 Zack Voell, "Tether Use on Tron Passes Ethereum as Low Fees Attract Small Transactions" (*CoinDesk*, January 21 2021), https://www.coindesk.com/markets/2021/01/20/tether-use-on-tron-passes-ethereum-as-low-fees-attract-small-transactions/

198 Fran Velasquez, "Justin Sun Says Hong Kong's New Licensing Regime Could Shift Policy in Mainland China, Eventually" (*CoinDesk*, March 2 20203), https://www.coindesk.com/policy/2023/03/01/justin-sun-says-hong-kongs-new-licensing-regime-could-shift-policy-in-mainland-china-eventually/

199 H.E. Justin Sun (Twitter, January 30 2023), https://twitter.com/justinsuntron/status/1619746238005649409?lang=en

200 John Cheng et al, "Hong Kong Plans to Legalize Retail Crypto Trading to Become Hub" (*Bloomberg*, October 27 2022), https://www.bloomberg.com/news/articles/2022-10-27/hong-kong-plans-to-legalize-retail-crypto-trading-to-become-hub

201 Annual share of Bitcoin trading volume executed in Chinese yuan from 2012 to 2018 https://www.statista.com/statistics/911260/china-annual-share-of-bitcoin-trading-volume-executed-in-chinese-yuan/

202 Primrose Riordan and Chan Ho-him, "How FTX used Hong Kong cash-for-crypto shop to turbocharge growth" (*Financial Times*, December 5 2022), https://www.ft.com/content/68dbe10a-fa38-443a-9790-dc96f2d8979a

203 Emily Washburn, "What To Know About Effective Altruism—Championed By Musk, Bankman-Fried And Silicon Valley Giants" (*Forbes*, March 8 2023), https://www.forbes.com/sites/emilywashburn/2023/03/08/what-to-know-about-effective-altruism-championed-by-musk-bankman-fried-and-silicon-valley-giants/?sh=2aba01a92362

204 "On Kelly and altruism" (*LessWrong*, November 25 2022), https://www.lesswrong.com/posts/XnnfYrqaxqvirpxFX/on-kelly-and-altruism

205 SBF (Twitter, December 11 2020), https://twitter.com/SBF_FTX/status/1337250708412801024

206 SBF (Twitter, December 11 2020) https://mobile.twitter.com/sbf_ftx/status/1337250710342127619

207 SBF (Twitter, December 11 2020), https://twitter.com/SBF_FTX/status/1337250716079931393

208 SBF (Twitter, December 11 2020), https://twitter.com/SBF_FTX/status/1337250720265867266

209 Tara Mac Aulay (Twitter, May 5 2017), https://twitter.com/Tara_MacAulay/status/860250532304240641

210 Gideon Lewis-Kraus, "Sam Bankman-Fried, Effective Altruism, and the Question of Complicity" (*The New Yorker*, December 1 2022), https://www.newyorker.com/news/annals-of-inquiry/sam-bankman-fried-effective-altruism-and-the-question-of-complicity

211 Reed Albergotti, Liz Hoffman, "Charity-linked money launched Sam Bankman-Fried's empire" (*Semafor*, December 9 2022), https://www.semafor.com/article/12/07/2022/charity-money-launched-sam-bankman-frieds-empire

212 Charlotte Alter, "Effective Altruist Leaders Were Repeatedly Warned About Sam Bankman-Fried Years Before FTX Collapsed" (*Time*, March 15 2023), https://time.com/6262810/sam-bankman-fried-effective-altruism-alameda-ftx/

213 Charlotte Alter, "Effective Altruist Leaders Were Repeatedly Warned About Sam Bankman-Fried Years Before FTX Collapsed" (*Time*, March 15 2023), https://time.com/6262810/sam-bankman-fried-effective-altruism-alameda-ftx/

214 Reed Albergotti and Liz Hoffman, "Charity-linked money launched Sam Bankman-Fried's empire" (*Semafor*, December 9 2022), https://www.semafor.com/article/12/07/2022/charity-money-launched-sam-bankman-frieds-empire

215 David Jeans *et al.*, "Meet Caroline Ellison, The 'Fake Charity Nerd Girl' Behind The FTX Collapse" (*Forbes*, November 18 2022), https://www.forbes.com/sites/davidjeans/2022/11/18/queen-caroline-the-risk-loving-29-year-old-embroiled-in-the-ftx-collapse/

216 Steven Ehrlich, Chase Peterson-Withorn, "Meet The World's Richest 29-Year-Old: How Sam Bankman-Fried Made A Record Fortune In The Crypto Frenzy" (*Forbes*, October 6 2021), https://www.forbes.com/sites/stevenehrlich/2021/10/06/the-richest-under-30-in-the-world-all-thanks-to-crypto/?sh=3fb8fe8b3f4d

217 Patricia Kowsmann *et al.*, "Troubles at Sam Bankman-Fried's Alameda Began Well Before Crypto Crash" (*The Wall Street Journal*, December 31 2022), https://www.wsj.com/articles/alameda-sam-bankman-fried-ftx-crypto-crash-11672434101

218 Patricia Kowsmann *et al.*, "Troubles at Sam Bankman-Fried's Alameda Began Well Before Crypto Crash" (*The Wall Street Journal*, December 31 2022), https://www.wsj.com/articles/alameda-sam-bankman-fried-ftx-crypto-crash-11672434101

219 Alexander Pack (Twitter, November 18 2022), https://twitter.com/alpackaP/status/1593308259087155201

220 Charlotte Alter, "Effective Altruist Leaders Were Repeatedly Warned About Sam Bankman-Fried Years Before FTX Collapsed" (*Time*, March 15 2023), https://time.com/6262810/sam-bankman-fried-effective-altruism-alameda-ftx/

221 Lantern Ventures https://www.lanternventures.com/

222 Frank Chaparro, "Alameda promised 'high returns with no risk' in 2018 pitch" (*The Block*, November 11 2022), https://www.theblock.co/post/186187/alameda-promised-high-returns-with-no-risk-in-2018-pitch

223 Toh Han Shih, "Now-Defunct FTX Drawn to Hong Kong's Crypto-Friendly Regulations" (*AsiaSentinel*, January 5 2023), https://www.asiasentinel.com/p/defunct-ftx-hongkong-crypto-friendly-regulations

224 Lakshmi Varanasi, Sarah Jackson, and Britney Nguyen "The rise and fall of FTX's Sam Bankman-Fried" (*Business Insider*, February 24 2023), https://www.businessinsider.com/ftx-crypto-king-sam-bankman-fried-rise-and-fall-2022-11

225 Sam Trabucco (Twitter, April 21 2021), https://twitter.com/AlamedaTrabucco/status/1385180941186789384

226 "For investigation and Inquiries: Guangying Chen, Binance, Bijie Tech and Changpeng Zhao (*Scambinance.com*), https://scambinance.com/investigations/109-for-investigation-and-inquiries-guangying-chen-binance-bijie-tech-and-changpeng-zhao.html

227 Lily Russell-Jones, 'Binance's Yi He: "My talent has always been trying to challenge myself"' (*City A.M.*, July 25 2022), https://www.cityam.com/binances-yi-he-my-talent-has-always-been-trying-to-challenge-myself/

228 Stan Higgins "Former Exec Hits Back at OKcoin Amid Contract Dispute" (*CoinDesk*, May 30 2015), https://www.coindesk.com/markets/2015/05/30/former-exec-hits-back-at-OKcoin-amid-contract-dispute/

229 OKCoin's response to CZ's lies and desperate nonsense https://www.reddit.com/r/Bitcoin/comments/37u6ca/okcoins_response_to_czs_lies_and_desperate/

230 Bryce Elder, "A brief-ish history of crypto audits" (*Financial Times*, December 12 2022) https://www.ft.com/content/d04a50e1-cffd-4712-827a-f554a43d39c5

231 "OKcoin's response to the allegations made by Changpeng Zhao" (*Reddit*), https://www.reddit.com/r/Bitcoin/comments/37u6ca/OKcoins_response_to_czs_lies_and_desperate/

232 "For investigation and Inquiries: Guangying Chen, Binance, Bijie Tech and Changpeng Zhao" (*Scambinance.com*), https://scambinance.com/investigations/109-for-investigation-and-inquiries-guangying-chen-binance-bijie-tech-and-changpeng-zhao.html

233 "Who owns Binance Casino: Guangying Chen (Heina Chen) or Changpeng Zhao?" (*Scambinance.com*), https://scambinance.com/investigations/131-who-owns-binance-casino-guangying-chen-heina-chen-or-changpeng-zhao.html

234 'Who Is Guangying Chen, and Is Binance a "Chinese Company"?'(*Binance*, September 1 2022), https://www.binance.com/en/blog/from-cz/who-is-guangying-chen-and-is-binance-a-chinese-company-2386330931319516973

235 Eva Xiao, "Three months after launch, this unbanked crypto exchange made $7.5m in profit" (*Tech in Asia*, December 1 2017), https://www.techinasia.com/cryptocurrency-exchange-binance

236 "Binance Whitepaper", https://www.scribd.com/document/369374867/Binance-WhitePaper-En#from_embed

237 Michael del Castillo, "Leaked 'Tai Chi' Document Reveals Binance's Elaborate Scheme To Evade Bitcoin Regulators" (*Forbes*, October 29 2020), https://www.forbes.com/sites/michaeldelcastillo/2020/10/29/leaked-tai-chi-document-reveals-binances-elaborate-scheme-to-evade-bitcoin-regulators/?sh=20448fcb2a92

238 "Binance Whitepaper", https://www.scribd.com/document/493563460/Binance-Coin-Whitepaper#download&from_embed

239 Binance
https://en.wikipedia.org/wiki/Binance#:~:text=The%20company%20was%20founded%20in,cryptocurrency%20tra
ding%20in%20September%202017.
240 Caitlin Ostroff and Patricia Kowsmann,"Texts From Crypto Giant Binance Reveal Plan to Elude U.S.
Authorities" (*The Wall Street Journal*, March 5 2023) https://www.wsj.com/articles/texts-from-crypto-giant-
binance-reveal-plan-to-elude-u-s-authorities-3a17ddeb
241 Michael del Castillo, "Leaked 'Tai Chi' Document Reveals Binance's Elaborate Scheme To Evade Bitcoin
Regulators" (*Forbes*, October 29 2020), https://www.forbes.com/sites/michaeldelcastillo/2020/10/29/leaked-tai-
chi-document-reveals-binances-elaborate-scheme-to-evade-bitcoin-
regulators/?sh=da34dec2a926&utm_source=substack&utm_medium=email
242 Tom Wilson, Angus Berwick, "How Binance CEO and aides plotted to dodge regulators in U.S. and UK"
(*Reuters*, October 17 2022), https://www.reuters.com/investigates/special-report/fintech-crypto-binance-
zhao/?utm_source=substack&utm_medium=email
243 Nikhilesh De, "New York AG Report Faults Crypto Exchanges for Manipulation Risks" (*CoinDesk*,
September 19 2018),https://www.coindesk.com/markets/2018/09/18/new-york-ag-report-faults-crypto-exchanges-
for-manipulation-risks/
244 Angus Berwick, Dan Levine and Tom Wilson, "U.S. Justice Dept is split over charging Binance as crypto
world falters" (*Reuters*, December 13 2022), https://www.reuters.com/markets/us/us-justice-dept-is-split-over-
charging-binance-crypto-world-falters-sources-2022-12-12/
245 Caitlin Ostroff, Patricia Kowsmann, "Texts From Crypto Giant Binance Reveal Plan to Elude U.S.
Authorities" (*The Wall Street Journal*, March 5 2024), https://www.wsj.com/articles/texts-from-crypto-giant-
binance-reveal-plan-to-elude-u-s-authorities-3a17ddeb
246 SPECIAL REPORT-How Binance CEO and aides plotted to dodge regulators in U.S. and UK
https://www.reuters.com/article/fintech-crypto-binance-zhao-idUKL1N31I15T
247 Tom Wilson and Angus Berwick, "How Binance CEO and aides plotted to dodge regulators in U.S. and UK"
(*Reuters*, October 17 2022), https://www.reuters.com/investigates/special-report/fintech-crypto-binance-zhao/
248 Tom Wilson and Angus Berwick, "How Binance CEO and aides plotted to dodge regulators in U.S. and UK"
(*Reuters*, October 17 2022), https://www.reuters.com/investigates/special-report/fintech-crypto-binance-zhao/
249 Angus Berwick and Tom Wilson, "Crypto giant Binance moved $400 million from U.S. partner to firm
managed by CEO Zhao" (*Reuters*, February 17 2023), https://www.reuters.com/technology/crypto-giant-binance-
moved-400-million-us-partner-firm-managed-by-ceo-zhao-2023-02-16/
250 Angus Berwick and Tom Wilson, "Crypto giant Binance moved $400 million from U.S. partner to firm
managed by CEO Zhao" (*Reuters*, February 17 2023), https://www.reuters.com/technology/crypto-giant-binance-
moved-400-million-us-partner-firm-managed-by-ceo-zhao-2023-02-16/
251 "Is Signature Bank Still Banking Binance.com?" (*Medium*, January 3 2023),
https://medium.com/@ExkrementKoin/is-signature-bank-still-banking-binance-com-e22b534ba983
252 Consumer warning on Binance Markets Limited and the Binance Group (*FCA*, June 26 2021),
https://www.fca.org.uk/news/news-stories/consumer-warning-binance-markets-limited-and-binance-group
253 Dave Michaels, "Crypto Giant Binance Expects to Pay Penalties to Resolve U.S. Investigations" (*The Wall
Street Journal*, February 15 2023), https://www.wsj.com/articles/crypto-giant-binance-expects-to-pay-penalties-to-
resolve-u-s-investigations-f1e3c9d2
254 Leigh Cuen, "Binance Warns Iranian Traders to Withdraw Crypto Amid Sanctions" (*CoinDesk*, November 16
2018), https://www.coindesk.com/markets/2018/11/15/binance-warns-iranian-traders-to-withdraw-crypto-amid-
sanctions/
255 Tom Wilson and Angus Berwick, "How Binance CEO and aides plotted to dodge regulators in U.S. and UK"
(*Reuters*, October 17 2022), https://www.reuters.com/investigates/special-report/fintech-crypto-binance-zhao/
256 Angus Berwick, Tom Wilson, "How crypto giant Binance became a hub for hackers, fraudsters and drug
traffickers" (*Reuters*, June 6 2022), https://www.reuters.com/investigates/special-report/fintech-crypto-binance-
dirtymoney/
257 Angus Berwick and Tom Wilson, "How crypto giant Binance became a hub for hackers, fraudsters and drug
traffickers" (*Reuters*, June 6 2022), https://www.reuters.com/investigates/special-report/fintech-crypto-binance-
dirtymoney/
258 Founder and Majority Owner of Cryptocurrency Exchange Charged with Processing Over $700 Million of
Illicit Funds (*DoJ*, January 18 2023), https://www.justice.gov/opa/pr/founder-and-majority-owner-cryptocurrency-
exchange-charged-processing-over-700-million
259 Tom Wilson, Angus Berwick, "Binance moved $346 mln for seized crypto exchange Bitzlato" (*Reuters*,
January 5 2023), https://www.reuters.com/business/finance/binance-moved-346-mln-seized-crypto-exchange-
bitzlato-data-show-2023-01-24/
260 Rohan Goswami, "Crypto is banned in China, but Binance employees and support volunteers tell people how
to bypass the ban" (*CNBC*, March 23 2023), https://www.cnbc.com/2023/03/23/binance-employees-volunteers-
tell-users-how-to-evade-china-crypto-ban.html
261 "FAQs" (RNS), https://docs.rns.id/support/faqs

262 Rohan Goswami, "Crypto is banned in China, but Binance employees and support volunteers tell people how to bypass the ban" (*CNBC*, March 23 2023), https://www.cnbc.com/2023/03/23/binance-employees-volunteers-tell-users-how-to-evade-china-crypto-ban.html

263 Binance (Twitter, October 21 2019), https://twitter.com/binance/status/1185989323293769728?lang=en

264 Soumen Datta, "Meet the Binance "Influencer of the Year 2022" Award Winners" (*BSC News*, 9 July 2022), https://www.bsc.news/post/meet-the-binance-influencer-of-the-year-2022-award-winners

265 Hasheur (Twitter), https://twitter.com/PowerHasheur

266 Tech Ranjan (YouTube), https://www.youtube.com/@TechRanjan/videos

267 Q8Three (Twitter), https://twitter.com/Q8Three

268 Fisayo Fosudo (YouTube), https://www.youtube.com/@FisayoFosudo

269 Kıvanç Özbilgiç (Twitter), https://twitter.com/kivancozbilgic

270 Deivide Guedes (YouTube), https://www.youtube.com/@deividiguedes

271 CFTC Charges Major Crypto Exchange Binance and Its CEO with Numerous Violations (*Practical Law Finance*, March 30 2023), https://uk.practicallaw.thomsonreuters.com/w-038-9837

272 Vicky Ge Huang *et al.*, "Crypto Firm Paxos Faces SEC Lawsuit Over Binance USD Token" (*The Wall Street Journal*, February 12 2023), https://www.wsj.com/articles/crypto-firm-paxos-faces-sec-lawsuit-over-binance-usd-token-8031e7a7?mod=Searchresults_pos1&page=1

273 Lyllah Ledesma, "Binance Mistakenly Mixed Crypto Exchange's Customer Funds With B-Token Collateral: Bloomberg" (*CoinDesk*, January 24 2023), https://www.coindesk.com/business/2023/01/24/binance-mistakenly-mixed-crypto-exchanges-client-funds-with-b-token-collateral-bloomberg/

274 Nikhil Kumar, "Founders of 'PayPal for criminals' Liberty Reserve are charged with money laundering" (*Independent*, 29 May 2013), https://www.independent.co.uk/news/world/americas/founders-of-paypal-for-criminals-liberty-reserve-are-charged-with-money-laundering-8635248.html

275 Jonathan Stempel, "Liberty Reserve founder must face $6 bln laundering case in U.S." (*Reuters*, September 24 2015), https://www.reuters.com/article/usa-cybersecurity-liberty-reserve-idUKL1N11T2G420150923

276 Aaron Wood, "QuadrigaCX Wallet Have Been Empty, Unused Since April 2018, Ernst and Young Finds" (*Cointelegraph*, March 2 2019), https://cointelegraph.com/news/report-quadrigacx-wallets-have-been-empty-unused-since-april

277 Umesh Bhagchandani, "What really happened to Gerald cotton?" (*South China Morning Post*, April 1 2022), https://www.scmp.com/magazines/style/celebrity/article/3172722/what-really-happened-gerald-cotten-netflixs-new-true

278 Tara Deschamps, "Crypto exchange Quadriga was a fraud and founder was running Ponzi scheme, OSC report finds" (*CBC*, June 11 2020), https://www.cbc.ca/news/business/osc-quadriga-gerald-cotten-1.5607990

279 "QuadrigaCX" (Ontario Securities Commission), https://www.osc.ca/quadrigacxreport/

280 "Self-Regulatory Organizations; Bats BZX Exchange, Inc.; Order Disapproving a Proposed Rule Change, as Modified by Amendments No. 1 and 2, to BZX Rule 14.11(e)(4), Commodity-Based Trust Shares, to List and Trade Shares Issued by the Winklevoss Bitcoin Trust" (Securities and Exchange Commission, March 10 2017), www.sec.gov/rules/sro/batsbzx/2017/34-80206.pdf

281 Andrew Hayward, "From 'Bitcoin Billionaires' to SEC Charges: A Brief Crypto History of the Winklevoss Twins" (*Yahoo!*, 14 January 2023) https://finance.yahoo.com/news/bitcoin-billionaires-sec-charges-brief-233829911.html

282 Seema Mody, Everett Rosenfeld, "Winklevoss twin predicts multitrillion-dollar value for bitcoin" (*CNBC*, December 9 2017), https://www.cnbc.com/2017/12/09/bitcoin-cameron-winklevoss-predicts-multitrillion-dollar-value-for-cryptocurrency.html

283 Annie Massa, "Winklevoss Twins Ignore Crypto `Winter,' Looking Toward 2019" (*Bloomberg*, December 11 2018), https://www.bloomberg.com/news/articles/2018-12-11/winklevoss-twins-ignore-crypto-winter-looking-toward-2019

284 Olga Kharif, "Billion-Dollar-a-Day Crypto Trader Finds Accolades Are Better Than Anonymity" (*Bloomberg*, November 13 2019), https://www.bloomberg.com/news/articles/2019-11-13/billion-dollar-a-day-crypto-trader-finds-accolades-top-anonymity

285 ZhaoDong@RenrenBit.com (Twitter, February 27 2020), https://twitter.com/zhaodong1982/status/1232818502026661888

286 Zhu Su (Twitter, April 13 2019), https://twitter.com/zhusu/status/1116951872214953988?lang=en

287 Morgan Chittum, "Caroline Ellison is cooperating with prosecutors after the collapse of FTX. New legal docs reveal how she acted on behalf of Sam Bankman-Fried." (*Markets Insider*, December 23 2022), https://markets.businessinsider.com/news/currencies/caroline-ellison-blamed-ftx-downfall-on-sbf-legal-documents-show-2022-12

288 "FTX Token Whitepaper" (Whitepaper.io), https://whitepaper.io/document/502/ftx-token-whitepaper

289 "Bitcoin Manipulation Abatement LLC v. FTX Trading LTD *et al.*" (United States District Court for the Northern District of California, San Francisco Division),

www.morrisoncohen.com/siteFiles/files/2019_11_02%20-%20Bitcoin%20Manipulation%20Abatement%20LLC%20v_%20FTX%20Trading%20LTD,%20et%20al.pdf

290 Ada Hui, "Ex-Kraken Trading Head Leads Crypto Quant Fund With $23M in Assets" (*CoinDesk*, June 19 2020), https://www.nasdaq.com/articles/ex-kraken-trading-head-leads-crypto-quant-fund-with-%2423m-in-assets-%242.3b-in-trades-2020-06

291 "FTT Token" (CoinDesk), https://www.coindesk.com/price/ftx-token/

292 Laurence Fletcher "Hedge fund admits half its capital stuck on FTX exchange" (*Financial Times*, November 11 2022), https://www.ft.com/content/726277bb-35a1-4d35-9df9-3e1cca587b77

293 Laurence Fletcher, "Hedge fund Galois closes after half of assets trapped on crypto exchange FTX" (*Financial Times*, February 19 2023), https://www.ft.com/content/a06b77bc-52ac-4901-98d7-8c567449262e

294 Jordan Finneseth, "Analysts point to overleveraged traders after Bitcoin flash crashes to $43K" (*Cointelegraph*, September 7 2021), https://cointelegraph.com/news/analysts-point-to-overleveraged-traders-after-bitcoin-flash-crashes-to-43k

295 Buttcoin, "FTX just brazenly admitted to manipulating leveraged liquidations." (Reddit), https://www.reddit.com/r/Buttcoin/comments/pjv86z/ftx_just_brazenly_admitted_to_manipulating/

296 Bitfinex'ed (Twitter, September 8 2021), https://twitter.com/Bitfinexed/status/1435390934045315074

297 Wolfie Zhou, "OKEx Confirms $9 Million Clawback After 'Enormous' Bitcoin Future Fails" (*CoinDesk*, August 3 2018), https://www.coindesk.com/markets/2018/08/03/okex-confirms-9-million-clawback-after-enormous-bitcoin-future-fails/

298 FTX website dysfunctional (FTX), https://help.ftx.com/hc/en-us/articles/360032509552-Leveraged-Token-Walkthrough

299 "LT Baskets Ltd." (RK Consultants), https://www.rkc.llc/post/ltbasketsltd

300 Bitcoin Manipulation Abatement LLC v. FTX Trading (November 2 2019), https://www.morrisoncohen.com/siteFiles/files/2019_11_02%20-%20Bitcoin%20Manipulation%20Abatement%20LLC%20v_%20FTX%20Trading%20LTD,%20et%20al.pdf

301 David Kimberley, "Attack On Binance Futures Platform a False Alarm" (*Finance Magnates*, September 16 2019), https://www.financemagnates.com/cryptocurrency/exchange/attack-on-binance-futures-platform-a-false-alarm/

302 Craig Adeyanju, "BitMEX Ends Year With Additional 13K BTC in Its Insurance Fund, Up 61%" (*Cointelegraph*, December 31 2019), https://cointelegraph.com/news/bitmex-ends-year-with-additional-13k-btc-in-its-insurance-fund-up-61

303 Antoine Le Calvez *et al.*, "The BitMEX Liquidation Spiral – Analyzing How Crypto's Nascent Market Structure Held Up During the Crash" (*Coin Metrics*, March 24 2020), https://coinmetrics.substack.com/p/coin-metrics-state-of-the-network-bf8

304 Colin Harper, "How Black Thursday reshaped the Bitcoin futures market" (*Decrypt*, April 22 2020), https://decrypt.co/26299/black-thursday-reshaped-bitcoin-futures-market-report

305 Huobi Group, "Huobi Launches New Futures Liquidation Mechanism to Hedge Against Market Volatility" (*Cision PR Newswire*, March 18 2020), https://www.prnewswire.com/news-releases/huobi-launches-new-futures-liquidation-mechanism-to-hedge-against-market-volatility-301026145.html

306 "How much were the first, second and third stimulus checks and when were they sent out?" (*AS.com*, March 17 2002), https://en.as.com/en/2022/03/17/latest_news/1647514558_032514.html

307 "The Man" (Wikipedia), https://en.wikipedia.org/wiki/The_Man

308 "Melvin Capital" (Wikipedia), https://en.wikipedia.org/wiki/Melvin_Capital

309 Robin Wigglesworth, Katie Martin and George Steer, "The Fomo rally: 'fear of missing out' helps fuel soaring markets" (*Financial Times*, November 12 2021), https://www.ft.com/content/637b2a59-f64d-46b6-a8a8-0072e3a936d2

310 Robert Leshner, "Expanding Compound Governance" (*Medium*, May 28 2020), https://medium.com/compound-finance/expanding-compound-governance-ce13fcd4fe36

311 Robert Leshner, "Compound Launches Money Markets for Ethereum Assets" (*Medium*, September 28 2018), https://medium.com/compound-finance/compound-launches-money-markets-for-ethereum-assets-f50920f04488

312 Tracy Alloway, Joe Weisenthal, "Transcript: Sam Bankman-Fried and Matt Levine on How to Make Money in Crypto" (*Bloomberg*, April 26 2022), https://www.bloomberg.com/news/articles/2022-04-25/odd-lots-full-transcript-sam-bankman-fried-and-matt-levine-on-crypto?leadSource=uverify%20wall

313 "Regulated Token Offerings (RTO)" (IBC Group), https://ibcgroup.io/services_old/regulated-token-offerings/

314 Community Growth – How It Works https://ibcgroup.io/services/

315 Ester Felez-Vinas, Luke Johnson, Talis J. Putnins, "Insider Trading in Cryptocurrency Markets" (*University of Technology Sydney*, August 8 2022), https://papers.ssrn.com/sol3/papers.cfm?abstract_id=4184367

316 "Former Employee Of NFT Marketplace Charged In First Ever Digital Asset Insider Trading Scheme" (The United States Attorney's Office, Southern District of New York, June 1 2022), https://www.justice.gov/usao-sdny/pr/former-employee-nft-marketplace-charged-first-ever-digital-asset-insider-trading-scheme

317 Stacy Elliott, "Alameda Allegedly Traded These 18 Tokens on Insider Info Through FTX" (*Yahoo!*, November 16 2022), https://autos.yahoo.com/alameda-allegedly-traded-18-tokens-212425478.html
318 Anatoly Yakovenko, "FTX Chooses Solana for Serum" (*Medium*, July 28 2020), https://medium.com/solana-labs/ftx-chooses-solana-for-serum-a-high-speed-non-custodial-decentralized-derivatives-exchange-c346a27c1f2b
319 SBF (Twitter, December 6 2020), https://twitter.com/SBF_FTX/status/1335531934269591556
320 Paul Jones, Lorenzo Giorgianni, "The Great Monetary Inflation" (Jameson Lopp), https://www.lopp.net/pdf/BVI-Macro-Outlook.pdf
321 Billy Bambrough, "A Legendary Hedge Fund Billionaire Just Flipped To Bitcoin—Calling It 'Better' Than Gold" (*Forbes*, November 11 2020), https://www.forbes.com/sites/billybambrough/2020/11/12/a-legendary-hedge-fund-billionaire-just-flipped-to-bitcoin-calling-it-better-than-gold
322 Kevin Stankiewicz, "BlackRock's Rieder says bitcoin can replace gold 'to a large extent' and crypto is 'here to stay'" (*CNBC*, November 20 2020), https://www.cnbc.com/2020/11/20/blackrocks-rick-rieder-bitcoin-can-replace-gold-to-a-large-extent-.html
323 Jeff John Roberts, "Software firm MicroStrategy makes a massive bet on Bitcoin with a $250 million purchase" (*Fortune*, August 11 2020), https://fortune.com/2020/08/11/buying-bitcoin-microstrategy-cryptocurrenc/
324 Nelson Wang, "MicroStrategy Reported Impairment Charge of $727K on Bitcoin Holdings in Q3" (*CoinDesk*, November 2 2022), https://www.coindesk.com/business/2022/11/01/microstrategy-reports-impairment-charge-of-727k-on-bitcoin-holdings-in-q3/
325 Noah Manskar,"Reddit user says post on $800M Tesla bitcoin buy was a hoax — and he was on LSD when he did it" (*New York Post*, February 9 2021), https://nypost.com/2021/02/09/reddit-user-says-post-on-800m-tesla-bitcoin-buy-was-a-hoax/
326 Elon Musk (Twitter, April 2 2019), https://twitter.com/elonmusk/status/1113009339743100929
327 Elon Musk (Twitter, January 25 2022), https://twitter.com/elonmusk/status/1485953263040188416
328 Elon Musk (Twitter, July 18 2020), https://twitter.com/elonmusk/status/1284291528328790016
329 Sam Trabucco (Twitter, January 14 2021), https://twitter.com/AlamedaTrabucco/status/1349538525218127872
330 Elon Musk (Twitter, December 20 2020), https://twitter.com/elonmusk/status/1340590280848908288
331 Rupert Neate, "Dogecoin value soars after Elon Musk says it will be accepted for Tesla goods" (*The Guardian*, January 14 2022), https://www.theguardian.com/technology/2022/jan/14/dogecoin-value-soars-after-elon-musk-says-it-will-be-accepted-for-tesla-goods
332 Elon Musk (Twitter, January 27 2021), https://twitter.com/elonmusk/status/1354174279894642703
333 Forbes Crypto (Twitter, February 5 2021), https://twitter.com/forbescrypto/status/1357366907985403910
334 Elon Musk (Twitter, February 10 2021), https://twitter.com/elonmusk/status/1359519541219500033
335 Elon Musk (Twitter, April 15 2021), https://twitter.com/elonmusk/status/1382552587099062272
336 All-In Podcast, May 13 2021, E32: Behind the scenes of Elon hosting SNL https://www.youtube.com/watch?v=GE0iWGNXKXw
337 Andrew Griffin, "Elon Musk says he still 'strongly believes in crypto' after contentious bitcoin tweets" (*CoinDesk*, May 14 2021), https://finance.yahoo.com/news/elon-musk-says-still-strongly-221830607.html
338 "China bans financial, payment institutions from cryptocurrency business" (*Reuters*, May 18 2021), https://www.reuters.com/technology/chinese-financial-payment-bodies-barred-cryptocurrency-business-2021-05-18/
339 Elon Musk (Twitter, June 4 2021), https://twitter.com/elonmusk/status/1400620080090730501
340 MacKenzie Sigalos, "Elon Musk walks back his fossil fuel worries, says Tesla will likely start accepting bitcoin again" (*CNBC*, July 21 2021), https://www.cnbc.com/2021/07/21/elon-musk-says-tesla-will-likely-start-accepting-bitcoin-again.html
341 Tyler Clifford, "Cramer calls Coinbase the 'real deal,' but warns investors to brace for a bumpy ride with the stock" (*CNBC*, April 13 2021), https://www.cnbc.com/2021/04/13/cramer-calls-coinbase-the-real-deal-warns-of-bumpy-ride-with-stock.html
342 Michelle Fox, "'Mr. Wonderful' Kevin O'Leary calls bitcoin 'garbage' in a takedown of the whole cryptocurrency industry" (*CNBC*, May 14 2019), https://www.cnbc.com/2019/05/14/mr-wonderful-kevin-oleary-calls-bitcoin-garbage.html
343 Andrew Heavens, "China vows to crack down on bitcoin mining, trading activities" (*Reuters*, May 21 2021), https://www.reuters.com/technology/china-says-it-will-crack-down-bitcoin-mining-trading-activities-2021-05-21/
344 Alun John, "Hong Kong to restrict crypto exchanges to professional investors" (*Reuters*, May 21 2021), https://www.reuters.com/technology/hong-kong-restrict-crypto-exchanges-professional-investors-2021-05-21/
345 Eric Lipton and Ephrat Livni, "Crypto Nomads: Surfing the World for Risk and Profit" (*New York Times*, July 23 2021) https://www.nytimes.com/2021/07/23/us/politics/crypto-billionaires.html
346 SBF (Twitter, July 25 2021), https://twitter.com/SBF_FTX/status/1419263708874694665
347 Tanzeel Akhtar, "Kraken to No Longer Offer Margin Trading for US Investors Who Don't Meet 'Certain' Requirements" (*Yahoo!*, June 10 2021), https://sg.news.yahoo.com/kraken-no-longer-offer-margin-181221848.html

348 Michael del Castillo, "The 'Great Bitcoin Exodus' has totally changed New York's bitcoin ecosystem" (*New York Business Journal*, August 12 2015), https://www.bizjournals.com/newyork/news/2015/08/12/the-great-bitcoin-exodus-has-totally-changed-new.html

349 Yessi Bello Perez, "The Real Cost of Applying for a New York BitLicense" (*CoinDesk*, August 14 2013), https://www.coindesk.com/markets/2015/08/13/the-real-cost-of-applying-for-a-new-york-bitlicense/

350 Marc Hochstein, "'BitLicense Refugees': ShapeShift, Kraken Talk Escape from New York" (*CoinDesk*, May 16 2018) https://www.coindesk.com/markets/2018/05/16/bitlicense-refugees-shapeshift-kraken-talk-escape-from-new-york/

351 Jeff Yeung, "A Single Ethereum Whale Has Spent $6 Million USD on CryptoPunk NFTs" (*Hypebeast*, August 1 2021), https://hypebeast.com/2021/8/cryptopunk-nfts-ethereum-whale-6-million-usd-purchases\

352 Hannah Murphy and Joshua Oliver, "How NFTs became a $40bn market in 2021" (*Financial Times*, December 30 2021) https://www.ft.com/content/e95f5ac2-0476-41f4-abd4-8a99faa7737d

353 Raynor de Best, "Sales volume of NFT collectible card game NBA Top Shot against the number of unique buyers from July 2020 to October 2022" (*Statista*, January 11 2023). https://www.statista.com/statistics/1266001/nba-top-shot-nft-development/

354 Angus Berwick, Elizabeth Howcroft, "From Crypto to Christie's" (*Reuters*, November 17 2021), https://www.reuters.com/investigates/special-report/finance-crypto-sundaresan/

355 Angus Berwick, Elizabeth Howcroft, "From Crypto to Christie's" (*Reuters*, November 17 2021), https://www.reuters.com/investigates/special-report/finance-crypto-sundaresan/

356 Matt Robinson, "Bored-Ape Creator Yuga Labs Faces SEC Probe Over Unregistered Offerings" (*Bloomberg*, October 12 2022), https://www.bloomberg.com/news/articles/2022-10-11/bored-ape-creator-yuga-labs-faces-sec-probe-over-unregistered-offerings#xj4y7vzkg

357 Leah Alger, "Yuga Labs' Leaked Financials Show Insane Profits" (*NFT Lately*, November 20 2022), https://nftlately.com/yuga-labs-leaked-financials-show-insane-profits/

358 "NFT Marketplace Competition Heats Up" (*Forkast News*, Q1 2022), https://forkast.news/state-of-the-nft-market/nft-marketplace-competition-heats-up

359 Lucas Matney,"NFT market OpenSea hits $1.5 billion valuation" (*TechCrunch*, July 20 2021), https://techcrunch.com/2021/07/20/nft-market-opensea-hits-1-5-billion-valuation/?guccounter=1

360 Department of the Treasury Financial Crimes Enforcement Network, "Application of FinCEN's Regulations to Persons Administering, Exchanging, or Using Virtual Currencies" (*FINCEN*, March 18 2013), https://www.fincen.gov/sites/default/files/shared/FIN-2013-G001.pdf

361 Nathan Reiff, "What Is the Grayscale Bitcoin Trust?" (*Investopedia*, January 21 2021) https://www.investopedia.com/news/why-buy-expensive-bitcoin-etf-instead-actual-bitcoin

362 Jacob Donnelly, "The bitcoin investment trust's GBTC begins trading on public markets" (*Bitcoin Magazine*, May 5 2015), https://bitcoinmagazine.com/markets/the-bitcoin-investment-trusts-gbtc-begins-trading-on-public-markets

363 BlockFi, "BlockFi Position in GBTC Reaches Disclosure Threshold" (*BlockFi*, October 27 2020), https://blockfi.com/blockfi-position-in-gbtc-reaches-disclosure-threshold

364 Elizabeth Howcroft and Hannah Lang, "What crisis? High-stakes crypto lending looks here to stay" (*Reuters*, September 23 2022), https://www.reuters.com/technology/what-crisis-high-stakes-crypto-lending-looks-here-stay-2022-09-21/

365 Krisztian Sandor, "Maple Finance's $54M of Sour Debt Shows Risks of Crypto Lending Without Collateral" (*CoinDesk*, December 12 2022), https://sg.news.yahoo.com/maple-finances-54m-sour-debt-035326041.html

366 Zhu Su (Twitter, May 25 2021), https://twitter.com/zhusu/status/1397051201246482433

367 Tim Copeland, "Su Zhu says his 'supercycle' price thesis was 'regrettably wrong'" (*The Block*, May 27 2022), https://www.theblock.co/linked/149111/su-zhu-says-his-supercycle-price-thesis-was-regrettably-wrong

368 Bob Simon, "A 1997 Prophecy: Bitcoin and the unfolding of how society will change coming to life with Bitcoin today" (*Bitcoin Magazine*, December 22 2021), https://bitcoinmagazine.com/culture/bitcoin-and-the-sovereign-individual-thesis

369 Anissa Gardizy, "Sam Trabucco, a Roxbury Latin and MIT grad, got rich trading crypto. Now he's the odd man out in the FTX saga" (*Boston Globe*, January 22 2023), https://www.bostonglobe.com/2023/01/22/business/sam-trabucco-roxbury-latin-mit-grad-got-rich-trading-crypto-now-hes-odd-man-out-ftx-saga/

370 "SEC Charges Ripple and Two Executives with Conducting $1.3 Billion Unregistered Securities Offering" (U.S. Securities and Exchange Commission, December 22 2020), https://www.sec.gov/news/press-release/2020-338

371 Paul Grewal, "Coinbase will suspend trading in XRP on January 19" (Coinbase, December 28 2020), https://www.coinbase.com/blog/coinbase-will-suspend-trading-in-xrp-on-january-19

372 Reef, "Our Official Response to Recent Events Regarding Alameda" (*Medium*, March 16 2021), https://medium.com/reef-finance/our-official-response-to-recent-events-regarding-alameda-a1978f7fbe57

373 Faithumoh422, "Reef Chain Designed to make web3 accessible to the next billion Users" (*Reddit*, February 27 2023),
https://www.reddit.com/r/CryptoKami/comments/11cyui0/reef_chain_designed_to_make_web3_accessible_to/
374 *Entrepreneur* Middle East Staff, "#CryptoConversations: A Chat With Reef CEO And Founder Denko Mancheski" (*Entrepreneur*, February 27 2022), https://www.entrepreneur.com/en-ae/finance/cryptoconversations-a-chat-with-reef-ceo-and-founder/421058
375 Steven Ehrlich and Nina Bambysheva, "Alameda And FTX May Have Taken Advantage Of Customers From The Start" (*Forbes*, November 17 2022), https://www.forbes.com/sites/stevenehrlich/2022/11/17/alameda-and-ftx-may-have-taken-advantage-of-customers-from-the-start
376 Soumen Datta, "SBF had detailed info on Alameda's finances as recently as March, Forbes reveals" (*CryptoSlate*, December 2 2022), https://cryptoslate.com/sbf-had-detailed-info-on-alamedas-finances-as-recently-as-march-forbes-reveals/
377 Zeke Fauk, "Inside the mind of the crypto billionaire who lost it all" (*Irish Examiner*, December 13 2022), https://www.irishexaminer.com/news/spotlight/arid-41025053.html
378 Jeff Kauflin, Emily Mason, "How Did Sam Bankman-Fried's Alameda Research Lose So Much Money?" (*Forbes*, November 19 2022), https://www.forbes.com/sites/jeffkauflin/2022/11/19/how-did-sam-bankman-frieds-alameda-research-lose-so-much-money/
379 Olga Kharif, "One of the Biggest Crypto Traders Is Tapping DeFi Loans for Funding" (*Bloomberg*, February 25 2022), https://www.bloomberg.com/news/articles/2022-02-24/one-of-biggest-crypto-traders-is-tapping-defi-loans-for-funding
380 Olga Kharif, "One of the Biggest Crypto Traders Is Tapping DeFi Loans for Funding" (*Bloomberg*, February 25 2022), https://www.bloomberg.com/news/articles/2022-02-24/one-of-biggest-crypto-traders-is-tapping-defi-loans-for-funding
381 Matt Levine, "Meme Stocks Were Too Good to Robinhood" (*Bloomberg*, June 28 2022), https://www.bloomberg.com/opinion/articles/2022-06-27/matt-levine-s-money-stuff-meme-week-was-too-good-to-robinhood
382 "DeFi Overview" (DappRadar) https://dappradar.com/defi
383 Annie Palmer, "Amazon is hiring a digital currency and blockchain expert, signaling a growing interest in cryptocurrency" (*CNBC*, July 23 2021), https://www.cnbc.com/2021/07/23/amazon-is-hiring-a-digital-currency-and-blockchain-expert.html
384 "U.S. infrastructure bill's cryptocurrency amendment to provide clarity on taxes – Yellen" (*Reuters*, August 9 2021), https://www.reuters.com/world/us/us-infrastructure-bills-cryptocurrency-amendment-provide-clarity-taxes-yellen-2021-08-09/
385 Sam Trabucco (Twitter, September 8 2021), https://twitter.com/AlamedaTrabucco/status/1435423614514319360
386 Suvashree Ghosh, "FTX's Federal Net Operating Loss Carryover Stood at $3.7 Billion" (*Bloomberg*, November 21 2022), https://www.bloomberg.com/news/articles/2022-11-21/ftx-s-federal-net-operating-loss-carryover-stood-at-3-7-billion
387 "Minutes of the Federal Open Market Committee" (Board of Governors of the Federal Reserve System, December 14–15 2021), https://www.federalreserve.gov/monetarypolicy/fomcminutes20211215.htm
388 Sahil Kapur and Benjy Sarlin, "Manchin says Build Back Better is 'dead.' Here's what he might resurrect." (*NBC News*, February 3 2022), https://www.nbcnews.com/politics/congress/manchin-says-build-back-better-dead-here-s-what-he-n1288492
389 "Yearender 2021: What Led to Bitcoin Price Fluctuation In 2021 " (*Outlook India*, December 23 2021), https://www.outlookindia.com/website/story/business-news-yearender-2021-what-led-to-bitcoin-price-fluctuation-in-2021/406465
390 Ephrat Livni, "Congress gets a crash course on cryptocurrency." (*The New York Times*, December 8 2021) https://www.nytimes.com/2021/12/08/business/house-financial-services-crypto.html
391 Pete Schroeder and Katanga Johnson, "Crypto executives urge light touch as Congress mulls new regulation" (*Reuters*, December 9 2021), https://www.reuters.com/markets/europe/us-risks-chilling-regulations-crypto-industry-warns-congress-2021-12-07/
392 Kate Rooney, "Congressional hearing on cryptocurrencies devolves into bitcoin bash fest" (*CNBC*, March 14 2018), https://www.cnbc.com/2018/03/14/congressional-hearing-devolves-into-bitcoin-bash-fest.html
393 "House Hearing on Financial Innovation and Digital Currency" (C-Span, December 8 2021), https://www.c-span.org/video/?516464-1/house-hearing-financial-innovation-digital-currency
394 Stephen Mihm, "FTX's Bahamas Headquarters Was the First Clue" (*The Washington Post*, December 7 2022), https://www.washingtonpost.com/business/ftxs-bahamas-headquarters-was-the-first-clue/2022/12/07/7dcc1686-7627-11ed-a199-927b334b939f_story.html
395 David Jeans and Sarah Emerson, "FTX Secretly Channeled A $50 Million Loan To Its Bahamian Bank Through An Executive's Company" (*Forbes*, January 16 2023), https://www.forbes.com/sites/davidjeans/2023/01/15/ftx-deltec-bank-jean-chalopin-moonstone

396 Max Reyes, "An Obscure Bank Found Its Key To Success. Then FTX Collapsed" (*The Washington Post*, December 12 2022), https://www.washingtonpost.com/business/on-small-business/an-obscure-bank-found-its-key-to-success-then-ftx-collapsed/2022/12/09/bc428e96-77c5-11ed-a199-927b334b939f_story.html

397 Stephen Gandel, "Crypto Firm FTX's Ownership of a U.S. Bank Raises Questions" (*The New York Times*, November 23 2022), https://www.nytimes.com/2022/11/23/business/ftx-cryptocurrency-bank.html

398 David Jeans and Sarah Emerson, "FTX Secretly Channeled A $50 Million Loan To Its Bahamian Bank Through An Executive's Company" (*Forbes*, January 16 2023), https://www.forbes.com/sites/davidjeans/2023/01/15/ftx-deltec-bank-jean-chalopin-moonstone

399 Jon Russell, "Terra is an ambitious crypto project to build a stable coin through e-commerce" (*TechCrunch*, August 29 2018), https://techcrunch.com/2018/08/29/terra/

400 Nicholas Platias, Eui Joon Lee, Marco Di Maggio, "Anchor: Gold Standard for Passive Income on the Blockchain" (Anchor Protoco*l*, June 2020), https://www.anchorprotocol.com/docs/anchor-v1.1.pdf

401 Anchor Protocol (Twitter, May 26 2021), https://twitter.com/anchor_protocol/status/1397400642566594563

402 Tracy Wang and Sam Kessler, "Jump Crypto Is Unnamed Firm That Made $1.28B From Do Kwon's Doomed Terra Ecosystem: Sources" (*CoinDesk*, February 18 2023), https://www.coindesk.com/business/2023/02/17/jump-crypto-is-unnamed-firm-that-made-128b-from-do-kwons-doomed-terra-ecosystem-sources/

403 Zack Seward, "Terra's Do Kwon Was Served by SEC New Lawsuit Shows" (*CoinDesk*, October 26 2021), https://www.coindesk.com/business/2021/10/23/terras-do-kwon-was-served-by-sec-new-lawsuit-shows/

404 Godfrey Benjamin, "Do Kwon Denies Allegations of Cashing Out $2.7Bn through DegenBox" (*Blockchain.news*, June 13 2022) https://blockchain.news/news/do-kwon-denies-allegations-of-cashing-out-2.7bn-through-degenbox

405 Andjela Radmilac, "Terra's (LUNA) Col-5 update is set to go live today" (*CryptoSlate*, September 29 2021), https://cryptoslate.com/terras-LUNA-col-5-update-set-to-go-live-today/

406 Kirsty Moreland, "Not Your Keys, Not Your Coins. It's That Simple." (Ledger, October 27 2022), https://www.ledger.com/academy/not-your-keys-not-your-coins-why-it-matters

407 The Intern, "Formation of the Luna Foundation Guard (LFG)" (*Medium*, January 20 2022), https://medium.com/terra-money/formation-of-the-LUNA-foundation-guard-lfg-6b8dcb5e127b

408 Brady Dale, "Jump and Three Arrows Lead $1B LUNA Buy to Secure UST Against Black Swans" (*The Defiant*, February 23 2022), https://finance.yahoo.com/news/jump-three-arrows-lead-1b-054508397.html

409 "A Community for #LUNAtics" (Terra), https://www.terra.money/community

410 Algod (Twitter, February 16 2022), https://twitter.com/AlgodTrading/status/1493900339300507652

411 Galois_Capital (Twitter, March 18 2022), https://twitter.com/Galois_Capital/status/1504611169994264577

412 Varuni Trivedi, "Terraform Labs CEO Bets $10M on LUNA's Bullish Trajectory" (*FXEmpire*, March 15 2022), https://sg.news.yahoo.com/terraform-labs-ceo-bets-10m-153826189.html

413 Danny Park, "Terra founder bets millions on LUNA's annual growth" (*Forkast*, March 16 2022), https://forkast.news/headlines/terra-founder-do-kwon-bets-LUNA-growth/

414 Damanick Dantes and Angelique Chen, "Market Wrap: Bitcoin Rallies as Crypto Holders Accumulate" (*CoinDesk*, March 29 2022), https://www.coindesk.com/markets/2022/03/28/market-wrap-bitcoin-rallies-as-crypto-holders-accumulate/

415 Krisztian Sandor, "Terraform Labs Gives $820M in LUNA Tokens to Luna Foundation Guard" (*CoinDesk*, April 15 2022), https://www.coindesk.com/markets/2022/04/14/terraform-labs-gifts-820m-in-tokens-to-LUNA-foundation-guard/

416 Daniele (Twitter, November 1 2021), https://twitter.com/danielesesta/status/1454885923980824577

417 Arman Shirinyan, "Maker Co-Founder: UST and MIM are "Solid" Ponzi Schemes" (*U.Today*, January 4 2022), https://u.today/makerdao-co-founder-mim-and-ust-are-solid-ponzi-schemes

418 MakerDao, "Parameter Changes, Core Unit Budget Distribution" (MakerDao, November 5 2021), https://vote.makerdao.com/executive/0x3381CaEaA980f78Aa1895f98E645e35cBDD4C593

419 "The Curve Wars Explained" (Flovtec, July 21 2022), https://www.flovtec.com/post/the-curve-wars-explained

420 Sam Trabucco (Twitter, May 9 2022), https://twitter.com/AlamedaTrabucco/status/1523381953239523328

421 Michael McSweeney, "Luna Foundation Guard says it will lend out $1.5 billion in BTC and UST to defend stablecoin peg" (*The Block*, May 9 2022), https://www.theblock.co/linked/145705/LUNA-foundation-guard-says-it-will-lend-out-1-5-billion-in-btc-and-ust-to-defend-stablecoin-peg

422 Do Kwon (Twitter, May 10 2022), https://twitter.com/stablekwon/status/1523733542492016640

423 Werner Vermaak, "Terra's LUNA and UST Crash Down to Earth: What Happened?"(CoolWallet, May 17 2022), https://www.coolwallet.io/terra-LUNA-and-ust-crypto-crash-what-happened/

424 Sam Reynolds, "Binance Restarts LUNA and UST Withdrawals After Brief Suspension" (*CoinDesk*, May 10 2022), https://www.coindesk.com/markets/2022/05/10/binance-suspends-luna-and-ust-token-withdrawals/

425 Stefan Stankovic, :"Terra's LFG to Deploy $1.5B to "Protect the UST Peg"" (*Crypto Briefing*, May 9 2022), https://cryptobriefing.com/terras-lfg-to-deploy-1-5b-to-protect-the-ust-peg/

426 Do Kwon (Twitter, May 10 2022), https://twitter.com/stablekwon/status/1524049689510694916?lang=en

427 Frank Chaparro, "Luna Foundation Guard seeks more than $1 billion to shore up UST stablecoin" (*The Block*, May 10 2022), https://www.theblock.co/post/145978/LUNA-foundation-guard-seeks-more-than-1-billion-to-shore-up-ust-stablecoin-sources
428 Daily Hodle Staff, "Three Arrows Capital Breaks Silence, Says That FTX and Alameda Hunted Their Positions During LUNA Collapse" (*The Daily Hodle*, November 14 2022), https://dailyhodl.com/2022/11/14/three-arrows-capital-breaks-silence-says-that-ftx-and-alameda-hunted-their-positions-during-LUNA-collapse/
429 Peter Hoskins, "S Korea says crypto-fugitive Do Kwon is in Serbia" (*BBC*, December 12 2022), https://www.bbc.com/news/business-63940181
430 "Securities and Exchange Commission v. Terraform Labs PTE. LTD. and Do Hyeong Kwon" (United States District Court, Southern District of New York, February 16 2023), https://www.sec.gov/litigation/complaints/2023/comp-pr2023-32.pdf
431 Sara Park, "U.S. investigative agency 'Tera' Jeong Aim... Do-hyung Kwon's 'money laundering' situation" (JTBC, June 9 2022), https://mnews.jtbc.co.kr/News/Article.aspx?news_id=NB12061975
432 Lee Do-yoon, "When Terra collapsed, 9 billion went to Kim & Chang" (*KBS*, April 13 2023), https://news.kbs.co.kr/news/view.do?ncd=7651051
433 Sangmi Cha and Hooyeon Kim, "Terra Co-Founder Shin, Nine Others Indicted by South Korea" (*Bloomberg*, April 25 2023, https://news.bloomberglaw.com/crypto/terra-co-founder-shin-nine-others-indicted-by-south-korea-2
434 Brian Evans, "Sam Bankman-Fried secretly transferred FTX customer funds to Alameda Research after his trading firm suffered losses in the spring, report says" (*Business Insider*, November 11 2022), https://markets.businessinsider.com/news/currencies/ftx-crash-client-funds-alameda-binance-sbf-sec-cftc-probe-2022-11
435 Ram Ahluwalia (Twitter, December 5 2022), https://twitter.com/ramahluwalia/status/1599573712810168320
436 Pete Syme, "Sam Bankman-Fried's secret 'backdoor' discovered, FTX lawyer says" (*Business Insider*, January 13 2023), https://www.businessinsider.com/sam-bankman-fried-secret-backdoor-worth-65-billion-court-hears-2023-1
437 Connie Loizos, "MobileCoin, a cryptocurrency advised early on by Signal's Moxie Marlinspike, has raised venture funding" (*TechCrunch*, March 10 2021), https://techcrunch.com/2021/03/09/mobilecoin-a-cryptocurrency-involving-signal-founder-moxie-marlinspike-just-raised-venture-funding/
438 Protos Staff, "Crypto whale stuck in $150M short squeeze during battle for tiny altcoin" (*Protos*, March 30 2021), https://protos.com/crypto-whale-short-seller-mobilecoin-ftx-ilikethecoin-gamestop/
439 CMS Intern (Twitter, March 29 2021), https://twitter.com/cmsintern/status/1376227532530454535
440 Jamie Crawley, "Alameda Research Shouldered FTX Loss of Up to $1B Following Client's Leveraged Trade in 2021: FT" (*CoinDesk*, December 2 2022), https://www.coindesk.com/business/2022/12/02/alameda-research-shouldered-ftx-loss-of-up-to-1b-following-clients-leveraged-trade-in-2021-ft/
441 Joshua Oliver and Kadhim Shuber, "Sam Bankman-Fried's hedge fund took big hit to prop up FTX exchange" (*Financial Times*, December 2 2022), https://www.ft.com/content/5e9dc424-aef4-4981-a4d7-e3c40e1e6085
442 Suvashree Ghosh, "FTX's Federal Net Operating Loss Carryover Stood at $3.7 Billion" (*Bloomberg*, November 21 2022), https://www.bloomberg.com/news/articles/2022-11-21/ftx-s-federal-net-operating-loss-carryover-stood-at-3-7-billion#xj4y7vzkg
443 FTX, "Our Liquidation Engine — how we significantly reduced the likelihood of clawbacks from ever occurring" (*Medium*, April 7 2019), https://ftx.medium.com/our-liquidation-engine-how-we-significantly-reduced-the-likelihood-of-clawbacks-67c1b7d19fdc
444 Maggie Fitzgerald, "Robinhood crypto wallet waitlist tops 1 million customers, CEO says" (*CNBC*, October 21 2021), https://www.cnbc.com/2021/10/21/robinhood-ceo-vlad-tenev-says-crypto-wallet-waitlist-tops-1-million-customers-.html
445 Kadhim Shubber and Joshua Oliver, "Crypto hedge fund Three Arrows fails to meet margin calls" (*Financial Times*, June 16 2022), https://www.ft.com/content/126d8b02-f06a-4fd9-a57b-9f4ceab3de71
446 Voyager Digital Ltd., "Voyager Digital Provides Market Update" (*PR Newswire*, June 27 2022), https://www.prnewswire.com/news-releases/voyager-digital-provides-market-update-301575492.html
447 Ryan Deffenbaugh, "Crypto fund Three Arrows has reportedly been ordered to liquidate" (*Protocol*, June 29 2022), https://www.protocol.com/bulletins/three-arrows-liquidation
448 Joanna Ossinger, Muyao Shen, Yueqi Yang, "Three Arrows Founders Break Silence Over Collapse of Crypto Hedge Fund" (*Bloomberg*, July 22 2022), https://www.bloomberg.com/news/articles/2022-07-22/three-arrows-founders-en-route-to-dubai-describe-ltcm-moment?leadSource=uverify%20wall
449 Rohan Goswami, "Voyager CEO made millions in stock sales in 2021 when price was near peak" (*CNBC*, August 3 2022), https://www.cnbc.com/2022/08/03/voyager-ceo-made-millions-in-stock-sales-in-2021.html
450 MacKenzie Sigalos and Rohan Goswami, "Sam Bankman-Fried's crypto firms had deep ties to Voyager Digital and its bankruptcy wipeout" (*CNBC*, August 9 2022), https://www.cnbc.com/2022/08/09/sam-bankman-frieds-alameda-voyager-digital-spar-in-bankruptcy-court.html
451 "Debtors' motion for entry of an order authorizing the debtors to redact and file under seal certain confidential information related to debtors' motion seeking entry of an order (i) authorizing the debtors to return collateral and

(ii) granting related relief" (United States Bankruptcy Court, Southern District of New York, September 19 2022), https://cases.stretto.com/public/x193/11753/PLEADINGS/1175309202280000000001.pdf

452 Shalini Nagarajan, "Voyager To Borrow $500M From Alameda Amid Industry Downturn" (*Blockworks*, June 20 2022), https://blockworks.co/news/voyager-to-borrow-500m-from-alameda-amid-insolvency-rumors

453 "Notice of response to Alameda/FTX Press Release" (United States Bankruptcy Court, Southern District of New York, July 24 2022), https://cases.stretto.com/public/x193/11753/PLEADINGS/1175307242280000000014.pdf

454 Prashant Jha, "Voyager Digital reportedly had deep ties with SBF-owned Alameda Research" (*Cointelegraph*, August 10 2022), https://cointelegraph.com/news/voyager-digital-reportedly-had-deep-ties-with-sbf-owned-alameda-research

455 Ryan Browne, "Crypto brokerage Voyager Digital files for Chapter 11 bankruptcy protection" (*CNBC*, July 6 2022), https://www.cnbc.com/2022/07/06/crypto-firm-voyager-digital-files-for-chapter-11-bankruptcy-protection.html

456 Callie Caplan, "Mark Cuban, Mavs partner with Voyager cryptocurrency platform in team's first international deal" (*Dallas News*, October 27 2021), https://www.dallasnews.com/sports/mavericks/2021/10/27/mark-cuban-mavs-partner-with-voyager-cryptocurrency-platform-in-teams-first-international-deal/

457 Samyuktha Sriram, "Mark Cuban Faces Class Action Investor Lawsuit After Promoting Crypto Firm Voyager Digital" (*Benzinga*, August 12 2022), https://www.benzinga.com/markets/cryptocurrency/22/08/28453962/mark-cuban-faces-class-action-lawsuit-for-promoting-crypto-firm-voyager-digital

458 Rohan Goswami, "FTX is paying $51 million in cash for Voyager assets, court records show" (*CNBC*, September 30 2022), https://www.cnbc.com/2022/09/30/ftx-is-paying-51-million-in-cash-for-voyager-assets-court-records-.html

459 "Q2 Market Observations" (Genesis, 2022), https://info.genesistrading.com/hubfs/quarterly-reports/2022/Genesis-Q2-Report-2022.pdf

460 Paul Kiernan, "Crypto Lender Genesis Had Sought Emergency Loan of $1 Billion" (*The Wall Street Journal*, November 17 2022), https://www.wsj.com/livecoverage/stock-market-news-today-11-17-2022/card/crypto-lender-genesis-sought-emergency-loan-of-1-billion-by-monday-573TThK17Ke15FYwJzLR

461 Statement by Digital Currency Group on Genesis Capital Chapter 11 Bankruptcy Filing (January 20 2023), https://dcgupdate.com/

462 Genesis Global Capital Update (*Genesis Trading*, January 19 2023), https://genesistrading.com/updates/genesis-global-capital-update-1-19-23

463 Yogita Khatri, "Babel Finance lost over $280 million in proprietary trading with customer funds" (*The Block*, July 29 2022), https://www.theblock.co/post/160230/babel-finance-crypto-lost-280-million-proprietary-trading-restructuring

464 Wolfie Zhao, "Leaked Recordings Suggest Crypto Lender Babel Leveraged Users' Funds in Longing Bitcoin" (*CoinDesk*, October 2 2020), https://www.coindesk.com/business/2020/10/02/leaked-recordings-suggest-crypto-lender-babel-leveraged-users-funds-in-longing-bitcoin/

465 CoinDesk Staff, "FTX US Gains 'Option to Acquire' BlockFi for Up to $240M" (*CoinDesk*, July 2 2022), https://www.coindesk.com/business/2022/07/01/blockfi-reaches-deal-with-ftx-us/

466 Benjamin Pimentel, "BlockFi agrees to sell itself to FTX" (*Protocol*, July 1 2022), https://www.protocol.com/bulletins/blockfi-ftx-crypto-sale

467 Tommy (Twitter, July 1 2022), https://twitter.com/Shaughnessy119/status/1542635063682207746

468 IPHawk (Twitter, July 2 2022), https://twitter.com/TheIpHawk/status/1542918858041921537

469 MacKenzie Sigalos, Rohan Goswami, "Crypto firm BlockFi files for bankruptcy as FTX fallout spreads " (CNBC, November 28 2022), https://www.cnbc.com/2022/11/28/blockfi-files-for-bankruptcy-as-ftx-fallout-spreads.html

470 Rohan Goswami and MacKenzie Sigalos, "BlockFi secret financials show a $1.2 billion relationship with Sam Bankman-Fried's crypto empire" (*CNBC*, January 24 2023), https://www.cnbc.com/2023/01/24/blockfi-secret-financials-show-1point2-billion-tie-to-ftx-and-alameda.html

471 MacKenzie Sigalos, "From $25 billion to $167 million: How a major crypto lender collapsed and dragged many investors down with it" (*CNBC*, July 17 2022), https://www.cnbc.com/2022/07/17/how-the-fall-of-celsius-dragged-down-crypto-investors.html

472 Joshua Oliver and Hannah Murphy, "US states clamp down on crypto yield products from Celsius Network" (*Financial Times*, September 17 2021), https://www.ft.com/content/de5d62e8-871e-465b-8ee1-35da08ec6379

473 Zeke Faux and Joe Light, "Celsius's 18% Yields on Crypto Are Tempting—and Drawing Scrutiny" (*Bloomberg*, January 27 2022), https://www.bloomberg.com/news/articles/2022-01-27/celsius-s-18-yields-on-crypto-are-tempting-and-drawing-scrutiny

474 Ryan Weeks, "Celsius pulled half a billion dollars out of Anchor Protocol amid Terra chaos" (*TheBlock*, May 13 2022), https://www.theblock.co/post/146752/celsius-pulled-half-a-billion-dollars-out-of-anchor-protocol-amid-terra-chaos

475 Kate Rooney, Paige Tortorelli and Scott Zamost, "Former employees say issues plagued the crypto company Celsius years ahead of bankruptcy" (*CNBC*, July 19 2022), https://www.cnbc.com/2022/07/19/former-employees-say-issues-plagued-crypto-company-celsius-years-before-bankruptcy.html

476 "Attorney General James Sues Former CEO of Celsius Cryptocurrency Platform for Defrauding Investors" (Letitia James, New York State Attorney General, January 5 2023), https://ag.ny.gov/press-release/2023/attorney-general-james-sues-former-ceo-celsius-cryptocurrency-platform-defrauding

477 "Terms of use" (Celsius, Last Revised: September 29 2022), https://celsius.network/terms-of-use

478 Dietrich Knauth, "U.S. judge says Celsius Network owns most customer crypto deposits" (*Reuters*, January 6 2023), https://www.reuters.com/business/finance/us-judge-says-celsius-network-owns-most-customer-crypto-deposits-2023-01-05/

479 Jim Cramer (Twitter, June 22 2022), https://twitter.com/jimcramer/status/1539532374463102980

480 Kadhim Shubber and Joshua Oliver, "Inside Celsius: how one of crypto's biggest lenders ground to a halt" (*Financial Times*, July 12 2022), https://www.ft.com/content/4fa06516-119b-4722-946b-944e38b02f45

481 "KeyFi, Inc, v. Celsius Network Limited and Celsius KeyFi LLC" (Supreme Court of the State of New York, County of New York, July 7 2022), https://regmedia.co.uk/2022/07/08/celsius_lawsuit.pdf

482 Jason Nelson, "Crypto Lender Celsius Countersues KeyFi for 'Gross Mismanagement'" (*Decrypt*, August 24 2022), https://decrypt.co/108079/celsius-keyfi-jason-stone-countersuit-money-laundering-theft

483 "Understanding Tornado Cash, Its Sanctions Implications, and Key Compliance Questions" (Chainalysis, August 30 2022), https://blog.chainalysis.com/reports/tornado-cash-sanctions-challenges

484 Lachlan Keller, "Vitalik Buterin says he used Tornado Cash to donate to Ukraine" (*Forkast*, August 10 2022), https://forkast.news/vitalik-buterin-says-used-tornado-cash-donate-ukraine/

485 "U.S. Treasury Sanctions Notorious Virtual Currency Mixer Tornado Cash" (U.S. Department of the Treasury, August 8 2022), https://home.treasury.gov/news/press-releases/jy0916

486 Emily Nicolle *et al.*, "Wintermute Hacked for About $160 Million in DeFi Operations" (*Bloomberg*, September 20 2022), https://www.bloomberg.com/news/articles/2022-09-20/wintermute-hacked-for-about-160-million-in-its-defi-operations#xj4y7vzkg

487 Jeff Kauflin, "With Sam Bankman-Fried's Hedge Fund Gone, Crypto Trading Firm Wintermute Emerges" (*Forbes*, December 20 2022), https://www.forbes.com/sites/jeffkauflin/2022/12/20/with-sam-bankman-frieds-hedge-fund-gone-crypto-trading-firm-wintermute-emerges/?sh=59c5a5232bbb

488 Jack Schickler, "Crypto Trading Firm Wintermute Given Seat on Key FTX Creditor Committee" (*CoinDesk*, December 16 2022), https://www.coindesk.com/policy/2022/12/15/wintermute-venture-cap-octopus-given-seats-on-key-ftx-creditor-committee/

489 Avraham Eisenberg (Twitter, October 16 2022), https://twitter.com/avi_eisen/status/1581326197241180160

490 "SEC Charges Avraham Eisenberg with Manipulating Mango Markets' "Governance Token" to Steal $116 Million of Crypto Assets" (U.S. Securities and Exchange Commission, January 20 2023), https://www.sec.gov/news/press-release/2023-13

491 Jesse Coghlan, "Mango Markets sues Avraham Eisenberg for $47M in damages plus interest (*Cointelegraph*, January 26 2023), https://cointelegraph.com/news/mango-markets-sues-avraham-eisenberg-for-47m-in-damages-plus-interest

492 Zhiyuan Sun, "Mango Markets hacker allegedly feigns Curve short attack to exploit Aave" (*Cointelegraph*, November 22 2022), https://cointelegraph.com/news/mango-markets-hacker-allegedly-feigns-curve-short-attack-to-exploit-aave

493 Aleksandar Gilbert, "Curve Releases Whitepaper for crvUSD Stablecoin" (*The Defiant*, November 23 2022), https://thedefiant.io/curve-crvusd-whitepaper

494 Kari McMahon, "'We came, we saw, we researched': Bankman-Fried considered closing Alameda in September" (*The Block*, December 13 2022), https://www.theblock.co/post/194604/we-came-we-saw-we-researched-bankman-fried-considered-closing-alameda-in-september

495 Kari McMahon, "'We came, we saw, we researched': Bankman-Fried considered closing Alameda in September" (*The Block*, December 13 2022), https://www.theblock.co/post/194604/we-came-we-saw-we-researched-bankman-fried-considered-closing-alameda-in-september

496 SkyBridge Capital, "FTX Ventures to Acquire Stake in SkyBridge Capital" (*PR Newswire*, September 9 2022), https://www.prnewswire.com/news-releases/ftx-ventures-to-acquire-stake-in-skybridge-capital-301621035.html

497 Andrew Asmakov, "Scaramucci's Firm Pauses Investor Redemptions for Fund With Bitcoin, Ethereum Exposure" (*Decrypt*, July 19 2022), https://decrypt.co/105436/scaramuccis-firm-pauses-investor-redemptions-fund-bitcoin-ethereum-exposure

498 Danny Nelson, "Scaramucci's SkyBridge Launching a Bitcoin Fund" (*CoinDesk*, December 22 2020), https://www.coindesk.com/markets/2020/12/21/scaramuccis-skybridge-launching-a-bitcoin-fund/

499 Prashant Jha, "Alameda Research FTT token transfer from September fuels wild speculations" (*Cointelegraph*, November 9 2022), https://cointelegraph.com/news/alameda-research-ftt-token-transfer-from-september-fuels-wild-speculations

500 Ryan Ozawa, "Caroline Ellison 'Knew That It Was Wrong,' Implicates Sam Bankman-Fried" (*Decrypt*, December 27 2022), https://decrypt.co/117989/caroline-ellison-knew-that-it-was-wrong-implicates-sam-bankman-fried

501 Kanjyik Ghosh, "Alameda, FTX executives knew crypto exchange was using customer funds - WSJ" (*Reuters*, November 13 2022), https://www.reuters.com/technology/alameda-ftx-executives-knew-crypto-exchange-was-using-customer-funds-wsj-2022-11-12/

502 Cheyenne Ligon and Tracy Wang, "Former FTX Executive Nishad Singh Planning to Plead Guilty to Fraud: Bloomberg" (*CoinDesk*, February 18 2023), https://www.coindesk.com/policy/2023/02/17/former-ftx-executive-nishad-singh-planning-to-plead-guilty-to-fraud-bloomberg/

503 Matthew Cranston, "FTX's inner circle had a secret chat group called 'Wirefraud'" (*The Australian Financial Review*, December 13 2022), https://www.afr.com/companies/financial-services/ftx-s-inner-circle-had-a-secret-chat-group-called-wirefraud-20221213-p5c5sx

504 Parikshit Mishra, "FTX's Sam Bankman-Fried Backtracks on $1B Political Donation, Calls It 'Dumb Quote'" (*CoinDesk*, October 14 2022), https://www.coindesk.com/business/2022/10/14/ftxs-sam-bankman-fried-backtracks-on-1b-political-donation-calls-it-dumb-quote/

505 Jesse Coghlan, "'Secretly circulating' draft crypto bill could be a 'boon' to DeFi" (*Cointelegraph*, October 20 2022) https://cointelegraph.com/news/secretly-circulating-draft-crypto-bill-could-be-a-boon-to-defi

506 James Thomson, "How the Mooch helped push the first domino in the FTX crash" (*The Australian Financial Review*, November 16 2022), https://www.afr.com/chanticleer/how-the-mooch-helped-push-the-first-domino-in-the-ftx-crash-20221116-p5byub

507 Ryan Salame FTX (Twitter, October 30 2022), https://twitter.com/rsalame7926/status/1586545907461398532

508 lightspeed mert (Twitter, November 9 2022), https://twitter.com/0xMert_/status/1590016419038916608

509 Rahul Nambiampurath, "Binance Hit By $570 Million Blockchain Bridge Hack" (*Investopedia*, October 7 2022), https://www.investopedia.com/binance-got-hacked-6748215

510 Ian Allison, "Divisions in Sam Bankman-Fried's Crypto Empire Blur on His Trading Titan Alameda's Balance Sheet" (*CoinDesk*, November 2 2022), https://www.coindesk.com/business/2022/11/02/divisions-in-sam-bankman-frieds-crypto-empire-blur-on-his-trading-titan-alamedas-balance-sheet

511 CZ Binance (Twitter, November 6 2022), https://twitter.com/cz_binance/status/1589283421704290306

512 CZ Binance (Twitter, November 7 2022), https://twitter.com/cz_binance/status/1589374530413215744

513 Caroline Ellison (Twitter, November 7 2022), https://twitter.com/carolinecapital/status/1589287457975304193

514 PastryEth, (Twitter, November 16 2022), https://twitter.com/PastryEth/status/1592744898666512386

515 PastryEth, (Twitter, November 16 2022), https://twitter.com/PastryEth/status/1592744916148289536

516 Caroline Ellison (Twitter, November 6 2022), https://twitter.com/carolinecapital/status/1589264375042707458

517 "United States of America v. Samuel Bankman-Fried, Superseding Indictment" (United States District Court, Southern District of New York, February 23 2023), https://www.documentcloud.org/documents/23688431-superseding-indictment-filed-as-to-samuel-bankman-fried-originally-filed-under-seal-on-22223

518 Matt Levine, "FTX's Balance Sheet Was Bad" (*Bloomberg*, November 15 2022), https://www.bloomberg.com/opinion/articles/2022-11-14/ftx-s-balance-sheet-was-bad

519 Joshua Oliver, "'Sam? Are you there?!' The bizarre and brutal final hours of FTX" (*Financial Times*, February 8 2023), https://www.ft.com/content/6e912f25-f1b7-4b19-b370-007fbc867246

520 Vicky Ge Huang, Alexander Osipovich, and Patricia Kowsmann, "FTX Tapped Into Customer Accounts to Fund Risky Bets, Setting Up Its Downfall" (*The Wall Street Journal*, November 11 2022), https://www.wsj.com/amp/articles/ftx-tapped-into-customer-accounts-to-fund-risky-bets-setting-up-its-downfall-11668093732

521 SBF (Twitter, November 9 2022), https://twitter.com/SBF_FTX/status/1590012128307875840

522 Alex Hern, "Binance to buy FTX in major cryptocurrency exchange merger" (*The Guardian*, November 8 2022), https://www.theguardian.com/technology/2022/nov/08/binance-to-buy-ftx-in-major-cryptocurrency-exchange-merger

523 Joshua Oliver 'Sam? Are you there?!' The bizarre and brutal final hours of FTX (*Financial Times*, February 8 2023), https://www.ft.com/content/6e912f25-f1b7-4b19-b370-007fbc867246

524 David Thomas, "Binance Walks Away From FTX Buyout, Citing Mishandled Funds and US Agency Investigations" (*BeInCrypto*, November 9 2022), https://beincrypto.com/binance-walks-away-from-ftx-buyout-citing-mishandled-funds-and-us-agency-investigations/

525 "FTX Digital Markets Ltd. (In Provisional Liquidation)" (PwC), https://www.pwc.com/bs/fdm#:~:text=On%2010%20November%202022%20the,as%20a%20digital%20asset%20business.

526 Joshua Oliver 'Sam? Are you there?!' The bizarre and brutal final hours of FTX (*Financial Times*, February 8 2023), https://www.ft.com/content/6e912f25-f1b7-4b19-b370-007fbc867246

527 Joshua Oliver 'Sam? Are you there?!' The bizarre and brutal final hours of FTX (*Financial Times*, February 8 2023), https://www.ft.com/content/6e912f25-f1b7-4b19-b370-007fbc867246

528 Neil Hartnell, "'FTX Bahamas Chief Confessed to Fraud" (*Tribune 242*, December 15 2022), http://m.tribune242.com/news/2022/dec/15/ftx-bahamas-chief-confessed-fraud-securities-commi/

529 Jesse Hamilton, Cheyenne Ligon, and Elizabeth Napolitano, "Congress' FTX Problem: 1 in 3 Members Got Cash From Crypto Exchange's Bosses" (*CoinDesk*, January 18 2023), https://www.coindesk.com/policy/2023/01/17/congress-ftx-problem-1-in-3-members-got-cash-from-crypto-exchanges-bosses/

530 Neil Hartnell, "Bahamas battles for control over $256m FTX properties" (*The Tribune*, December 13 2022), http://www.tribune242.com/news/2022/dec/13/bahamas-battles-control-over-256m-ftx-properties/#:~:text=%E2%80%9CFTX%20Property%20Holdings%20is%20a,never%20has%20done%20business%20here.

531 Thomas Barrabi, "Sam Bankman-Fried's parents staying in Bahamas, fear his legal fees will 'wipe them out'" (*New York Post*, December 12 2022), https://nypost.com/2022/12/12/sam-bankman-frieds-parents-fear-his-legal-fees-will-wipe-them-out/

532 Jack Schickler, "Sam Bankman-Fried's Mother and Brother Not Cooperating With Financial Probe, FTX Lawyers Say" (*CoinDesk*, January 27 2023), https://sg.news.yahoo.com/sam-bankman-fried-mother-brother-172209477.html

533 Statement from the Attorney General (*Government of The Bahamas*, December 12 2022) https://pacer-documents.s3.amazonaws.com/33/188450/042120682086.pdf

534 Email from Sam Bankman-Fried to Ryan Pinder (Filed December 14, 2022), https://www.ledgerinsights.com/wp-content/uploads/2022/12/FTX-SBF-Bahamas-email.pdf

535 Zhiyuan Sun "FTX partially resumes withdrawals, blockchain data shows " (*Cointelegraph*, November 10 2022) https://cointelegraph.com/news/blockchain-data-show-ftx-appears-to-have-resumed-withdrawals

536 Nikhilesh De "Bahamas Securities Regulator Says It Didn't Order FTX to Reopen Local Withdrawals" (*CoinDesk*, November 13 2022), https://www.coindesk.com/policy/2022/11/13/bahamas-securities-regulator-says-it-didnt-order-ftx-to-reopen-local-withdrawals/

537 Felix Ng, "Fear of 'angry people' drove Bankman-Fried to open withdrawals for Bahamians" (*Cointelegraph*, November 30 2022), https://cointelegraph.com/news/sbf-reveals-what-was-behind-ftx-s-reopening-of-bahamian-withdrawals

538 SBF (Twitter, November 10 2022), https://twitter.com/SBF_FTX/status/1590709195892195329

539 Glenn L. Friedman *et al.*, "Prager Metis Opens First-Ever CPA Firm in the Metaverse" (Prager Metis, January 7 2022), https://pragermetis.com/news/prager-metis-opens-first-ever-cpa-firm-metaverse/

540 Joe Schneider, "First accounting firm with HQ in metaverse is sued over FTX meltdown" (*Bloomberg*, November 24 2022), https://www.bloomberg.com/news/articles/2022-11-23/first-accounting-firm-in-metaverse-sucked-into-ftx-meltdown

541 Jean Eaglesham and Patricia Kowsmann, "FTX Auditors Doubled as Crypto Industry Cheerleaders" (*The Wall Street Journal*, November 17 2022), https://www.wsj.com/articles/ftx-auditors-doubled-as-crypto-industry-cheerleaders-11668709049

542 Mike Truppa, "FTX Telegram admin claims exchange hacked" (*The Block*, November 12 2022), https://www.theblock.co/post/186289/ftx-claims-it-has-been-hacked-of-all-of-its-funds-website-and-mobile-app-compromised

543 Aktriti Sharma, "FTX officials appear to confirm potential hack to apps - CoinDesk" (*Yahoo!*, November 12 2022), https://finance.yahoo.com/news/ftx-officials-appear-confirm-potential-062927996.html

544 Tobi Opeyemi Amure, "FTX Collapse Worsens After a $600 Million Hack And Criminal Charges" (*Investopedia*, November 14 2022), https://www.investopedia.com/ftx-got-hacked-6828458

545 Arjun Kharpal *et al.*, "FTX-owned service being used to launder hundreds of millions 'hacked' from FTX, researchers say" (*CNBC*, November 21 2022), https://www.cnbc.com/2022/11/21/ftx-theft-hackers-start-to-launder-477-million-of-stolen-crypto.html

546 Gary Wang (GitHub), https://github.com/garywang

547 Thomas Barrabi, "FTX lawyer tied to poker scandal reportedly flipped on Sam Bankman-Fried" (*New York Post*, January 5 2023), https://nypost.com/2023/01/05/daniel-friedberg-flips-on-ftxs-sam-bankman-fried/

548 Josh O'Sullivan, "FTX hacker identity discovered by Kraken Exchange team" (*CryptoSlate*, November 12 2022), https://cryptoslate.com/ftx-hacker-identity-discovered-by-kraken-exchange-team/

549 CMC News, "Securities Commission of The Bahamas denies asking FTX to mint millions in tokens" (*Caribbean National Weekly*, January 4 2023), https://www.caribbeannationalweekly.com/news/caribbean-news/securities-commission-of-the-bahamas-denies-asking-ftx-to-mint-millions-in-tokens.

550 MacKenzie Sigalos, "Sam Bankman-Fried reportedly denies fleeing to Argentina, says he's still in the Bahamas" (*CNBC*, November 12 2022), https://www.cnbc.com/2022/11/12/sam-bankman-fried-reportedly-denies-fleeing-to-argentina-says-hes-still-in-the-bahamas.html

551 Jon Boon, "Spurs owner Joe Lewis lives on a £112m boat, is friends with Tiger Woods and gave The Nolans their first ever gig" (*The Sun*, February 16 2023), https://www.thesun.co.uk/sport/5186973/joe-lewis-tottenham-owner-yacht/

552 Antoine Gara *et al.*, "FTX held less than $1bn in liquid assets against $9bn in liabilities" (*Financial Times*, November 12 2022), https://www.ft.com/content/f05fe9f8-ca0a-48d5-8ef2-7a4d813af558
553 Jeff John Roberts, "FTX's balance sheet from hell" (*Fortune*, November 15 2022), https://fortune.com/crypto/2022/11/15/ftxs-balance-sheet-from-hell/
554 Testimony of Mr. John J. Ray III (House Financial Services Committee, December 13 2022), https://docs.house.gov/meetings/BA/BA00/20221213/115246/HHRG-117-BA00-Wstate-RayJ-20221213.pdf
555 Rohan Goswami, "Never seen 'such a complete failure' of corporate controls, says new FTX CEO who also oversaw Enron bankruptcy" (*CNBC*, November 17 2022), https://www.cnbc.com/2022/11/17/ftx-ceo-shreds-bankman-fried-never-seen-such-a-failure-of-controls-.html
556 "FTX Trading Ltd." (Kroll), https://restructuring.ra.kroll.com/FTX/
557 "Superseding Indictment, United States of America v. Samuel Bankman-Fried" (United States District Court, Southern District of New York, February 2 2023), https://www.documentcloud.org/documents/23688431-superseding-indictment-filed-as-to-samuel-bankman-fried-originally-filed-under-seal-on-22223
558 Gretchen Morgenson, "This little-known firm with a weird website was central to the misappropriation of FTX customers' money, regulators say" (*NBC News*, December 27 2022), https://www.nbcnews.com/tech/crypto/north-dimension-ftx-bankman-fried-rcna63175
559 "North Dimension" (Web Archive), https://web.archive.org/web/20221111031650/https:/northdimensioninc.com/category-market.html
560 "Jury Trial Demanded, Securities and Exchange Commission v. Nishad Singh" (United States District Court, Southern District of New York, February 28 2023), https://www.sec.gov/litigation/complaints/2023/comp-pr2023-40.pdf
561 "Superseding Indictment, United States of America v. Sam Bankman-Fried" (United States District Court, Southern District of New York, February 23 2023), https://www.documentcloud.org/documents/23688431-superseding-indictment-filed-as-to-samuel-bankman-fried-originally-filed-under-seal-on-22223
562 "Jury Trial Demanded, Securities and Exchange Commission v. Caroline Ellison and Zixiao "Gary" Wang" (United States District Court, Southern District of New York, December 21 2022), https://www.sec.gov/litigation/complaints/2022/comp-pr2022-234.pdf
563 "Amended complaint for injunctive and other equitable relief and for civil monetary penalties under the Commodity Exchange Act and Commission regulations, Commodity Futures Trading Commission v. Samuel Bankman-Fried *et al.*, (United States District Court, Southern District of New York, December 21 2022), https://www.cftc.gov/media/8021/enfftxtradingcomplaint122122/download
564 "Jury Trial Demanded, Securities and Exchange Commission v. Nishad Singh (United States District Court, Southern District of New York, February 28 2023), https://www.sec.gov/litigation/complaints/2023/comp-pr2023-40.pdf
565 Babafemi Adebajo, "FTX Is Upgrading Its Matching Engine" (*Coinspeaker*, October 10 2022), https://www.coinspeaker.com/ftx-matching-engine/
566 "United States Attorney Announces Charges Against FTX Founder Samuel Bankman-Fried" (The United States Attorney's Office, Southern District of New York, December 13 2022), https://www.justice.gov/usao-sdny/pr/united-states-attorney-announces-charges-against-ftx-founder-samuel-bankman-fried
567 "CFTC Charges Sam Bankman-Fried, FTX Trading and Alameda with Fraud and Material Misrepresentations" (Commodity Futures Trading Commission, December 13 2022), https://www.cftc.gov/PressRoom/PressReleases/8638-22
568 Benjamin Weiser, "Prosecutor in Bankman-Fried Case Made a Career of White-Collar Cases" (*The New York Times*, December 13 2022), https://www.nytimes.com/2022/12/13/business/damian-williams-ftx.html.
569 Joshua Oliver, "'Sam? Are you there?!' The bizarre and brutal final hours of FTX" (*Financial Times*, February 13 2023), https://financialpost.com/fp-finance/cryptocurrency/sam-are-you-there-the-bizarre-and-brutal-final-hours-of-ftx
570 David Yaffe-Bellany, "How Sam Bankman-Fried's Crypto Empire Collapsed" (*The New York Times*, November 14 2022), https://www.nytimes.com/2022/11/14/technology/ftx-sam-bankman-fried-crypto-bankruptcy.html
571 David Yaffe-Bellany, "How Sam Bankman-Fried's Crypto Empire Collapsed " (*The New York Times*, November 14 2022), https://www.nytimes.com/2022/11/14/technology/ftx-sam-bankman-fried-crypto-bankruptcy.html
572 "Amended Complaint for Injunctive and Other Equitable Relief and for Civil Monetary Penalities Under the Commodity Exchange Act and Commission Regulations, Commodities Futures Trading Commission v. Sam Bankman-Fried et al." (United States District Court, Southern District of New York, December 21 2022), https://www.cftc.gov/media/8021/enfftxtradingcomplaint122122/download
573 Joshua Oliver, "'Sam? Are you there?!' The bizarre and brutal final hours of FTX" (*Financial Times*, February 8 2023), https://www.ft.com/content/6e912f25-f1b7-4b19-b370-007fbc867246
574 Dave Michaels *et al.*, "Alameda, FTX Executives Are Said to Have Known FTX Was Using Customer Funds" (*The Wall Street Journal*, November 12 2022), https://www.wsj.com/articles/alameda-ftx-executives-are-said-to-have-known-ftx-was-using-customer-funds-11668264238

575 Kara Scannell and Allison Morrow, "Stanford scholars co-signed Sam Bankman-Fried's $250 million bail deal" (CNN, February 15 2023), https://edition.cnn.com/2023/02/15/business/sam-bankman-fried-bail-cosigners-stanford
576 Kelsey Piper, "Sam Bankman-Fried tries to explain himself" (Vox, November 16 2022), https://www.vox.com/future-perfect/23462333/sam-bankman-fried-ftx-cryptocurrency-effective-altruism-crypto-bahamas-philanthropy
577 Cheyenne Ligon, "DOJ Claims Sam Bankman-Fried Tried to Influence Witness Testimony, Asks for Communications Ban" (CoinDesk, January 28 2023), https://sg.finance.yahoo.com/news/doj-claims-sam-bankman-fried-024137349.html
578 "Declaration of Daniel Friedberg in Support of Amended Objection of Warren Winter to Debtors' Application for an Order Authorizing the Retention and Employment of Sullivan & Cromwell LLP as Counsel to the Debtors and Debtors in-Possession Nunc pro Tunc to the Petition Date" (The United States Bankruptcy Court for the District of Delaware, January 19 2023), https://restructuring.ra.kroll.com/FTX/Home-DownloadPDF?id1=MTQzODk5NA==&id2=-1
579 Rohan Goswami and MacKenzie Sigalos, "Lawyers and advisors in FTX bankruptcy have billed nearly $20 million for 51 days of work" (CNBC, February 8 2023), https://www.cnbc.com/2023/02/08/ftx-bankruptcy-fees-near-20-million-for-51-days-of-work.html
580 Oluwapelumi Adejum, "FTX defends move to appoint law firm Sullivan & Cromwell as advisor" (CryptoSlate, January 18 2023), https://cryptoslate.com/ftx-defends-move-to-appoint-law-firm-sullivan-cromwell-as-advisor/
581 Jody Godoy and Luc Cohen, "FTX's Singh pleads guilty as pressure mounts on Bankman-Fried" (Reuters, March 1 2023), https://www.reuters.com/legal/ftxs-singh-agrees-plead-guilty-us-criminal-charges-lawyer-says-2023-02-28/
582 "Securities and Exchange Commision v. Nishad Singh" (United States District Court, Southern District of New York, February 28 2023), https://www.sec.gov/litigation/complaints/2023/comp-pr2023-40.pdf
583 Emma Roth, "Sam Bankman-Fried accused of sending a $40 million crypto bribe to Chinese officials" (The Verge, March 29 2023), https://www.theverge.com/2023/3/28/23660076/sam-bankman-fried-accused-bribe-chinese-officials-ftx
584 Nivesh Rustgi, "FTX Debtors Say 'Hubris, Incompetence, and Greed' at Root of Exchange's Collapse" (Decrypt, April 10 2023), https://decrypt.co/125818/ftx-debtors-say-hubris-incompetence-greed-root-exchanges-collapse
585 SBF (Twitter, August 1 2019), https://twitter.com/SBF_FTX/status/1156696100729806849
586 Elizabeth Warren et al."(United States Senate, December 5 2022), https://www.warren.senate.gov/imo/media/doc/2022.12.05%20Letter%20to%20Silvergate%20Bank%20re%20FTX.pdf
587 Zacks Equity Research, "Signature Bank (SBNY) to Reduce Crypto Exposure by $8-$10B" (Yahoo!, December 7 2022), https://finance.yahoo.com/news/signature-bank-sbny-reduce-crypto-130301487.html
588 "Metropolitan Bank Holding Corp. to Exit Crypto-Asset Related Vertical" (Metropolitan Commercial Bank, January 9 2023), https://investors.mcbankny.com/news-events/news/news-details/2023/Metropolitan-Bank-Holding-Corp.-to-Exit-Crypto-Asset-Related-Vertical/default.aspx
589 Board of Governors of the Federal Reserve System et al., "Joint Statement on Crypto-Asset Risks to Banking Organizations" (Federal Reserve, January 3 2023), https://www.federalreserve.gov/newsevents/pressreleases/files/bcreg20230103a1.pdf
590 Brian Deese et al., "The Administration's Roadmap to Mitigate Cryptocurrencies' Risks" (The White House, January 27 2023), https://www.whitehouse.gov/nec/briefing-room/2023/01/27/the-administrations-roadmap-to-mitigate-cryptocurrencies-risks/
591 Hannah Lang, "U.S. Federal Reserve rejects crypto-focused bank's application to be supervised by the Fed" (Reuters, January 27 2023), https://www.reuters.com/business/finance/us-federal-reserve-rejects-crypto-focused-banks-application-be-supervised-by-2023-01-27/
592 "Kraken to Discontinue Unregistered Offer and Sale of Crypto Asset Staking-As-A-Service Program and Pay $30 Million to Settle SEC Charges" (U.S. Securities and Exchange Commission, February 9 2023), https://www.sec.gov/news/press-release/2023-25
593 Nic Carter, "Operation Choke Point 2.0 Is Underway, And Crypto Is In Its Crosshairs" (Pirate Wires, February 9 2023), https://www.piratewires.com/p/crypto-choke-point
594 Angus Berwick and Tom Wilson, "Crypto giant Binance moved $400 million from U.S. partner to firm managed by CEO Zhao" (Reuters, February 17 2023), https://www.reuters.com/technology/crypto-giant-binance-moved-400-million-us-partner-firm-managed-by-ceo-zhao-2023-02-16/
595 "Silvergate Capital Corporation Announces Fourth Quarter 2022 Results" (Silvergate, January 17 2023), https://www.silvergate.com/Archives/edgar/data/1312109/000131210923000020/ex991si4q22earningsrelease.htm
596 Michael del Castillo, "Signature Launches Institutional Payments Using Permissioned Ethereum Blockchain" (Forbes, December 4 2018), https://www.forbes.com/sites/michaeldelcastillo/2018/12/04/signature-launches-institutional-payments-using-permissioned-ethereum-blockchain/

597 Yueqi Yang and Eva Szalay, "Signature's Signet Provided Path for Tether Holders" (*Bloomberg*, April 5 2023), https://www.bloomberg.com/news/articles/2023-04-04/signature-s-signet-provided-path-for-tether-holders#xj4v7vzkg

598 Hugh Son, "Why regulators seized Signature Bank in third-biggest bank failure in U.S. history" (*CNBC*, March 13 2023), https://www.cnbc.com/2023/03/13/signature-bank-third-biggest-bank-failure-in-us-history.html

599 Jeremy Allaire (Twitter, March 13 2023), https://twitter.com/jerallaire/status/1635059033634906112

600 Protos Staff, "Did Justin Sun's diplomatic immunity get revoked?" (*Protos,* March 21 2023), https://protos.com/did-justin-suns-diplomatic-immunity-get-revoked/

601 Protos Staff, "Justin Sun's Grenada post grants diplomatic immunity — in Switzerland" (*Protos*, December 22 2021) https://protos.com/sun-grenada-his-excellency-justin-crypto-tron-diplomatic-immunity-switzerland/

602 Omar Faridi, "Justin Sun's Tron controversies: plagiarism, Teslas, Warren Buffett, kidney stones, and a deleted apology" (*CryptoSlate*, July 29 2019), https://cryptoslate.com/justin-suns-controversies-plagiarism-teslas-warren-buffett-kidney-stones-and-a-deleted-apology/

603 Hu Yue *et al.*, "Buffett Lunch Winner Barred From Foreign Travel" (*Caixin Global*, July 24 2019), https://www.caixinglobal.com/2019-07-24/exclusive-buffett-lunch-winner-barred-from-foreign-travel-101443031.html

604 "SEC Charges Crypto Entrepreneur Justin Sun and His Companies for Fraud and Other Securities Law Violations" (U.S. Securities and Exchange Commission, March 24 2023), https://www.sec.gov/litigation/litreleases/2023/lr25676.htm

605 Reuters, "SEC sues Tron founder Justin Sun, Lindsay Lohan, other celebrities over crypto sales" (*SCMP*, March 23 2023), https://www.scmp.com/news/world/united-states-canada/article/3214504/lindsay-lohan-and-jake-paul-among-celebrities-charged-touting-cryptocurrency-social-media

606 Kim Dong-ho, "Kwon Do-hyung on the run, "The United States has no jurisdiction"" (*YNA*, April 4 2023), https://www.yna.co.kr/view/AKR20230403139000009

607 Ava Benny-Morrison *et al.*, "Do Kwon Charged With Fraud by US Prosecutors in New York" (*Bloomberg*, March 24 2023), https://www.bloomberg.com/news/articles/2023-03-23/do-kwon-charged-with-fraud-by-us-prosecutors-in-new-york

608 Turner Wright, "South Korean authorities seize $160M in assets tied to Terra employees: Report" (*Cointelegraph*, April 3 2023), https://cointelegraph.com/news/south-korean-authorities-seize-160m-in-assets-tied-to-terra-employees-report

609 Prashant Jha, Do Kwon converted illicit funds from LUNA to Bitcoin: S.Korean prosecutors (*Cointelegraph*, April 7 2023), https://cointelegraph.com/news/do-kwon-converted-stolen-funds-from-luna-to-bitcoin-s-korean-prosecutors

610 "CFTC Charges Binance and Its Founder, Changpeng Zhao, with Willful Evasion of Federal Law and Operating an Illegal Digital Asset Derivatives Exchange" (Commodity Futures Trading Commission, March 27 2023), https://www.cftc.gov/PressRoom/PressReleases/8680-23

611 "Commodity Futures Trading Commission v. Changpeng Zhao *et al.*, (The United States District Court for the Northern District Of Illinois, March 27 2023), https://www.docdroid.net/60YAbCz/cftc-binance-pdf#page=3

612 Lydia Beyoud *et al.*, "Jane Street, Tower and Radix Are Unnamed 'VIPs' in Binance Case" (*Bloomberg*, April 6 2023), https://www.bloomberg.com/news/articles/2023-04-05/jane-street-tower-and-radix-are-unnamed-vips-in-binance-case?leadSource=uverify%20wall

613 "CFTC Charges BitMEX Owners with Illegally Operating a Cryptocurrency Derivatives Trading Platform and Anti-Money Laundering Violations" (Commodity Futures Trading Commission, October 1 2020), https://www.cftc.gov/PressRoom/PressReleases/8270-20

614 "Federal Court Orders BitMEX to Pay $100 Million for Illegally Operating a Cryptocurrency Trading Platform and Anti-Money Laundering Violations" (Commodity Futures Trading Commission, August 10 2021), https://www.cftc.gov/PressRoom/PressReleases/8412-21

615 Luc Cohen, "Crypto exchange BitMEX co-founder gets 6 months house arrest for U.S. charges" (*Reuters*, May 23 2022), https://www.reuters.com/legal/government/crypto-exchange-bitmex-co-founder-gets-6-months-house-arrest-us-charges-2022-05-23/

616 Shawn Tully, "How Binance really operates: The world's largest crypto exchange boasts vast profits, hefty influencer payouts, and a ticking time bomb on its balance sheet" (*Fortune*, March 28 2023), https://fortune-com.cdn.ampproject.org/c/s/fortune.com/2023/03/28/binance-cftc-lawsuit-bnb-coin-social-media-influencers/amp/

617 Binance, "Binance Annual Revenue Grew Tenfold In The Last Two Years, But Not Without Challenges" (*Binance*, January 12 2023), https://www.binance.com/en/feed/post/157884

618 Ian Curran, "Binance chief steps down from Irish firms at centre of US lawsuit" (*The Irish Times*, April 6 2023), https://www.irishtimes.com/business/2023/04/06/binance-chief-steps-down-from-irish-firms-at-centre-of-us-lawsuit/

619 Brandy Betz, "Abu Dhabi Starts $2B Initiative to Back Web3 Startups" (*CoinDesk*, February 15 2023), https://www.coindesk.com/business/2023/02/15/abu-dhabi-starts-2b-initiative-to-back-web3-startups/

620 Samuel Wan, "Coinbase CEO says leaving the US for UK is 'on the table'" (*CryptoSlate*, April 19 2023), https://cryptoslate.com/armstrong-coinbase-leaving-the-us-for-uk-is-on-the-table

621 "The Sovereign Individual" (Wikipedia), https://en.wikipedia.org/wiki/The_Sovereign_Individual

622 Stephen Clark, "Falcon 9 deploys 56 Starlink satellites on SpaceX's 20th launch of the year" (*Spaceflight Now*, March 24 2023), https://spaceflightnow.com/2023/03/24/falcon-9-rocket-deploys-56-more-starlink-satellites-on-spacexs-20th-launch-of-the-year

623 Martin Gruenberg, "Remarks by FDIC Chairman Martin Gruenberg at the Institute of International Bankers" (Federal Deposit Insurance Corporation, March 6 2023), https://www.fdic.gov/news/speeches/2023/spmar0623.html

624 Mehmet Caner *et al.*, "Finding the Tipping Point—When Sovereign Debt Turns Bad" (The World Bank, July 2010), https://documents1.worldbank.org/curated/en/509771468337915456/pdf/WPS5391.pdf

625 Jesse Hamilton, "U.S. Federal Reserve's Real-Time Payments System Coming in July" (*CoinDesk*, March 16 2023), https://www.coindesk.com/policy/2023/03/15/us-federal-reserves-real-time-payments-system-coming-in-july/

626 "What Is EIP-4844 in Ethereum and How Can It Benefit Users?" (Binance Academy, February 14 2023), https://academy.binance.com/en/articles/what-is-eip-4844-in-ethereum-and-how-can-it-benefit-users

627 Marko Mihajlovic, "What Is EIP-4844?" (*Academy Shrimpy*, March 13 2023), https://academy.shrimpy.io/post/what-is-eip-4844-how-proto-danksharding-reduces-gas-fees

628 "Cryptocurrency Ownership Data" (TripleA), https://triple-a.io/crypto-ownership-data/

629 "Bitcoin Halving" (*Coinwarz*), https://www.coinwarz.com/mining/bitcoin/halving#:~:text=When%20is%20the%20Next%20Bitcoin,to%203.125%20Bitcoin%20per%20block

630 "CME Group Self-Certifies Bitcoin Futures to Launch Dec. 18" (CME Group, November 30 2017), https://www.cmegroup.com/media-room/press-releases/2017/12/01/cme_group_self-certifiesbitcoinfuturestolaunchdec18.html

631 "Coinbase Global, Inc." (United States Securities and Exchange Commission, February 25 2021), https://www.sec.gov/Archives/edgar/data/1679788/000162828021003168/coinbaseglobalincs-1.htm

INDEX

Printed in Great Britain
by Amazon

23552190R00229